The Hardest Challenge

By Bruce Chapin

Teachers Insurance and Annuity Association
College Retirement Equities Fund

First printing December 1990

Published by
Teachers Insurance and Annuity Association
College Retirement Equities Fund
730 Third Avenue
New York, NY 10017

ISBN 0-9613704-2-4

Library of Congress CIP data available

FOR
My Mother and Father

My advice to bereaved mates: Lean into the pain. Let it run its course. It is the hardest challenge life can deal you.

—Woman, age 60, widowed two years

ACKNOWLEDGMENTS

Heading the list of those I thank is TIAA-CREF itself. It is ever mindful that every dollar it spends makes a significant contribution to its charter purposes of strengthening educational institutions ''by providing annuities, life insurance, and sickness and accident benefits'' especially suited to their needs, and ''by counselling such institutions and their employees concerning pension plans or other measures of security.''

TIAA-CREF has always viewed its counselling purpose broadly. Since the 1940s, it has published several books surveying and collecting its participants' retirement experiences to counsel those approaching retirement. Those volumes met with such a successful reception that when Steve Weisbart, manager of the Educational Research Division, proposed the idea for a similar research project and volume on the experiences of widows and widowers, it was quickly adopted. I am grateful to Steve for offering me the opportunity to distill that research into this book, and to him and Bob Perrin, Executive Vice President of the External Affairs Area, for the combination of patience and firmness with which they oversaw the project.

The substance of the book I owe to the services of Jim Mulanaphy and Ina Hillebrandt. Jim, the head of the company's Division of Policyholder and Institutional Research, conducted the 1987 mail survey from which the book originated. The skill and tact with which he and his colleague Stuart Whalen fashioned the questionnaire for the survey were proved by the quantitative results the survey fetched (very ably tabulated and analyzed by Kevin Gray and Jeff Cuiule) and, much more important to me, by the qualitative ones—the words which came back on those questionnaires. Ina, of Hillebrandt Consultants, was engaged to lead the discussion groups that supplemented the survey (she appears as the ''Q'' among the speakers). Again, the results bore witness to her finesse at that work: her attentiveness to what individuals wanted to say (and often wouldn't without being prodded) and her rather uncanny awareness of where the group wanted to go (some of the best dialogue unrolled when she found some pretext to leave the group alone at the right moment).

In putting together what Jim and Ina passed on to me, many others had a hand. Elaine Olimpio was a help right from the beginning and remained so to the end. Diane Loughran, who had to leave TIAA-CREF in mid-1990 to attend to the birth of her twins, was a wonderfully judicious critic, before and even after that event. Jane Porcino deserves the credit for compiling the Bibliography and the "Resources." And I am grudgingly grateful (what else can they expect of an author?) to my copyeditors, Nancy Inglis and Rose Krieger.

Finally, when it came to the nitty-gritty, I was blessed by two marvels: Peggy Eberhart and Joan Watson, in their respective roles of secretary and publications specialist.

Bruce Chapin
Assistant Publications Officer
TIAA-CREF

New York, NY
November, 1990

CONTENTS

Our Purpose

This book is for TIAA-CREF policyholders like you who have lost their spouses, and it was written for two reasons. As to the first, we'll let someone else speak for us, as we shall throughout:

> **John**: *What a book or any sort of counselling does, whether it is about death or things close to death, like drug addiction, alcohol, is to say, "You're not alone. You weren't singled out for this experience for some reason—like, God got up on the wrong side of bed and decided He was going to nail* you." *You close the book and say, "Somebody else has gone through that too." It's just a matter of sharing. You're not going to get answers, you're not going to get redemption. It's experiencing it.*
> —*New York, #2*

It's this simple service above all that this book hopes to perform. Being told "you're not alone" in this way may seem absurdly abstract when you may never have felt so keenly *all* alone—more alone, perhaps, than you ever imagined it was possible for a human being to feel. But knowing that others have felt this way and hearing how they dealt with it may be one of the many ways you can begin to deal with it too.

And that leads to the other reason for this book: the abundance of experience we could pack into it, the thoughts and feelings of more than a thousand people like you. Almost all were the widows and widowers of TIAA-CREF policyholders who wrote responses in the spring of 1987 to a questionnaire that, among other things, asked them "what it is like to survive a spouse." The remainder—less than a

1

hundred in all, but also all widows and widowers—were participants (like John quoted above) in a series of nine discussion groups that TIAA-CREF sponsored across the country in the fall of 1987 as a follow-up to our mail survey.

What they had to say proved an extraordinary mixture of the reflective, the passionate, and—yes—the occasionally funny that explored grief from its most desolate moments to its most mellow and even exultant ones. And the dialogue that emerged from the discussions sometimes beautifully complemented—or countered—the "monologue" of the answers to the questionnaires. We have done our best to let these words come through with as little interference from us as possible.

By doing so, we've tried to underscore what we think is one of the most important messages sent by this group collectively as well as by so many of its individual members: there is no set of prescriptions for meeting "the hardest challenge." Instead, the multiplicity of ways that people go about it is astonishing, something that the previous literature has not always fully appreciated. For this very reason, we hope their examples will give reassurance and fortitude both to those of you who feel beset by people giving you the "right" advice and to those of you who feel in utter want of it.

What does this book not try to do? Perhaps of most importance to many of you, it does not pretend to be a manual that systematically instructs you about such tasks as settling an estate, securing financial or emotional counselling, or finding a job. People had a lot to say in passing about this "practical" side, and we tried to include as much of it as we could. But you can find on the market some admirable books for widows (and widowers too in some cases) that deal with these matters in abundant detail. Bearing titles like "handbook" and "guide" and complete with "agendas," checklists, and worksheets, some amount to virtual works of reference. Rather than try to emulate them, we've set out a generous sampling in the Bibliography at the end of this book. For the same reason, we've also appended a list of other practical "Resources," like the names and addresses of service organizations that surviving spouses have found helpful.

Firsthand accounts from people in your situation, then, are what you'll be listening to here. Those of women will predominate, for the simple statistical reason that the preponderance of surviving spouses are widows—in the nation as a whole and therefore among the people we randomly selected to represent it (see the box at the end of this chapter for the exact proportions). But we've tried to include the comments of men wherever we could, with the intention of making the book meaningful to widowers too.

From men and women alike, you will be hearing a medley of voices, speaking in unison on certain larger themes but often disputing each other, not only over the little things but the big ones as well. They address all the topics you might expect: the sorrow, the fear, the anger, the guilt, the loneliness, and the ways in which the survivors were helped (or *not* helped) in coping with them by family, friends, society at large, God, and—ultimately—themselves. We parcelled out most of their comments into Chapters 1 through 7, which move more or less from the most immediate and pressing tasks of adjusting to the loss to the longer-range ones.

By splitting apart people's stories in this way, however, we risked losing the individuality of what they had to say along with its totality. So we've tried to counteract this with a "Prologue" and an "Epilogue" that preserve some of the most eloquent of these stories as nearly word-for-word as we could, without any comment. Much of the Prologue consists of raw suffering relived, because it focusses on the pain that people felt in the aftermath of the death. The Epilogue, by contrast, shows how people were able to live with that pain and even triumph over it. You might liken the Prologue to letters home from soldiers in combat and the Epilogue to the war memoirs of veterans, written in peacetime. And if you feel too much in the midst of your own battle with grief, you may want to skip the former—or, after reading a bit of it, go directly to the latter to put it in perspective.

A note on how we've ''identified'' the people quoted here. Those who were responding to the TIAA-CREF mail survey (which was of course confidential) are characterized by sex, age, and the number of years since their spouses died (thus, ''Woman, 66, 3''—or ''NA'' for the handful of cases where the last two items were lacking). First names are used for the participants in the discussion groups (which also guaranteed confidentiality), and we note the location of the groups and the order in which they were scheduled, if there were more than one (thus, ''Miami, #2'').

Of those in the survey who responded to the essay questions, 1,018 (95.6%) were women and 47 (4.4%) were men. All the discussion groups were composed of women, except for Los Angeles, #1 (evenly mixed) and New York, #1 (all men).

For the reason you might expect, the discussion groups excluded people whose spouses had died within the previous six months; the similar cutoff for the survey was a date of death less than two years before.

Prologue

It seems to be a period for which—no matter how long you have been expecting it— there is no preparation—

There is the loss of identity—someone has been depending on you—somehow or other you have meant something—then there is nothing—

There is the physical loss—the gentleness of a touched hand—a pat on the head—few people realize how desperate a lack this is—almost the worst—

Then the silence—as you think, "I will tell him this—ohh no . . ."

The negation of you is something out of which you have to crawl inch by inch—with the help of others and the love of God.

—Woman, 82, 10

Sylvia: *Well, my husband—I went into the kitchen—he was sitting in the living room just as happy as he could be, I heard him laugh. I heard a strange noise and I went in and he was dead. That's a traumatic situation.*

Q: *What did you do?*

Sylvia: *What did I do? I first ran to him and called him and I tried to get him out of the chair and he was a great big man and I couldn't move him. I ran to the front door screaming and the neighbor heard me and called the paramedics. And he was dead and I held him.*

At first you're in complete total shock. Then you go through—I think I went through every emotion that there is in the human body. I felt everything. I felt despair, I felt like I had been cheated and

5

robbed, and I felt like I hated people for their having their husbands and mine was gone, and I wouldn't believe it, and I used to go out and look in the car and see if he was coming back. I went in and I took his bathrobe and slept in it. And I went berserk . . . for a long time.
Q: How long ago was this?
Sylvia: *Five years.*

—Los Angeles, #1

Margaret: *My husband wanted to go on a trip, to go back and touch base with all kinds of relatives across the country. He wanted me to go with him. I felt I couldn't take off from work. Also it wasn't a trip I* wanted *to go on. I took him down to the bus station on a Monday morning, and he was to call me on Tuesday when he got there. I got a call on Tuesday to say that I better get to Texas. He was dead.*

I was 52, and my husband had just had his 58th birthday. So, along with the loss and the shock—and we had been married thirty-one years at the time—was also the guilt. Would anything have been different if I had been there with him?

You go through all sorts of different things. I was working. I was a state employee, with a very, very good position. I ran immediately back to work, and in many ways I didn't let it touch me for several years. And when it finally did, I fell apart. I was making something in the kitchen, and a box of oatmeal fell on the floor, and I heard a crazy woman screaming, "How dare you leave me! You promised me a lifetime!"

—Los Angeles, #2

Q: Let me interrupt. How many people were angry when their husbands died? One, two, three, four. What were you angry about?
Ida: *I was angry because a man who was never sick a day in his life—*
Peggy: *Yes, but where does that anger come in?*
Ida: *A man who was never sick a day in his life, and all of a sudden he says, "I don't understand a goddamned thing that's on television! What are they talking about?" Here was a man who was highly educated, lived a good life, never had any problems with anything. And all of a sudden he doesn't know what's going on in the world. Had a brain tumor. Came on just like that. With no warning whatsoever.*

So I was angry: how that could happen to a man who was healthy and enjoying life up to the hilt! The result is, I don't go to the cemetery and look at the dirt in the ground to see where a nice young man is lying for no reason at all! I'm still angry.

—*Miami, #2*

Elaine: *I felt that my life was over. I woke up the next morning, I thought, "I've got absolutely nothing to live for."*
Q: *What did you do?*
Elaine: *Oh, what did I do? I didn't do anything for a long time. You know, you're busy with people coming in. And then, little by little, the company keeps getting lesser and lesser and you find you have to go out and make new friends. You realize who your friends really were and who needed you more than you needed them [laughter and murmurs of agreement from rest of group]. You become the oddball. "Is my husband going to start fooling around with this woman?" Or, "Do we have to pick her up for dinner?" "Do we have to pick up her check?" "There but for the grace of God go I, I don't want to see her because I may be in that position." You've got to go out and make new friends.*

So you go out during the day. You join an organization or you do volunteer work, whatever it may be. But when you come home and turn that key in the lock, you know you're alone. If it's a rotten day, there's no one to say, "Well, what do you care, dear? Tomorrow's another day. We have each other and nothing else matters." And if it's a good day, there's nobody to share it with. And that's rough! If you can't share, you've got nothing.
Margaret: *It's the trivial things.*
Elaine: *That's right. The laughter, the love, you pass by him, you slap each other or pat each other, whatever. It just isn't there.*
Kaye: *It's just the sharing that you miss.*
Elaine: *That's right.*
Kaye: *It's the sharing of everything.*

—*Los Angeles, #2*

Sylvia: *And I just wanted somebody to sit and talk with, that could understand what it was I was feeling. Not to say, you know, "Don't cry, you must be strong." Which is what I got from my rabbi and* *everybody else. "You've got to be strong, you've got to be strong, got to be strong" [pats self on head ironically], and inside you are dying but outside strong.*

Betty: *Oh, God. Positive and strong.*

Sylvia: *There was a woman at work—I came home, I cannot tell you how I felt—who said, "I hope when it becomes my turn that I can handle it as well as you." And I wanted to* scream, *to* scream! *I couldn't say a word. I could find absolutely nothing to say.*

Everybody said, "You've got to get away and do things." My doctor, whom I had known for years and who knew my husband, said, "Sylvia, you should go on a trip." I said, "Who should I go on a trip with?" "Just . . . go on a trip."

Sara: *Rhetoric!*

—*Los Angeles, #2*

Laura: *I can't go to a dance, it would kill me. I went to one party five years ago, it was in the family. Everybody got up to dance and left me sitting at that table alone. [to Frieda] At least you had a lady sitting with you. I was alone. I spent three hours in the ladies' room. I wouldn't come out. But that's beside the point. I didn't really expect any of them to ask me to dance, but just watching them dance and sitting on the side and remembering how important I was to somebody . . . and to these people there, I'm dirt! That's exactly how I felt.*

—*Miami, #1*

Q: *Gladys? Did you go through these feelings? The numbness?*

Gladys: *I'm still going through it.*

Q: *What do you do about that?*

Gladys: *Try to run as much as I can. I cannot stay alone. I try to find someone to have dinner with every night. There will come a time when I may have to do it by myself. I have no working skills. I do volunteer work. I was a very dependent social butterfly, that's what my husband wanted. He was in the legal profession. He wanted a hostess. He wanted the entertainment. He wanted all the superficial things, as I see them now, and they were wonderful, they were beautiful, and I loved it.*

But he would never teach me. When the time came when he was ill,

I asked him to teach me to take care of myself. He said, "Your son is being trained." Well, my son has a life of his own. He's 34, 35, he has a new wife and a new baby and he's a pilot and she's a director and they're very involved and busy with their life.

My affairs have not been settled. My family have not been entirely supportive. They don't want to see me cry. They want to see me where I was before, and I can't give them that. I'm just beginning to try, with the help of a psychologist. And I'm not the beneficiary of their love and their attention. They have somewhat abandoned me in some ways. Not entirely, but some ways.

I'm very hurt; I'm very alone. I have friends, not nurturing friends. I have made a network of new friends. They don't want to hear it anymore. They don't want to hear. I've got to smile, I've got to laugh. The facade has to be superficial, and I try. I get in the car and I go home and I cry.

So I'm going through it. I can't wait to fall asleep at night, I can't stand to wake up in the morning. And when that changes, maybe I will change too.

—Los Angeles, #2

Chapter 1

Grieving

"It Was As Though I Died Too"

One woman in our survey goes right to the heart of it: "My husband's sudden death was really a death of love!" Grief, of course, is what we go through when we lose what we love. Some have argued that we react with a measure of grief to any change in our lives—even a welcome change. But the loss of someone we love is the most profound, and most profoundly unwelcome, change we can suffer. If love—along with work—is what gives our lives meaning, then "the death of love" has the power to kill that meaning. And a life without meaning is no life at all.

You can hear the terror this lack of meaning holds for this survivor, a physician:

> *Without my spouse, there is nothing I am able to enjoy in the same way, even my wonderful four children! Everything is "half-a-measure" or less—nothing feels the same. Life without the love and intimacy and mutual interdependence with a spouse is a terrible thing—a terrible, terrible thing. So I say I am not coping because I hate the way I feel. It doesn't feel like life as I knew life.*
>
> —*Woman, 66, 3*

She is right—it isn't "life as I knew life." Perhaps this is why the survivor sometimes feels, "It was as though I died too." Advises one, "Figure there will be eighteen months to two years when you will feel like a cold, dead person yourself" (woman, 59, 17). Observes another, "It is shocking how our culture forces you to act like nothing has happened, when the reality is that your life has stopped" (woman, 58, 3). And to a third—who despite more than a decade of widowhood

11

found it "very stressful" to answer our questionnaire—it seemed the cessation of everything:

> *From a loving, happy marriage of many years, many friends and places to go together, many things to do, all of a sudden, I was alone. I felt my life was ending.*
> —*Woman, 75, 14*

If your spouse's death did not leave you feeling dead yourself, it may nevertheless seem to have done actual physical violence to your sense of self:

> *At first it is as though you'd had very intense surgery. Everything is different. You feel as if there is nothing to live for, you don't want to do anything. You want to try to be yourself again.*
> —*Woman, 83, 15*

The truth smoldering in the proverb "man and wife are one flesh" may have flared up searingly, as it did this for this woman:

> *Losing my husband was losing the best part of myself. It encompassed loss of identity, lack of confidence in myself, loss of meaning to life, loss of desire to live, and extreme loneliness even with the support of others.*
> —*Woman, 48, NA*

The woman whose words gave this book its title and whose husband died a "horrendous hospital death" characterizes herself as a "survivor-victim" enduring a pain that is "excruciating, immobilizing, self-alienating" (woman, 60, 2). Another likens it to "a part of you being lost or taken"; and yet another, a man, to the loss of "your other hand."

Comparing the loss of a husband with that of a parent or sibling, these two agree:

> *Evelyn: It isn't like mother and father. It's different. I mean, my friend lost her mother and she said, "Well, I went through the same thing." I said, "No, Jenny, it isn't the same. A husband is different. You love your mother, you love your father, but your husband is your partner."*
> *Edith: Your husband is an extension of you. Edith and someone else. You're not an Edith alone.*
> —*Boston, #1*

Lee, a man in another group, meditates on ''how your wife becomes a part of you and you become a part of your wife, spiritually, mentally, physically, you're a part of each other, and you never realize that until the day that one of you is gone'' (New York, #2). It seems like such a tired old truth—until you feel its force personally. We define ourselves to a greater or lesser extent in terms of others, and nowhere more so than in marriage:

One feels half of himself/herself is gone. One feels there will never in the rest of your life be anyone with whom to communicate completely or who understands completely.

—Woman, 73, 12

So grief leads you into dwelling on how, in carrying off your husband or wife, death has damaged *you*. And dwell on it you must, most widows and widowers agree:

Advice: Grieve. My first grief was connected to the frustration of realizing how unfulfilled his life—and even more, our lives were. No matter that his life was quite fully realized—and he achieved a degree of eminence—the overriding sensation was of a life cut short (he was 57) and, even more, of all those years ahead when we would finally be coming together in new ways: those years simply sliced off and discarded.

—Woman, 59, 2

But grief also offers the way *out* of this state, the means for making ''the journey from your own seeming death back to life'' (woman, 69, 2). If grief has suddenly suspended your life, it eventually enables you to ''begin your life again''—one of the exhortations survivors most often get from others and, sooner or later, are able to pass on to others in their turn:

Live! After the shock you have to realize you cannot die too.

—Woman, 58, 2

Don't put yourself in the grave with your spouse.

—Woman, 51, 2

Marilyn: *You can't just stop living because someone close to you has stopped living. That's my feeling* now. *It wasn't my feeling in the* *beginning, but it is my feeling now.*

—*Boston, #2*

Marilyn follows up with an account of how it took "a full year before I was human again." Again and again, survivors describe their emergence from grief as the regaining of their identity and humanity, as feeling "normal" and "whole" once more, being a full-fledged "person" again instead of that forlorn freak, "half a couple." But they also stress, almost unanimously, that they achieved this *because of* their grief—not in spite of it:

Don't suppress grief and depression. It is probably useful, if you don't cry easily or don't express anger easily, to have some professional help. The people I know who seem to have come through grief and then bloomed were those who really experienced all the anger and sadness of the loss fully and expressed it.

—*Woman, 62, 12*

We'll explore what this means at greater length in Chapter 7, where we contrast the necessity of "getting through it" to the notions of "getting used to it" or "getting over it." It's enough to say here that, when we are "grieving," we are not just recoiling from our loss but also learning how to adjust to it and, at best, accept it. Through grief, we reinvest our lives with meaning again. It is the avenue to self-regeneration. It is how we manage the change that death has brought into our lives, and not merely how we react to it. So grief—like love—is a complex of emotions, subsuming a host of more concrete, and often contradictory, feelings. Like love too, it has social and moral as well as emotional dimensions, for it is a course of action as well as an expression of emotion. It can even become a code of conduct.

None of this is new—these ideas have become the commonplaces of "the literature of bereavement." And of course there are still people who dismiss grief as self-indulgence, among them a handful of ours:

Grief is a fruitless, self-serving emotion.

—*Woman, NA, NA*

To me, one suffers grief only because she pities herself or feels some guilt toward the deceased.

—Woman, 76, 8

Mourning heavily does not bring the loved one back. It only makes life unpleasant to those dear ones who are concerned and are helpless to better the situation, and it very often ruins the health and shortens the life of the mourner.

—Woman, 81, 15

There is also somewhat greater agreement that prolonged grief can be harmful. But survivors much more often grant grief a positive role:

Grieve constructively—let yourself feel the pain—somehow it helps.

—Woman, 69, 2

As another explains further with a commonly used analogy,

Accept the fact that the loss is going to hurt—a lot. And be open to the help people want to give you—even if it makes you weep. The weeping is a natural part of grieving. And you must *grieve.*

Losing a mate can be likened to receiving a big bruise. It hurts terrifically at first—pains almost beyond endurance, but it begins to heal. Even as it heals there's hurting, tenderness, sensitivity. But as the process continues, the hurt becomes less—and less. Sometimes you almost forget the hurt until the day comes when you realize that you feel normal again.

Oh, you don't forget what happened and you cherish the good memories, but most of the hurting is gone, and you are free to get on with your life.

—Woman 81, 4

At its most paradoxical, grief can end up restoring to you at least some of the love stolen from you. It did for the woman who urges others,

Talk about your loss, talk about your love, recognize you lost the person not the love.

—Woman, 67, 16

"We're All Different"

"No one can understand *your* grief" (woman, 68, 2). Such an uncompromising statement—seeming to leave the survivor in complete isolation—is extreme (though certainly understandable, coming as it does from the widow of a suicide). But it does reflect a more broadly held view, which we can sum up as "We're all different." Different not only because the crisis that faces each of us differs in its particulars, but also because each of us must grapple with them differently.

The research specialists at TIAA-CREF who designed our survey tell us that people who are asked for advice on questionnaires habitually issue "disclaimers" like those below, but we think it goes deeper than that in this case. You be the judge, on the basis of examples culled not only from our survey but our groups as well:

I do not have advice to offer other widows. Being a survivor is a unique and dreadful experience with which each individual must cope in his own way.

—Woman, 64, 4

All have different problems and each person is an individual—for there are no carbon copies.

—Woman, 75, 3

I have thought long and frequently about this and have concluded that there are as many kinds of widows as there are marital relationships. What is helpful for one may be nearly intolerable for another.

—Woman, 57, 3

Being realistic, there is no advice one can give to really help another. Even sisters are so different that their responses to death are totally different. My sister took her husband's death in stride and went right on living as before. I, on the other hand, felt that a hole had been torn out of my life and I can't repair it even after 15 years of widowhood.

—Woman, 78, 15

The fact that *everyone* is different—you and everybody else around you—makes losing a spouse not only one of life's hardest challenges but one of its hardest to simplify as well. The setting you're in is one of a kind:

Some nine years after the death of my husband I have reason to think that there is no "same experience" for widows and widowers. About the only common element is that you are the survivors. There may be grown children, younger children, or no children. Financial circumstances can vary greatly.

—Woman, 71, 9

And, however you handle matters, you have no assurance that others will behave as you hoped:

Each person reacts differently—and their families and friends respond in different ways.

—Woman, 60, 3

Which leads us, inescapably, to this:

Each person has to find his own solution—there is no right and no wrong way to handle each situation.

—Woman, 54, 2

That's what this group concludes after arguing about whether it's possible to mitigate grief by travel or a move to a new locale:

Sara: So you can't run—
Kaye: You can run, but it goes with you.
Sara: It goes with you.
Gladys: I don't agree with that, either. Everybody's different.
Q: Excuse me, I'm going to jump in for a minute. I don't always do this, but I'm going to posit something to you: that what works for one person doesn't necessarily work for another.
Gladys: Exactly.
Sara: That's right.
Q: So there's no right or wrong?
Gladys: Oh no, absolutely not.

—Los Angeles, #2

You are a complicated person in a complicated world, engaged in a *very* complicated task, which cannot be reduced neatly to rule and formula:

There aren't any set answers. Each individual has different strengths. Some of us need support groups; some have loving families. Some grief is very private, some needs to be shared.

—Woman 76, 3

These warnings seem the fruit of heartfelt experience, and their validity is borne out when people do give advice (which they do profusely). That advice, on a given issue, often takes every conceivable position, some of them squarely opposed. As an example (and to pick up on the last thought of the person just quoted), take one of the most commonly debated questions about grief: how open should you be about expressing it?

Do not go around with a sad face—you can lose friends this way. Cry when you are alone.

—Woman, 75, 15

Don't keep your grief contained inside you. Cry, talk with a friend.

—Woman, 62, 16

Don't burden others with your loss; they too have burdens to bear. We do not have to look far to find those who carry crosses heavier than ours. Try to forget self and think of others.

—Woman, 77, 3

Grieve with friends and family—it helps them as much as you.

—Woman, 55, 7

We've deliberately let the extremes clash above, because neither one nor the other emerges a clear winner in our survey. In fact, people taking the opposite approaches sometimes report that they have arrived at an identical goal, like the ''support'' these two sought from those around them:

I feel very fortunate to have a close family (mother, siblings, and my own children), all of whom have continued to be very supportive. Don't make unrealistic demands on those around you—only you can know the inner feelings of loneliness you experience at having lost the person with whom you expected to share the rest of your life. Don't inflict your sorrow on others unnecessarily, or you may find yourself without much company! A happy countenance makes others feel better and, ultimately, brings its own rewards.

—Woman, 59, 3

Don't hide from, or deny, the painful feelings of loss, share those feelings with those close to you. Reach out to others, not only for closeness and companionship, but understanding and solace. Don't be afraid to ask for help with any problems, either practical or emotional. What helped me the most was continued emotional support of family and friends.

—*Woman, 72, 9*

Of course many people are able to stake out a middle ground between extremes:

I think one should talk as naturally as possible about the deceased spouse (when referring to death, calling it by name and avoiding euphemisms), without unduly dwelling on the loss or emphasizing the "Poor Me" aspects. But one should have other topics. And it's just as well not to think of oneself primarily as widow or widower.

—*Woman, 68, 7*

Some urge you to confide your grief fully with others, but only with those who know you best or who are most likely to be receptive:

Discuss your personal feelings only with a good friend. Friends are concerned, acquaintances get bored.

—*Woman, 68, 10*

Realize that only those who have lost a mate can appreciate what you are experiencing—and will be truly supportive. Others will show immediate sympathy for a short while and expect you to be back "to normal." Don't inflict your sense of loss and grief on these friends and acquaintances.

—*Woman, 60, 3*

Find someone with whom you can share your grief—continuingly. A close friend who feels the loss keenly; someone you know who is going through (or has fairly recently gone through) the same experience. Some people find a widows/widowers group helpful. I had a close friend whose wife died the same week as my husband, and we had our own close-knit "group."

—*Woman, 72, 3*

Others distinguish "crying" from "talking" (note how often

they are conjoined by the people quoted earlier):

> *You deal with death by not crying on everyone's shoulder. You do your crying in your home. (But I talk about my husband to other people because I loved him very much).*
>
> —*Woman, 69, 4*

> *It's so helpful also just to be able to* talk *about your loss, talk about good times. Many friends shy away from this, thinking this is too painful for you. A grieving spouse needs an outlet for her thoughts and emotions—if allowed to have it, he/she will better be able to cope. However a widow or widower must be able to be good company and easy to be with. My way was to do my crying and keep my hysteria confined to my home—and to present a smile when I was out with friends. I managed to cope, but it took years.*
>
> —*Woman, 67, 10*

Some find "talk"—at least some kinds of it—a benefit to others as well as themselves:

> *Keep your feelings of loneliness to yourself—except for sharing them with those who want to and are able to provide emotional support. Most survivors seem to have enough to handle without listening to the sorrows of others—and that is what I found unpleasant about support group therapy. So, though one* can *gain comfort from someone who has been bereaved and talks about grief, usually it brings back one's own grief. But talking about and thus sharing the good times of the past with a survivor is often helpful to both parties.*
>
> —*Woman, 69, 22*

Still others appear ready to "talk" about all of it, even at the risk of alienating friends:

> *The most important advice to widows/widowers is to talk as much as possible about what they are feeling. It is extremely therapeutic and healing. Most people don't want to listen about the death of a spouse, but this is* the *healing process.*
>
> —*Woman, 38, 2*

Her faith in the curative powers of talk—and we'll see in the next chapter how loneliness is so often summed up as the lack of "some-

one to talk to''—is shared by this woman, who luckily finds hers
abundantly reciprocated:

> *In my case, the advantage was having a very close family, excellent
> in-laws, many friends, and coworkers of my husband who re-
> sponded almost 100%. The reason I state this is because I had to
> talk! And everyone responded in kind and no one pretended it
> didn't happen. We all feel free to discuss my husband.*
> —Woman, 60, 3

So how you ultimately answer the question may ''depend on the
person'' entirely—that is, on how you and the others in your life
interact:

> *Elaine: You have to speak with someone who understands, who
> isn't going to say to you, "Stop crying. Everything's going to work
> out all right." It's a lot of nonsense. You have to cry. You have to
> mourn. You have to be with people who understand.*
> *Betty: But you have to cry alone; otherwise people just shoo away.*
> *Elaine: It depends on the people.*
> —Los Angeles, #2

> *Q: Yes, widows or widowers, what kinds of things do you talk to
> them about?*
> *Connie: It all depends upon the person. I know people who immediately
> want to cling to you. I hate that—that just puts a wall up in front of me.*
> *Isabel: That's usually a woman, though.*
> *Bea: No, there are men like that too.*
> *Connie: I guess my nature just doesn't agree with theirs.*
> *Bea: You are an independent person. I am too, I can't stand the
> clinging vines.*
> *Connie: A lot of people do. They frighten me because I feel so bad
> for them.*
> —New York, #1

Would Connie have rejected Elaine with scorn and fear (for her
attitude is a mix of both) as a ''clinging vine''? Perhaps—which is
why, in feeling your way toward ''what's best for you,'' you should
be prepared to make mistakes, one way or another:

> *Q: I want to ask you to respond to a different thing. What's the stupidest*

thing you did, that somebody should avoid? What are the screwups?
Peggy: *Wearing your heart on your sleeve was my mistake. I was told by a sister-in-law, "You wear your heart on your sleeve. You don't tell us about all the nice things you do, you only tell us about the sorrow that you're having." And I learned a lesson. I put my hat and coat on and walked away from her apartment, walked right out, never spoke to her again for the hurt that it caused me. But I learned a lesson the hard way.*
—*Miami, #2*

I lived day to day and postponed my grieving—This was the mistake—My advice is join a group right away—deal with the loss—get rid of their personal belongings—cry, scream—whatever—I did not cry for two years—then I joined a grieving group—it was wonderful—I hurt so those two years, but let no one know—not even myself.
—*Woman, 51, 5*

To further illustrate how "we're all different," consider another question that grief poses to everyone who passes through it. Being stuck with a frightful change and the puzzle of how to deal with it may lead you to wonder how much you—consciously and methodically—should try to change in response to it. So you may start asking yourself how much of your "old" life you will try to preserve and how much of the "new" you will try to bring into it.

Again, it seems to boil down to who you are:

Each person is different; some will find solace in the familiar, others in new experiences.
—*Woman, 74, 9*

Some declare themselves staunchly in favor of trying to keep things "the same":

For me, it was extremely important that I could keep many things (my home, my routine, my friends) the same. This helped to reduce the trauma.
—*Woman, 63, 2*

I believe that getting back to a regular routine of daily living, doing things that you had done before the loss of your spouse, is the very best way to cope with your loss.
—*Woman, 67, NA*

It's very important to be stubborn about maintaining the pattern of your own life. For example, I've played the cello—as an amateur—for years. It makes me very angry when well-meaning people say, "Oh, I'm glad you're keeping up your cello." As if this would be a time to give up your most important activity!

—Woman, 68, 5

But, as another widow (64, 6) notes, although it "can be comforting eventually, the familiar is painful at first"; and for some this pain is uppermost:

Some are comforted by familiar surroundings; I personally found them too painful. I chose to move for both financial and emotional reasons.

—Woman, 56, 4

Things that were a comfort and a commonplace in the years that my husband and I were together (32 years) are often now such a reminder of loss that they sadden rather than support me. Getting out to see new things and places has been a useful preoccupation, not so much helpful as less hurtful than much else I do. My husband and I were very close in our profession as well as our personal lives. I still find it difficult to walk where we used to walk, despite the fact I feel I need some continuing exercise.

—Woman, 57, 3

Like the question of how open you should be, this one finds some people who can hold the extremes almost exactly in balance:

Physically, spouse is gone, but memories survive and these can help make the loss less painful. Find new interests to fill void without discarding past ones. Take the steps; it is scary at first; but life has much to offer. Each new venture can complement your life before and provide an opportunity to fulfill dreams you both had previously—but now one doesn't have a partner and so goes on alone.

—Woman, 68, 15

But most people don't—and perhaps can't—divide their allegiances so evenly. Look at how this woman, although she acknowledges the necessity of "changes," makes the "old" the bedrock for them:

I consider myself fortunate that I had a job which made it possible for me to stay in my house and live pretty much as I had before being widowed.

I realize that this may not be possible for everyone. Then, too, others may find more comfort in being able to get away or make great changes in their lives. I can speak only for myself, of course, but I have found the sense of continuity in my life—job, friends—to be a stabilizing force. Then one can add changes gradually, as one is ready for them.

—Woman, 61, 8

Another woman, perhaps because of the benefit of decades of widowhood, positively embraces the ''new'':

Travel if you can, make new friends in new surroundings. Get out of painful old ruts if possible. Do things you've ''always wanted to do,'' things perhaps your spouse would not have wished to engage in.

Remember at all times, difficult though it may be (and it seems impossible at first), that you will *feel better. Grief is like a terrible disease, but if you are good to yourself, throw out remorse, guilt, and morbid recollections, it will eventually be healed. But give yourself at least a couple of years. It takes* time.

Get new *hobbies, don't hurry into any move, but consider an eventual shift from the old scenes you shared with your spouse. And remember: you owe it your departed spouse to build a new, happy, and productive life. Nothing will ever be the* same, *but life can be exciting and worthwhile again.*

—Woman, 66, 26

''Nothing Will Ever Be the Same''

We've quoted our last contributor at some length because she touches upon some additional themes with which we'd like to close this chapter. According to her, you must acknowledge that ''nothing will ever be the same'' and yet go on to achieve ''a new, happy, and productive life.'' As another admonishes,

A widow or widower cannot expect things to return to normal—life will never be the same. But the survivor must make a new life for his or her self. You don't forget the past, but you can't live in the past.

—Woman, 67, 2

The standard advice, which you've probably heard all too often. And when you have, you've probably asked yourself, ''But how do I get from 'here' to 'there'?'' From past to future, from emptiness to fullness, from that which was lost to that which should be found? How do you make the passage across such a gulf, between two such incompatible states of mind? How, in other words, do you "recover"?

Some say you never do:

Family and friends and faith have been a great help to me. However, after many years of happily married life, I don't know how anyone can fully recover from the loss of a loved one. It leaves an everlasting void.
—Man, 81, 3

Echoes a woman (69, 6), "You do adjust to the void in your life—but never completely recover." Another (65, 3) pronounces it "an irreparable loss from which you never recover." Some seem resigned to having their grief be a permanent part of their lives:

I still feel the grief process is not "complete" and it may never be.
—Woman, 43, 2

My husband has been dead for seven years, and I still miss him beyond measure. I live in a "sea of widows" in this retirement home. Some forgot very easily, and with some there's an inner mourning which will last until they're dead.
—Woman, 73, 7

Sentiments like these you might assume to be coming from people who feel they're faring the worst. But every single one of them rated themselves on their questionnaires as among the 40% in our survey who reported they were "coping fairly well" with their loss—not the highest of the three possible scores they could have awarded themselves, but not the lowest either (the totals for the others: 52% "coping well" and 6% "not well").

So "recovery"—as other books about grief have observed—may be a somewhat misleading word to describe what happens for many who adjust. A "wound" that "heals" may not be the right metaphor for everyone. "Reconciliation" and "acceptance" are perhaps more accurate names for the process—and certainly less ambitious and less intimidating ones. The awareness of loss—the knowledge that "nothing will be the same"—may stay with you to the end. But what our people seem to be stressing is that it need not be incompatible with "making a new life.''

We'll look more closely in Chapter 7 at the various ways people make their ''old'' lives—the past—at home in the present. But a bit more here on the possibility for a ''new'' life. If such a thing is attainable, what is the route to it? Some people who have studied bereavement have identified various ''stages'' or ''phases'' through which a survivor must travel. And some survivors use them as roadmaps:

> *My husband died suddenly and unexpectedly of a heart attack in November of 1985 while we were with friends attending a production at the University Theatre. I am now able to recognize the stages of grief which I have experienced.*
>
> *At first, it was absolute daze and unbelief. It was difficult to make the necessary decisions. I didn't want to see anyone, even the members of my closely knit family. Then, I entered into what is described in the literature as Stage II—that of deliberate activity. Here, I completely redecorated my house—even though it was not particularly necessary.*
>
> *When this was accomplished, I believe that I came to Stage III, which has been described as ''Hitting Rock Bottom.'' My anger was beginning to play itself out, and I asked, ''Why me?'' It is very natural to feel sorry for yourself and to look with envy at those around you who have their loved ones.*
>
> *I am now in the stage of loneliness. Even when I am with family and friends, I continue to feel so* alone. *I hope that this will pass, but I try so hard not to let anyone know. I realize that the future stages are those of Acceptance and Hope. I am not there yet.*
>
> *—Woman, 70, 2*

Of course, if a ''scenario for grieving'' like this helps you to make sense of what you're going through, it's all to the good. But it also has its dangers, and many survivors are adamant against gauging one's progress by such supposed mileposts:

> *First of all, recognize that all people go through grieving in stages and it is all different depending on your personality.*
>
> *—Woman, 53, 2*

> *I'm a social work person. These professionals think according to a ''program for grief.'' There are no programs except the individual*

psyche's own idiosyncratic one. The most that can be said is, "Please stop assuming I'm at stage X."

—*Woman, 73, 9*

Remember that everyone meets this traumatic experience in a different way; don't be too hard on yourself if you don't seem to be getting over your loss as quickly as you "should" (there are NO "shoulds" in this kind of experience).

—*Woman, 72, 3*

"Adjustment" may be possible but, they caution, don't expect it to arrive "on schedule":

For me grief was intense for nearly two years. I would advise newly widowed people to take time to grieve and not try to carry on as if nothing had happened. Grief is necessary, and adjustment comes in time—but that time is different for each person.

—*Woman, 68, 2*

The loss and readjustment take much *longer for some of us than can possibly be anticipated. And one is* not *wallowing in grief through all that time, but is rebuilding a life and five years is not an unreasonable time to go through the stages (I think.) And that's based not only on my experience, but that of several of my friends. If one has a shorter progress that's great, but widows(ers) need to know that it can take a long time, even though one seems to be coping well.*

—*Woman, 62, 12*

Don't look for sudden revelations or watershed moments either:

Understand that the grieving process takes a long time—don't expect to wake up one day and find it to be over.

—*Woman, 67, 3*

Finally, don't be surprised by relapses:

Dorothy: *I get along fine for months at a time, I'm doing great, and I look at my husband's pictures and think, "I'm still living," and I don't let it get to me. And then I have moments when I get tense, or there's stress from my family, and I'm down like a . . . [trailing off].*

—*Miami, #1*

Gladys: It was my first trip, and we had a wonderful time, and this one friend said to me, "Well, the old Gladys is back, and we love it." But I can't keep it up.
Elaine: Well, you have to push yourself.
Fay: Yes, but you take three steps forward and one step back.
Gladys: Or vice versa.

—Los Angeles, #2

This is not to say you can't make progress and don't know it when you do:

It really isn't all cut-and-dried, as some of the questions imply. If I had answered them one year ago, my answers would have been much different. It's been two years now and it's still not good—but getting better and a little easier.

—Woman, 67, 2

And it can even dawn on you that you are undergoing some fundamental changes in outlook:

I have a clearer sense of what I, and I alone, want, where I am headed, and how I will get there. As much as I had carved out a life independent of husband and family, it was so subtly and intricately tied to a family constellation that it is only now after he has left (the children left before his death) that I can more clearly see not only the road ahead, but where it is going. It has taken two years, and I expect this clarity of purpose to continually be refined.

—Woman, 59, 2

But be prepared to be like a traveller on foot, to whom changes in the landscape are so gradual you're sometimes not conscious of them until you're past them.

One of the commonest ways people realize, upon reflection, that they are "getting better" is when the memories seem to help more than they hurt:

We had an exceptionally good marriage. I feel very fortunate to have been married to such a fine person for over thirty years, and I am now used to remembering the good times we had together rather than the fact that she is no longer alive.

—Man, 59, 2

Don't dwell on the "old" days and how you looked and what you could do, but feel happy with your wonderful memories.

—Woman, 81, 16

While life can never be the same, what appreciation for the years shared, the cherished memories which abide!

—Woman, 75, 7

And the good memories can inhere in the simplest of things:

Fran: *My daughter talks about her father every day of the week. There isn't a day goes by she doesn't talk. Like we'll all be watching television programs, and she'll say, "Oh, this is a program Daddy would have liked." We'll go to a movie, and she'll say, "This is a movie Daddy would have liked."*
Julia: *That's all right. I know the television programs my husband used to like. The last show we watched was the miniseries* North and South. *And every time I see one of the actors from it on TV, I think of the picture and the kick he used to get out of it. A lot of things that come back don't all have to be sad.*

—Boston, #2

Perhaps this is what a lot of the "adjustment" is all about, at a much more profound level than might first appear: learning to live—and live comfortably—with the memory rather than the reality of the human being:

Grief has its own timetable, and being allowed to grieve in one's own way is part of the slow healing process. People who have not experienced this great loss are often impatient with the widowed. A new life cannot be forced upon a person, nor can you expect that in a short time one can adjust to living with a memory rather than a person.

—Woman, 64, 6

There is more to it than this, however, because there is one person you are still living with: yourself. And learning how to do *that* comfortably may prove even more difficult than learning to live with the memories. With the death of your spouse, your role changed instantly from "husband" or "wife" to "widow" or "widower," and you may feel revulsion at the very word itself:

Gladys: I can't think of myself as a widow. It's a horrible, horrible feeling!

—Los Angeles, #2

One fact that makes it horrible—and makes it feel as if part of you is literally missing—is how marriage has built up "years of shared identity," as one woman (78, 11) puts it, in which "your own individuality and interests may have been subordinated" to another's. In fact, some such "subordination" is essential for a marriage to work at all. And the more you anchored your life to that of your spouse, the more adrift you may find yourself, like this wistful woman:

My late husband and I talked, lived, ate, and slept his work. When he was gone, so was everything else, his friends, his work, his social life. One should make a point of having interests of one's own before the tragedy occurs.

—Woman, 59, 12

What faces you afterward, however, may go beyond merely developing "interests of one's own" to finding out things about yourself you had forgotten—or had never known before. Women especially tend to come to this awakening:

Betty: I felt very lost because, even though I was a businesswoman before I married, I was quite happy to leave my job to become a wife and mother. Like women of my generation I was happy to project myself through my husband. Because I projected myself so much through him—happily—when I lost him, I just was lost for a while. I had to find myself. I didn't feel like a complete person.

—Los Angeles, #2

And the experience is not limited to those who assumed the traditional marital role:

Sylvia: In handling business, money, taking care of family, there's been a lot in my favor. I've always been able to handle that. I have lived outside of me and I'm really good at that, taking care of anybody's problem, whatever it is. But I've never learned how to go inside and take care of me. And that is something I am working on now, and it is very frightening.

—Los Angeles, #2

Thanks perhaps to the timeworn masculine ideal of self-certainty, men seem less likely to question themselves in this way; instead they are more inclined to assert, "Look to yourself—it is really all we have" (man, 65, 3), with more apparent confidence as to who that "self" is. But "husband" is as much a role as "wife," and, to the extent that any union with a spouse entails a merging of identities, widowers as well as widows must redefine who they are, now that they are alone.

At any rate, some people claim this is exactly what they set out to do, as this woman says she did about three months after her husband's death, after an extended visit with friends:

> *On the way home on the train I thought: "You had over forty-one years of wonderful life as Mrs. John Doe. Now it's time to see what you can do with the rest of your life as Dorothy Doe."*
>
> —*Woman, 76, 4*

And they do report that their grief has not only finally let them "become a person again" but "their own" person at that:

> *Take time to become your own person. It takes courage!*
>
> —*Woman, 62, 4*

> *Become your own person—not be just Mr. So-and-So's widow and live in his shadow.*
>
> —*Woman, 67, 10*

As a part of coping with your loss, then, you may need to "cope with yourself," as this woman bids:

> *Cope with yourself—face what has to be faced. Learn to like yourself enough that you can live with yourself alone.*
>
> —*Woman, 72, 7*

In Chapter 7, we'll look at how people have tested this old maxim: that living *by* oneself entails at best learning to live *with* oneself. And accomplishing that may take a change in oneself, as this woman intimates:

> *Develop your own resources as an individual, rediscovering who you are (if necessary), and be willing to change.*
>
> —*Woman, 72, 7*

Such a change—on top of those you are already struggling with—may seem so far beyond you that it's a cruelty even to suggest it. But, in the course of that struggle, you may eventually find that it's happened to you without your realizing it—until there comes a day when you, like many survivors, can say "nothing will ever be the same" of yourself, as you can about so much else in your life. As one woman asks, in something like wonderment,

> *Who was the "self" that had just lost a spouse? Is this "I" that "self"? No.*
>
> *—Woman, 73, 9*

Chapter 2

Taking the Blow: "It's Just an Open End"

Molly: My husband dropped dead dancing. He just loved to dance. He always said, "I hope I die dancing." He did, he got his wish.
Beulah: Where were you when he was dancing?
Molly: Well, I was at the party, and I was with somebody, and he was dancing with somebody and down he went. There were three priests there, and he went right down in their lap.
Q: And how did you feel?
Molly: I don't know what happened to me. It just hits you—just like that. It's just an open end.

—Boston, #1

A death is an "end," no doubt about that. But usually, when we encounter an end, we are meeting something that stops us from going further, like a locked door in a hallway or a sign reading Road Closed. But then we can retreat, go back the way we came, into a past we know. An "open end," on the other hand, leaves us staring into space—a future into which we must go forward. But go forward to what? The signposts and landmarks we had counted on finding will be gone. We are face to face with a void.

This chapter is about the jolt of confronting that open end—the shock of it, the numbness, the emptiness, and then the rush of emotions that may come pouring in afterward. As Molly says, "shock" may not do justice to what hits you right off. She continues,

I couldn't recognize it. I don't know whether it shocked me or what it did to me. Then we had to go to the hospital and I was still in a daze, like somebody hit me over the head and I didn't come to.

A sense that "it is impossible to put into words what it is like to lose one's spouse and face structuring a life style alone" (woman, 79, 10) often makes people grope, like Molly, for figures of speech:

> *Q: Virginia, how did it go for you, was it sudden?*
> **Virginia:** *Fifteen minutes.*
> *Q: And then, what did you do next?*
> **Virginia:** *It seemed as though . . . I was in the fire.*
> —*Boston, #2*

> *When my husband died suddenly, I felt like I was on a merry-go-round going ninety miles an hour and no way to get off.*
> —*Woman, 73, 7*

> **Sylvia:** *I was used to being very strong and, all of a sudden, I am putty, I'm falling apart.*
> —*Los Angeles, #2*

> **Edith:** *I can equate with her, I know where she's coming from. She's coming out a pit, trying to look over the edge of it.*
> —*Boston, #1*

Similes and metaphors like these are the shortcuts intuition tries to make in coming to an understanding of the inconceivable fact that husband or wife has gone—and gone in an instant, no matter how long the preceding decline. "It just didn't seem possible a person could go that fast," muses Marian (San Francisco) over what it was like to have her husband, who had been "very sick for five years," die in her arms. When Edith (Boston, #2) is asked what she felt at the time, she almost seems to put herself in her husband's place: "Too fast. You're there one minute and you're not there the next. You're not even prepared to feel anything." Or sometimes even to think properly:

> *After almost fifty years, to be without the company of my husband, I was desolate, the silence, the emptiness around me, I felt amputated, I was not whole—a silent world, I could not think straight.*
> —*Woman, 82, 4*

Life has transformed itself irretrievably, and our incomprehension at "the finality of death"—that phrase that is so banal in the abstract but so crushing when it becomes concrete—may know no bounds.

Disbelief is the universal reaction to sudden death, as it was for Pat, whose husband was in the hospital for routine surgery:

We were at home, the three of us, and one son was making the pasta and the other was getting the wine and we were sitting at the table really enjoying it and the phone rang, and I said to the older son, "Get the phone and tell them I'll call them back," and I paid no attention to what he was talking about. My younger son and I just went on conversing with one another. And then Bobby, the older one, came in with a very strange look on his face. He said, "That was Dr. So-and-so. Dad just died." And we couldn't believe it because three, two hours before, the head doctor had told my husband, "I'm going to move you, you're getting along so well."
Q: What did you do?
Pat: I said, "I don't believe it, I don't believe it." And then I went into the bathroom. I thought I was going to faint. My sons picked me up and took me into the den, and I kept saying, "I don't believe it."
—Los Angeles, #2

But the survivors of the terminally ill often report themselves just as stunned, like Hannah, whose husband died of a long-standing problem with blood clots "*exactly* the way the doctors had said that he would" years before and who had then "told my son the truth about his father" (only to hear in return, "The doctors don't know what they're talking about"). So she believes she and her spouse "were prepared—most people are not." Yet of the moment itself she says,

It's fortunate for the one who goes because it's "1, 2, 3, Bingo! Out!" But the survivor really remains in a—how shall I say it?—in an outer space. You can't believe it.
—Miami, #2

A good many survivors agree that the manner of death—sudden or expected—doesn't alter the incredulity with which we meet it:

Q: Did he die suddenly?
Emily: No, he was sick for many, many years. But I didn't believe that he would die when he died. My daughter screamed at me one day, "Daddy is dying!" I said, "Don't say that, it's not so," because he had been going to the hospital so many times and he always came back. This last time, that was it. But I would not believe, I wouldn't accept it.

Peggy: *The fact that you have years to get used to the idea that he's going to pass away—does that make it any easier when it happens?*
Emily: *No, no.*
Peggy: *Mine went like that [snapping fingers]! I left in the morning, by the time I got to where I was going, he was gone. It doesn't matter, really, because you don't believe that it's going to happen. For someone who had never been ill, you just—*
Emily: *You just—you just don't accept it, you will not accept it.*
—Miami, #2

Betty: *He died sitting next to me on a plane, and I couldn't believe it because it was so sudden. I couldn't say the word "dead" for instance. I'd go to a bank and do some business, and when they said "die," the whole thing became real and I would* flood.
—Los Angeles, #2

Of course, if a fatal disease or disability has lasted long enough, or been hard enough on victim or caregiver or both, this can override the tendency to disbelief. When it does, it may allow the survivors-to-be to prepare for the death to some degree, practically and even emotionally. So, when death comes, you may count it as a blessing for both of you. We've devoted a separate section—on death as a relief (pages 79-87)—to the comments of such people, because they clearly formed a significant group among the one-third of those we surveyed who reported their spouses succumbed to "a long illness" (with about another third each reporting "suddenly" or after "a short illness"). But the more common response to terminal illness, it appears, is to deny the inevitable, as these survivors admit:

Ruth: *The five years that he was ill, I knew that he was going to die. They told me that. That there was no getting back on it, and it happened within the month they had told me. So they weren't steering me wrong. But I never believed it would happen. Somehow you feel this can't happen to you. It just isn't in the books. We had always talked that I would be the one to go. Not him.*
—Miami, #2

My husband had chronic bronchitis which got gradually worse over a long period of time. He continued to work but would have periodic critical episodes. When you consider that he was an economist, I am shocked at how little planning we did; but the truth is that although I knew he was seriously ill, I was very heavily into denial. I just never believed—really—he would die.

—*Woman, 62, 12*

In any event, most people concur that there is no way you can fortify yourself against the emotional onslaught:

My husband was sick twelve years and I thought I was prepared. Nothing prepares you for the total devastation you feel—can't imagine the pain!

—*Woman, 43, 2*

We say "most people" because, as usual, some exceptions stand out, even among those caught without warning, like these two:

I am sure the biggest help was our attitude before my husband's death. We talked about death, joked about it, and knew it was a part of life. Too many people avoid the subject. In thirty-five years of marriage, we had lost many close relatives and friends, of all ages, and each time you have to adjust a little more.

—*Woman, 60, 3*

My husband and I talked freely about death and what he—or I—would do if left alone. Recalling those conversations has helped me to adjust and cope with financial and other decisions. It has been, at times, like having his advice even now six years later.

—*Woman, 83, 6*

Another, whose husband also died suddenly, likewise asserts, "Preparation for your adjustment begins with your marriage":

If you live as many wish they had lived, it is much easier to bear. I had no regrets of the way we lived—a loving, caring fifty-plus years. We did not put off until tomorrow things we wanted to do. We traveled extensively even though it was expensive. Always just the two of us. We had discussed the role of the survivor after such a pattern. I'm glad I'm the one to bear the loss myself. Perhaps my whole philosophy is summed up by what I wrote right afterwards (and do not remember doing), "Today, R. went on ahead." I can cope!

—*Woman, 80, 6*

This clear-eyed approach served her well and may be right for others, as the woman who says "I hate the way I feel" in Chapter 1 (page 11) speculates:

> *I think the actual agony of death and final separation is something spouses should talk about together while they are both alive—perhaps that might be some small measure of preparation for the unlucky one who survives.*
>
> *—Woman, 66, 3*

But of course whether this would have helped most people or not (and there's no evidence it necessarily would), it's too late now, and regrets on this score are pointless.

Not so pointless, perhaps, are regrets about a lack of a different sort of preparation: the practical planning for the eventuality of death. If it was done properly for *them,* many survivors give thanks to the support it lent them in their battle on the emotional front. Advises one to "those who may some day be faced with the loss of a spouse,"

> *Be as informed and prepared as possible about the practical matters. (No one can be prepared for the emotional factors.) My late husband kept a file labeled "If I Die" containing information and instructions, and I will be eternally grateful for his love and consideration which made a very difficult time somewhat easier.*
>
> *—Woman, 54, 4*

Another describes how her previous involvement with her husband in all the details of planning his estate now gave her "a feeling of at least some control, the best antidote I know to the helplessness in the face of an overwhelming situation that I have observed in some contemporaries" (woman, 69, 4). Whether or not your spouse was able to smooth the way for you in this fashion, you may want to do so for your eventual survivors, like your children. We'll say a bit more about this under "Estates" in Chapter 4, but now we'd like to look further at exactly how people find themselves overwhelmed.

No matter how prepared you believe you may have been, your spouse's death may leave you feeling buried by an avalanche of details. One woman complains,

> *One of the worst things is feeling so overwhelmed with practical things*

to take care of that you don't have time to grieve and get your feelings together.

—*Woman, 62, 2*

The formalities of dealing with the death itself can be grueling even when they go as they should. When they don't, they can drag you into emotionally brutalizing bureaucratic entanglements. Just the paperwork alone can do it, as this exchange attests:

Q: What kind of business did you have to do?
Ann: Well, I had to arrange for the burial, and I had to take care of paperwork. If you had any legal papers—you had to have his name taken off of your home, for instance. And there are a thousand things to do. You have to write in for all the death certificates. It's just a horrible experience.
Leonard: They wouldn't even give me a death certificate for several weeks. I couldn't even collect the insurance because the insurance people said, "You have to present a death certificate."
Edwin: Well, what was the reason?
Leonard: Something about the coroner's report. Finally, when I got after them about it and said that I wanted to have a death certificate, they sent me one that said "doctor's possible mistake" [spreading hands in disgust].
Edwin: That's what happened with my son. They held his body for a week or two until we got the death certificate. They had to find out if he had narcotics or anything like that in his system. So we had to wait a while before they paid off on his insurance.
Leonard: The same thing with me. I had the funeral set for a certain time and then they held it up. The coroner wanted to examine my wife one more time. I think they were trying to decide whether the doctor actually made a mistake or not. So I couldn't even bury her. I had to call the funeral off and do it all over again.

—*Los Angeles, #1*

Edith also found the autopsy to be a symbol of how society is apt to put its own interests ahead of the well-being of the survivor:

I had no guilt, but the hospital almost put guilt on me. Now, I know what he died from; it was fast, it was his heart, it gave out. But right away they hit you with an autopsy. They say, "Well, don't you want to know—for your son's, for your grandchildren's sake—what he died from?" But I didn't allow it. I said, "No, I don't want to hear about it. What you write on the certificate is what he died from."

—Boston, #1

And the pressure to act quickly may add to the strain, as it did for this woman:

There was a feeling of urgency to get everything taken care of in short order. I wish I had had the presence of mind not to tie it all up in such a hurry. At the time of death it seemed resolution was a necessary process.

—Woman, 49, 2

Heap these new demands on top of all the other problems of daily living and, no matter how much assistance you may get with them from others, you probably feel under siege. What might normally have been just nuisances become magnified into crises and crises into something worse; and they all may seem to start multiplying with uncanny rapidity, as in this litany of small and not-so-small travails:

Events conspired to keep me facing each day as it came. Earlier in the year before my husband died, we had had a few crises—broken water pipes after a freeze-up, car breakdown, and IRS audit as a result of the fire loss [a campus fire over a year earlier had destroyed all her husband's books and research data]. And only about a week before my husband's death, there was smoke and soot all through the house because of an oil burner problem.

After he died, there seemed to be one thing after another that needed attention, or a new crisis. Having just completed an insurance claim for the water damage, I couldn't face having someone in to clean up the smoke damage and making out another insurance claim. But I did have to clean the downstairs, at least, before the memorial service. Federal and state taxes were due, my son joined the unemployed in April, my car continued to have a series of problems, and it seemed as if everything that could break down in the house did so in the next six months—to name a few, the refrigerator, the washer, first with a broken belt and then the gasket on the front load door blew out (with the washer full of clothes and water, of course), the shower didn't work, a water pipe and the faucet had to be replaced in the kitchen.

In addition, there were estate matters to work on, my mother-in-law to look after, finances to figure out and bills to pay. There were a few mornings when I thought to myself, as I trudged up to my office on the campus, "And my husband died of stress!"

—Woman, 68, 8

"Coping with all these things," she observes wryly, amounted to "a kind of therapy, but not really the sort one might recommend."

Her suspicion that everything which *could* have gone wrong *did* is not an uncommon one. Here is another recital of events that conveys how completely a husband's last illness and death can make a jumble of a previously well-ordered life:

Margaret: *Well, everything happened that year. My husband was at home ill—a bad heart. I was working. And I was mugged on the way to work. Thrown down in the street, lost all my credit cards, everything I had. I continued on to work—I didn't even want the police to come that morning to write up a report because it might disturb my husband. My legs were bleeding, [laughing] my wig fell off, pedestrian picked it up [laughter], because it was Monday morning and every Tuesday morning I went to have my hair done so by Monday I'd have to wear a wig. And—I look back on that— don't believe that all happened to me.*

Then—by this time my husband had been taken to the hospital—trying to get my American Express and my Visa cards straightened out, they were charging on his, and I was getting bills, and they would connect me with the fraud division. Between the correspondence and the credit cards and the running to the hospital . . . there were a million things like that! I look back at the nightmare of it all!

Then he died. And when I took his remains out to Pittsburgh, had him buried in my father's family plot out there, I was robbed. My apartment was broken into. My silverware was stolen—oh, I don't know all the things that were lost.

My daughter and son came up for the funeral. My daughter stayed for a few days, and she said, "If you don't leave this apartment and get a smaller one where you might be safer, I won't go back to Florida with my husband." So between moving and writing the fraud division [laughing] about the credit cards, trying to write thank-you notes for condolences I had received, going to work every day and . . . angry . . . and . . . I look back on it and I wonder if it was I? Did I go through it all?

—Miami, #2

If, in telling her story, she seems to linger more over the loss of her credit cards than of her husband, you should not be surprised. The death of a spouse dislocates life so jarringly that any lesser deprivations may take on a disproportionate size—especially when it's easier to talk about them than about the larger one.

Margaret's story also points up something else: the phenomenon of multiple losses. The laws of chance make it inescapable that some people will suffer a string of misfortunes that appear to defy those laws, including the deaths of those dear to them. Tales like these—depressingly—are not as unusual as you would hope:

> *Our 16-year-old had earlier lost her sight and was diagnosed as having M.S. Then my husband had a stroke and he was in a coma five months before he died. During this period I lost my 43-year-old brother to cancer and my mother to a heart attack.*
>
> *—Woman, 51, 5*

> *Q: How long has he been gone?*
> *Lil: Ten years, but my brother-in-law had died ten weeks before my husband. And I'd be with my sister and saying, "You'd better pick up the pieces, you know; let's go bowling." Around ten weeks later she was telling me the same thing. Then my brother died; right after that, his wife died. And friends, I had a friend that died suddenly too. For a while it seemed all I did was go to wakes and funerals.*
>
> *—Boston, #2*

> *Rose: I didn't only lose my husband. I lost sisters and brothers just before that. I lost three of my sisters and brothers in three weeks! And then I had one sister left who I really socialized with a lot. We were very close in age. And she died nine months before my husband. There were five of us, and I'm the only one left. It was such a tragedy that a lot of my friends couldn't understand it, really.*
>
> *—San Francisco*

They may have been the victims of the caprices of chance. But some clustered deaths may not be mere coincidence: cases where the stress caused by one death appears to have induced another, through the agency of the proverbial broken heart. This is what Ann thinks happened to her husband after the death of their 14-year-old daughter, from a brain tumor that had paralyzed her for a year and a half:

My husband began to brood. He couldn't live. He just couldn't go on. He actually killed himself by brooding over it—within three months he had a heart attack and I lost him.

—Miami, #2

Here, the shock of loss may well have been lethal. But, as we'll see in the next section, that shock may protect you as well as endanger you.

Shock

"Shock" is the word almost invariably used of bearing the brunt of the death: "First comes the shaking and shock, and then the tears and screams" (woman, 64, 2). It's mental stress at its most intense and extreme; at the same time it packs a wallop as if it had dealt you a physical blow (in fact the roots of "shock" go back to a French word meaning "to strike"). And it expresses itself in some visceral ways. Shaking is indeed one. Mary, who had to drive back to Boston from the Cape after she heard the news, says, "My knees knocked all the way home" (Boston, #1). Screaming is another, as it was for Irene after she was told:

But when everybody left, I wanted to be alone. I went into the den and I screamed. I just kept screaming.

—Los Angeles, #1

But these are the gut responses which generally pass fast. More long-lasting is an emotional state usually characterized as "numbness" and "emptiness":

Fay: *I don't care if you expect it, I don't care how you see your husband deteriorate, when it happens it's a shock. You go numb and you're entitled to be hysterical.*

—Los Angeles, #2

Another woman (57, 3) sums up what she felt as "empty, no feelings, no desire to eat." Raymond (New York #2) compares it to going "into a trance. I couldn't believe it happened. I didn't want to eat. I didn't want to do anything."

The total apathy he experienced often grips people at this time, as it did Edith, who explains that ordinarily

I'm a very capable person. I was president of one of the largest organizations in my area. I could get up and talk to five hundred women and say, "We need money, we'll collect the money." And, "We'll do this, we'll do that, checks will go here and checks will go there."
                                                                                    —Boston, #1

But when death invaded her own household, she confesses,

Right away, I'll tell you, the pile of bills was like this [raises hands to demonstrate] and the checks were like this [does so again]. And I just left them there on the dining-room table.

Others recall that, if they acted at all, they acted like robots:

It seemed almost an automatic process filing all of the paperwork. I didn't fully comprehend all I had done for some time.
                                                                                    —Woman, 49, 2

Recommends another, of the first days,

Find someone who can walk you through the whole procedure. As organized as I consider myself, I was in such a daze that I functioned like a zombie.
                                                                                    —Woman, 62, 2

Sometimes this inability to make the mind focus on things becomes protracted, as it did for the woman who recounts how she was plunged into

deep shock for quite a while. My children and neighbors helped a lot because I could not concentrate while I was recuperating from the shock.
                                                                                    —Woman, 62, 3

"Cognitive scatter"—including "memory loss and indecision"—is the expressive name one woman gives to it, and she says that, when combined with the obtuseness of her supervisor, it defeated her efforts to complete her Ph.D.:

My eldest, who is now finishing his doctorate, said recently if he had been older he would never have let me drop out. My husband had

*been my source of encouragement and support; after his death I seemed
to lose focus and I had a* lot *of cognitive scatter. No one explained
what this was. I got some counselling, but it didn't restore motiva-
tion. Some faculty were very supportive, but my committee chair-
man never acknowledged I'd been widowed, and three months after
Floyd's death I was really hassled about some minor details in my
plan of study. The effort it had taken to write and submit it was monu-
mental, and I could never seem to get enough energy to redo it.*

—*Woman, 62, 12*

Writers about grief have generally agreed that, in addition to being
our first reaction to death, shock is also our first line of defense against
it and that the numbness which envelops us, despite its frightening
side-effects, is a buffer against more terrible pain. By spinning us off
into ''an outer space'' where ''we can't recognize it,'' so the
reasoning goes, shock enables us to get through such preliminary
ordeals as the funeral, the burial or cremation, the negotiating with
lawyers, Social Security, insurance companies, and so on. And this
contention may be true for a good many, as it was for this woman,
who, distraught as she was, rose to what others expected of her:

*Total devastation! I was surrounded by family and friends and I did all
the things I knew had to be done—but it was all very mechanical. I
couldn't eat. I lost weight. I was in complete control of my emotions
when around friends, who often commented on how ''great'' I was!
When alone, I was hysterical and cried for hours!!*

—*Woman, 75, 7*

And some say the trauma did spare them full awareness of the reality
of what had happened for a good while:

*Fay: I think when it happens, you're numb. You don't really know
what's going on and it takes a long time before you realize that he's
gone. You feel that, at any moment, he's going to walk through that door.*

—*Los Angeles, #2*

In a calculated subterfuge, this woman *willed* herself to believe it for
a time:

This ploy *worked for me at first:* pretended *my husband was out-of-
town on a business trip, for a few days.*

—*Woman, 66, 7*

Six months is mentioned as a typical duration for shock:

I lost my husband almost two years ago. It is a horrible experience. The shock stayed with me about six months, then the realization and loss sets in.

—Woman, 64, 2

The same went for Virginia, who ascribes her delayed reaction to being absorbed in caring for her three children:

Virginia: It took me six months to actually realize it. Then all of a sudden it hit me.
Q: What happened?
Virginia: I just fell apart. Now, when he died, I had three boys at home, which had helped tremendously.
Q: How did that help you?
Virginia: Well, they were always there and always very active, and of course there was nobody else to take them here and there, so it was up to me to do it. It just took up my mind and my time.
Q: And then, six months later, what happened?
Virginia: I just couldn't understand it, I couldn't figure out why, and everything just seemed like . . . as if there's no point to this.

—Boston, #2

"You blunder along in grief for at least six months" is the vivid way another puts it, who describes herself as feeling "numb and useless" during the time (woman, 70, 4). So the shock may be a kind of balm—a "gift of nature," as one writer about grief terms it. Yet there is no guarantee that shock will dampen everyone's pain. "Numb" is scarcely the word you'd apply to this woman, even though she was exhibiting the same bewilderment and disorganization that the preceding people did:

Simply put, it is terrible! I wished I were dead too. The pain is so deep, you can't sleep. I could not make important decisions or balance a checkbook for six months. I did not accept investment advice for six months, which actually cost me a lot in the long run. What they were saying didn't seem important at the time. I did not trust my judgment. I wondered how survivors made it without the support I had.

—Woman, 63, 3

And although she appears to believe it was a mistake in her case, her instinct not to trust her own judgment may be sound for most in her situation. You'll note that what unites people's descriptions of what they mean by shock is a profound mental disorientation and disequilibrium. And it's one that can persist for years rather than months:

Do not move and do not sell home or other property (bonds, etc.) for at least one year, and better, not for two years. You need to get over the shock to think straight. Do not marry again for one to two years for the same reason!

—*Woman, 73, 9*

And while you are struggling to think straight, to "understand it," to "know what's going on," you may feel you're in a frame of mind that borders on, or crosses over into, mental illness. Edith (Boston, #1) describes the whole process as "sorting out" and, when asked what she went through to do it, says with grim obliqueness, "Let's put it this way—you're not well when you're sorting out." Others are more direct:

Friendships and friend networks are really important, especially the first year or two after losing a spouse. Most people I know who have been through it go a little crazy. It's smart not to make any more major decisions than absolutely necessary because one may not be totally compos (standard advice and TRUE).

—*Woman, 62, 12*

The utility of this standard advice (as indeed it is) we'll examine at greater length in the next chapter. Here, we simply want to emphasize the reason for its possible validity: "You're not emotionally ready to make a rational decision" (woman, 38, 2). A repeated message of survivors is this: you may be in more psychological peril than you realize; beware of trusting yourself too much and steel yourself for the unexpected, for delayed reactions, and for sudden resurgences of the sort that beset Melba for the first year:

Well, I say, the first year, forget it. You're not even living. I remember that first year, and it was hard.
Q: What's the worst part about it?
Melba: Well, you could be in a crowd and all of a sudden it would hit

you, or you could be driving along—boom! And there's nothing you can do to stop it. But if you live through the first year, you're doing all right, I think.

—Miami, #2

The awareness that "there's nothing you can do to stop it" can be the most frightening aspect of all, and you may feel it's gone so far beyond your control—or lasted so long—that you need help from people more knowledgeable about how to contend with it. That seems very much to be so with this man, who cries, fully three years later,

This is a terrible situation. I adjusted to the Army, to the Korean War, and to the 48th MASH. I remember the ones that didn't and were led away crying, hysterical, or frozen with terror. Lila's death recalled all that and has made me feel that my time for shellshock has arrived. Remembering her strong will and optimism has helped me not to give in, but I think that I am faltering.

—Man, 57, 3

Clinically, he may be right on target when he diagnoses himself as a case of combat fatigue, of shellshock. And he recognizes he should no longer be trying to handle it alone:

Anyway, I plan to look for groups that deal with this. Up to 1986, I think I was on quiet hysteria. Now that this is wearing off, and I have to face this awful loneliness, "hang on" or "put up with it," I'd like to meet others and see what they are doing.

A similar kind of panic seems to have frozen this woman, who now regrets not having "sought professional help" and urges others in like predicaments to do so:

The first year I think I was in a fog and very frightened. I had two girls about to graduate from high school about a year apart. The fear of how I was going to make sure they went further with their education (as they so much wanted to do and as my husband wanted for them) was overwhelming.

—Woman, 53, 2

At least she can locate an origin for her fear, but others cannot and find it all the scarier for that, like the woman (63, 3) who discloses, "I was absolutely petrified to be in a group of more than six persons, even though they were my best friends.'' She reports, ''I've overcome this''—again on her own, although she too wishes she'd had the benefit of ''counselling.'' People's experiences with various forms of counselling—from support groups to clinical treatment by a professional—are surveyed in the last part of Chapter 5.

Other Symptoms of Stress: From ''Hypochondria'' to Hallucinations

Grief has the power to disrupt the interplay between mind and body, and, when it does, both body and mind can behave in peculiar ways. Some of them we've heard about already, like insomnia and loss of appetite, and we'll glance at a few more here. There may be pain, pure and simple. The pain may be signalling that there is something physically wrong with you that requires physical intervention—like surgery—to correct, even though, as Sharkey surmises here, it may have had its origin in mental and emotional strain:

> **Sharkey:** *I went into a deep depression and I was in stress, everything combined. And then I had a back operation for a ruptured disc. Three months after my husband died, I had pain in my leg. A friend got me to a doctor at Massachusetts General, and right away they gave me a myelogram and they found out exactly what was wrong. I was on the operating table the next day. But it was all due to stress and depression.*
> **Edith:** *I think stress does an awful lot of it.*
> **Evelyn:** *And you don't even realize it.*
>
> *—Boston, #1*

Or it may be the product of pure imagination. That is what Lee's doctor told him of his pounding heart:

> *I used to go to bed at night and hear my heart go, ''Pow, boom, boom,'' like a son of a gun. And I went to the doctor and he says, ''Well, you're still under pressure, you know.''*
>
> *—New York, #2*

Marlene, the survivor of a suicide, was told the same of an attack of panic that made her pass out:

They didn't say what happened, but I suppose everything built up inside of me, and one time I passed out. I had a seizure. They said nothing was wrong with me—it was more or less just anxiety.

—*Miami, #1*

Edith was the victim of an illusion not unknown to the survivors of the terminally ill—that they have contracted the disease that killed the spouse:

Right after, I had to go to the doctor because I thought I had the same thing. You know, it's ridiculous, but it's true. You take on their illness and you have real pain when it's really not there. So you go, and they tell you you're fine.

—*Boston, #1*

She theorizes, shrewdly we think, that "it's part of the mourning period to identify with your spouse's illness." But why? Could it not be from the wish we've heard several times now—the wish that "I were dead too"? You are alive and your spouse is not, and this, as we've seen, is a fact shock may not let you believe yet. Wishing yourself dead too is one way of sidestepping it. So is its opposite: wishing your spouse back to life, a wish that may also manifest itself in startlingly physical ways that verge on hallucinations:

Fay: You have a couple of people in, and you're accustomed to having him make the coffee, and you sort of expect him in the kitchen making the coffee. And that isn't so.

—*Los Angeles, #2*

Julia: Now, we had twin beds the last few years, and it is strange, some mornings I'd get up and I'd start to say something. And then I'd look over the room: "Oh . . . he's not there."
Q: How did you feel?
Julia: Well, it was . . . a down *feeling.*

—*Boston, #2*

The simplest reminders of your lives together can be enough to trigger these lapses. The time of day, for example:

Virginia: Every night, for a while, I'd look at the clock and I'd

*say, "Time for him to come home." Then, after about six months, I
came out of it.*

—Boston, #2

Or a trip to the supermarket:

Marilyn: *Buying food, I will forget that he is not in the house any more,
and I will actually pick up a favorite food—I don't buy it, I pick it
up—and for a split second I say, "He likes this." Then I'll say, "My
God, what am I doing?"*

—Boston, #2

And of course dreams, the classic routes to wish-fulfillment, can
serve as gateways for the same fantasy:

*Even several years later, I found myself thinking, "I must ask him
about that," or, "I'll tell him I saw So-and-so when I get home." There
were also dreams in which he was there, even though in the dream I
knew he was gone, but (as dreams will do) there was some way he
had been allowed to come back.*

—Woman, 73, 19

These illusions are the work of disbelief and its more vociferous
partner, denial, operating instinctively. Fay acknowledges it in her
own case:

*My husband was a healthy man, a strong man. He was rarely ill, rarely
had a cold. And then when he had cancer—I just couldn't understand
how a healthy man can get something like that. He walked three or four
miles a day, twice a day. So it's very difficult to accept. And today, in
the evening, I think he's in the bedroom, you know, that he's gone to bed.
You just think he's still there.*

—Los Angeles, #2

Perhaps none of the examples we've seen so far would fit the
definition of the full-fledged hallucinations that are cited in the
clinical literature on bereavement; but the apparitions that haunted
Raymond might well qualify:

*Two years ago, I found myself in a very, very strained situation. I
saw faces of people. I saw them every night when I closed my eyes.*

Not only my wife but other people too. This went on for about twelve days, and finally I went to my doctor.

—New York, #2

He managed to find relief—but from something prescribed by a friend rather than his doctor, who tried

to give me some Valiums and other things I didn't want. Then a friend of mine told me that if you make believe a curtain is being drawn down over that face, it will go away. And I did and I swear it worked. I didn't see that face any more. I saw the curtain, but I pulled the curtain down myself. It might sound weird but it did happen.

It's a pity all the symptoms of stress are not susceptible to home remedies like these. Many of the reactions we've noted already—like apathy, insomnia, indifference to eating, "cognitive scatter," sudden panic—and others to come later in this chapter—like weeping and feelings of anger, worthlessness, and guilt—are characteristics of depression, anxiety, or the two combined. And they can create so much havoc in a life as to demand medical diagnosis and treatment. So perhaps this is the place to underscore this woman's warning:

The whole gamut of emotions will come—love, hatred, fear, loneliness, unworthiness, and all of this is normal. What is not normal is to let it control you more than temporarily.

—Woman, 86, 7

But perhaps it's also the place to reiterate that temporarily may mean quite a long time indeed and to repeat what has become a dictum of books about the experience: the loss pitches you into such emotional turmoil that nothing you are feeling can readily be branded abnormal. *Not* to have these feelings, or to repress them, may lead to trouble too. As one woman confides:

Grieve as much as you want. It will help later. I did not and am still having a rough time.

—Woman, 55, 3

And her sentiments are almost uniformly shared when people talk about the particular expression of grief considered next—crying.

Tears

Tears are the primordial way of venting grief, and some societies still encourage women, and even men, to let them flow freely in public, as part of communal rituals of mourning. But not, of course, in the West generally and in the United States in particular, where the license for public mourning does not extend much beyond the casket or the graveside.

This taboo may account for the distaste with which some react to the thought of doing any crying in the presence of someone else, even people close to them. In Chapter 1, we saw the extreme positions which people can take on the matter when we looked at the debate over "How open should you be?"

> *Smile—no one wants to be around a depressed person. Cry, and cry loud if you must, but do it alone.*
> *—Woman, 81, 21*

> *Talk about your life together. Don't hold in your thoughts and feelings. Cry alone and also openly with friends and family. It is quite normal, and your grief will pass quicker if you share it.*
> *—Woman, 73, 9*

The reticent ones are probably contending with the fact that tears *do* represent a loss of emotional control, if we yield to them involuntarily (as we usually do). And no one likes to lose control in front of other people.

That's why we refer to resorting to tears as "breaking down," and why people who do advocate openness so often warn us not to be afraid and ashamed:

> *Don't be afraid to call close friends for support when you need it—there's nothing like a good friend's company to help you over a "hump." Don't be ashamed to cry—you need to.*
> *—Woman, 55, 2*

> *Don't be afraid to cry a lot in public and in private. It's not easy!*
> *—Woman, 65, 2*

Some weeping can be so vehement, however, that it may only leave others abashed and helpless; and, for it, privacy is probably the best setting, as it apparently was for the woman (69, 2) who says, "I tried to do my own wild crying on my own."

People are almost unanimous about two aspects of crying—its necessity and its value, whether done by oneself or in the company of others:

> *Q: Lydia, when you lost your husband, what kinds of things did you do for yourself?*
> *Frieda: [anticipating] She cried.*
> *Lydia: I cried. I'm still crying every day.*
> *Dorothy: We all cried.*
> —Miami, #1

A lone holdout does inveigh against all crying with an almost Biblical fervor:

> TEARS PROFIT US NOTHING. *They take strength which is needed in abundance in order to cope. They blur the vision and dull the mind. We must have clear vision and clear minds to make proper decisions and successfully think our problems through and assume our responsibilities.*
> —Woman, 77, 3

But the rest with something to say about it take quite the opposite position:

> *One must cry, in the night, with family, in a friend's arms.*
> —Woman, 75, 3

> *Accept the fact that it is OK to grieve—to weep. If you didn't mourn, it would say that your relationship wasn't very meaningful.*
> —Woman, 72, 3

Crying, in other words, can be constructive—as the phrase "a good cry" has always implied. "Cry a lot," commands one woman (69, 10). Another (50, 3) repeats the immemorial belief that it's a form of self-purification: "Tears are a catharsis." In fact, researchers have recently found some scientific support for this idea in the fact that tears appear to purge the body of chemicals it manufactures in response to stress. One woman (74, NA) even recommends a means of facilitating them:

Watch "tearjerker" movies on TV. It helps to release the tears.
                                                              —Woman, 74, NA

And another passes along the pretext she concocted for hers:

Don't be ashamed of crying—it does help. At first I felt it was a weakness in me. On days I couldn't stop the tears, I made onion soup, so that when my adult children came to see me, I had a good excuse for the red eyes. They caught on after a while. Anyone wanting onion soup, let me know, because I have a freezer-full—and I do make good onion soup.
                                                              —Woman, 74, 3

In talking about crying, people often portray it as something which they may have tried to resist but to which they are now surrendering:

Don't fight *sadness—give way to it—cry, yell, whatever, when alone. Essential to work it through.*
                                                              —Woman, 70, 4

Weeping may therefore be a way of relaxing, for a moment, our will to disbelieve, a way of working through to the truth in sudden bursts of emotional energy, as this woman suggests:

I miss my husband very much. I loved him very deeply. Do not hold back the tears and the grief. It hurts very, very much. Admit it!
                                                              —Woman, 53, 2

For this reason and others, even men undoubtedly find crying helpful, although they may be traditionally adamant against letting anyone see them at it. It may be a measure of the continuing strength of male attitudes on the subject that not a single man in our survey or groups even alluded to it.

We should end this section with the cautionary note we have sounded before in discussing the potential benefits of painful emotions. Depression can make itself known not only in listlessness and lethargy but also in the upheavals of crying jags:

Mary: *For two years after he died, I cried and cried every night. And finally I got sick from crying. You know, that can really affect your nerves.*
                                                              —San Francisco

With that caveat, we'll go next to a painful emotion that everyone agrees has no redemptive aspects.

Loneliness

Most survivors single out loneliness as the worst of their tribulations—the most all-pervasive; the most insidious and relentless; and, sadly, the most intractable. It heads the list of the problems enumerated by our survey participants. "The greatest enemy," one brands it (woman, 67, 2), adding the assurance that "eventually you learn to have a little fun again." But many say that it continues to darken their lives long after the other shadows have receded:

> *The loneliness of losing your "Best Friend" is the hardest part to cope with, and time really doesn't help that part any.*
> —*Woman, 56, 2*

> *As for the loneliness, nothing changes that—you live with it every day.*
> —*Woman, 62, 2*

The years that may pass without alleviating it can be formidable:

> *Do not be distressed if getting adjusted to the loss takes much, much longer than you and many others expect. (Three years for me were very painful ones, and the loneliness continued even after that.)*
> —*Woman, 67, 8*

> *Losing a spouse is the most traumatic, devastating experience of my life thus far. After six years I feel I am coping well with the situation by keeping busy, but the loneliness never really goes away.*
> —*Woman, 61, 6*

> *I have been a widow for eight years. The most difficult situation for me is the "aloneness" of being a "single" instead of a "couple." I still miss my husband dreadfully and I have no solution to the problem of loneliness.*
> —*Woman, 67, 8*

One woman, who was widowed at 46, relates,

> *I returned to college for a master's degree, then taught for five years and was an administrator for twelve before I retired in 1983. I was*

therefore forced into a new life and career. Nonetheless, in the twenty-two years since my husband died, I have never ceased to regret not being part of a "couple." In fact, C. S. Lewis probably expressed it best when he wrote after the death of his wife, "Her absence is like the sky—spread over everything."

—Woman, 69, 22

Some even discover that time deepens loneliness:

After almost three years, the loneliness and longing are more rather than less. Time may dull the constant acute pain of the earliest weeks and months. But the pain still recurs very frequently, and the longing and loneliness get worse with time.

—Woman, 66, 3

I must truthfully say that there are still times when the loneliness becomes more and more unbearable. I sometimes wonder if it will ever cease; but so far, NO!!

—Woman, 73, 4

After reciting some of the usual palliatives, another woman declares that none of them assuages the pain:

They just divert it temporarily—and the lonesomeness increases like a cancer, unseen, but there.

—Woman, 57, NA

In particular, age, with its encroachments on energy and mobility, may serve to exacerbate it:

I'm more lonely now than when my husband died eleven years ago, because at my age I have to slow down a little.

—Woman, 75, 11

The loneliness may also be of an intensity that far surpasses the other versions of it that you've known:

Noreen: It's all right through the day when you're with people and having fun, fine. But when you close the door at night, you're alone. And, in the morning, it's just the missing of that person. I mean, no one can explain it. No one knows unless you've been there yourself.

—Los Angeles, #2

Wedlock is, after all, the cornerstone of the social structure—of the families, clans, tribes, and nations that we have always found essential to the conduct of life. And there may be no more primal a fear than that of being alone, isolated and helpless, cut off from the human family. A spouse is one of our first bulwarks against this fear, and, when death breaches it, the fear rushes in with a force you may not have felt since childhood, if ever:

> *When I, an only child, was orphaned at the age of eight, my guardians stressed that I was going to spend a good part of my life alone and would have only myself to depend on. Also, unlike many women of my generation, I was a working wife and "family financial administrator" because my husband's extremely busy schedule left him little time or energy for such matters. Therefore, when my husband died suddenly, I did not find dealing with the practicalities of estate settlement and the like, or the hassles of daily living, very difficult. However, the sudden cessation of so many years (thirty-eight) of close, happy companionship was traumatic. Although I returned to my teaching as soon as possible, I found the time by myself almost overpowering. I was ALONE, as my guardians could never have described it to me.*
>
> *—Woman, 73, 14*

Some sense of this is what prompts other people to make sure that, in the emergency of the first hours or the crisis of the first days, the survivor has human company. They often do so as automatically as they would cover an accident victim with a blanket, like the policeman Irene found standing on her doorstep:

> *He asked, "Are you alone?" And I said "Yes." "Could you get a friend?" "For what?" "Well, I came to tell you some sad news. Your husband passed away."*
> *Q: What happened next?*
> *Irene: Well, a friend of mine on the corner came over immediately when I called her, and some of the neighbors came over, and they consoled me. My daughter came. They finally located her, and she came at twelve o'clock and stayed with me the rest of the night.*
>
> *—Los Angeles, #1*

As another Irene explains, simply having someone else around created an aura of animal reassurance:

My sister-in-law, one of his sisters, stayed with me because I have no children. That really helped out—having somebody stay in the house with me.
Q: What did that do for you, Irene?
Irene: Well, it gave me some support. I wasn't alone. I suppose, if I had had to stay alone, I could have. But it did make it easier for me to have someone with me.
Q: Do you remember any particular thing she said or did that made you feel better?
Irene: No, just her presence.

—Boston, #1

Of course, as usual, we can find at least one person who was able to dispense with this reassurance, whether because of the shock or more deliberately we can't tell:

Sylvia: I wanted to be alone.
Q: You did?
Sylvia: I did. I wanted to be alone. I went ahead with all the business that I had to do. Really, I didn't even remember doing it. But I carried on, and no, I didn't want people.

—Los Angeles, #1

Others, however, want people at the time so desperately that their need may become pathological, as Sarah relates of someone who eventually needed institutional care:

I have a friend that was extremely intelligent and had a keen sense of humor and seemed to be with it. When she lost her husband, her life stopped at that point completely. She had no incentive to go on, and I would visit her almost daily. She could not be alone. She would dial friends every hour on the hour. She had to have every moment filled in with other people.

—New York, #1

Although the presence of others may afford some immediate comfort, it's bound to be temporary, as Evelyn laments in discussing with Edith the custom in Judaism of "sitting shiva," perhaps the most systematic of the approaches to grief prescribed by the major Western faiths. Edith explains to the group how the Jewish ritual tries to ease the survivor into the reality of being alone as gradually and gently as possible:

My religion helps us. We have a way of dying and handling death that is very satisfactory to me. It gives us a week with a lot of people. You can't even think. You are exhausted, and it is good for you. You just want to sleep. You know, "Let them go home!" And after that you've got a month that they don't really leave you alone. You know they're there, friends and relatives, and you should start taking control of yourself in that month. And then for eleven months after his death, every night or every morning you say a prayer. But after the eleven months, it's against my religion to mourn. You've got to be through with it. You've got to have a memory, but not a mourning memory. And I think this is the healthy way to cope with death.
—Boston, #1

But Evelyn rejoins right away,

That doesn't help everybody because I'm of the same religion and it's fine, but then they all go home. And you're still left with the problem, whether it be right after the funeral or a week later.
Edith: *But you have all these people there.*
Evelyn: *Yes, I did too. But then afterwards the dawn came. I was still left alone in a big house. My daughter went back to New Jersey and my son went home to his family. My son said,"Mother, come stay with me." What was that going to do? I'll be with him, with the kids, but I still had to come back home. I had friends and my friends were wonderful to me, but I was still in a big house all by myself.*

"Afterwards the dawn came"—it's the awakening experienced by most: finding that you're all by yourself in a house suddenly made too big by another's absence:

All the pouring out of sympathy at the time of death—then nothing.
—Woman, 73, 17

After the death, relatives, neighbors, and friends were very attentive. Then, within a week's time the hard fact struck home—utter loneliness!!!
—Woman, 73, 4

Because loneliness is such an important part of grief, we'll spend much of Chapters 3 and 4 illustrating how people have been able to fend it off and, in Chapter 7, how they have learned to live with it and come to regard "being alone" as quite another thing than "being lonely." But here, you'll note, the two conditions melt into one overall misery, as people begin to discover how a spouse's presence may have permeated their lives in ways they were never conscious of until now:

Lee: My doctor used to say, "Do you have any sisters or brothers?" I said, "Yes I've got a sister." He said, "Good idea: go to your sister's, then come back." So that's what I did. But when I came back, I missed everything I took for granted.

—*New York, #2*

It's tough being sick alone and not having anyone around to get ice water or a cup of hot soup. It's all the little things—the companionship!

—*Woman, 67, 3*

I fear growing old alone, being sick alone, facing surgeries alone, even though I have many interested adult children. Being without a spouse, even with family support, is a complete change in a person's life.

—*Woman, 58, 4*

And along with everything else, it's a world of shared emotions that has disintegrated. So all the events of everyday life—even those that might give pleasure—may seem to conspire to make it worse:

Sad things make me sadder and beautiful things make me sad without the chance to share the beauty with my spouse.

—*Woman, 66, 3*

Not surprisingly, nighttimes can be especially bleak:

Evelyn: No one is coming home at night.
Sharkey: Yes, to be alone at night is the worst. During the day you survive, but at nighttime it's just terrible.

—*Boston, #1*

The dead of night drove it home the hardest for Sylvia the two times she felt the tremors of a Los Angeles earthquake. During the first,

> *There was me and a dog and a house. Although I was frightened, I called family, my son, my sister, all over, to make sure everyone was all right. I found the aftershock on Sunday more frightening, because it was in the middle of the night. And while there are many times one feels all alone, there is something about the middle of the night where one feels more alone. At eight in the evening you can make calls, and you are doing something, you're acting, you are in charge in some way. Whereas at four o'clock in the morning I could only deal with me, and it was frightening and lonely.*
>
> —*Los Angeles, #2*

She's identified *one* of the ways being alone can be so lonely—it can prevent you from verifying that you matter in the lives of others. But there's a corollary that may be even harder to accept: the knowledge that you will never matter as much to others—even family and close friends—as you did to your spouse. This may be what Lee is expressing, with the widely recurring image of the door that, closing behind you at the end of the day, heralds an empty evening:

> *But it's rough when you're home alone and that door closes, you're by yourself. And I think the better your marriage was, the harder it is, because when you were together all the time and you're left alone, your family doesn't make up for your partner.*
>
> —*Miami, #1*

Over and over, loneliness is distilled in the lack of "someone to talk to":

> *The most difficult problems I experienced were having no one to come home to; no one to discuss daily events with; the maddening silence at home, especially on weekends.*
>
> —*Woman, 72, 3*

Marriages may be life's longest-running dialogues, with your spouse in the role of "that regular person to bounce ideas back and forth," as Roger says in amplifying what Murray means by "you lost your other hand actually" (New York, #2). We have noted earlier how easy it is to slip into the illusion that he or she is still listening:

We had always discussed everything important, and I found myself many times going down the hall to an empty bedroom to ask his opinion.
—*Woman, 71, 7*

A similar yearning troubled this woman, who says that, after forty-two years of marriage, ''I missed most that we talked to each other a lot'':

I was with my husband when he died—of a massive heart attack—and when he was taken away, even after the funeral, I felt desperately, for a very long time, that I should be looking after him.
—*Woman, 69, 6*

Some people have a refreshingly straightforward response to these fancies: yield to them. After one woman (63, 2) advises other widows, ''Talk about your deceased spouse,'' she adds, ''Don't be ashamed to speak to him.'' And another woman certainly wasn't (though she concludes her confession with an amusing twist of hard reality):

What is it like to survive my husband? Loneliness! How can you share thirty-three years of marriage and not feel this? My answer was to just cope with it every day. I found myself talking to Bob a lot the first year, and still do when I really want to share happiness or sadness with him (I also scrubbed the kitchen floor a lot).
—*Woman, 59, 2*

In Chapters 6 and 7, where we examine how people have been able to find comfort in their memories of their spouses, we'll find many—and not necessarily the superstitious—who have come to the conviction that the departed have in fact not left them altogether.

The loneliness often stems from something even deeper than the absence of talk, and, because it does, some people describe aloneness as an almost palpable sensation and the silence as not only wordless, but soundless as well:

What is hardest for me? The silence. Not just ''No Conversation.'' The SILENCE! The first year is tough. People say it won't be so difficult after that. I have found the second year and since harder. I've had to accept that this is the way it is going to be for the rest of my life.
—*Woman, 69, 3*

She's mourning the bare fact that no one is around the house, making those familiar noises; and, to mask it, some people keep a radio or television playing constantly. Again and again, survivors marvel at how *physical* a void the spouse has left. What triggers the cruelest pangs are often the times of day when some of the most common-place, but also the most casually intimate, moments of your life together occurred, moments that may not have necessitated much in the way of words, just an appreciation for the other's being there:

> *My biggest problem was getting used to the idea of "aloneness"—the last thing at night and first thing in the morning and while eating a meal at home or in public.*
>
> —*Woman, 60, 5*

> *It's tough! The loneliness is almost too much to bear, especially in the evenings and waking up alone.*
>
> —*Woman, 67, 3*

"The empty-bed syndrome," one woman (68, 4) labels it, noting she found it "the hardest to cope with." And she's probably referring not to sex but to mere touch, as this other woman clearly is:

> *The thing I miss most about losing my sweetheart is that I have no one to talk with about my innermost feelings, no one to touch; a hand to hold; an arm to hold on to.*
>
> —*Woman, 59, 3*

And the measures by which survivors try to compensate can be as poignantly primitive as the nature of what's missing:

> **Dorothy:** *You know, I still sleep with a teddy bear. I have a stuffed teddy bear. And it's not funny, because I was so used to sleeping with him, my hand still goes out and I'm . . . [trailing off]. That teddy bear is all beat up, but it's my security blanket.*
> **Laura:** *I take a pillow.*
> **Dorothy:** *That's all right. A pillow is good, too.*
> **Lee:** *There really is no answer.*
>
> —*Miami, #1*

Lee is of course correct in this particular instance, and about the larger problem. And this woman explains exactly why:

He is gone two and a half years, and the ache has hardly lessened. I
am lonely, but not for others—only him.

                                                        —Woman, 64, 2

If you long *only* for your spouse, others can never fill the gap.
Organized social activity, friends, and family—ultimately all must
fall short:

Associating with widows, bridge, short trips, etc., all help, but living
alone is sheer agony.

                                                        —Woman, 75, 3

Comfort is found to some extent in group activities and friends. But
realize that survival emotionally is very hard. One can be very lonely
with family and/or friends.

                                                        —Woman, 74, 9

Friends, travel, and keeping active—volunteer work and being with
people—were of most help to me. But my husband died three years ago,
and I still miss his companionship as much now as I ever have. My
feelings are not morbid, but the loneliness remains.

                                                        —Woman, 76, 4

And she's not being morbid if she finds *his* companionship
irreplaceable. It is and always will be, for "the loneliness is emotional, not social," in the words of a woman whom we've quoted
several times before, because she details her sufferings from it more
copiously and passionately than anyone else in our survey:

I am starved for the emotional intimacy and sharing of everyday things
that can never be replaced by social interaction. Work, socializing, or
whatever are all "diversions"—to give you respite from the intense
loneliness.

                                                        —Woman, 66, 3

In fact, she goes on, the company of others may even compound it:

Social situations are lonely and empty without him even though other
friends or relatives are around. This absence is so intense in such social
situations that I feel even lonelier.

We'll close with the most obvious potential cure for loneliness, so obvious that you are probably wondering why we haven't brought it up already:

> *Remarrying is the best thing widows or widowers can do for themselves in the long run. It's the loneliness that gets you down after the grief is gone.*
>
> —Woman, 58, 10

We've refrained because we've reserved the whole ticklish subject for Chapter 6. We'll only comment here that, although it can work wonders (as it appears to have done for the woman above), acquiring a new spouse—or a new sexual partner—will no more magically banish loneliness than friends or family will. To the extent that loneliness is simply a pining after what has been permanently lost, it may very well last as long as you will.

Anger, Hatred, and Envy

The trio that are the subject of this section are perhaps the most unsavory characters included in this chapter's lineup, and they are all close relatives. So it may be tempting to identify them and hustle them back to their cells as speedily as we can. But because they are a side of ourselves that we aren't very eager to scrutinize, it may be worth tarrying over what others have to say about them—and hearing the reluctance with which they do.

Aggression is what fuels anger, hatred, and envy alike. And the impulse to *act* that they embody sets them off from shock and loneliness, which prey on us at our most passive and leave us decidedly on the defensive. So some writers about grief have viewed these aggressive feelings as forces for good, a sign that we are beginning to emerge from the trance of disbelief and to confront reality, if only just to beat our fists against it. Emotions like anger—and guilt, the subject of the next section—do clearly spring from an urge to make sense of what has taken place, to assign causes to it.

We are angry when we are injured, and our anger swells when we can find someone to blame for that injury. One of our first targets may be the most seemingly irrational:

Marlene: *When I get upset and I look at my husband's picture,*

sometimes I cuss him out.
Frieda: *Oh, I've done that. I get so mad at him for going.*

—*Miami, #1*

Ann was dumbfounded when her daughter voiced a similar resentment:

> *My daughter was very angry when her father died. You know what she said? "Mother, it wasn't fair of him to go off and leave us." Well, that shocked me. Because death is something none of us choose for ourselves. And I couldn't make her understand that. Anyway, she was very torn about it.*
>
> —*Miami, #2*

But this sense of abandonment, of being deserted and even betrayed, can oppress adults as painfully as it can children. Listen to Ruth, who was sick so frequently that she always assumed she would die before her husband:

> *Many times we would joke around, and he would say, "Don't worry, when you're gone, I promise you, I'll never get married." "Well," I'd say, "I don't care what you do when I'm gone." He'd say, "No, I'll never find anyone I could argue with as well as I can with you." So when he died, I felt it was wrong. I was angry with him. He left me. All this burden. All these things on my shoulders. I had never, never had anything like that happen to me. My boys always protected me, my husband always protected me. I didn't know how to do any-thing when I was left alone.*
>
> —*Miami, #2*

And the anger can harden into something that survivors can frankly call hatred:

> *Do not be surprised if you have moments when you feel hatred to your loved one because he left you behind.*
>
> —*Woman, 86, 7*

Sylvia: *And I had another emotion. I don't ordinarily hate, because there's nobody in this world I don't like. But I hated my husband. I hated him for dying. I said, "Why did you do this to me? Why did you do this?"*
Lillian: *That's something I've never been able to understand.*

Ina: Did anybody else have that feeling?
Bud: I did.
Sylvia: I really did and I was so heartbroken over feeling like that.
—*Los Angeles, #1*

Sometimes this anger may have its roots in something real, such as a spouse's failure to take precautions against what caused his or her death—usually "his" because it's a commonly perceived male failing:

I think men don't go to doctors as often as women. Women take care of themselves better. I really was very bitter when my husband died, because he would never go to a doctor. And he could have prevented it. But a month before he died, we had been on a trip, a cruise, and he got deathly sick. And the doctor asked, "Does he have a heart condition?" I said, "I don't know. He never goes to the doctor." Now, that makes you bitter.

—*San Francisco*

"What else is new?" exclaims Hannah, when Ruth says, "I was angry with him because he didn't take care of himself when he should have" (Miami, #2).

If your marriage was not entirely satisfactory, your memories of what was wrong may vex you terribly. Bad marriages are a subject into which those who filled out our questionnaire were understandably reluctant to venture—as, for that matter, were the participants in our groups. But Edith may be hinting at it here, when she was asked whether, after eighteen months, her anger had subsided:

That anger? Well . . . [long pause], I just don't let myself think about anything in the past that wasn't really good. I've gone forward, but I'm not all the way there.

—*Boston, #1*

And Connie's anger is still very much alive three years later, when she confirms Sarah's conjecture that the death of her alcoholic husband may have come as a "relief":

Connie: Yes, actually. It is not nice to say, but it is true. I think I would eventually have killed him myself [laughter].
Sarah: Thank God you were spared the necessity.

Connie: *You are right. I told that to the doctor, and he laughed.*
—New York, #1

More often, however, there is no ''justification'' for the way you may feel, save for the fact that he or she did indeed ''leave'' you—which of course, emotionally, is plenty of justification. And the anger may encompass many more objects than your spouse. Right after the death, some are furious, rightly or wrongly, with those responsible for his or her care—with ''doctor, hospital, diagnosis,'' and all the rest, as one woman (62, 3) fumes. Anger may emerge as the envy of others who still have their spouses—and may be increased by how little they appear to appreciate what they have:

Lilian: *Afterwards, I went down South to visit with my parents. And I would hear women in the restaurants saying about their husbands, ''Oh, he's such a bum! I hate him!'' And I thought, how could they think that way? They didn't realize how fortunate they were.*
—Los Angeles, #1

Finally, anger may spill over into the world at large, as it did for Edith when she found herself raging at an anonymous ''them'' to bystanders in the cemetery:

Edith: *Anger? Are you kidding? I went to the cemetery with my son and I yelled at everyone there: ''How dare they do this to me!'' But I felt better. And my son said, ''Feel better, Mother? OK?''*
—Boston, #1

At its most all-embracing, it can extend to the entire cosmos, in ways that mystify those who have not experienced it, like Elizabeth (Miami, #2), who asks Ruth in utter puzzlement, ''Were you angry with him, the world, or God, or who?''

Sometimes the answer is all three—him, the world, and God. People in the grip of this kind of anger are prone to lash out at the ''injustice'' of what death did to them. Instead of deploring the unfairness of a spouse, they may denounce the inequity of a universe, as this woman is essentially doing:

My husband died suddenly from a first heart attack. He never had a serious illness, and we thought he was in perfect health. We were

enjoying our freedom from financial worries and family worries, as our children were all emotionally and financially settled. I greatly resented his being taken by death when we were so happy.
—Woman, 68, 2

This kind of bitterness often afflicts the survivors of a sudden death; and, when it does, it is no good observing to them that, if they and their spouses had been leading healthy and happy lives, the fact might be something to be thankful for. They may eventually come around to this view. But not now, any more than those made miserable by envy will find consolation in perfectly sensible reflections of this sort:

People our age have so many maladaptive life patterns. My friends who envy women who still have their husbands often don't give themselves credit for helping out their own for twenty to sixty years.
—Woman, 73, 9

If you had sixty years together, it may make it much worse than having had twenty.

Most of those who have been struggling with these emotions agree that they're transient and that, when you have finally shaken them off, you're well rid of them. As to how much good they do in the meantime, however, people differ. We've seen Edith "feeling better" after her outbursts in the cemetery, but also Sylvia "heartbroken" over the hatred she briefly bore her husband. And consider John (New York, #2), who had lost his wife suddenly in his 30s. He exemplifies how dangerous anger can be when it threatens to dominate one's personality, especially a man's personality, more predisposed to aggression and less tolerant of frustration than a woman's. Anger can be a powerful spur toward alcohol and drugs, and so it was for John. A year and a half later, he says he needed "more than anything a relief from the rage that I felt," a rage which lured him into "a lot of drinking and craziness"—and into asking a question that may be one of grief's most demoralizing and destructive dead ends: "the center of it, what it got down to, I was trying to say, 'Why me?'"

We'll look further in Chapter 7 at how this question may be our touchstone in the extraordinarily difficult task of separating "productive" grief from "self-pity." As for John, although he concedes that he still cannot "feel really peaceful" about his loss, he did find the relief he sought in friends and professional counsellors, including one of the most old-fashioned—a parish priest. With others, the anger just burns itself out on its own, as it apparently did with Ann:

> *And so, you're angry: you're hurt and, after you're hurt, you get angry. And then you say to yourself, "Well, but you have to accept it. This is the way it is."*
>
> —*San Francisco*

Guilt

Guilt is much more complicated than anger. Guilt is a species of it, among other things, but a convoluted one because the anger is directed at ourselves. Guilt also gets snarled up with other emotions that are anger's opposites, like shame—including shame that we may have given way to anger. And guilt denotes an objective fact as well as an emotion: it can signify both the wrong that we have done and our remorse about it. We are guilty not only *about* something but also *of* something.

Of what do survivors think themselves guilty? First, of simply having survived. It seems absurd that something which is so clearly not a wrong in any meaningful moral sense could inspire self-reproach—until we recall how fervently some wished "that I were dead too." And this type of existential guilt may be sharpened when you find that you are not only alive but even—occasionally—enjoying it:

> **Grace:** *When I started dating after I lost my husband, I had a guilt feeling, that I shouldn't be doing it.*
> **Q:** *Did anybody else go through that?*
> **Frieda:** *Yes, the first date.*
> **Dorothy:** *Not even a date. I felt guilty when I laughed. I said, "Why am I laughing? I have no right to be enjoying myself." I got over that.*
>
> —*Miami, #1*

As Dorothy implies, it may be fairly easy to surmount such feelings of being disloyal to your spouse after he or she is gone. More difficult are the occasions, real or imagined, when you may think you failed your spouse before then.

Occasions of that sort clearly bothered this woman, who after three-and-a-half years allows,

> *I have by no means completely adjusted to the emotional aspects. In particular, I have difficulty with guilt feelings for sins of omission as well as those of commission. Since I have not discussed this with other widows or with professional counsellors, I have no idea if this is a common difficulty.*
>
> *—Woman, 71, 4*

From the evidence of both our survey and our discussion groups, it's very common. One of the injunctions survey participants most often pass on to those who are still married is this:

> *Be your spouse's very best friend and lover. Live each day as though it will be your last one together, so you will have no regrets about things spoken or unspoken.*
>
> *—Woman, 69, 2*

The prevalence of this advice may thus be proof that guilt feelings are widespread. But what does it say about their origin?

Sentiments like these could be coming from people who are dwelling on what were serious flaws in their marriages. Just as plausibly, however, they could reflect a relationship that was very near to being entirely satisfactory, and we suspect the truth for most is more likely to lie in this direction. As we noted in the last section, if our people were the survivors of unhappy unions, they generally don't own up to it (much less go into detail about it). Most describe themselves as just the opposite. Take this woman, the wife of a minister and former college president, who now recalls her life with him with an obvious serenity and is among the majority of survey participants who gave themselves the highest of the three possible marks for adjusting. Yet she was badly beleaguered by guilt:

> *My husband died quite suddenly as we were preparing to go on vacation. We were in the process of rewriting our wills and trying to finalize them before leaving. We went to bed with some differences unresolved. His sudden death in the middle of the night left me in a state of shock, but when that wore off, I needed professional help. For some reason I blamed myself and could not forgive myself. When I realized that, the healing began.*
>
> *—Woman, 83, 6*

The disagreement over the wills clearly sparked her guilt. But can it fully account for its intensity, an intensity that demanded counselling? That seems likely only if the fact of his death had somehow magnified the disagreement into its cause.

And why not, in her subconscious at least? It sounds like half-baked theorizing from a psychology textbook, but what else could explain the power that, say, a trivial domestic squabble, which might have been set to rights the next day, can wield over the memory when that next day is no longer available? Words, no matter how casually or hastily spoken, can resonate terribly in retrospect, as Marilyn knows:

> *Every man and woman has arguments, you know you do, you have words with your mate. And when you can't say, "I'm sorry"—because they are taken from you so quickly—you do go through a very bad time. You say, "Gee, I wish I hadn't said that!" And you go through "I wish I had" or "I wish I hadn't" for a very long time, because you do have guilt, you can't help it.*
>
> *—Boston, #2*

And the words not spoken can be just as tormenting, as Pat discloses in rebuking herself for a supposed failure to recognize what was coming:

> *The sad thing was that when my son Bobby came out from Connecticut, he found, on his father's desk, a legal sheet with the plot number of the grave in Indiana, where he was going to be buried, and also a list of the pallbearers that he wanted. My husband had a premonition, he must have, you know, that he was going to die.*
>
> *But I never saw it—I never paid any attention to what was on his desk unless he'd ask me to look for something there. And my son said, "Look at this!" And I said, "Well, he mentioned the plot number of the grave many times." There's a huge plot back there for his family. We counted twenty-two headstones. There are two left, one is his and one is mine—it just happened that way.*
>
> *Anyway, my son wasn't upset, but he said, "Didn't you know about this?" And I said, "No." Had I known about it, the day that I took him into the hospital for just a final checkup, had I known that I was never going to bring him back home, things would have been different. I would have talked to him about it. Instead of saying, "Everything is going to*

be fine. Bobby will be here in three days."

Oh, and then he said, "Don't forget to ask Father Reilly to call on me." And I said, "Oh, I was hoping you'd ask for Father So-and-so." Because his favorite priest in our parish is not one of my favorite priests. Another one is. He said, "Well, I like Father Reilly." And I said, "Fine." And I just took everything very lightly, you know. I just wish I had known so I could have said more to him.

—Los Angeles, #2

Regardless of whether she's right or wrong in constructing her hypothesis of a premonition from these clues, she is caught up in an exercise that is futile, even though it may also be inescapable. She and Marilyn—intelligent and articulate women both—are engaged in hopelessly wishful thinking on two counts: wishing that they "had known" and that, if they had, "things would have been different." Two totally impossible aspirations, but by entertaining them, as some writers on grief have suggested, we may be instinctively seeking to regain the sense of control over the life of another that death deprived us of. We might have made a difference—if not by postponing the death, then at least by sweetening its memory.

With this kind of guilt, we're also trying to explain the inexplicable, as we are when we get angry. If our spouse wasn't responsible, then we were. Either way, we now have a reason for the death. But anger is likely to leave us feeling impotent, because its object, if it's our spouse, is no longer here, or, if it's God or the world-order, may appear very remote indeed. The object of our guilt is conveniently close at hand and can be punished with no damage to anyone but ourselves.

These twin urges—to seek a cause and to reassert control—are what make reveries about "if only . . ." so seductive and so tenacious. A final illness is especially likely to act as a catalyst. Some survivors, like these two, can find solace in the help they were able to give their spouses during it:

I was very much in love with and loved by my spouse. When he became ill, I did everything I could to make him comfortable and happy. Having done these things, I had no regrets.

—Woman, 56, 4

Do not feel guilty that you survived. Accept death as a natural part of life. Be glad you could help your spouse during the final illness.
—*Woman, 65, 7*

But such peace of mind is apparently rare. Look at how persistently the doubts gnaw at Irene (and we're quoting her at length just to show that persistence), despite her knowledge of all the reasons they're unwarranted. She did all she could, and there was no further action she could have taken because she had neither the knowledge nor the power to take it. Nevertheless, the questions keep nagging, for the perfectly sound psychological reason she posits as she begins her story:

I think that whoever is with the person that passes away, whether it's your mother, father, brother, husband, sister, whoever is with them in control of the situation, there is always some guilt that comes up. There's something that maybe you should have done that you didn't. Even though at the time you're doing everything possible.

I was visiting my husband in the hospital about two days before he passed away. The nurse came into the room. She took his blood pressure and she said, "You're running a low blood pressure, so I'm not going to give you the Hydralazine because that lowers it more."

So then, two days later when I was there, another nurse came into the room and she took his pressure. And I said, "What is it?" And she told me, and I was shocked. I said, "Isn't that low?" And she said, "No, for him it's not low." So I said to her, "Are you going to give him the Hydralazine? Because the nurse before said she wouldn't." And this nurse said, "Yes."

Well, who knows more, she or me? So it just didn't hit me. And then the next night the doctor called me up and said he passed away. I felt guilty because I knew his blood pressure was low and yet the one nurse gave him the pill that the other nurse didn't. Though, actually, I didn't know. And if she didn't know, why should I know? I thought she knew what she was doing. That's what I have a guilt feeling about. And yet it was nothing in my control, so actually I shouldn't feel guilty. But it always bothers me.
—*Boston, #1*

All this self-recrimination in spite of the fact that she's in possession of the most decisive rebuttal to it:

But of course it probably wouldn't have made any difference. He really didn't have much life in him anyway. His heart was very, very low. He couldn't even walk. He was practically dead then.

However much we know it wouldn't have made any difference, the obsessiveness with which we fret about what might have been testifies to how hard—sometimes impossible—it may be to eradicate these regrets. It's even harder when you *do* know you might have made a difference, as Sharkey did when she and her husband decided against risking the life of their son on the chance of saving his:

I feel guilty because, when he had the choice to have a transplant, my son was a candidate. But we discussed it and we thought that we didn't want him to go through the agony of the operation of giving a kidney to his father. What if something happened to him? *And you know, if you lose one kidney . . . But now I feel, "Well, why didn't we do it?"*
Connie: *The operation might not have been successful.*
Sharkey: *I don't know. But I'm always thinking, "Maybe, if he had that kidney, he would have been alive today," and it's always going through my mind.*
Q: *You made a good decision with what you knew at the time. And it wasn't only your decision.*
Sharkey: *No, it was his decision also.*

—*Boston, #1*

Her awareness that the decision was as much her husband's as hers may make her dilemma less lacerating, but it doesn't show her a way out of it. That can only be done through the final realization that it's all beyond remedy now, a realization that should lift the burden even if the decision had been hers alone. "What's past is past"—if you can say that resolutely (and, in Chapter 7, we'll be looking at some people who can), you have probably vanquished your guilt. It may then dawn on you that it was not *really* guilt at all, not the sort we might feel if we stole something. Throughout history, as a regulator and reformer of human conduct, guilt has played a hugely constructive social and moral role, but in our lives as individuals it can do so only with respect to how we behave in the future. And the guilt we feel as survivors is trapped forever in the past. This woman may be suggesting the essential artificiality of such emotions in grief by her use of quotation marks when she says, ''Realize that it is perfectly natural to go through the 'hate,' 'guilt,' etc.'' (woman, 48, 7). Another woman sees guilt as a hindrance to real emotion, when she says she's trying

> *to be joyful or sorrowful when my feelings tell me to, to be resentful*
> *and desperate, and not be guilty about it. Don't lament the imperfec-*
> *tions of yesterday. ''If only'' is out.*
>
> —*Woman, 73, 9*

Until we've attained this frame of mind, however, ''if only'' may seem an implacable opponent. Some of the standard tactics for wrestling with it are those this group uses with Lydia below: realism (Frieda), fatalism (Lee), and counterattacking with guilt-free memories (Dorothy and Ida). All these points of view—along with Lydia's self-castigation—can be accommodated within your mind all at once, for, as Marlene and the rest note, there is nothing like guilt for stimulating an inner debate:

> **Lee:** *Everyone goes through the same guilt feelings—that you could*
> *have done this when he was alive and you could have done that. I don't*
> *think there's any answer because, for every person, you have to find*
> *your own way. What's good for one may not be good for another.*
> **Lydia:** *I feel guilty because my husband had a cold and he left for work*
> *Saturday morning and I told him, ''Don't go today because you don't*
> *feel so good.'' And he answered me something—I didn't understand*
> *what—and he walked out. Then they came with the news.*
> **Frieda:** *But why do you feel guilty?*
> **Lydia:** *Because I didn't hold him back.*
> **Frieda:** *You told him not to go. You couldn't hold him down. He's a*
> *man.*
> **Lydia:** *I should have screamed, ''Don't go!''*
> **Lee:** *When the Man Upstairs wants you, you go whether you say yes or*
> *no. It was probably his time, and you can't stop that.*
> **Dorothy:** *The guilt feeling—I got over that. I keep saying to myself,*
> *''Oh, you were the best God-damned wife that ever was.'' And I really*
> *was.*
> **Marlene:** *I talk to myself a lot.*
> **Laura:** *We all do. We all talk to ourselves.*
> **Ida:** *Everyone goes through that guilt complex. But then you have to*
> *look at the good that you did.*
>
> —*Miami, #1*

As we'll see in Chapter 7, a strong religious faith can be an enormously helpful ally on this front.

Finally, as Marilyn's tale below illustrates, you must be on your guard against others who try to exploit your guilt, your anger, or both—an attempt from which she rightly recoiled:

> *When my husband went to work in the morning, he fell right out of the elevator at the office, and that was it. There was no one there who knew CPR. And the doctor at the Medical Center told me if someone had given him CPR he might have been alive. That . . . [incredulously] was not the right thing to say! Sometimes doctors are very heartless. Then he said, "Do you want to do anything about it?" I'll never forget what I said: "Do* what? *What* are you suggesting? *Do you want me to sue someone because they didn't give him CPR?"*
>
> *—Boston, #2*

Happily, there was a more benign sequel: without any intervention from her, everyone in the office learned CPR, and she even took a course in it herself.

This is not to say—as we'll see shortly—that you'll inevitably feel guilty over a spouse's death. When the topic came up in some of our groups, some people disavowed such feelings, and we have no grounds for disbelieving them. Women, as some researchers have speculated, may have more of a propensity to guilt than men (virtually none of our men alluded to the subject), and children more than either—a problem we'll glance at in Chapter 5. And guilt can rack one group with especial fierceness:

> *Coping with suicide is an added blow. You never get over the feelings of guilt—that, too, you have to learn to live with.*
>
> *—Woman, 68, 2*

The Bibliography cites several books written exclusively for those grieving over a self-inflicted death.

As we've seen several times, survivors often feel most vulnerable to guilt about supposed derelictions—"Why didn't I say such-and-such to the doctor?" in Elaine's words (Los Angeles, #2)—when they were "in charge" of their spouses' last hours or days. We'll conclude with a reaction that may outweigh all the others when those last hours or days have stretched into months or years.

Relief: The Special Case of Terminal Illness

Guilt may plague you in the aftermath of a spouse's prolonged final illness for all the usual reasons, as this woman recognizes:

> *The care of a terminally ill spouse is emotionally, physically, and mentally exhausting. Forgive yourself of things you wish you had or could have handled better. And thank God you were able to do all that you did during this time of your spouse's and your life.*
>
> —*Woman, 45, 2*

But in cases like hers, the guilt may be triggered by one emotion in particular:

> *My husband died of ALS [Lou Gehrig's Disease] after five years. The last year was bad as he had lost the use of his arms and legs. I had him at home, and I grew terribly tired—and cranky with him. His death came as a relief to us both, but because of this I felt quite guilty for a long time. I am fine now.*
>
> —*Woman, 74, 7*

And, in fact, the illness may have put you through a trial so agonizing or interminable—or both—that your relief may be completely untinged by regret:

> **Beulah:** *I had no guilt, probably because I had devoted fifteen years to caring for him almost constantly. And in the end he was in pain, and in a way it was a relief. And you know, if he had his choices, that's what he would have wanted. Fifteen years of being an invalid!*
>
> —*Boston, #1*

Gil was "happy" and Joe "thanked the Lord" when their wives died, as they explain in their intertwined accounts:

> **Gil:** *My wife was an Alzheimer's victim and came from a family that had it before her. As a matter of fact, her mother had it, and we took care of her in Beverly Hills. And then a younger brother got it, and a younger sister, and then she came down with it. She was ex-*

pected to live about seven years and part of that time she was bedridden. It was a long-drawn-out proposition. But I knew the experience of others with nursing homes and I didn't want that. So I took care of her at home with the aid of a visiting nurse. And I was emotionally drained by the time she did pass on. It was a relief, for her benefit and mine; I was happy that she passed on because she was very bad. She had to be spoonfed for years.

Q: Joe is nodding on that one.

Joe: Yes. My wife—it's hard even after [referring to his tears]—was, oh, she was a lovely person. But she was sick, sick for so long that when she went I thanked the Lord for it. I knew if she lived longer she would be getting worse and worse all the time. So I said, if it was the Master's time to call her, that's good enough for me. Because she was just going down, down, down, and I couldn't stand to see her suffer like that. It was just like Gil's wife, only my wife could talk. Gil's wife couldn't talk to him.

Gil: Only through the eyes, that was the only recognition.

Irene: Gil was the most devoted husband. I'm his neighbor, and everyone prayed for him and her both, because he was so devoted to her.

Gil: All the same, I had to be happy when she died, because it was a miserable way to live.

—Los Angeles, #1

"A blessing for both" is how such deaths are commonly greeted:

Richard: You're so helpless when someone is dying of something terminal like that. I mean what help can you really give them?

Murray: There is only one good point. When someone is struggling and you see their suffering, it's a blessing for that person when death comes. You say, "Thank God!"

Richard: Yes, we all say that when the person dies—"Maybe he's better off, God bless him."

Murray: He is better off.

Noel: It's also a blessing for the person that they leave behind even though they don't want to admit it.

Murray: It is a blessing for everyone.

—New York, #2

Numbered among everyone may be a whole family that has become caught in the disease's vortex, not just the spouse:

> *Ann:* *He had a very strong constitution because he lasted longer than the doctor expected. But it was a blessing when he went because there was no hope for him and he was suffering. I was suffering. The children were suffering. We didn't have a day and we didn't have a night without it.*
>
> —*Los Angeles, #1*

Many terminal illnesses ravage their victims mentally even worse than they do physically, and this may create an emotional distance between spouse and the sufferer long before the death. This woman may be hinting at it:

> *My situation was atypical. The length of my husband's illness gave me plenty of time to adjust, and we had pretty much gone our separate ways, which softened the blow of his loss.*
>
> —*Woman, 81, 5*

This man is much more blunt:

> *It was a relief when my wife died. Due to her illness (heart and diabetes), she was compulsively and militantly aggressive. The last years were unbearable.*
>
> —*Man, 76, 5*

And so is this woman:

> *Inasmuch as my husband's death was due to heart trouble (ischemic) and strokes, my answers apply only to those widows who have been caring for a long period for someone who has marked mental deterioration and great personality change. By the time he died he was a stranger. My grieving had been done years before.*
>
> —*Woman, 69, 6*

What researchers have called "anticipatory grief" may supplant the lost intimacy and may make it easier for survivors to adjust afterwards. Such was clearly the case above—in fact, her experience would seem to contradict the standard warnings in books on bereavement that no one in her situation can expect to accomplish all their grieving beforehand. This man—"very happily married for forty-two years"—discovered he could not:

I knew far in advance of my wife's terminal illness, so I was prepared for some of the consequences and had everything in order. But no matter how well you plan, there is still a pattern of adjustment that everyone has to go through. You have to accept that life has to go on.
                                                              —*Man, 73, 7*

The same went for this woman:

As he had Alzheimer's disease, I knew I had lost him several years before he died. This didn't help much when death became a reality.
                                                              —*Woman, 75, 5*

Indeed, as we saw at the outset of this chapter in discussing disbelief and denial, some people stave off the realization that a condition *is* terminal until the last possible moment, like Lillian:

My husband died from cancer of the liver. He talked to the girls about his going, but he never talked to me about it. Apparently he didn't want to hurt me. And I knew he was sick, but I kept telling myself he was going to recover. He had had about eight chemotherapy treatments, and they didn't have the awful effects on him that they had on others. After about the fourth treatment, the doctor said the liver was shrinking. And so I just kept myself smiling and thinking that he was going to get better.

And then he was at home after that, and I had a woman there, a health aide, helping me. It was very difficult for me because we always did everything together. We traveled a lot. We'd go walking after dinner. He was a very energetic man. He had immense vitality. He'd get up at about 5:20 in the morning, get dressed, make breakfast for himself and me. And then he would walk from the house to Burger King, and he'd get the express bus to his office. He was an architect.

Anyway, from being an energetic person, he started to rest an awful lot and did very little walking. And then one day he asked the aide if she would help feed him. Well, after he did that, I went out and I walked about three streets away. And I cried my eyes out because I knew I couldn't make myself think he was going to get better. That was too much—that he should ask somebody to help him like that, a man who never took any help, always did everything for himself.
                                                              —*Boston, #1*

Still, as Edith reminds her,

> *We widows who have had our husbands sick for a long time do better than those who were devastated immediately with death, when you get it just like* this *[claps hands], with no preparation. I mean, we never really prepare for death, but we should. And when the doctor says to you, "I don't know whether we can bring him through," it's time to prepare, whether it takes six months or a year.*

And others confirm that, by the time death finally arrived, they had been through the worst:

> *I was blessed with adequate resources and enough experience to handle them reasonably. My children were independent and very supportive during their father's illness. I was completely in charge of the family's affairs during the last year of his life when he suffered from the effects of a brain tumor. My grief had come a year earlier, and, when death finally came, it was a relief, and I was ready for new activities.*
> —*Woman, 73, 12*

> *I suspect my period of deep mourning was shorter than the experience of many husbands devoted to their wives because I had been secretly mourning my wife for at least two years before she died. She had ALS and every month lost another function or physical capability although her spirit remained courageous and her mind clear to the very end.*
> —*Man, 67, 2*

In addition, a physical separation enforced by the illness may make the final one easier to bear. Clara, whose husband's mind became so "befuddled" that he required care in a nursing home for sixteen months (where she nevertheless continued to visit him every day), confesses,

> *So when he passed away, he was away from me, and the adjustment wasn't quite as drastic as it was with Rose. Because I more or less expected it. And the morning that they called me from the home and told me, when the phone rang, I knew exactly what it was.*
> —*San Francisco*

Stories of final illnesses often revolve around the selflessness of people like Joe and Gil who balked at putting spouses into nursing homes and stoically endured anguished years of caring for them personally. But the question of whether to place a spouse in an institution is never morally clear-cut. This woman credits her decision to do so virtually as her salvation:

> *My husband died six years after a series of strokes left him speechless and crippled. He had been a brilliant professor of philosophy at the college for thirty years. He was ten years older than I. It was a nightmare for us both.*
>
> *I tried taking care of him at home. Doctor friends urged me to put him in a nursing home, which I did, and I went to work at the college library. It was this life, that I had established and that I could go on with after his death, that helped me the most.*
>
> —*Woman, 76, 24*

Terminal illness is normally such misery for both parties that it's hard to conceive it might have any redeeming aspects, but we've seen one already: the opportunity to prepare for life alone that some of those quoted above say it gave them. The woman whose husband became "a stranger" to her is quite forthright about it:

> *My advice is, if the spouse has a long illness, use that time to plan one's life after he/she has died. It's good emotional therapy while caring for him. Do all one can to make his life easier, but recognize that one's own life will not stop with his death. This is very hard for most people to do. My being a nurse made it easier.*
>
> —*Woman, 69, 6*

Another woman, whose husband was stricken ironically by the very maladies it was his life's work to combat, describes how her assumption of sole responsibility for the household sustained her the most during his illness:

> *My husband, who had been one of the foremost neurosurgeons in the country, had a series of cerebral accidents and was mentally and physically incapacitated over six or seven years—until finally he was completely bedridden, after some major strokes. I always was able to keep him at home with nursing care during the day. During this long time I gradually learned to take care of the management of our affairs, the bills, insurance, etc. I had advice and help when needed from three wonderful sons, but I took over all responsibilities eventually. I really felt that I had lost my husband years before he died. So that, when he finally did go, I was glad that his sufferings had stopped. I*

know the fact that I could take care of things for him helped me bear this long grieving.

—Woman, 76, 9

Some had the good luck to have their spouses as partners in their planning. Says one woman, whose husband was claimed by a long illness,

I think the fact that my spouse and I had discussed with each other our inevitable separation—and the preparations we made for that event—made my transition to widowhood much easier.

—Woman, 75, 5

Another woman agrees gratefully,

I was financially secure but emotionally distraught. However, I was in an exceptionally fortunate situation since the extended illness enabled my husband and me to plan for our (or my) future years. At the time of his death we had been accepted as residents of a Life Care Community for just over a year. We had given up our large home together with its responsibilities and had quietly settled into a much more relaxed way of life.

—Woman, 77, 11

A husband's heart problems spurred this couple to a new awareness of their mortality—hers as well as his:

Because my husband had a coronary condition that held no hope of recovery, we long knew that he might precede me in death. We were not morbid about this, we rarely spoke of it, but we had a "tacit understand- ing." We shared every facet of our financial status, modest as it was, and we knew full well what demands would be made whenever death should come to either of us. We had made wills, chosen the place we wanted for burial, etc.

—Woman, 77, 2

Those who could lay such plans often knew it was the last course of action they were undertaking as a couple, and some find the memory of it very moving, like this woman who encourages others to do it:

It helps not to have to make these decisions under stress, and there can

be something triumphant in experiencing the execution of the plans you made with your spouse.

—Woman, 69, 2

Terminal illness sometimes made survivors remarkably grateful for another chance that it gave them: just the chance to be of help. Those of us who haven't undergone the experience, and can only surmise how grueling it must be, find it hard not to marvel at this gratitude. Far from nursing a grudge for their months or years of servitude, some, like Al, give thanks for them:

Death was the end of a confining illness, an illness that got very bad. I had a woman taking care of her five days a week from nine in the morning until five at night, when I took over. And I stayed with her during the weekends, Saturdays and Sundays and holidays— which in itself was quite confining but well worth it. She deserved it. And then, after the end came, I was freed from these restraints. Fortunately I have many good friends and I have many invitations to social affairs and to lunches and dinners and the like. That has helped alleviate the loss. But while the confinement lasted six years, I wish it could continue today. I don't regret a moment of it.

—New York, #2

Note how these are the words of a gregarious man, not someone who was totally dependent on his wife for companionship. A woman who "knew from day one there was no hope," but who succeeded in keeping her husband at home for all but the last four days of his final ten months, felt likewise—and so apparently did her children:

What helped me most was that I gave him the very best care I was capable of. The last two months of his life I had a lot of help from Kaiser-Hospice and the Cancer Society—moral support in addition to physical help. And the last month, when he had to have twenty-four-hour care, our sons took turns staying overnight to care for their dad. So we were all very much involved in my husband's illness.

—Woman, 68, 6

In Chapter 6, we note that many survivors, when pressed as to why they have rejected the idea of remarriage, commonly give this reason, among others: their dread of having to tend another spouse during a struggle with a fatal disease. Yet they often hasten to add that they'd gladly do it all over again for the one they lost.

Finally, a terminal illness may have afforded to some a chance that a sudden death could not: the chance to say goodbye. When the sick spouse is not preoccupied (as some commonly are) by his or her own plight to the exclusion of everything else, or too physically or mentally incapacitated, anticipatory grief can be a shared experience:

> *My husband was diagnosed as inoperable, uncurable, and terminal. He was expected to live three to four months, he lived fourteen months. During that time we were able to truly say goodbye to each other. The most helpful thing is to have that.*
>
> *—Woman, 51, 2*

And that's what her husband's asbestosis gave to Nora:

> *He was a very healthy, healthy builder, a great builder. All at once he was diagnosed with this, and they gave him four months. Four months to the day, he was gone. But the point was, he really wasn't ready. He was a very active, very strong person. Near the end, he was in the hospital for about seventeen days, and he just started going down. But he really didn't want to turn loose.*
>
> *And I remember sitting with him one Sunday morning and bringing up the history of us. He couldn't speak, but I could press his hand and he could press mine back. And I told him about what the two of us had done. We had been together for forty-five years. We'd brought up three beautiful children. Two girls. One is a doctor now; the other has a master's in education. My son is the other baby— he does this and that, but he's a nice boy [laughter]. The grandchildren, we had five beautiful grandchildren. And that theatre or community center that we had been working on together. He had been making the plans, drawing them up, and so forth. I think I relieved him of all of that, and I explained to him it was time that he went on now, because he was suffering so much. But that I was going to do it, I was going to do it. And then, after I had done it, he was going to be so proud of me.*
>
> *—San Francisco*

As we'll see when we pick up on her story at the end of Chapter 4, that's exactly what she did. And we trust he is.

Chapter 3

Being by Yourself, I: "Do Nothing . . ."

Do not make any changes in your life, or any major decisions (about what to sell, where to move, etc.) before two years are up, if not absolutely necessary for financial reasons. Sit tight.

Keep busy at interesting and worthwhile activities that broaden your mind and keep you on your toes. Don't sit before "Soap Operas" and vegetate! It's better to wear out *doing interesting things and having a good time with interesting people than to sit and* rust out, *being miserable feeling sorry for yourself! Plan ahead so you have something interesting and exciting to look forward to. Viva the Good Life!*

—Woman, 78, 12

Up to now, we've emphasized how often one survivor will give advice that runs directly counter to that of another. We've keyed this chapter and the next to what are perhaps the only two pieces of wisdom that are agreed upon by almost *all* survivors. One counsels acting and the other refraining from it, but they are not in conflict. The two admonitions—"keep busy" yet "do nothing"—dovetail quite snugly.

They both address a single question: how—and how fast—do you try to resume control over the practical matters of life? The house or apartment is still obstinately there. Meals must be made and bills must be paid. You may have a lawn to mow, a car to keep going, a salary to earn, a child to school. Only now, managing all of this has gone from a joint endeavor to something you must do singlehandedly. The prospect may be daunting to the point of looking hopeless:

Sometimes it seems overwhelming—the survivor cannot expect to carry out all the responsibilities that used to be shared.

—Woman, 67, 2

But this very fact may be be enticing as well. Your spouse's death may have transformed the way you've been accustomed to living so ruthlessly that you may be tempted to retaliate by transforming it even more:

> *Margaret: My advice is, sit back and wait. Don't make any changes. Until you think it over. Because your mind changes so much, and things happen so fast. At the time, you're angry, you're hurt, you're all mixed up emotionally, and you want to strike out at the world and do this and do that.*
>
> *—Miami, #2*

It's a temptation to be resisted, practically everyone agrees (and, again, take heed of that "practically"—we'll let the exceptions have their say in due course). One out of every seven we surveyed made "do nothing" an explicit counsel, and we saw the grounds for their belief in the preceding chapter:

> *Don't make any serious changes in your life for at least two years—if you can possibly avoid it. You are not thinking clearly, or operating normally—and you need to get your perspective back before you really know what you want to do.*
>
> *—Woman, 65, 2*

But acting rashly is not the only danger. An even more sinister temptation lurks in the opposite corner—not acting at all.

In the last chapter also, we saw how apathy can settle over many survivors like a fog:

> *Although I go through the motions of a normal life and "carrying on as usual," I find all the joy, the fun, the* raison d'être *is gone. There is a great feeling of detachment—a feeling of not* really *caring, but I try not to let it show.*
>
> *—Woman, 72, 2*

At least she is "going through the motions," out of an awareness that

> *you* must *accept the fact that you will never see your beloved spouse again, and start your new life, even though you don't want to.*

A similar sense of inertia weighs this woman down:

> *What it's like to survive a spouse: it's a struggle to continue to live a life alone when it was planned and designed to be enjoyed by two. All responsibilities are now yours alone as are all decisions. Everything is done with a feeling of emptiness and no incentive for carrying on. Life truly becomes a "day at a time" effort.*
>
> *—Woman, 75, 2*

But without that effort life may become something even bleaker: an absence of even the motions.

"Sitting around" is the way it's usually characterized, often in front of a TV set (as the woman at the start of this chapter depicts it). It's definitely not the same as sitting back or sitting tight. "Giving up" is perhaps its nearest synonym. And keeping busy is the antidote almost universally prescribed for it:

> *It is an effort to get out and get into activities, but, for me, the only way to adjust has been to keep very busy with worthwhile activities— church, little theater, some classes, League of Women Voters, a local soup kitchen. There's no limit to things that need to be done and are rewarding.*
>
> *—Woman, 69, 3*

> *My children, one hour and six hours away respectively, were a great help, but my decision was to be independent. Therefore, I made new friends—most widows like me; took courses; learned a new craft—ceramics; brushed up on my bridge; and soon found that, though I was alone, I was not lonely. For me, keeping busy helped me adjust to the great loss in my life.*
>
> *—Woman, 75, 10*

> *I forced myself to go back to my volunteer work, church activities and community involvements within a few weeks after the funeral. The activity and responsibility was a blessing! It was my salvation.*
>
> *—Woman, 75, 7*

Virtually everyone in our discussion groups called it their lifeline too:

> ***Clara:*** *Because I was working at the time, I was keeping busy. And I worked for a year after he was gone. Since then I've been very active in*

the church and I hold several positions in it. I sing in the choir, so I go to choir practice on Wednesday evenings, and we have our women's group, and I do volunteer work at the Food Bank in Alameda on Mondays and then other afternoons if they need me. So keeping busy really helps.

Q: What does keeping busy do for you?

Ann: It's the answer to everything.

Q: If you didn't keep busy, what would happen?

Rose: You have too much time to think of everything if you're not busy. You're just vegetating—that's terrible!

—San Francisco

Keeping busy is how you start to fill all this time with the right things. Doing nothing is how you avoid filling it suddenly with the wrong ones—until you regain the confidence that you can discriminate between the right and the wrong. In this chapter and the next, we'll survey what survivors recommend 1) doing nothing *about* and 2) keeping busy *with*. Among the latter, you may be relieved to hear, is the intelligent watching of TV.

On Decisions: "Take Your Time"

"Changes"—and the making of the "decisions" that will bring those changes about—are what people who say, "Do nothing," usually have in mind. That does not mean, of course, that these changes should never be made. Hence the qualification very often added: "Do nothing—right away."

"Right away," however, may stretch from months into years:

Q: Is there something that you might advise other people, Loretta?

Loretta: I would be very careful about everything for a while. Just sit tight. Don't sign papers, don't do anything. Be very careful.

Leonard: For six months at least.

Loretta: Yes, very careful.

Leonard: At least six months. Don't change anything.

—Los Angeles, #1

Take time to assess how to live alone. Do not be pressured into moving or changing your residence until you feel reasonably sure it is what you really want to do. Take at least the first year to make any changes.

—Woman, 77, 13

Don't make any changes for at least three years, i.e., selling your home, remarrying, or traveling extensively.

—Woman, 59, 12

The same "big" changes are cited again and again:

Please don't make any major decisions for at least six months—like:
   A. selling your home
   B. your car (buy or sell)
   C. changing jobs
   D. moving
   E. spending any large amounts of money.

—Woman, 45, 2

And we'll investigate how people have approached each of these (remarriage, the one salient omission from her list, we'll postpone to Chapter 6). For a moment, though, we'd like to dwell on the insistence with which some survivors warn against interjecting *any* more change into a life that has already been so convulsed by it.

"Take your time" is their watchword, and they aren't talking solely about "major" decisions:

Connie: *One of the things I remember—it was always in the back of my mind—that a widow should never make a decision for at least a year. Any decision.*
Rae: *Very true.*
Q: *Has anyone else ever heard that?*
Bea: *I have.*
Ida: *I heard it endless times.*
Q: *Isabel?*
Isabel: *Yes, definitely. Don't rush, don't rush.*
Bea: *That's the worst thing in the world.*
Isabel: *Take your time. Like, if you want to move,*
don't *move, wait.*

—New York, #1

Here the very desire to make a decision is a warning it shouldn't be made, a paradox that, if allowed to direct your life, would bring it to an abrupt stop. But in another group, Margaret illustrates the kind of decision Connie has in mind—and the skewed perspective that made it a misguided one:

> *Margaret: You have a tendency to say, "I'll get rid of this, I'll get rid of that, because I'll never do such-and-such again."*
> *Peggy: People do—you're right! The good china, the good silver, they give it to the kids.*
> *Emily: She's right.*
> *Margaret: All my silver was gone, but I thought, "It doesn't matter, I'll go out and buy flatware, stainless steel, and make that do, I'm never going to entertain again."*
> *Ruth: That's wrong.*
> *Q: And now?*
> *Margaret: And now, I've gotten rid of so many things that . . .*
> *Ruth: You're sorry?*
> *Margaret: Sorry—because I* am *entertaining again. So don't get rid of your things.*
>
> —*Miami, #2*

So people who say "take your time" mean "take it easy," over the little affairs of living as well as the large ones:

> *Take it easy. Don't expect too much of yourself.*
> —*Woman, 66, 9*

> *Be good to yourself. Make only the decisions you* have *to make.*
> —*Woman, 51, 2*

> *Always remember the acute grief and desolation will pass in time; be patient with yourself; the sorrow and loss will always be with you. Don't try to do or cope with too much too soon.*
> —*Woman, 66, 6*

"Time heals." Survivors differ sharply (as we'll see in Chapter 7) over how true this adage may be about grief overall, but they generally vouch for it when your practical problems are the issue:

> *Like yourself—and take good care of yourself. If you cannot keep up with some things, don't worry or fret—let time help heal the loss.*
> —*Woman, 55, 2*

Simply allow time to clarify the basic fact that your wife is no longer living and you are alone. Physical, mental, and social adjustments dealing with this fact cannot be rushed, but at the same time should not be resisted. Time is truly one's best friend.

—Man, 66, 2

Time was what restored to Edith a sense of her place in the world, and note that it is a place she defines in terms of the practical—her vocations:

There is no question time and patience do make it easier. And as more time goes by, your coping mechanism gets stronger, and you go forward with yourself. Because you realize you too are on this earth for some reason, whether it is to be a mother, grandmother, volunteer worker, or just working for yourself, to buy clothes.

—Boston, #1

We don't want to leave the impression that absolutely everyone is an advocate of time and patience. Occasionally—but very rarely—people insist that time must do their bidding instead of the other way around:

Don't postpone doing things you want to do. Time goes by so fast that, if you wait, the opportunity may be gone. Be adventuresome rather than conservative.

—Woman, 75, 9

And here and there you come upon someone who seems utterly nonchalant about even big decisions:

Do not fear making a major change in your life such as a move. Cut down on responsibilities that are burdensome. Do not fear making decisions even though you may make a few mistakes. (It takes about four years to feel independent!)
New address—I just moved 1,200 miles.

—Woman, 72, 8

But such breezy self-confidence (perhaps born of age and considerable experience as survivors) is as hard to find as it is exhilarating to hear.

Taking your time—and "being good to yourself"—may be mandatory if the death has depleted you physically as well as emotionally:

> *Because I had handled the details of our finances during most of our marriage, I had no problems with finances or taxes after my husband's death. But I was surprised to find that I was very, very tired. Apparently my husband's poor health for a long time and final illness had been more of a strain than I had realized. For that reason I took it very easy for some time, not even trying to make plans ahead—they almost made themselves.*
>
> *—Woman, 73, 6*

Intelligent choices are easier to make when you are sound in health as well as in spirit:

> *Recognize the fact that your body suffers along with your psyche. Give yourself time to adjust to a new way of life before any decisions, such as moving, etc., are made. If you own your home (or, if not, if you have lived there for some time), stay there for the time being.*
>
> *—Woman, 69, 9*

While you are recuperating, you have the license for a judicious amount of self-indulgence:

> *Accept help from relatives and friends. Eat what you can and exercise. Pamper yourself. Slowly, independence and the ability to cope will come.*
>
> *—Woman, 82, 24*

It's a time when you should not feel ashamed of putting your own interests ahead of those of others—even those you love. One woman (who nevertheless closes with the benediction "Thank God for my kids, neighbors, and friends!") urges,

> *Be yourself, don't give all of yourself to your children. You are #1 now, and you have to take good care of you.*
>
> *—Woman, 55, 3*

Finally, some survivors remind us that "doing nothing" can reward us with an outcome which we so often hope for when we're lazy—problems that solve themselves:

There will be times when you doubt your own wisdom—just do what has to be done today and push the other worries into tomorrow. They will probably disappear.

—Woman, 77, 20

If possible, do not make any hasty moves— give time a chance to work for you; so often solutions I never dreamed of have turned up unexpectedly for me, in a beneficial way.

—Woman, 84, 9

These serendipitous solutions don't necessarily materialize out of nowhere, however. They may be the fruit of changes in ourselves:

Many problems can be outgrown.

—Woman, 76, 12

Time is the most important part. Take lots of time to make decisions about what to do with your life. As time goes by, you will probably change your mind about some of the things that seemed so important immediately after your spouse's death.

—Woman, 53, 2

And these inward changes may persuade us, as things gradually fall into place, that changes in our external lives aren't called for after all:

Ruth: What I would tell somebody is not to make too many changes in her life—when this very big change has happened. Because a lot of women pick themselves up and change their lives entirely. They sell their homes, and—
Elizabeth: Too late!
Ruth: Too late they turn around and see that this is not what they really wanted. But if they were given the time to quietly make adjustments in their lives, in their environment, they would find that things sort of fall into place, and many times they don't want to change their home. They don't want to change their style of life. They like it.

—Miami, #2

But what if you *do* want changes? You have basically two choices. After due deliberation, you can make up your mind and go ahead with those changes, preferably with no nagging glances backward:

> *Take time to make a decision, and once you have, let it go; don't re-decide the same thing over and over. Be confident that you made the best decision based on both the knowledge you had and your feelings about the situation at the time.*
>
> —*Woman, 59, 3*

Or you can ask for advice. And, as we'll see next, advice is a subject about which survivors are even more ambivalent than the rest of us.

Advice

One of the most intimate matters in marriage may be one of its most seemingly prosaic: shared decision-making. You may miss this side of it as much as any other:

> *We were very close and did everything together. All expenditures were discussed before we made them. I am still adjusting to the idea that I have to make my own decisions without having my husband to discuss them with.*
>
> —*Woman, 53, 2*

You may have forgotten what people who must make decisions on their own know so well—what a necessarily lonely enterprise it is:

> *I think my greatest problem has been making decisions alone. I talk things over with my family, but the decisions have to be made by me.*
>
> —*Woman, 74, 3*

If you no longer have someone to take the step with you, you, like the woman above, should ideally have someone to consult about the merits of taking it—or simply to inform you of the various directions in which you can move. So one injunction often heard is to rely on advice and not try to go it alone:

> *If you don't know how to handle a problem, financial or otherwise, seek help from someone who has the knowledge. Don't be timid about it.*
>
> —*Woman, NA, NA*

> *Move slowly, make no hasty decisions, and balance every potential step with advice from trustworthy neighbors, old friends, or business partners and senior colleagues.*
>
> —*Man, 69, 3*

Don't try to be too independent—use the help that is offered or hire people so that you don't feel overwhelmed by responsibilities.

—*Woman, 79, 6*

Independence may be your goal, but advice is the route to it:

In areas about which you know little or nothing—i.e., finances, car maintenance, house maintenance, taxes, Medicare—you must seek help, be it from friends, relatives, or professionals, until you can become self-reliant.

—*Woman, 67, 4*

Others know what's best to do, but they may mistakenly assume you do too. So you must speak up:

If you have questions, ask—people (and organizations) want to help you find the answers and they will help you. Give them a chance. Do not try to "do it all" by yourself.

—*Woman, 62, 3*

Accept all invitations and offers of help. Call on your friends, neighbors, and relatives. They want to help and can't know what you need unless you tell them.

—*Woman, 65, 2*

Now, as usual, we'll turn to a different set of survivors, who have discovered that people are all too ready to tell you what you need:

Once widowed you are bombarded with advice. I think everyone should follow their own inclinations after thinking them over for a time. Moving will not eliminate loneliness. A year does not automatically end grief. It is a continuing process which each individual must deal with herself *or* himself.

—*Woman, 71, 5*

Another woman also repeats some of the platitudes with which she has been peppered by the "well-meaning," a euphemism survivors like to use about people they think are unconsciously serving them ill:

Make no important decisions for several months. Well-meaning friends will offer such advice as "Sell your house—it's too big," "Take an apartment," "Live with a relative or friend."

—*Woman, 78, 21*

And this woman has some brusque advice in her turn—spurn them:

Don't take advice from well-intenders—take your time about decisions.
—Woman, 67, 3

Another woman complains about having to put up with

receiving advice on what I should do with my life by well-meaning
persons who have not experienced the loss of their spouse.
—Woman, 61, 6

Such gratuitous counsel proved an actual hindrance to her because of the difficulty she found in disregarding it:

I had to learn to make decisions on my own feelings and not feel guilty
if another's suggestions are not my wishes.

This woman appears to have had fewer qualms:

By trying to please and follow the advice of everyone, you may please
nobody—least of all yourself. Follow your own instincts.
—Woman, 49, 9

From fighting your instincts to following them—how can we reconcile these two extremes? It's not enough to speculate that people taking the former stand received sound advice, whereas those taking the latter did not. More probably, their conflicting positions may reflect the fact that the giving and receiving of advice can be an emotionally ambiguous situation, in which even a placid surface may conceal some rather treacherous undercurrents. In asking for advice, or any other kind of help, we are confessing to a certain lack of knowledge or power, something we may find unsettling. Her very realization of her ignorance about money matters, this woman reveals, held her back from rectifying that ignorance:

Be knowledgeable about family financial affairs! I had never balanced
a checkbook or paid a bill before my husband died. Had no idea of how
to cope with insurance, taxes, or household expenses. The prospect of
dealing with money was totally bewildering. The first year I felt I was
in a deep pool and barely able to keep my head above the water. I wish

I had learned earlier to ask for help, but it was very hard for me to do that when I felt so ignorant and uninformed. (I'm sure this is why I did not ask anyone at TIAA-CREF for advice or assistance.)
—Woman, 60, 3

In any quest for advice, we must surrender a degree of our autonomy, no matter how slight, as Elaine postulates:

You know, I think that asking for help is, in a way, losing your independence. You have to want to accept it, and that's very difficult.
—Los Angeles, #2

"Losing your independence" greatly exaggerates it, as she herself acknowledges by that qualifying "in a way"; but she does discern why soliciting advice can be so hard. Asking for it, of course, is only the start. Once you get it, what then? Accept it, and you're in the giver's debt; decline it, and you may put yourself in his or her bad graces.

Correspondingly, the dispensing of counsel may indeed be born of the wish to help, but it also can spring from the desire to dominate, either subtly or crudely. This may explain the wariness with which some of those we've quoted greet the "well-intentioned." (It may also explain why so many people are more fluent at advising than condoling—psychologically, many of us may feel more comfortable assuming authority over survivors than achieving empathy with them, an act which obliges us to put them first and ourselves second.)

In any case, emotional complexities like these may account for the emphasis placed by so many on maintaining a balance between being open to others and acting on your own:

All I can say is listen *to everything people say, but* do whatever seems to be best for you.
—Woman, 73, 2

Listen to advice from family members (and accept help), read up on managing finances, and make your own decisions.
—Woman, 69, 4

Accepting advice and preserving your independence need not be incompatible:

When one becomes a widow, one must develop self-reliance. Take time, heed your inner voices, listen carefully and cautiously to advice, and remember the possible long-term consequences of following your own and other plans.

—Woman, 78, 16

Avoid sudden, impulsive changes like selling home quickly, moving, changing jobs, or making very different new "friends." Of course some may have to make decisions more quickly, but they should seek competent, trustworthy advice. However, we must follow our own instincts, too, if such are well thought-out, for each of us is different.

—Woman, 62, 5

Stay receptive, in other words, but don't feel obligated:

Listen to advice and suggestions from family and friends. It is not necessary to abide by these hints and suggestions, but others may have good points.

—Woman, 72, 3

And don't let bad mentors discourage you from searching for good ones:

Remember there is a lot of superficial and phony advice, but you must keep trying until you find the helpful counsel you need.

—Woman, 53, 2

Still, always keep in mind that your own interests are paramount and that it's up to you exclusively to decide how they are best served—and then see to it that they are:

Accept all offers of advice and help, but rely on your own judgement. Always remember it is your life, your money, and no one has as much interest in it as you do.

—Woman, 54, 4

Never believe that anyone else will be as interested in your financial and emotional security as you are. You (and only you) are responsible for your quality of life.

—Woman, 59, 17

Finally, plan:

Limit major changes (job, financial, moving) for months until sure of future plans. But do plan for the future (with flexibility).

—*Man, 61, 3*

Planning is advanced by many as one of the best ways of ensuring that you stay in control of your affairs. For one thing, it allows you to view advice in its proper context—your life in the long run:

Do nothing in haste. Do not sell your home immediately. Think about the long-range plans rather than the immediate impact.

—*Woman, 66, 10*

Make no major decisions (i.e., jobs, residence) for about a year. Establish short- and long-range goals.

—*Woman, 54, 3*

As a necessary prelude to planning, you must gauge how much latitude you have to act on whatever advice comes your way:

Take sufficient amount of time to sort things out—do not jump into anything before thoroughly understanding what you want to do with what options you have, and this takes time.

—*Woman, 52, 7*

With this kind of groundwork laid, you can be a better judge of both the suitability and practicality of any changes pressed upon you.

Unfortunately, the best of plans won't necessarily direct you to the best sources of advice. Some found them in the family:

Little advice was given, but our only son assisted with discussions, suggestions, and alternatives for some concerns. The help was greatly appreciated, but the decisions were left for me to make. This family support was of paramount importance to me.

—*Woman, 73, 3*

For the reasons just discussed, his respect for her freedom of action seems to have meant as much to her as the "help" he actually gave her (and note how she doesn't like to characterize it as "advice"). A similar tact was shown by another woman's sons—in contrast to the

condescending lectures apparently delivered by some of her other
relatives:

> *On financial subjects, I have found "hired" people much more helpful
> than relatives—my brother and brother-in-law, who in the end don't
> want to be responsible. They both make me feel incompetent. My grown
> sons have been helpful and given me good advice. Perhaps this is
> because they know I'll make up my own mind in the end.*
>
> *—Woman, 68, 5*

Her preference for seeking guidance from professionals rather
than from family or friends, especially with regard to finances, is
shared by other survivors:

> *Financial decisions: you may listen to well-meaning friends, but act on
> sound advice from reliable sources—attorney, accountant, etc.*
>
> *—Woman, 73, 14*

> *Try not to be influenced by "do-gooders." Seek qualified professionals
> like lawyers, undertakers, realtors, insurance agents, and accountants,
> as well as house-repair and car people.*
>
> *—Woman, 62, 5*

Aside from not being amateurs, they are acting as your paid servants,
and your dealings with them will not be charged with the emotional
overtones generated by an involvement with kin:

> *My advice is to make your own decisions. Listen to the family, then
> proceed as your inclinations dictate. Don't become dependent on them
> or allow them to become dependent on you. For business advice, go to
> a professional you trust outside the family.*
>
> *—Woman, 77, 20*

> *Let a tax lawyer handle financial affairs; it's worth every penny it
> costs. (It keeps well-meaning relatives' and children's advice to a
> minimum, and helps you on the road to being your own person in charge
> of your own affairs.)*
>
> *—Woman, 70, 8*

And, although their fees may make inroads on your budget, you can
see to it that they don't ambush it:

Professional advice and help are superior to calling upon friends. An accountant and lawyer are almost musts for widows, certainly within that first year. (Widows should ask in advance what the fees will be per hour, making clear that this is a consideration.)

—Woman, 68, 7

Enlisting the aid of professionals, however, can have its drawbacks too. For one, it can be unnerving if it's all new to you:

Expert advice is crucial in those first months of adjustment. One has to recognize and accept that one will be dependent upon outsiders if there is no immediate family nearby to help. If you've never had to go to strangers for assistance, this can be difficult and bewildering.

—Woman, 64, 6

It's almost proverbial that you shouldn't stint on quality when you engage a professional:

Be sure of the people with whom you do business. Get the best professional help you can possibly get when professional help is needed.

—Woman, 74, 22

And winnowing out the good from the bad on short notice—as many survivors are forced to do—cannot be approached casually:

If other widows/widowers need an attorney or accountant, I advise them to proceed with caution in their selection, if they do not have someone they know. There are good attorneys and bad; the same for accountants.

—Woman, 77, 3

Some attest vigorously to the truth of that last observation, like the man who proclaims,

Don't put full faith either in brokers or insurance men! Surviving spouses must do their own homework and have a full understanding of every decision made. My lawyer was in gross error ($68,000) on the estate total because he did not understand the basis for estate taxes on TIAA-CREF.

—Man, 60, 3

It's nice to have a lawyer who's your friend, but it's vital to have one who's your fiduciary, the disinterested guardian of your welfare:

> *Right away—have a lawyer you both* like *and* trust.
> —*Woman, 72, 7*

With professionals, then, don't let the servant play out the old scenario of usurping the master's place. Stay on top of things by asserting yourself:

> *Even if you have a lawyer or accountant or financial advisor helping you, it is your responsibility to protect your interests. Take a firm stand, never be intimidated, and never hesitate to ask questions.*
> —*Woman, 77, 3*

> *Get good professional advice and consider* all *options. Ask questions.*
> —*Woman, 56, 2*

As each of the last two instructions indicate, it's not a matter of bossing them around but of ferreting out all the various means by which they can be—and perhaps haven't been—aiding you. Some survivors refer us to a variety of professional advice that, at best, can be the least self-serving and most cost-effective of all—books:

> *There are excellent books available which can be very helpful and offer impartial advice from someone with no vested interest in your decisions.*
> —*Woman, 54, 4*

> *When tough decisions have to be made, go to the library and immerse yourself in as many books as you need in order to make decisions with which you are comfortable.*
> —*Woman, 59, 17*

Of course, books are no substitute for someone who knows the particulars of your situation—and has the power to act on your behalf when you, either legally or practically, cannot.

In the next sections, we'll see some specific cases where advice has paid off—or backfired; but we'd like to conclude our survivors' advice on advice by coming back full circle to their most persistent admonition:

I feel now that the most important thing for anyone is not to be rushed. If at all possible, live in your new situation for a while. It is not necessary or vital to decide right now—and even better if you can put finances, etc., on hold, until you can get your new status into perspective. You are very vulnerable and easily persuaded and should wait.
—Woman, 60, 3

She may be ruing her own vulnerability here, for she volunteers that, if she had followed this course "for at least six months, I know I would have made a lot of my decisions differently." Some admit that when they did act, they capriciously flouted what they *knew* to be their best interests. So Hannah did with her finances, despite having been tutored in them by a husband who was a lawyer and businessman:

Therefore, I felt I was fortunate, that I had been trained, and he was a superb teacher. But, when he died, I went into reverse and made the greatest errors. As a matter of fact, I think I lost my marbles and allowed myself to be influenced. Every mistake I advised people not to make—don't ask me why!—I turned around and did it [laughing]. I needed six *psychology classes [with a nod to a participant who just mentioned that she was enrolled in one].*
—Miami, #2

Only two exceptions to the general rule are commonly invoked—when either your health or your finances pose a crisis that requires immediate action. One man mentions a third possibility—when a decision has been made beforehand:

Decisions of lasting importance (such as where to live, how to dispose of property, etc.) should be postponed if possible, unless made in advance.
—Man, 77, 2

As we saw in the last chapter, some people's dilemmas had a way of simply evaporating with time. Or so this woman would like to think:

As for the newly widowed, I can offer only the teaching of my own experiences: listen to advice, but make your own decisions, and, in line with that, take your time in making them, since many problems have a way of providing their own solutions.

—Woman, 73, 14

But she adds, wistfully, "Good advice, if only I could follow it."
We'll see next what survivors themselves advise doing and not doing
about some of their major quandaries: what to do with their spouse's
belongings and their own, most notably their cars and their houses.

Your Spouse's Belongings

Your spouse's personal things—the clothing, toiletries, jewelry,
and the like—may pose the most gnawing reminders of what is
missing, of his or her physical presence. More than memories may
cling to them—smell, in particular, in the case of clothes, perfumes,
and after-shaves. And they may exert a powerful spell over some, like
Sylvia in the Prologue, who recalls sleeping in her husband's bathrobe (not an uncommon way, according to books on grief, of trying
to replicate a spouse's embrace).

But its very power gives many reason to regard the spell as
dangerous and to exempt the disposing of personal effects from the
list of actions that can wait:

> *Get rid of inexpensive personal items like clothing quickly; take time*
> *with valuables.*
>
> *—Woman, 65, 9*

> *Dispose of personal items, such as clothes, as soon as possible. Do not*
> *dispose of extra automobiles, houses, etc., too hastily, as you find later*
> *that you were in a state of shock and did not realize it.*
>
> *—Woman, 63, 2*

Some books on grief endorse their viewpoint, arguing that by making
a relic of a threadbare garment, you are obstructing the work of
making room for your spouse in your memory—the proper place for
a shrine if one is needed.

One woman in our survey appears to agree when she advises
others not to repress their grief as she had done:

> *My advice is deal with the loss right away—get rid of their personal*
> *belongings.*
>
> *—Woman, 63, 2*

Giving them away is a speedy, and socially beneficial, solution:

Noel: All my wife's clothing and jewelry—not that it was valuable jewelry—I gave to Covenant House because a lot of the residents there didn't have decent clothing.

—New York, #2

Murray did the same, out of a feeling that otherwise he would be creating the equivalent of the locked room that is the staple of novels, where everything is kept ''just as it was'' after a death or some other calamity:

I got rid of—I gave to a charitable organization all of my wife's clothing. I didn't want to make a mausoleum in the house, so every time I'd come in, I'd remember.

—New York, #2

Inevitably, there's an opposing camp:

Take your time—time helps through it all. Do not make quick decisions about changing your financial situation, your lifestyle, or getting rid of your spouse's belongings.

—Woman, 62, 3

Another woman sees nothing macabre about keeping such mementos about, although she seems aware you can overdo it:

I feel my late husband's presence. I don't shut him out; I keep some of his things around—to a degree.

—Woman, 68, 2

Lil is quite unrepentant about how she's consecrated her husband's chair at the dining table, regardless of what others might infer about her state of mind:

You know, it's crazy, after all these years, but if I have someone in for a meal, they can't sit in my husband's chair. Now that's a weird thing. I wouldn't let anybody sit there. I still won't.

—Boston, #2

And who's to say some genuine comfort can't be squeezed from sleeping in a spouse's bathrobe—at least for a while?

The little dispute we've just presented revolves about one of the main issues confronting all survivors, one that we viewed in a rather abstract context in Chapter 1: how much of the old do you try to preserve and how much of it do you scrap? Here the question concerns something very concrete and should be fairly easy to settle, because what could more plainly bear the stamp of obsolescence than your spouse's clothes? But even the answer to this is not easy—and it becomes harder as your definition of your spouse's "belongings" widens from clothes to furniture and cars, then to parts of the house that were particularly his or hers, and perhaps to the house itself.

Sometimes, we can rearrange things to suit ourselves readily enough, as this woman literally did in a rather neat compromise between the old and new inside the house:

> *Don't rush things. Take your time in disposing of your spouse's belongings. Do, however, rearrange your home so that the familiar objects are still there, but not in their accustomed places.*
> *—Woman, 74, NA*

But in other cases, we must rearrange our lives a bit to suit an object. Widows, in particular, most often encounter such an object in that combination of servant and tyrant, the automobile.

Cars: A Special Problem for Widows

Lydia sold an automobile with the same shudder that she might have cast away a new jacket that her husband had bought right before his death. But as Frieda points out, by not getting a replacement, she may have sold more than that:

> **Lydia:** *My husband bought a car about a week before he got killed. The car was brand new and it had 237 miles on it. I couldn't get in the car after he got killed. I took a $2,500 loss to sell it.*
> **Laura:** *Do you drive, Lydia?*
> **Lydia:** *I drive, but I haven't got a car now. I couldn't—when I'd get in that car, my heart would . . . [fluttering hands].*
> **Laura:** *Well, that's understandable. But you should have sold it and got another car.*
> **Marlene:** *Or traded it in.*

Frieda: *Your car is your independence.*

—Miami, #1

Other widows may not have found their cars evoking such painful feelings, but may still have viewed them as "his"—and disposed of them accordingly. Or you may have succumbed to the advice of "well-intenders."

In any case, at last we have a consensus:

Don't sell your car if you are a licensed driver. I'm pretty much left out of many programs because I can't get to them. I can't call friends all the time.

—Woman, NA, NA

Be independent, as much as possible. Be able to drive your own car. (A must—otherwise you're confined and dependent on others.)

—Woman, 62, 3

Be sure you drive a car. I've seen some widowed friends have a miserable time because they don't drive.

—Woman, 72, 9

It's a chorus composed entirely of women's voices, of course. It was not so many decades ago that driving was still widely held to be a male marital prerogative—with deplorable consequences, in Ruth's opinion:

You see some very sad cases. I have a girlfriend that lost her husband about four or five months ago. She gave up driving a car. And I spoke to her and I pleaded with her to be stronger. I think her husband drove the car. That's another thing that's wrong—women not driving the cars. When they have husbands, the husband drives them everywhere, and they just feel that they don't have to. It's true, while he's alive, they don't have to. But they sure as hell need to when he's gone.

—Miami, #2

In extreme cases, some women simply never learned to begin with:

Learn to drive! I never did and I find it a terrible and expensive handicap! It keeps me from going to concerts, plays, etc. Either I go

alone and take a cab or depend on friends to take me. And with the latter,
I do not like to presume too much on their kindness.

—Woman, 83, 2

More commonly, as was apparently true of Ruth's friend, they did drive but in widowhood found their skills (or nerve) had atrophied— either because they had largely ceded control of the car to the husband when he retired and they began going almost everywhere together or because he had always appropriated certain types of driving to himself:

In our nearly fifty years of married life my husband preferred to do
the out-of-town driving. Now I'm afraid to drive expressways or
do night driving.

—Woman, 72, 6

Finally, maintaining the car, if the husband had borne responsibility for it, may have intimidated these women just as much as driving it. The world of garages and mechanics is still a mysterious and menacing one for some of them:

One has to learn many new things that your partner did, like looking
after the car. (I still dislike getting the gas for the car.)

—Woman, 74, 13

Seems like all garages want to take a woman for a ride (if you know what
I mean!).

—Woman, 61, 5

Of course we can add, "And a man, too." And being unwillingly without a car should become rarer and rarer for women. After all, we live in a time in which many wives are much more knowledgeable about cars than their husbands. Nevertheless, plenty of widows among an older generation find themselves in the predicament; and one of our discussion groups, when asked what they would pass on to others, put this at the top of their list:

Peggy: *A car is a very important thing. Learning to drive a car is of*
utmost importance, especially when you live in Florida.
Ida: *You must drive. If you drive, you've got a friend. But if you don't*

drive, you are alone.
***Peggy:** You're dead.*
***Ida:** And you're at the mercy of other people. Sometimes they'll do you a favor, they'll take you shopping. But nine times out of ten, they'll sneak away so they don't have to encounter you. You must learn to drive.*
***Peggy:** Even just for local driving. To get to the doctor, the dentist, the market.*
***Ida:** Don't give up your car, even if you have to hire somebody to drive you shopping. Your car is your friend.*

—Miami, #2

And the social isolation and dependency they predict for widows without this particular "friend" is a real threat:

***Dorothy:** You don't go out of the house?*
***Laura:** Oh yes, I go, you know, shopping and stuff like that.*
***Catherine:** You don't go to any clubs or anything?*
***Laura:** No, never.*
***Catherine:** Do you drive so you can go places?*
***Laura:** No. My grandkids pick me up to go shopping, stuff like that.*
***Catherine:** I would never depend on my grandchildren. They have lives of their own. They don't want to be bothered. That's why I keep my car. I'd starve before I'd give up my car.*

—Miami, #1

Laura's morose "stuff like that" says it all.

The way out of her plight is not hard. Learn, if you don't know how. You may not need to resort to professionals. The students of this woman's husband, for example, hit upon an inspired way of repaying their debt to him in kind:

My husband had lung cancer for eight months and he taught at Stanford until two days before his death. His students held a meeting to see what they could do for me, and they decided to teach me how to drive our car. Six of them were my drivers, and one would come to my home each day. And the big day came when I passed the test. They held a party for me in the evening, and the cake was topped with a little Mustang.

—Woman, 81, 16

If your ability has rusted a bit, polish it up gradually:

> *If you need practice in getting back into driving, try to get someone to search out an area where you can do so and also work out with you easy routes for routine trips.*
>
> —*Woman, 79, 6*

You may not even need help, as Lillian discovered when she stubbornly held out against the wishes of her family:

> *The other thing my children didn't want me to do is drive a car, because they said I was too old. So they wanted me to sell the car. But I said, "No, I'm not going to do it," and I didn't. And then one day I said to myself, "I'm going to take the car and drive around here and see how I feel about it." I felt like a prisoner of war—I was never a person who could stay in the house all day. I have to get out. And I found that I'd go out around ten o'oclock when there is very little traffic and I'd do my marketing or whatever and, after, I'd come back home. But, if I'd listened to them, I would have had to stay in the house, and I would be completely demolished. So I'm glad I didn't.*
>
> —*Boston, #1*

So, if you're a widow, and unless age or other handicaps genuinely prevent you from getting behind the wheel (or if you live somewhere that lets you do all the getting around you need by other means), keep the car. Aside from mere transportation, it can be a passport out of loneliness:

> *I drive—so at times when I would get lonely, why, I would just get into my car and travel to one of my children or my aunt for a few days.*
>
> —*Woman, 67, 2*

And a car can even deliver you from the doldrums by letting you deliver the less mobile elsewhere:

> ***Virginia:*** *I didn't have any children to take care of, but I was doing for neighbors, driving them here, driving them there, so that kept me busy.*
> ***Bud:*** *She had a car, and that's very important because other people don't drive.*
> ***Virginia:*** *Yes, the ones that didn't drive, many of the old ladies, I'd take to the market.*

Sylvia: You were very popular [laughter].

—*Los Angeles, #1*

Money: Spending It or Investing It

Money has two uses—it can buy us goods or services or make us more money. More than a few of us have sometimes found the supply on hand for these purposes to be woefully meager. So our only recourse has been to go slow. Going slow may be especially vital for survivors, who may have been left much poorer—or richer—than they were before. In the next chapter, we'll see how people fared in the routine business of managing their money from day to day. Here we want to give the floor briefly to people who mostly urge you to refrain from doing anything more than that for the time being.

Laying out large sums—or locking them into something—is often coupled with moving as prime examples of actions that should be held in abeyance:

Don't make hasty decisions on moving or spending or investing any money you receive from your spouse's death.

—*Woman, 60, 3*

For starters, you may need to determine how much scope you have for either. This in turn will engage you in a fiscal exercise to which you may be largely or wholly unaccustomed, especially if you are a widow—comparing what is going out to what is coming in:

Take your time and don't make big changes in your life style hastily. Sit down and survey your needs and your income to cover those needs.

—*Woman, 60, 2*

The figure of the widow (or widower) bilked by the con man is entrenched in folklore, but like all stereotypes, it has its roots in fact:

Do not make any sudden financial decisions before two years have passed. Your vulnerability can easily be mistaken for something else.

—*Woman, 62, 3*

Gullibility is no doubt that ''something else.'' And we are issued the standard alerts against brothers-in-law bearing stock tips—or seeking handouts:

Don't *allow anyone to play on your sympathy—a relative or anyone else. You probably have cash now. There are untold people who want to help spend it.*

—Woman, 85, 12

While you're biding your time, she continues, you can use it to increase your knowledge:

Look into the proposition, but remember, you don't know how long your money must last. This is a time when you must be selfish. If you don't know about something, go take a course or find a good financial advisor. I took courses in income taxes, stocks and bonds, and real estate. Know what you're doing!

Some degree of expertise—or the sheer resolve not to let people get any further than your doorstep—is especially important if you find yourself besieged by ''professionals'':

Some real estate agents were very aggressive, and one agent came to my home two days after my husband died and presented me with his card. Financial advisors kept coming to my home, one man six times!

—Woman, 81, 16

Others remind us, however, that our worst advisors may be ourselves:

Don't spend your income (or insurance money) too quickly. Live within your income. (I went on a buying spree; now I regret it.)

—Woman, 61, 5

Melba went on a similar binge:

Q: OK, tell us some of the mistakes that people make.
Melba: I would advise anybody, ''Don't even move for a year. Don't do anything.'' Because I bought new furniture. Had to get rid of that bedroom, first thing. Had to do that. Things like that, things that could have waited, you know?

—Miami, #2

Furniture—and a house that begs to be remodeled—are particularly mentioned by widows as inducements to extravagance:

Q: You were talking about credit cards. You said, "Get rid of the credit cards," and somebody else said, "Yeah, yeah."
Connie: *A widow, as I said, the first year, she goes haywire. I had a sister who did that, her husband died, and I don't know what happened to her. She decided to buy everything new, and it's not that she has money. It is just she had a feeling—*
Jean: *She had a credit card!*
Connie: *That she needed new furniture, needed new lamps, needed new everything, she was just going bananas.*
Q: So you would guard against that?
Connie: *Again, I say a widow should wait a year. Wait, don't buy the furniture, but give yourself a chance to calm down and get organized.*
—New York, #1

Nothing can seduce us into living beyond our means faster than credit, and charge cards may have given Connie's sister an opening she might not otherwise have had. Bad experiences with credit obviously befell these two:

Do not have credit card accounts!
—Man, 70, 4

Don't get into debt! It's better to do without!
—Woman, 76, 6

You shouldn't go so slow, however, that you come to a complete standstill where one isn't called for. Money harbors an enormous power to frighten us, and survivors in particular, especially those faced with living in suddenly straitened circumstances, may be petrified by their finances:

The financial worries are endless. I'm scared to use any insurance money as I'm only 43 and know it has to last hopefully for another forty years.
—Woman, 43, 2

And in some cases their anxieties may exceed rational bounds. Of our survey group, 26% gauged their "overall financial situation" to be "worse" than it was previously, but 53% deemed it "about the same," and 21% actually judged it "better." Books on grief abound with instances of widows, especially, who are consumed by fears about money despite being quite well off. This woman hints as much about herself:

> *The worry of not having enough to live on in the future was a big problem, the but I am becoming more relaxed about that. I was obsessed with "saving every penny I could" for a while!*
>
> *—Woman, 61, 6*

We'll see more such anxieties, justified or not, in the next chapter. So perhaps it's best to close this part with an example to counterbalance our previous ones—a woman who feels that *not* having moved faster worked to her long-term financial detriment:

> *Here is what I wish could have been different:*
>
> Long-term planning*: I hadn't known that I would get Social Security (or that the children would) and, when I did, that it would be so much more than I expected. I wish I had invested more of it for them. Also that we had made concrete plans for improving the house and adding a rental unit. I was afraid to spend really large sums so I dribbled it away; yet $5,000 spent remodeling the house would have been good and brought in some income.*
>
> *—Woman, 62, 12*

A Job: Keeping It If You Have One

If most survivors are chary of experimenting with their money, they are even more so of doing it with a job that may have been bringing some or much of that money in. Work—paid or not—is one of the most highly-rated means of "keeping busy," so we're reserving much of what people have to say about it for that section below. But almost 40% of the people in our survey were in paid employment when their spouses died, and among them we found no one who quit (because insurance proceeds or an estate settlement enabled them to, for example) and few who even eased up for a bit. Quite the contrary:

> *I went back to work, and very soon, where I had caring coworkers. Also, in that way my salary continued too.*
>
> *—Woman, 70, 11*

Continue working. Resume work as soon as possible. It structures daily life.

—*Woman, 55, 7*

I was lucky to continue working on my own terms. It got me up and out of the house and with people. I think I kept my sanity because of my work and my boss.

—*Woman, 63, 3*

As you can see, financial motives may not have been paramount with these people. To be sure, a salary may give you the wherewithal to "do nothing" about the rest of your life:

I consider myself fortunate that I had a job which made it possible for me to stay in my house and live pretty much as I had before being widowed.

—*Woman, 61, 8*

But a job can contribute to your well-being in so many ways that, if you don't have one, survivors often make getting one the single exception to their rules against immediate major changes:

Keep your job if you have one. If not, then get one.

—*Woman, 61, 5*

No one advocated abruptly leaving an old job—even temporarily. A break from work apparently did this woman good, but note how she advises waiting for a while before taking it:

Make no major decisions for twelve months. If possible, if you work, take some time off after about three months.

—*Woman, 55, 3*

A job may actually offer you a respite:

Work hard—it gives your mind and heart a rest from grief.

—*Woman, 66, 6*

Some did scale their old jobs back a bit:

We had no children; therefore, I have very little family to rely on. The thing that helps most is staying busy, and I have been fortunate to have stayed on part-time at my former place of employment.

—Woman, 66, NA

But others returned to jobs they'd left:

Leonard: *I went back to work for one year in order to get things off my mind, just to forget. It wasn't that I couldn't have used the money, but the main reason was just to take my mind off my troubles and my wife's dying.*

—Los Angeles, #1

And still others used old jobs as stepping-stones to new ones, like this nurse:

Be busy with purposeful work. I took a half-time educational leave from my job to attend school shortly after my husband's death. It was a wise move—new environment, new people, new ideas to think about. It will also mean a positive career change.

—Woman, 52, 2

As usual, the fact that we encountered no one who made a spouse's death the occasion to retire is no proof you can't do so successfully. But the only person who reported toying with the idea was glad she went no further:

"Do not make a basic decision for at least one year after the death of your spouse"—for me, this advice was very sound. Few of us have experience in meeting the problems caused by the death, and decision-making must be carefully weighed. I almost made a major error—but pulled back in time and continued my career. For three more years.

—Woman, 59, 3

Retirement can be attended by stresses of its own, and they compounded those of widowhood for this woman:

I had retired just before my husband became ill. So I also had problems of adjusting to retirement. It would have been more difficult physically if I were still working, but infinitely easier psychologically and emotionally.

—Woman, 73, 8

Despite the fact that TIAA-CREF's reason for being is to provide for its people in retirement, we know from previous surveys that ''Work until you drop!'' is the stubborn motto of some of them:

> *I have only one piece of advice for either a widow or widower, and that is to keep on working as long as the condition of his or her health permits—and even longer. People who have to work beyond retirement age in order to augment their incomes are more fortunate than they sometimes realize. Of course I recognize that many people do not have the kind of work that can be pursued into old age. But, wherever it is at all possible, they should stay at the job. I know no better therapy for the loneliness of widowhood—and indeed for the anxiety and loneliness of advanced age, even while one's wife or husband is still alive.*
>
> —*Woman, 82, 12*

Our jobs may do a great deal to confer upon us a sense of who we are, and this is undoubtedly why people like her so fiercely resist the idea of surrendering them. Our self-esteem may be very tightly bound up in our work:

> *It is well to try to keep or get a paying job. Work is therapeutic, and pay is good for one's self-image.*
>
> —*Woman, 62, 8*

> *Strengthen your identity. Success in own profession helps here.*
>
> —*Woman, 78, 8*

At a time when we have been stripped of our identities as ''husbands'' or ''wives,'' an occupation may be a path to self-preservation—quite literally. Ruth found it so when she returned to her job of bookkeeping:

> *It gave me a chance to invest money that I wouldn't have been able to, and I now am more or less self-supporting in every way. Which makes me feel great. My boys used to help me, and now I don't have to worry about that. I kept my home. I have a three-bedroom house, and everyone that wants to come is welcome. The children, the grandchildren. My son is coming down with his wife from Alaska and they have a place to go and I feel great.*
> **Peggy:** *You haven't lost your identity.*

Ruth: *Oh, no, I have not!*

—Miami, #2

Ruth has also led us directly to a dilemma many people don't resolve as tidily as she did: what to do about where they live.

The House: Sell It or Keep It?

For many survivors, as we'll see in the next chapter, "getting out of the house" epitomizes how they regenerated their lives—and, in some cases, retained their sanity. Any home shared with a spouse becomes a repository of emotions that, once you are alone again, can be a comfort—or a torment. Add to this the unaccustomed duties of maintenance and finance that you may be newly saddled with, and you may well ask, "Why not get *rid* of the house?"

By this time, we know the standard answer well:

If you own your home (or, if not, if you have lived there for some time), stay there for the time being.

—Woman, 69, 9

If possible, give yourself plenty of time before making any radical change in living arrangements.

—Woman, 78, 11

Follow your usual routine and remain in your own home for at least a year—until you know what you want to do.

—Woman, 69, 4

This caution may have been inspired by something we've also seen before—overzealous advice-giving. And, as usual, many are able to congratulate themselves on remaining obstinate:

I would advise everyone not to do anything in a hurry, to take time to think things over, to find out what would be best for you. I had lived forty-five years in my home, and when my husband died, I had a lot of advice from everyone. They wanted me to sell my home and move into a home for "senior citizens." But my health wasn't too bad, so I decided to stay in my home as long as possible.

I had seen what such moves could do. When my sister's husband died, everyone was telling her to sell, and she did. And in three months she had moved into a trailer. But she was never satisfied, terribly lonesome and crying all the time. I'm very happy that I did what was right for me.

—*Woman, 74, 5*

Those who refused to budge at all—and they include two-thirds of those in our survey—obeyed a variety of impulses. Sheer unwillingness to change was one—in this case, an unwillingness born of courage rather than timidity:

I am 79 and do not find life easy living alone in the country. But I do not want to leave this house and all my belongings.

—*Woman, 79, 2*

This woman, younger and in easier circumstances, enjoys the feeling of command she gets from staying with what she knows:

If you have been rather well-situated and kept your home, don't sell it!!—you will be happier. I'm the boss here, and I'll always want to remain in my comfortable home of forty years.

—*Woman, 69, 6*

Some, like Ruth quoted at the end of the last section, prize their homes for being of use to others as well as themselves:

Try not to change your life-style, and please don't bemoan your fate. Stay in the same home you enjoyed with your spouse and keep up with the same friends by entertaining them there.

—*Woman, 82, 17*

My husband died unexpectedly from a stroke while on sabbatical before he ever had a chance to enjoy the fruits of his many years of teaching. He especially wanted to get rid of the house and travel. For now, I am glad we kept it, so it can be of some use to my children and grandchildren (and six cats).

—*Woman, 67, 2*

I believe that staying in my home helped. It gave a home to a niece and family who needed it for a year, and I have helped other relatives in time of crisis.

—*Woman, 69, 5*

And of course underlying these reasons is a shared pleasure in the familiar, whether articulated or not:

> *As long as you can, stay in your former home—the one with the happy memories.*
>
> —Woman, 75, 5

> *We bought a home and four acres and spent a lot of time planting, he doing the heavier work, digging stony ground. The blooms that come each year and the place in general are one of the biggest comforts.*
>
> —Woman, 60, 3

Nora equates her house with herself:

> ***Ann:*** *Have you thought of getting rid of that big house and getting into a smaller one?*
>
> ***Nora:*** *Yes, but, then, my husband built the house, and we all lived there together ever since the children were little, and that's a part of you. You know, it's built in* you *there somewhere. You didn't just go out and buy the house. It took us about eighteen months to build that house. And you can't get rid of a part of you.*
>
> —San Francisco

She and it form a bastion of stability in a neighborhood she reluctantly concedes is not what it was:

> *The kids have said, "Sell the house. Move up to a better neighborhood." There's nothing wrong with my neighborhood—that's where I've been all the time. Well, the neighborhood* has *changed. But then I haven't, and it's still my house. So, as I tell them, I don't ever intend to leave my neighborhood unless I go feet first.*

A good many who did ultimately say goodbye to their old homes stress how long they lingered before doing it:

> *Don't rush into any change in your life-style (unless your finances force a change). I have now, after three years, decided to sell my house because I can't keep up the day-to-day repairs (lack of knowledge) and yard work (lack of enthusiasm) and to rent a large apartment with the interest from about $100,000 in CDs.*
>
> —Woman, 63, 4

I stayed in my home for six years and moved to a very nice condominium complex where I now have very good friends. I think it is wise to wait quite a while before selling a home. In my case I knew when the time had come. I was glad to be relieved of so much work.

—Woman, 81, 16

Fairly urgent practical concerns—the chores of upkeep—were prodding both of them, but they held off until they sensed "the time had come." So did Loretta, who explains that otherwise events would have seemed to have taken the upper hand and evicted her:

Loretta: Don't sell your home right off.
Q: Why do you say that?
Loretta: Because you'd make a mistake. You want to get away from it, as far as you can, but that's the biggest mistake you could make. Because your home is there, you settle down finally, and then you make the decision to go away. I had a big home and I knew I couldn't take care of it. But I stayed a year and a half, and then the time was right for me to sell it, and it was a happy move. Otherwise, I would have felt like I had just been shaken out of my home, like I'd been thrown out. I think it's a good thing to stay put.

—Los Angeles, #1

This woman let the familiarity of her home cushion her in just the same way—until she was sure she was ready:

There is a great temptation to make decisions immediately upon the death of one's spouse. I was very glad that I did not sell my home; the adjustment would have been much more difficult in strange surroundings, away from friends. After many years, the time came when it got to be too much of a responsibility, and I have recently moved to an apartment, but in the same neighborhood.

—Woman, 75, 19

Note that her move didn't carry her out of the neighborhood—a possibility that is considered in the section following this one.

Also testifying to the wisdom of acting deliberately are the tales of some of those who didn't:

Rae: I sold my house too soon and I am sick every time I think of it. But you can't go back, we have to go ahead. That's why thinking is a

great thing—not in haste, haste is terrible, you repent it, but nothing can be done, after.
Eleanor: Ten years from now, what you would sell now would be worth so much more—
Rae: Well, I sold it eight years ago for practically nothing. And when I hear the prices today . . . sad, it's really sad.
—New York, #2

Her lack of financial foresight appears to be what she's deploring most, but we've heard enough to know that her regrets could also be grounded in her emotions. In retrospect, a house forsaken, no matter how willingly, can transform itself into yet another loss on top of the larger one. So it would be tempting to exhort everyone to sit tight.

There is another opinion, however—a minority opinion, granted, but we can see it emerge in this debate between Bud and Sylvia on their experiences in moving to a retirement community after their spouses died:

Sylvia: I think that I would have been much happier when I first moved here, had I moved in with my husband. Because when you lose your home, I mean, when you give it up, then there's that horrible, let-down feeling that you're all alone in a strange place. So I think people are better off if they moved in with their spouses. When the spouse is gone, they still maintain their home and they're happy.
Loretta: Some disagree with that because of the associations, the remembering, too. They like a new life.
Sylvia: Well, but you're never going to erase the memories. They're there forever.
Q: Bud?
Bud: Well, in the apartment buildings we owned, we lived in one of the units. And after my wife died, why, I had plenty of entertainment. But there were too many memories. When I went out in the daytime, it didn't bother me to come home. But when I came home after dark, it did, because it was all memories and I'd have a little lump in my throat again. So I had my apartment up for sale.
—Los Angeles, #1

Some flatly deny that you can distance yourself from your memories as he apparently did:

Do not move. Your memories are with you wherever you live.
                                                    —Woman, 75, 15

Sara: *When my husband died, everybody said to me, "Sell your house, get an apartment." And my first reply would be, "But no matter where I go, I take everything with me."*
                                                    —Los Angeles, #2

But Noel exuberantly disputes that view:

I think where you live is important too. I recently moved in the last year, and I have a place in the West Village on Barrow Street. I've planted flowers for the first time in my life, and I have a backyard and a lot of light in the apartment. It's not always easy to move out of an apartment, especially in New York. But if you live in drab surroundings—especially if you lived there with that person you were married to for many years—a change of scenery I think is paramount in changing your feelings about your own life. It helped me. I love my apartment. That's why I very rarely go out.
                                                    —New York, #2

And we meet his counterparts among the women. The same Lillian who rebuffed her children's advice to sell her car (page 114) proved of an equally independent mind when it came to her residence—only now she was being counselled *not* to sell:

My children wanted me to stay in the house. And I didn't want to because I'm a scaredy cat. To stay in the house alone was not for me. So then they said, "Well, why don't you rent it?" And I said, "I don't want the responsibility of having to take care of heating and so forth." Then they decided to go look for a place for me. And they went and they saw an apartment and they put down a deposit on it. And then they showed it to me. I thought it was very nice. I liked it. So I moved there June 2nd. And it's pleasant there, well-kept.
                                                    —Boston, #1

So there may be good cause for divesting yourself of the house, now or later. Most commonly cited is advancing age, which persuaded many to seek places that made less strenuous demands on them—and possibly on others:

I sold my home to make it simpler for my children when I die or if and when I can't take care of myself—less worries both for me and them.
                                                                    —Woman, 71, 4

I sold our house after a year and a half because physically (health) I couldn't take care of the garden/yard and routine maintenance. It was in excellent shape, and, before it went downhill, I felt it wise to sell.
                                                                    —Woman, 69, 3

Others foresee the eventuality of such changes:

I am living in the suburban home we raised our children in, and they still come home often to visit. But when I am no longer able to drive, I think I would prefer to be in the city, where I could walk or take public transportation.
                                                                    —Woman, 59, 3

I have a mortgage-free home where I hope to live for as long as health permits. Then, when necessary, I will sell it and seek refuge at a proper place where care and attention are available. Presently I have two long-time friends who have power of attorney and are fully aware of all of my circumstances.
                                                                    —Woman, 77, 2

The "refuge" she envisions is probably one of the retirement communities that have become fixtures of the American scene over the last four decades. People are drawn to them, of course, by the appeal of living in quarters that are smaller and more flexible than the typical family house, with the nuisances of maintenance usually shifted to the community's management. And they may also be attracted by other features ranging from communal dining and organized recreational activities to nursing care and other health services on the premises for those who become ill or incapacitated— sometimes guaranteed (at considerable cost) by "life-care" contracts signed at the time of entry. People who had opted for a life in communities like these comprised 10% of our survey and, in the discussion groups, everybody in one (Los Angeles, #1) and several in the others. Given their number, we anticipated some grumbling—about promises not kept, services not performed, or a milieu that disap- pointed (at worst, some of these places have been portrayed as virtual ghettos for the elderly). But we heard none, except by hearsay—whether through chance or as a faithful mirror of prevailing reality, we cannot of course tell.

Those who reported entering retirement communities before their spouses died were uniformly thankful for it, like this woman who had done so a year earlier with her husband because of his illness:

I know that few people can anticipate the necessity of such drastic change, and that most who can might not be financially able. I am most grateful to have been so fortunate and to have been living among congenial people, many of whom had already adjusted to the loss of a spouse.

—Woman, 77, 11

This woman had enjoyed a full six years with her husband in a similar setting and likewise found it a great resource after his death:

I was very fortunate in being able to cope after my husband's death because I live in a retirement community. After more than ten years here, I have made many friends among the two thousand residents. There are many, many activities offered where you can find ful-fillment according to your talents.

—Woman, 76, 4

Those who came afterwards seemed just as pleased:

If you are over 65, move into a retirement community or home. Take part in the programs offered and possibly do volunteer work in the home, for friends needing help. Do not wait until you're too old to enjoy new surroundings and activities.

—Woman, 85, 10

And they eventually included the Sylvia who said on page 126 that she was disconsolate at first:

So I moved to Leisure World—moved there to die, and instead I've had more fun than I've had in my life.

—Los Angeles, #1

No one complains of an overly regimented existence or an environment that is too confining. Here is someone who plainly values her freedom of action and doesn't find it cramped:

I have always been independent—that helped! Personality and friend-
ships have much to do with "coping." I chose (after two years) to move
to a life-care community where I can have privacy in my apartment if I
wish—and friends all around the complex when I am lonesome.

—Woman, 71, 4

In fact, retirement communities appear to have expanded rather than
narrowed some horizons. Several found their social lives enriched:

Q: Who else came in after their spouses died? What was the reason,
Lillian?
Lillian: Well, I knew if I lived in an apartment by myself, I'd crawl into
my little shell. I'd known about Leisure World, and it had the outdoor
living that I wanted, the swimming. Just to be able to walk out on the
street and see other people's beautiful gardens—to have a garden. And
the feeling you get, walking along, seeing pleasant people, everybody
says, "Good morning."
Leonard: Even at twelve o'clock at night [laughter].

—Los Angeles, #1

Frieda: It's only for older people—there's nobody there younger
than 70. I don't know how many people live there, but look how many
friends I've got! Everybody talks to everybody else. This morning, as I
was leaving, a woman got hold of me—she's going to have some of us
up in her apartment. She thinks that we ought to entertain in each
other's apartments. And we do.

—Miami, #1

Many were liberated from worries about their personal safety. Edwin's story of how he abandoned a deteriorating neighborhood is
typical:

Q: Edwin, why did you come in?
Edwin: Well, I had a friend living here, my daughter's mother-in-law.
And I lived not too far away, and it was getting rough in the neighbor-
hood, break-ins and what-not. Although they never seemed to bother my
house, because I was prepared for them. I said, "They'll come in, but
they'll never go out." And it was a three-bedroom house with a big yard,
and I figured, why should I do all this? So I said, "Time to go," and I
put my house up for sale and got $112,000 for it.
Q: How did you feel once you got here?

Edwin: *Fine. I felt more secure than on the outside because I knew eventually I would have shot somebody who did come into the house.*
—Los Angeles, #1

A burglary convinced Anne and her sister to relocate to apartments in the same complex, and she happily relates what happened shortly after they did, when, in a hasty departure for a weekend, they left a front door ajar, with a key in it:

We came back Monday, we found the key in the door, the door was open like we left it, and our mail was lying there on the floor. Can you imagine anything more secure? Nobody had walked in. I'll tell you, we were happy then and we are happy now.
—Los Angeles, #1

Frieda, like several others, appreciates the devices her community uses to safeguard the physical well-being of its residents:

There's one problem with it—it's expensive. But I think if we can afford it, we do get our money's worth, because I have never had such care and consideration in my life. Not only do we have that emergency thing in case we need help, but there's a button—oh, I forgot to push it this morning!—there's a button on my wall. When I get up in the morning, I'm supposed to push that. Nobody answers it, but if I don't push it by eleven o'clock or eleven-thirty, they're going to phone to make sure I'm all right.
—Miami, #1

Her words are a reminder, however, that if you are considering life in a retirement community, you must be prepared to accept the two facts about it which necessitate that ''care and consideration.'' You will be surrounded by people who are old; everyone we have quoted on the subject is at least a septuagenarian. And a good many are likely to be infirm or ailing, even though they may be able to joke about it:

Leonard *[to our moderator]: For your information, in Leisure World we have clubs according to diseases of different kinds, dozens of them. So we have the Arthritis Club, the Emphysema Club, and so on.*
Q: *Does anybody here belong to any of those clubs?*
Virginia: *Yes, we belong to all of them [laughter].*

Gil: *It's all one big club—an old-age club!*

—Los Angeles, #1

So selling the house may be merited for a number of good reasons. One-third of those in our survey, after all, did so. But perhaps we should reiterate once more the conclusion of most: if you feel any flickers of indecision, wait. Syd explains how she has pieced together her "own life" from the resources right at hand, her home and her neighbors:

> *I have a private home, in which I've been living alone now for the last four years. I've been very lucky with my neighbors and my friends. My neighbor in the back, when she goes shopping, says, "Give me a list, I'll do your shopping for you." I drive a car, but I also have other friends that drive who pick me up. My friends right now are all widows, and we have a lot in common—we play cards, we go out to dinner. There is a community center which I belong to, I go to the pool. And you make your own life.*
>
> *—Miami, #2*

She then contrasts her situation to that of some who ventured further afield—to retirement communities that proved all too much like "one big club":

> *You take some people that I know who have sold their homes and gone into a condominium. You come in, you're somebody in left field. They're a close-tied group, they don't admit strangers right away. And you really have a tough time breaking into a condominium unless you're very outgoing and make friends easily. If you are a quiet, retiring sort of person, it's tough, and you're not happy. So everybody has to find their own level.*

We have seen how fears for their safety were partly what impelled Edwin and Anne out of their houses and into retirement communities, but others devised stratagems that let them feel secure enough to remain where they were. Nora, whom we saw clinging fiercely to her house in a neighborhood increasingly bedeviled by crime (page 124), tried to allay her anxiety at first by mechanical means:

> *I was terribly afraid to live in my house, which is rather large, and everybody was gone but me. And walking around through that house,*

I was terror-stricken. Someone was breaking in—I had three or four different break-ins. And I was begging people to come spend the night with me. You didn't want to say you were afraid, but you were urging them, "Come and stay with me." And someone finally suggested, "You'd better get one those home security systems," or whatever, with the loud noises and all that. So I had all that done, and it did relieve some of the pressure of being so afraid there by myself.

—San Francisco

Next she progressed to a human equivalent:

Then I went little further and started advertising in Project Share. You've heard of that organization? You get someone like yourself to come to share your home with you. That went on for a few years. And I finally got so I could stay in the house by myself if I had a teenaged boy who would come and spend the night and go home the next morning.

Rather than paying others to keep them company, a few homeowners got others to pay them:

If you are able to rent a room, someone in the house is a comfort.

—Woman, 64, 7

Worries about your safety and your finances may not be all a boarder can help to relieve:

My biggest asset is my lovely four-bedroom house, so I have taken in young people from the local Opera Festival each summer, and they added so much to my life. This September I took a young schoolteacher for the winter months, and she is such a joy. We share the refrigerator, and she cooks for herself. What she pays me helps with the taxes. It is helping both of us. This is something that we older citizens can do to keep our own independence and yet bring young people into our lives.

—Woman, 74, 3

But those contemplating experiments like hers should remember that the results may not be uniformly positive:

I hate living alone. I never had to before. So I've had a series of roomers—interesting if not very satisfactory ventures.

—Woman, 70, 4

Widows, of course, are especially apt to be preoccupied with warding off intruders and other potential wrongdoers. A bold front is this woman's tactic, backed up by a lot of wariness:

Stay alert when you come in and go out of your living quarters. Walk with confidence and never behave in any way to make yourself appear vulnerable. Do not walk afraid. *However, always try to know when to use caution.* Don't ask for trouble.

—*Woman, 73, 11*

A bit of camouflage is enough to reassure Clara:

Two of the things I did after my husband passed away: I left the phone listed in his name; and also I have his name, with mine, on my mailbox. So strangers don't know that I'm by myself, and that gives you a sense of security.

—*San Francisco*

Marlene puts her faith in her dog and some equally vigilant neighbors:

I have a big dog, so when he barks, I look to see what he's barking at. And the few people that live close to me, we all look out for each other if we happen to see a strange car or whatever. Which is good, neighbors should do that.

—*Miami, #1*

Hannah installed an even more elaborate set of alarms than Nora did:

I have always had my own home, but because of the peculiar era that we live in today, I had to put in a burglar alarm. Not really so much for the items in the house—for what are diamonds?—but for me. And I also hook into a terminal. I have two silent alarms. And, if I feel sick or feel I need help, I can reach one of the alarms very easily because it's right by my bed. And when there's a silent alarm, the terminal knows who to call.

—*Miami, #2*

Note how naturally she moves from crime to a peril that preys even more on the minds of survivors who remain in their houses—that an illness or injury will leave them as helpless as a turtle on its back.

Earlier, she had explained,

> *As one gets older and one loses friends—and I've lost three of them, one right after the other—I have become a little bit afraid. One can have a mini-stroke and not be able to move. I don't want to be found on the floor alone.*

Alone—and perhaps dead. Something to counter this threat is what Molly discovered she was really seeking—and what she got—after she rallied her neighbors together to do battle with the other one:

> *I live alone in a house on a block that is just one block. Now, I've been living there twenty-one years and I knew who most of my neighbors were, but I didn't really know them, if you get what I mean. I decided to have a crime-watch meeting in my home after hearing about some of the things that were going on. I was amazed! There were eighteen people on my block who came to my meeting. Men and women. And we had a very nice officer who explained to us a lot of the things to do and not to do. We made a list with everybody's name and phone number. Everybody got a copy.*
>
> *—Miami, #1*

And the aftermath left her equally amazed:

> *Since then, I have had so many neighbors come and ring my bell and just ask, "How are you?—I haven't seen you." And I'm amazed, just amazed that these neighbors—who I never spoke to before—have come forth and really are concerned about me. Now, my next-door neighbor has the key to my house. If for some reason I don't talk to her during the day and she calls and I don't answer, she comes into my house just to see whether I'm alive or dead. And I think it's very important that at least one person has a key to your home.*
> **Dorothy:** *We have that in the condominium.*
> **Catherine:** *We have that, the buddy system.*

That same system instills as much confidence in Hannah as her electronic ones:

> *It gives a sense of security knowing that somebody is looking for you every morning. When I go to the beauty parlor, I have to call my neighbor and tell her, "Don't worry about me, Margot, I'm going to*

the beauty parlor."

—*Miami, #2*

The telephone may not be quite as indispensable to human communication as phone-company ads like to suggest, but the daily peace of mind of some survivors pivots upon it:

> **Lee:** *I check in with my mother every day. She lives alone, and not a day goes by that I don't call her. If she's going to be late or she's going to be someplace, she always lets me know. And someone always knows where I am, and I think that's the key to it all—the buddy system in case of any emergency.*
>
> —*Miami, #1*

Some subscribe to the "telephone reassurance" services offered by social-service organizations and government agencies, including some police departments:

> **Laura:** *Call the police station and say you want to be put on their list. Each morning, you're supposed to call in—"Hello, this is Danny, I'm fine." That's all. But if they haven't heard from you by about ten o'clock, they call you. And if there is no answer, there's a number on file for the neighbor, and they call the neighbor. And if the neighbor doesn't know where you are, they will dispatch a police car there to find out.*
>
> —*Miami, #1*

But Syd has worked out a little ritual with a neighbor that does without the phone altogether:

> *I have a neighbor, her backyard meets my backyard, and so she has keys to my house. Every morning she comes through her backyard, raps on my window just to make sure I'm all right. If she doesn't see me, she comes around the front, rings the doorbell. Then if there's no response, she opens the door. I have two other friends that have keys—everybody has a key to my house.*
>
> —*Miami, #2*

One doesn't bridge backyards with this kind of trust overnight—a consideration that of course should not rule out giving up your house, but which may give you pause before you do. We'll leave the topic with a final story from one woman that puts the dangers of acting too quickly in sharp relief, because if anyone could have been expected to know what she was doing, you would think it would have been she. Clearly a businesswoman to her fingertips, she and her husband (a professor of music)

> *had worked together for twenty years (in our spare time from teaching) buying property—renovating, renting for a short time, then selling on a contract basis. Within a year after his death, I sold the large eight-room family home, a duplex, two cars, held an estate sale—and left with seven installment-sale mortgage contracts. Within the last two years, I have bought a condo for myself; purchased two townhouses as rental units; invested funds in a small local business; and continue to handle the estate business on my own.*
>
> —*Woman, 73, 4*

Yet she goes on to lament,

> *In retrospect now, I think if I had to do it all over again I would not have sold my home—at least, not so soon. All advice from family and friends was "wait at least a year before making a decision." I think a longer time would have been more advisable. It all happens too quick!!! If one can financially do so, keep the home much longer and remain in familiar surroundings.*

We'll go next—and last—to "familiar surroundings" in a larger sense.

The Locale: Move or Stay Put?

Leaving a dwelling behind may not entail giving up your locale—the setting that may have become as much of a "home" for you as a house. Here we'll examine the pros and cons of doing both.

First, the proponents of caution, including the proverbial one year's wait:

> *Get a perspective on things before making any serious changes like moving. The chances are your roots and friends are where you have lived. They will give you solace.*
>
> —*Woman, 76, 13*

> *As a small-town attorney, I encounter many recently widowed people.*

The standard advice not to make serious decisions quickly is good. The dependence on neighborhood friendliness, the storekeeper, mailman, etc., should not be underestimated. Relocation should be preceded by careful evaluation over a period of time.

—*Woman, 59, 3*

For an older person it truly takes time to mourn a loved one, adjust to living alone, and deal with one's own mortality. An established routine offers, unrecognized at first, support in a traumatic situation. I think moving from one's home the first year alone would only increase the confusion. When I grocery-shop, walk in my neighborhood, or go to church, I meet friends.

—*Woman, 70, 2*

Friends and your home ground, if not your home, should take precedence over whatever might lure you elsewhere:

If one lives where the winters are cold, I believe that friends and community ties can be much more important than the advantages of a milder climate.

—*Woman, 71, 9*

Don't move away from old friends, group activities, and community projects unless absolutely necessary—even to live nearer to adult children.

—*Woman, 76, 17*

And the urge to escape is futile:

Do not move away—this thing follows you wherever you go.

—*Woman, 72, 11*

Now compare the sentiments you've just read to these:

For me, it was good to get away, not to stay in the same environment or house.

—*Woman, 59, 11*

Move to be near family (mine a son, daughter-in-law, and two teen-age grandsons), so you are not lonely and have others to think of.

—*Woman, 82, 4*

Create a "new life" in a new location if possible. Near children if possible. I've just moved from California to Maine to be nearer mine.
—Woman, 68, 2

I moved to be nearer to my children—and be away from the many memories of my husband's long sickness.
—Woman, 87, 2

The standoff we have arrived at is an inevitable one. Long-distance moving poses the question of how much of the old you are willing to exchange for the new in its starkest form—as very much of an either/or proposition, without compromises. This does not mean that, if you're inclined to the new, you should plunge into it; as this woman suggests, an acquaintance with the new is best made without hurry:

Get involved in something new. Move, so you don't surround your-self with painful memories, but not in haste. Take a long time—it's part of doing something new.
—Woman, 48, 6

What we ultimately do decide—if we have the luxury of waiting—hinges on our view of how we best fit into the world, and these views can be as opposed as the different sets of political values that make one of us a liberal and the other a conservative. And the fact that they are squarely at odds with each other is no sign that one is any more intelligently held and deeply felt than the other.

You can glimpse that depth of feeling in the almost awkward intensity with which this woman pleads with us not to make a break with the past:

I believe one of the most important things that a person who has lost a spouse can do is to go on trying to live his or her life in a way as close as possible to the kind of life which the two of them had had together. By that, I mean that the person left should go on, if at all possible, to a great extent, with the same friends, the same interests, and the same general activities, which the two of them had had in unison. In that way, the whole continuity of life will not seem so much to have been lost or broken, and you will not feel so terribly alone for so long a time.
—Woman, 80, 3

Although she doesn't say so, she'd clearly regard moving as inconceivable. To John, at the other extreme, it is *not* moving that is inconceivable:

> *I moved right after. I got into a smaller apartment. I found that mandatory.*
>
> *Noel: Did moving change your attitude also?*
>
> *John: Yes, I looked at it as a given—right off the bat. I said, "You've got to get out of here."*
>
> *Q: How did it change your attitude?*
>
> *John: Well, it gave me a sense of newness. Trying to leave the memories and the associations was the big thing. You know, the pizza joint. There was a pizza joint we used to go to. You associate that with her. You get that with friends and family too, although it's more the little things, the familiarity of the laundry. You know, you'd go down to the laundry together. So it seemed time to go, and—[to Roger] as I was thinking when you mentioned moving out to California—just get away from the whole thing. I don't know if that's escaping or not.*
>
> *Q: Is it OK to escape?*
>
> *John: Yeah, I think at times you have to.*
>
> *Roger: I think it's starting over again.*
>
> *John: It keeps your sanity.*
>
> —New York, #2

John is referring to Roger's earlier announcement of his hopes for a "new life" in California, plans that he emphasizes were already evolving before his wife's death:

> *Roger: I'm planning on moving. I'm living in an apartment that is going co-op, and I've been waiting for that day to happen, so I can move to California and start a new life out there.*
>
> *Q: Where in California?*
>
> *Roger: Probably Los Angeles. I have a lot of friends out there. I just think that for me it would be good. I'm not happy in New York particularly, and I don't think it has anything to do with my situation now. We were thinking about this before.*

For an apartment dweller like John in a big city, however, a move across town may be as effective as one across the country in exorcising the past.

Those who share John's and Roger's view that a major change of place is a prerequisite to "starting over again" are outnumbered by those who don't—including those who once did but had a rueful change of heart:

Do not move from your community too quickly. I made that mistake and was miserable the first year.

—Woman, 79, 20

Even more regretful were those who felt they had been forcibly uprooted:

My difficulty was that I was unable to stay in our home—an isolated one in rural Vermont—because of the difficulty of maintenance and because of loneliness. In moving to a new environment, five hundred miles away, I was unable to maintain contact with old friends and habits.

—Woman, 79, 3

I had to move across country and establish a completely new "life-style" because I was completely alone 1,500 miles from my family. If you can maintain your home and can stay in a familiar area, the adjustment would be much less traumatic.

—Woman, 74, 3

Ann describes how stranded she felt without her job and friends after her husband's illness brought her—unwillingly, but inescapably—halfway across the continent:

I'm not a native Californian. I come from Cleveland, actually. My husband had not been well, and he had a very bad heart attack. And the doctor said to me, "If you don't get him out of Cleveland, he's not going to last the winter. Therefore, you don't have too many alternatives."

My children lived in California; and every time we'd come to visit they would say, "We're here, and what are you doing there?" And I would answer, "Baby birds have to leave the nest, but that doesn't mean that Mama Bird and Papa Bird have to fly after them." Ha! You know that old saying "Man proposes and God disposes"? I called the children and told them what the doctor had said, and they said, "There's no question, come on out."

Well, I had a wonderful job—a dream of a job which I hated to leave. I'd been there for fifteen years. Anyhow, to make a long story short, we came out to California. I hated it! How can you say you hate California [laughter]? I hated it! The first year I was—you leave all your ties behind you and you come to a strange place and you know nobody. And I—wise guy!—had said before we left, "You know, the children have their lives to live, and we're not going to intrude on them. We're going to have to make lives of our own." Well, the children found us an apartment in Oakland, and, three times that first year, they sent me back to Cleveland because I couldn't adjust to not knowing anybody. I would pick up the telephone—just to see if it was working!

—San Francisco

Searching for reassurance in a dial tone—it's one of the bleakest pictures of social isolation imaginable. Fortunately, as we'll see in the next chapter (page 247), she found a "lifesaver" in resuming her college education before her husband's death—and completing it afterwards.

Aside from depicting how hard it is to construct an entirely new social life (a task probably made doubly difficult by having her ailing husband at home), Ann's story reveals how unpredictable can be the outcome of the commonest occasion for moving—to be nearer family, usually grown children (and often their offspring), but sometimes siblings and even parents. Ann herself now delights in being with her family:

There are many times when you get very lonely, but you don't get lonesome, and I think the difference is because you have children around. I have five grandchildren and three great-granddaughters. And I thank God that I'm around to celebrate some of the nice things that come up in their lives.

The 74-year-old woman quoted right before her, whose move after the death was just as disruptive, concedes nevertheless,

It is a great comfort to be near family—near but not *with.*

Maintain your emotional self-sufficiency as well, another woman stresses:

Don't move immediately; allow a year or so to think about your

situation. Then, if possible, live near one of your children (daughter preferably) and grandchildren—but don't count on them to fill your time.

—*Woman, 67, 10*

Both are undoubtedly alluding to the tendency of some survivors to make undue demands upon their adult children. That, and their children's reactions to it, is a topic we'll cover in Chapter 5.

Several report success moving not only near siblings but *in* with them to boot, perhaps because it is easier to establish a relationship with them as coequals than it is with children:

I was fortunate to be able to move from a New York apartment when I closed our business to my widowed sister's home in California, where we share expenses.

—*Woman, 76, 8*

I moved to a small western town where there is less dining out, less entertainment, and less need for formal clothes. People are more friendly and informal. I would not advise everyone to move, but I had a sister with whom I could live and am a small-town person at heart. We have community concerts and adult education classes; also active church groups.

—*Woman, 80, 13*

Much of their satisfaction clearly stems from their happiness with the ambience of their new locales (note how the first underscores "home"). And being a member of her sister's household may have gained the second an entree to small-town society, something that frustrated another woman:

If possible, don't live in a tiny town. It takes a long time for them to take you in, and there are fewer activities.

—*Woman, NA, NA*

So even if your main motive is to settle near your own, take heed of where they live. This woman, who held off for eight years before moving four hundred miles to be near her children, found her new environment as congenial as she'd hoped:

I am comfortable in a small city with a large university, simple traffic, a wealth of cultural activities, and friendly people.

—Woman, 78, 11

No matter how well planned, every big decision is in part a gamble, and moving long distances is one of the biggest decisions—and thus one of the biggest gambles—of all. This woman moved to be near family not once but twice, the second time when the first failed to pan out:

I even moved across the country (3,000 miles) and attempted to live near my only sister and other maternal relatives. The result was that I did not fit into that social and family structure any more. I remained one year and moved back across the country to be near my husband's children and grandchildren, feeling much closer to them than my own blood relatives.

—Woman, 73, 4

In this instance, a sister couldn't offer the closeness that children could—stepchildren at that, apparently. On the other hand, another woman ventured to relocate near her *parents*, rather than her children—and found it paid off right away:

After a happy marriage of thirty-four years, I found it hard to be alone and to make decisions for myself. My parents lived in another part of the country, and I moved, as soon as matters were settled, to be near them. My two children were grown and had their own lives to live and did not need me.

As I had been teaching school, I almost immediately found a teaching position. Planning for the students occupied my thoughts and energy. Then, too, in a medium-sized city I quickly found a group with similar interests and made new friends very soon.

My advice to other widows would be to move to a small or medium-sized city that has no memories connected to your husband. Then get a job you would like or become involved in community work helping others—either through a church or club.

—Woman, 77, 4

We've quoted her in full, however, to show just how much of her life she had to reorchestrate—and with what decisiveness and foresight she went about it. There's an equally impressive example on pages 488-89 of the Epilogue.

Such self-certitude is not granted to us all. Some of us may not be sure exactly what is impelling us to leave or stay put. Another Ann ruminates over why she moved—and kept on moving, not to be nearer family, but away from them and away from the friends and the past she felt were failing her (see pages 318 and 321). She later wonders, however, whether she was not more afraid of herself than she was of them:

After my husband died, I had to get out of that town. I grew up in that town, I knew everybody. I can't stand pity. I run from it. I never could stand to hear anybody say, "Oh, Ann . . . ." So I had to get out of there. And after leaving, I lived a little bit all over—Arizona, Colorado. I finally moved to California, I lived in many parts of the state. I couldn't find myself. I was running from myself.

—*Miami, #2*

Her perplexity is an appropriately indecisive note on which to conclude this chapter. Again, in Chapter 5 we'll delve into relationships with family and friends—and how they can wither or flourish. In the meantime, we'll go on to the tricks by which people, on their own, keep the little affairs of life going, regardless of what they have decided about the big ones. Tricks as simple as this (with a final nod to our departing subject):

Continue to correspond with former friends if a move to a new area is necessary.

—*Woman, 77, 4*

Chapter 4

Being by Yourself, II: . . . But "Keep Busy"

"Keep busy"—or words to that effect—was by far and away the front-runner among the pieces of advice elicited by our survey questionnaire: 490 people (46% of those responding) urged it. Here is a sample:

My best advice is to keep busy. This was mandatory in my case, as there were then three teenage children facing college, so I had to continue working. As my children have matured, I have found them to be my best friends. At age sixty I began the study of the cello and now play in the local symphony. I also do volunteer work and am active in the church. There are many, many things one can do as a single person.
—Woman, 73, 19

Keep BUSY! Take educational courses. Enter volunteer activities (hospital, library, social service). Make new friendships and re-activate old ones. Find a hobby and pursue it vigorously. Read. Help other people at least once a day. Talk daily to a friend or someone you may feel is lonely.
—Woman, 76, 10

Play golf, bridge, help with blood banks, hospital guild—anything to keep you out with other people. Get together with other widows, talk to them on the phone. In other words, keep busy.
—Woman, 72, 5

Virtually anything will serve, survivors say:

For spouses left alone: get involved in something. *Find an activity you enjoy or volunteer for church or community work.* Keep busy.
—Woman, 72, 3

Get down to it right away:

> *The important thing is to keep as busy as possible. For weeks I wrote thank-you letters, went through filing cabinets, anything that would keep me too busy to think about myself.*
> —*Woman, 74, 9*

And plug away at it no matter how little you may feel like it, in mind or body:

> *Keep as busy as possible despite the fact that deep grief is no good for physical energy.*
> —*Woman, 65, 11*

"Keep busy"—with its slightly scolding, schoolmarmish ring—may strike you as a pallid panacea. But then how to account for the urgency, sometimes even passion, with which the directive is put forward, as if its value far transcends the ordinariness of the activities involved—bridge, golf, writing letters, talking on the phone? You can spy some of the deeper reasons above. Keeping busy combats loneliness by getting you together with other people. It helps take your mind off yourself—and therefore away from pitying that self. At its most fundamental, however, it just affirms that you are alive, as this woman suggests:

> *Try not to be alone too much and dwell on the past or what might have been if your spouse had lived. Get busy with life—get involved.*
> —*Woman, 59, 3*

In the most literal sense, "keeping busy" signifies motion, movement, "keeping going." The alternative, as we noted in opening the last chapter, is the kind of inactivity symbolized by "sitting around," a paralysis that is the semblance of death. An organism's ability to move under its own power is one of the tests scientists have traditionally used to validate that it is indeed living. To this group, reminiscing over the fate of a locally prominent media "personality," "keeping going" is proof that life is not over:

> *Ida: She's retired now. She used to be a gorgeous woman, a brilliant woman. And the day she retired, she became an old woman.*

Q: Hold on! Is there a lesson in that?
Peggy: Sure!
Ida: Yes, keep going!
Peggy: You've got to keep going.
Ida: Keep going. Crawl, but keep going.
Margaret: And don't feel that your life is over.
—*Miami, #2*

We can see this elemental purpose in Molly's sketch of how she deals with a bad day (note how "keeping busy" frames it):

Q: Molly, how do you handle it?
Molly: Well, I try to keep myself very busy. I do a lot of volunteer work. I do some exercising and I do a lot of walking. I have a lot of friends. You never get over it, and every once in a while you go into a room and have yourself a good cry. We were married almost fifty years, and it was a shock, an awful shock. Sometimes it gets you. Some days it's bad, some days it's sore. When it's bad I put on my hat and coat and go out, take a walk. You'll never get over that feeling—it's terrible, it's dreadful! But you have to keep busy and you have to keep going.
—*Boston, #1*

Molly's response to an emotional setback—"going out, taking a walk"—embodies the will to live. And this ulterior purpose is what counts, never mind the immediate one:

My advice is, don't sit thinking about the past and feeling sorry for yourself, your life must go on, so keep yourself busy and your mind occupied. I found that working jigsaw puzzles and crossword puzzles helped me a great deal. Any hobby would help.
—*Woman, 80, 9*

"Working puzzles" as the road to recovery from the death of someone you loved? It sounds preposterous, but in the context we've just outlined, it makes eminent sense. Another woman is driving at the same thing when she lets one item dominate her checklist:

1. Keep busy!
2. Feel free to remember; to enjoy.
3. Stay in touch with friends and relations.

4. Find something to do for other people.
5. Keep busy!
6. Don't let your unaccustomed chores throw you.
7. Keep busy!

—Woman, 50, 3

Intelligent, purposeful movement is what is meant by "keeping busy," an animal vitality—not "vegetating":

Keep up personal interests and seek new ones—keep the mind occupied and busy with living, versus existing.

—Woman, 64, 6

Virginia chronicles how keeping busy kept her going—through six years of widowhood and on into marriage with the husband now sitting next to her:

Well, when I became a widow, I looked at it this way: I wasn't the first widow and I won't be the last. So I picked up my life and I started to travel. And I was alone for six years, but I was never lonely because I kept busy. And I think that's what keeps us going, is keeping busy and getting interested in things. And I managed very well, and I met Bud through an introduction, and we've been very, very happy. He's a wonderful husband. He's a nice guy, too.

—Los Angeles, #1

"Get Out of the House"

If keeping busy is the ultimate solution, where do we begin? How do we set life going again when it's been brought to a standstill? By a simple act of locomotion that is recommended almost as often as keeping busy, and often in the same breath:

Try to get out of the house every day, if only to go to the grocery store or to take a walk.

—Woman, 80, 5

Get out and do things. It's no good sitting home grieving. Life can be good again.

—Woman, 63, 3

Do not stay home and brood. Get out, call friends, plan something

for your weekends (the hardest times) other than staying home alone.
—*Woman, 65, 2*

The house, or apartment, is the center of the circle that circumscribes our lives. We sally forth from it at the start of the day and fall back to it in more or less orderly fashion at day's end. So it's a refuge. But when a spouse's death has disrupted this ebb and flow, the house has the power of becoming something else—a prison. Jean just holed up in hers:

After my husband's death I remained in my house for a year, not going anywhere. I was so grief-stricken that I refused to go. People called me and came over and visited. I had a wonderful family. But I just didn't feel like going anywhere.
—*New York, #1*

The house is where the inclination to sit around tugs at you most strongly:

Become involved in some useful undertaking, whether civic, educational, or religious. While this cannot take the place of a good companion, it is better than sitting at home asking oneself so many questions that now will never be answered.
—*Woman, 88, 2*

Asking questions that never will, or can, be answered—like "Why me?" is a sure way of engendering self-pity, and the house is seen as a breeding ground for it:

Make an effort to get out. Staying home feeling sorry for yourself only makes things worse.
—*Woman, 62, 3*

Do not withdraw, *but try to get out of the house. Don't sit around feeling sorry for yourself. You are not the first person who has faced this sorrow.*
—*Woman, 75, 2*

Marilyn recalls how the syndrome got its grip on her:

For the first year, I was a basket case. I didn't want to do anything for the year. I just stayed in the house. I never went anywhere. I was dragged out to dinner with my friends, and then I would come right home, and that was that. I wanted nothing that would make me happy, I think. I just wanted to wallow in self-pity.

—Boston, #2

Sitting around, moreover, can be conducive to something far worse than self-pity:

Lillian: *You have to get out. You* have *to get out.*
Molly: *Some days you don't want to, but if you stay in the house—*
Lillian: *You will go out of your mind.*

—Boston, #1

Depression in particular may be what we're courting:

Keep occupied—if you get depressed, get out of the house.

—Woman, 70, 4

Depression very typically drives its victims to their beds, and that may be why some pair getting out of the house with an even more rudimentary task of daily living:

If you don't work—get dressed by nine, ten, eleven, or noon each day and get out of the house at least once a day—the grocery store, a meeting, eating out, etc.

—Woman, 66, 7

Your bathrobe can be an invitation to chronic self-neglect (not to be confused with an occasional festive interlude of the sort Noreen mentions); and self-neglect feeds self-pity:

Elaine: *You said, "Whatever you do, get out of the house." I say, "Whatever you do, get out of your bathrobe."*
Gladys: *Good point!*
Q: *Tell us a little about why you say that?*
Elaine: *Because after a while you start feeling sorry for yourself.*
Sara: *You* look *like a wreck.*
Elaine: *You start feeling sick. Whereas if you get into your clothes, you say, "Gee, I've got to go somewhere, I've got to do something," and you feel better about yourself.*

Noreen: I must be different, then, because I enjoy "jama-days," I call them, where I just sit down and do anything I want.

Elaine: Oh, that's different, because you've set the day aside to be home doing nothing. But if you do that day in and day out, you're going to go nuts.

Fay: I still get dressed, even if I stay home. And my makeup is on. That's right, never have a naked face.

Q: Never a naked face?

Fay: Never [laughter].

—*Los Angeles, #2*

"Feeling better"—about yourself and the rest of the world—is the upshot of getting out for several reasons. When we emerge from the house, we necessarily mingle with the rest of humanity, if only to "be around" them—and that in itself tends to disarm self-pity and its emotional allies, especially when you see that some are just like you:

To be able to get out of the house and be around people helped me a great deal.

—*Woman, 65, 9*

Force yourself to get out of the house and do something. Realize you are not alone—there are millions of us.

—*Woman, 65, 3*

And for many of us, just the experience of open space can produce an expansiveness of mood:

Richard: If I feel lonely I just go out. I walk down to Soho and I walk back. It's good for me; I meditate nicely and put my head together.

—*New York, #2*

Lillian: I like to be outdoors, and I go swimming every day. It's the idea of the sunshine. You feel that you have to—because our place is small—get out of a small area into the outdoors and the sun and the fresh air and talking to other people. Sitting in our pool I can . . . [searching for words] get out of my bad thoughts.

—*Los Angeles, #1*

Connie feels exactly the same, for exactly the same reasons:

Connie: I think you have to keep after it and get out—to meet other people. Then, when you come home, you're tired. And you can cope with the evening, you can watch television. But you can't stay in the house all day watching that television—all those crazy programs! No, it's true, so get out. Now sometimes, I might have a little nap, but I go out at four o'clock. I leave my house. I go out and I walk to the corner. Everybody is coming home from work, and it makes you feel altogether different.

Q: Can you put into words what it is doing for you?

Connie: It puts me in a different frame of mind. I'm not saying, "I should be cleaning this, I should be doing that."

—Boston, #1

In drawing the conventional portrait of those who shut themselves in as captives of their television sets, she observes how she has been freed to enjoy hers. The same goes for Virginia, whose daily regime is full of the selective viewing of TV:

Q: What's a typical day for you?

Virginia: Well, I get myself out of there. I get to the health club in the morning, come back, watch my soap opera, wait for the mailman, go to the swimming pool, maybe there's something to do in the evening, maybe there's a better show on TV, and things like that. I'm very content.

—Los Angeles, #1

Contentment like hers is hard-won, however. We saw how survivors could be of two minds about the house when it came to deciding whether to sell it or keep it. No other inanimate object, as we all know, can conjure up stronger feelings, and the death of a spouse can stir these feelings into volatile mixtures of aversion and attraction. For Lee, they're all aversion:

I'd leave my house and I'd go to work, and the whole day I wouldn't think of things. Then, of course, I never wanted to go home. I'd drive around, I'd go shopping. I hated to come home. I hated my house. And I think everybody goes through the same thing. It's universal.

—Miami, #1

It's not, as Sylvia demonstrates:

*I would go to work and come right home. I felt very safe in the house.
My home was my refuge. I didn't run outside. I ran inside. That's where
security was. Everything was the same. I could walk in the house and
lock the world out. And that's how I made it.*

—Los Angeles, #2

The very sameness that made the home a refuge for her was probably
what made Lee flinch from hers—and perhaps from the fact that it is
"the same" in all respects but the most vital one.

Sylvia herself, in a striking bit of self-recollection later in the session,
reveals how much more ambivalent her feelings actually were. Her
children were trying to persuade her to visit them in other parts of the
country:

Sylvia: *I didn't go, but it was for a very good reason. I wanted to run
out of the house. I knew if I left the house I would never come back.
Never, ever, ever, in a million years.*
Q: *What would be the problem with that?*
Sylvia: *[looking startled and after a long pause] I don't know, I
hadn't thought about that. You know, it's something I've never dealt
with. No, no—part of it I do know! I had a sister, younger than me, who
committed suicide eight years ago. She would try to run. She did—she
probably knew every hotel and every motel in Southern California. You
can't run. If you could, it would be marvelous. You could close this door,
and all the pain you could leave in here. You would be another person.
But you can't. So when I say "run," you may physically run, but you
haven't run from anything because it's all still with you. It's all there
waiting for you.*

Her sister's frantic desire to escape—from what, we are never
told—led to self-destruction; and that precedent inspired Sylvia to
"run" for sheer safety in the opposite direction.

Grace, on the contrary, implies that she was rushing *from* suicide when she fled the house:

Q: *Grace wanted to say something.*
Grace: *I just want to say that I was 29 when I lost my husband. And
he was 29. I had two young children, 6 and 5. And I loved my husband
dearly and my children also. And I had to get out of the house after he*

died. I could not stay in or I would have—I don't know what would have happened to my life. I had to get out, and I don't mean with men. I dated later on, but just to get out of the house and be among people and friends. Because I got to the point where I didn't even want to live at times.

—Miami, #1

But it was not merely getting out that came to her rescue, but also a solitary pastime that could only be pursued inside the house:

But by myself, going to the priest and talking to him, and getting out, going shopping, looking in the stores, and doing a lot of sewing, which was terrific therapy for me. Sewing is like taking a tranquilizer. I mean you could get at a sewing machine, and you could just think of nothing but sewing and forget about the whole world and your hardship and your sorrow. And this really helped me overcome losing him at such a young age.

The lesson? If the house is no longer the same haven that it was before the death, the object is to prevent it from turning into a prison, yet preserve and foster what makes it a refuge until, at best, it becomes again what it once was—genuinely a home to you. It has reverted to that for these two, who can embrace the prospect of coming back after "going out" (which has so much more leisurely a ring to it than "getting out"):

Why do spouses want to move out of their homes because "there are too many memories?" Memories are so comforting. It is so comforting to me to be able to remain in the same home we were in when he left, a home and surroundings he enjoyed so much. I never think about being alone. I love the peace and quiet—I don't want a TV or radio blaring! When I have to go out for a while, I look forward to returning home.

—Woman, 77, 3

I did not change anything at home and I live more or less the same way as when he was with me. I was sociable before; now I prefer to be more by myself and my very good memories. I often visit friends who need help. I go out with friends or have them home, I visit my family, but I do not need to be entertained. I feel very comfortable at home alone—I never feel "alone"—reading, listening to music, or playing my guitar (I play classical guitar) for my pleasure. We did that often together.

—*Woman, 82, 4*

They can positively savor the ways in which their homes remind them of their lives with their husbands—and neither seems mawkish about it.

"Getting out of the house," therefore, does not constitute the bare act of striding out the front door but the whole task of reestablishing a meaningful rhythm in our daily round from dawn to dusk—and then to dawn again.

The Days

Time itself may seem to loom up in front of you every day like a blank wall:

Simply try to face each day, one day at a time.

—*Woman, 76, NA*

And those days may creep along inch by inch:

Take it a day—or a minute—at a time at first.

—*Woman, 66, 7*

"One day at a time"—the phrase has become a commonplace, partly the result of having been adopted as the motto of Alcoholics Anonymous. And it has a protean ability to take on different meanings depending on its context. Among survivors, it crops up constantly. Often it bears the message it most frequently does for AA participants. Recovery over the long term demands concentrating on the here-and-now (that's all we have the strength for), progressing in painfully small steps, and not trying to achieve too much too soon:

Connie: Take one day at a time.
Molly: One day at a time.
Connie: You think you're never going to be able to do it.
Molly: But you do it.

—*Boston, #1*

Learning to live alone is the worst part, but, if you take it one day at a time and keep busy, you will eventually adjust.

—*Woman, 74, 12*

At best, "one day at a time" can express an unfettered enjoyment of the everyday—something we'll come to in Chapter 7. At worst, it voices an utter indifference to it, the "numbness" of sensibility we saw in Chapter 2, in which "one day at a time" melts into a leaden succession of them:

It still seems unreal. It's one day at a time and it's difficult to make decisions. I keep thinking I should be doing something else, but I just go along.

—*Woman, 61, 2*

I can't make up my mind about my house, so I just live day to day.

—*Woman, 60, 3*

The grieving process took at least eighteen months. During that period I lived from day to day, not caring whether tomorrow came or not.

—*Woman, 57, 3*

For people in this frame of mind (observe how much fresher their grief is than that of the previous group), time has become an inert heap of minutes and hours, with no future to it, and they would just as soon junk what is so often praised as life's most precious commodity:

If you are young enough to keep working, do so. This keeps you going during the day at least. It's difficult for older non-working persons—anything to kill the time, kill the day.

—*Woman, 75, 4*

If the death has stripped time of its potential, you must somehow restore that potential to time, and day by day is how many survivors say you should go about it:

First year is difficult. Keep busy. Stop looking back. Make each day important.

—*Woman, 62, 3*

"Making each day important" demands some forethought and

willpower—at a minimum, the resolve to make each day memorable for something, and therefore different from the last:

> *Find something each day for which to be thankful. Find something each day that will make you laugh.*
>
> —*Woman, 86, 7*

And if you are in no mood to be gratified or amused? Then perhaps getting out will put you into it:

> *Take each day one at a time—go out each day and make an effort to talk with someone (shopping, visiting, etc.).*
>
> —*Woman, 56, 2*

For one woman, even such casual human contact is fundamentally "creative"—and she's right:

> *Create something—see or talk to other people* every *day.*
>
> —*Woman, 67, 4*

This man lets such creativity extend to some harmless false pretenses:

> *Even if you have a washer and dryer, take your clothes to a laundromat and talk—but not too much about your spouse's death.*
>
> —*Man, 61, 3*

And if you can't talk face-to-face, there are substitutes. The phone is one:

> *Get out of the house for a while each day or at least telephone family or friends daily.*
>
> —*Woman, 67, 5*

> *I make good use of the phone whenever I feel like talking to my children and friends. My family have not forgotten me and let me know it. That has really been a plus for me.*
>
> —*Woman, 66, 3*

The mail is another:

> *Get out and do something for someone else. If you can't get out, write*

letters to friends.
                                            —Woman, 73, 8

Do not withdraw from people. I write at least one letter each day.
                                            —Woman, 82, 7

My daughter and I write a letter to each other every day.
                                            —Woman, 73, 8

To keep the lines of communication open (and her mind at ease), this woman *must* use letters instead of the phone:

Since I am quite deaf, I write letters to friends and relatives instead of telephoning—jokingly I say, "A letter a day keeps the psychiatrist away."
                                            —Woman, 86, 8

By trying to make our time significant to ourselves and to others, we are reasserting our control over it. And we are often exhorted to tighten that control even further by planning—if only so that we can lift our heads off the pillow in the morning more willingly:

Each night before you go to sleep, plan at least one thing for the next day—it will help get you out of bed.
                                            —Woman, 80, 5

Lee's doctor literally prescribed him a regimen of planning:

Q: What were the kinds of things you needed?
Lee: Activity, mainly. I had professional advice. And I was told that there was a time for grieving and then you have to put it aside and go on with your life.
Q: Did that make sense?
Lee: Yes, and so the doctor told me to plan what I am going to do a week in advance, activities for each day. And that's what I've done and it has worked quite well in helping me adjust.
                                            —New York, #2

For these two, the whole art of keeping busy lies in planning:

Now that you are alone, you must think through an agenda that keeps your mind and body busy.

—Woman, 85, 23

Make commitments to be busy, occupy time, mind.

—Woman, 71, 11

By committing ourselves, we create imperatives to act that we cannot easily undo. But that's just what makes such commitments so intimidating. We saw earlier (pages 118-122) how survivors with jobs tended to treasure those jobs. And these two did so because their work relieved them of the task of planning their days:

> **Peggy:** *Employment was the thing that saved me from going out of my mind. I had a very good job. I knew I had to get up every morning and go to work. I had no time to feel sorry for myself. And that was my salvation.*
> **Syd:** *It was the destination which was great.*
> **Peggy:** *[nodding] I had somewhere to go every morning.*
> **Ruth:** *It's a wonderful thing when you can get up every morning and you know what you're going to do that day. You don't just sit and say, "Well, should I go to the mall or should I go to see a movie or should I call up a friend?" No, you say, "Today I'm going to work." I loved that job so much! I was so happy there.*
>
> *—Miami, #2*

The very "lack of choice" can be liberating, as long as (an important proviso) you like your job in the first place:

> *Keep working if you enjoy work. Of my friends who were working when we were widowed, all have agreed that the structure was helpful, the lack of choice about whether you got out of bed was a lifesaver, and that having a job (unless it's one you hate) takes you out of your self-pity and inertia.*
>
> *—Woman, 62, 12*

If you don't have a paying job (or can't find one—more on this later in the chapter), then volunteer work can be a means of introducing the same kind of constraints into your day. Elaine expostulates with Gladys, who is complaining of the torture of getting up:

> **Elaine:** *But you have to plan something to get up for.*

Gladys: There's something to get up for, but I'm not interested. I mean, I can go to the health club—
Elaine: Yes, but you've got to look forward to something that you are interested in, that you want to do.
Gladys: Years ago, in my young married life, I worked with spastic children, and that is something I would like very much to do. But apparently there is no place to go to do it.
Elaine: Well, if you want to work with children, then you've got to go get children to work with. Now, I've got a book out and I've been doing programs for different organizations. And sometimes I feel, "Well, gee, I want to sleep in today." But I can't sleep, I've got a program to do. I've got to get up.

—Los Angeles, #2

If you don't have obligations like these to dictate how your day will go, then planning becomes more crucial—and more difficult. The burden of ordering your time falls on you. Some approach their social lives with the same sense of duty they would a job:

Plan a social activity every day (meet with someone).

—Woman, 68, 3

This woman's club represents the same sort of daily destination the workplace does for others:

I belonged to a senior citizens club which gave me a destination to walk to each day.

—Woman, 73, 7

And of course weekends (like nights, as we'll see next) throw everyone into the same quandary—trying to make use of free time when this "freedom" may be the last thing you want:

Gladys: Somehow or other, I have made a network of what I call new friends in the last year. And one or two of us try to make the weekends mean something. For instance, I volunteer on Sunday morning—because what else will I do with Sunday morning?

—Los Angeles, #2

Plan to have a special activity (like hiking) on Saturday and be with friends on Sunday afternoons—invite them to your home.

—*Woman, 73, 15*

Laying plans like these—and then executing them—would seem an innocuous enough proposition, but as we'll see further in Chapter 5 (where we consider human relationships in more detail), it demands a herculean effort from many survivors. "Every day" is again and again portrayed as a battle:

How can I give advice when every day is a struggle to live the life of a single person after fifty years of sharing one's life?

—*Woman, 75, 3*

And it is a battle with yourself above all:

I found it necessary to force *myself to participate in physical—and mental—activities. Walking, hiking, and reading were the biggest sources of survival.*

—*Woman, 68, 4*

Keep your familiar routine as much as possible. Make yourself do things even when you don't feel like it.

—*Woman, 69, 2*

Nevertheless, it is a battle you may find yourself winning:

I use my willpower; I discipline myself. Keep plodding, you will be surprised at how much you can accomplish.

—*Woman, 77, 3*

At first I forced myself to travel and be involved, but now it is a regular part of my life.

—*Woman, 76, 4*

Postponing the fight may just make it worse:

Continue your usual activities as soon as possible after your loss. The longer you wait, the harder it is.

—*Woman, 84, 14*

Getting back into the swing of life as soon as possible helped. It is hard whenever you start. The longer it is postponed, the harder it is. It is very necessary to "get out and do" and forget your own troubles for a time. Keep your chin up. Things do get better.

—Woman, 73, 4

And frightened though you may be, you may find your terrors unfounded:

It's up to you to "make things happen." One has to force herself to get out. I was so scared and have found there's "nothing to fear but fear itself."

—Woman, 70, 5

One often-praised weapon in the struggle to make things happen—to make life "eventful" again—is the list:

Write a "to do" list and make a plan for every day—even simple things like making a phone call or writing a letter. Write it down and do it.

—Woman, 48, 4

Such a list serves Pat as both a plan of action and a record of it:

Q: Plan your days. Do you have anything to add to that?
Pat: I was doing that for quite a few years even before my husband died. I was very involved in a lot of volunteer work, but I was also losing my memory. So I started keeping a sheet, "Things to Do Today," and as I do them, even if it's just a telephone call or going to market, I check it off. And those that I don't do get carried over to the next day. It's like a diary, and I have kept those sheets. They come in handy. If something was promised you a week after you bought it and you didn't get it, you can go back and check the day that you were in the store.

—Los Angeles, #2

Betty has converted her calendar into an arsenal of possibilities—most of them never to be drawn upon, but ready for use all the same:

When I read the newspaper and look at some of the events in it, I will jot them down on my calendar no matter how far in advance they are. And then each day when I look at my calendar, I'll see that maybe it's something I don't want to do, maybe it's something I can't

do, but a lot of times I will go to these lectures or whatever.
—*Los Angeles, #2*

Besides ordering the day, such planning can stamp it with a distinctive shape that sets it off from the one that's gone and the one to come. This woman sorts out some of her chores by the points of the compass:

Spread errands so daily trips have direction.
—*Woman, 78, 12*

This woman blends the venturesome with the cautious—but again with the unstated aim of making each day unique. She warns us against trying to make each day too "important":

Tackle one difficult task a day, not bunch them together—such as meeting with a lawyer or banker in matters relating to spouse, or seeing to the maintenance of the home.
—*Woman, 47, 2*

But she also invites us to flirt with the untried:

Plan something for each day. Live one day at a time. Follow your interests. Try some things that are new, that you didn't do with spouse.

Another also tries to flavor her time with the same mixture of known and unknown:

Try to keep as busy as possible—things you like to do and things you've never tried.
—*Woman, 58, 10*

Ideally, we shall reacquire the knack of giving the entire day a direction, one leading into the future—which of course planning of any sort forces us to focus on instead of the immediate present or the past. And eventually we may be able to "look forward" in the more felicitous sense:

Plan for a trip. You need something to look forward to.
—*Woman, 80, 5*

Try to keep something just ahead, such as a visit to children or a trip of some kind.

—Woman, 72, 10

Or, as this woman says (with disarming circularity):

Plan a special treat three to six months after death of spouse to plan toward.

—Woman, 64, 2

Noel says that he drew upon his talents for planning—and upon an admitted penchant for putting himself first—to repattern his days completely:

If you can't cope with the immediate changing of your own lifestyle, it's rough. I think you have to find your own niche, and maybe I'm luckier than a lot of people. It's not that I didn't love my wife, but my daughter said my being selfish has probably helped me a lot. When I say "selfish," I mean that I think of myself. I have my day planned. I know what I'm going to eat that night, what I'm going to cook that night.
Q: Is that all new? You weren't like that before?
Noel: No, it's all new. I used to go out a lot, but I don't much anymore. I used to go out to dinner almost three or four nights a week, socializing and drinking a lot. There were more people over to the house. I was always a good cook, so I still have people over once in a while. But now I stay home and read and work. I look forward to every day because I know what I'm going to do that day. And, strange to say, now that it's over, I feel I'm entering a new phase in my life, in which I've found an inner peace with myself.

—New York, #1

But most scarcely went to such deliberate lengths to reorganize their lives. Ida, for example, makes no ambitious claims; she just unassumingly relates how she reintroduced structure into her day by building on what was already there:

Well, you go into a tailspin at first, almost a depression. But, luckily for me, I had friends that rallied around, and you take up things little by little. You join things. You travel a bit after a while, and then I like to read, so I joined a private library. I like to write, so I took some classes, just to encourage me to do more, you see. I was in the theater—well, the business end of it—and I joined the American Theatre Week as a volunteer. I joined the international group where you teach English to foreigners. You have to structure your day so that you can fill it in somehow with things other than just the chores which you used to do in your lunch hour. You sort of stretch it out. And somehow time goes, and you're reconciled to what has happened. That's it as far as I am concerned.

—New York, #1

The extraordinary assortment of things she's found to do belies her modesty. She has triumphed over the day and made "time go" again—"little by little."

The Nights

The approach of dark is as dreaded by many survivors as the break of day. Evenings are of course when most couples reunite after a day spent apart, and we saw in Chapter 2 (pages 61-62) how coming home for the night also brings home the aloneness anew, regardless of how you passed the day:

I found that my co-workers were exceptionally thoughtful, but my evenings were very difficult.

—Woman, 63, 8

Betty: *During the day I find I keep quite busy doing volunteer work, taking courses, or things like that. It's the nights that are gruesome.*

—Los Angeles, #2

Lee: *I have a few friends, but when they've left, that's when the whole thing starts, ten or eleven o'clock.*

—New York, #2

Your regular sleeping habits may have been an immediate casualty of the loss, as they were for Raymond:

I went to sleep, and I still do sometimes, at eight o'clock in the evening. I don't like the evenings. I don't go out. I get up at five-thirty or six in the morning and do housework then. I sleep very badly. I wake up maybe at one o'clock, go back to sleep again about two or three. Put the radio on, listen to the news. So I haven't been sleeping as

well as I used to. And I won't take naps.
—New York, #2

One nostrum against insomnia is to make the rigors of your day defeat those of the night:

Work physically if possible so you are tired, so tired you can sleep.
—Woman, 61, 2

All the advice in the world is not going to help the "always alone" feeling, but keeping busy helps the time to pass. I work hard, so I'm tired enough to go to sleep at once when I go to bed.
—Woman, 67, 3

The blessings of exhaustion can flow from caring for children or going to a job:

Q: So how did you handle it?
Judy: Probably because I had four kids.
Angela: Kept you busy?
Judy: They kept me busy constantly. And then when my son started school, I went back to work part-time just to keep the days going, so at nights I could sleep.
—Boston, #2

But although depleting yourself like this works for some, it doesn't for others:

Noreen: I have a suggestion. Why not keep very busy during the day, so that you're tired at night and you go right to bed?
Gladys: [with a groan] Not me! I have unlimited energy.
—Los Angeles, #2

Dorothy: I won't say that I'm walking on air . . . , but I've got a lot of plans and, at least in the daytime, I'm occupied. I'm an athletic person, and I make myself so tired in the daytime that at night I don't mind being in the house.
Lydia: Well, I get out too, but I play the radio the whole night.
—Miami, #1

And Dorothy admits her own recipe doesn't always succeed with her, either. To Lee's account of how her mother crams her days with shopping and socializing at clubs, she retorts,

> **Dorothy:** *I've been doing that for years. It's not the days that bother me. I'm busy all day long. Comes the night, I regress.*
> **Lee:** *So then at night you do all the things you could have done during the day. You clean—*
> **Dorothy:** *I don't believe in cleaning!*
> **Lee:** *I can iron, I can wash, I can do everything in the middle of the night.*
> —*Miami, #1*

Lee's inversion of the normal order of events reflects how much the death of a spouse may turn days and nights upside down, from the time when the former were dedicated to work and the latter to play. We just witnessed how Raymond did his housework at five-thirty in the morning as something of a stopgap; Noel exalts it into a principle:

> *I love to shop. I do my shopping at eight o'clock in the morning in the supermarket. I've got my list made up and I speed through. And I do all my own cleaning in the house. I wax my furniture once a week. I do that in the morning before I go down to work. I find by getting my housework done early in the morning, I call people up at seven o'clock in the morning on Sunday and invite them over for brunch. They say,"What are you doing up? I just got in." "I just did my floor." But, again, I usually don't stay up past ten o'clock at night.*
> —*New York, #2*

The surprise of his friends on these occasions may not be that of unalloyed delight; but it's hard not to smile at his pleasure in having successfully rescheduled his life.

Like Raymond, Noel goes to bed early in part because he is not allured by the idea of going out at night. But many other survivors are, and they are very annoyed when they are stymied. Betty complains of her inability to get to a support group:

> *I haven't gone very often because I don't get out at night now, because I don't drive at night. And I guess most of us don't get out at night alone.*
> —*Los Angeles, #2*

As her group begins to turn into a symposium on the difficulties of getting out at nighttime, Elaine fastens upon another reason that keeps widows in particular indoors then:

> *Most of my friends are married. Now, I can see them during the week, during the day, but in the evening they want to spend the time with their husbands.*
> *Gladys: Well, they have to.*
> *Elaine: Sometimes we go out together in the evenings. But there are so many . . . complications. And you say, "Oh, heck, go alone? I'd just as soon not." And then you don't go.*
> —*Los Angeles, #2*

Gladys doesn't let night-driving or the specter of just being alone stop her, but it takes some gritting of the teeth and a dash of West Coast fatalism:

> *I go to a lot of movies. Fortunately, I do drive at night. I don't like coming home to the garage at ten-thirty or eleven o'clock at night. But a friend said, "If you want to go out, you're going to do it," and I do it. And I just say, "Well, it's not in my karma to get hurt."*
> —*Los Angeles, #2*

But even her faith in her karma falters now and then:

> *Gladys: I can do things during the day, but I'm always looking for things to fill my nighttime. Now I'm taking classes. I take Harvey Stromberg's class in political science. I'm taking a philosophy class with Mia Fivas. You've probably all heard of her. Isn't she marvelous? And I've taken classes at UCLA, but now I'm afraid to go at night to UCLA.*
> *Elaine: And they do have some of the greatest things at night—concerts, lectures.*
> *Gladys: Well, I don't like to go alone.*
> *Q: Excuse me! Maybe you two will call each other up.*
> —*Los Angeles, #2*

Our moderator's proposal that they join forces is one that Elaine and her friends have already adopted, with a variation that spares them from having to return alone in the dark:

*Well, I'm lucky. I have some friends that I can do some things with,
too. And when we go out at night, we stay at each other's homes and
then we don't have to drive home at night. Of course, you've got to
have people whose interests are compatible with yours.*
—*Los Angeles, #2*

And of course, if you must be alone, the phone can offer the same
escape from your isolation that it can during the day:

Tom: *Another thing that was very helpful to me is being from a
large family. When nighttime comes is when you miss your wife the
most. And if I went into any kind of dive or a depression, I would phone
one of my brothers or sisters and have a protracted conversation, and
it seemed to help.*
—*New York, #2*

But trying to get out at night—being with others in person or over
the phone—may not be all to the good. The nights may frighten you
most for the very reason that you are left alone in them. If learning to
live alone is what being a survivor is all about, then perhaps the nights
are the best, if also the hardest, place to begin. This woman belatedly
acknowledges it:

*I'm just now, four years later, trying to cope with the aloneness—
joining organizations was never my interest. I usually spend daytime away from home. Although I don't like it, I am coping with the
evening hours—crocheting, knitting, watching TV, etc.*
—*Woman, 76, 4*

There is such a thing as keeping *too* busy:

Keep busy, but don't get exhausted.
—*Woman, 55, 3*

*Try to accept any invitation—it may be more appealing than you might
think. But don't continue to "run" all the time—it's very wearing.*
—*Woman, 57, NA*

By "running" you may be fleeing something you shouldn't:

Face grief, do not try to bury it by engaging in frenetic activity.
—*Woman, 60, 3*

So, although tiring yourself out may be an effective sedative, like sedatives of the real variety it should serve as a temporary expedient:

> *If need be, seek professional help, or at least obtain some sleeping pills, to be used when absolutely necessary only.*
>
> —*Woman, 71, 9*

Something more easygoing, like winding yourself down, is what's really called for. And keeping busy is counterbalanced in the advice of some by what they style "quiet time":

> *Remain or become* productive, *either in a job or hobbies, preferably both.* Keep busy—*regular schedule, but include some private/quiet time.*
>
> —*Woman, 54, 3*

Mary steers a discussion about keeping busy into this same backwater:

> *Marian: It really pays to keep busy. I love to crochet. I have made more afghans! We raffle them off for the church or the lodge. It's just good to keep busy.*
>
> *Q: [at an easel] I'm going to write some of this down. The first thing everybody's been saying is, "Keep busy." I've heard a lot of that. "Be needed." "Volunteer." "Travel."*
>
> *Clara: That's mine. I like that [laughter].*
>
> *Q: Then we've got a crocheter here.*
>
> *Mary: But you also have to have a quiet time.*
>
> *Ann: Yes, sometimes I close the door and turn off the phone, and I just want to be, you know . . .*
>
> *Marian: Read a good book or something.*
>
> *Q: But why do you need that?*
>
> *Rose: You're busy, busy all the time. My daughter says, "Mother, you're so busy. Don't you ever sit down and relax?" And I think you need to do that once in a while. I don't do it very often, but once in a while.*
>
> *Diane: Yes, I think you need that.*
>
> *Mary: For your nervous system.*
>
> —*San Francisco*

The word Ann leaves unspoken is probably "alone," absorbed in solitary pursuits that are an end in themselves (note how Marian's crocheting is a bit different because it is tied in with a group activity). And Ann and Rose amplify on the good those pursuits do the "nervous system":

> *Q: What does it do for you?*
> **Rose:** *Relaxes you.*
> **Ann:** *I do needlepoint because I can empty my head of everything and just watch a needle going down and coming up, going down and coming up. You concentrate on it and you don't have to think about anything else. And I think that revives you and gets you going again.*

"Quiet time" can thus be both soothing and stimulating, and although this group may be talking about indulging in it during the day, the night, that naturally quiet time, is an even better occasion. Of course, you must enjoy being alone to get the most from it:

> *Find something interesting to do that involves other people; but also, on occasion, enjoy being alone: read, ponder, sew, look around you.*
> *—Woman, 84, 5*

So perhaps you can set aside some nights for practicing how to be alone without positively hating it. Take that most "passive" of activities, watching television. John, for a time, approached it in a truly passive fashion, as another opiate to deaden the sensibilities:

> *I found that, late at night, I had become a TV addict. You get into any sort of diversion. Some of it not healthy—drinking, some drugs.*
> *— New York, #2*

But to Al it's an active affair that engages the intellect:

> *I think selective viewing of television is a big help. Not this random turning on, just seeing whatever's there. Actually, there is a great deal on television in your range of interests that is worth seeing. And I believe in tuning into something if I'm at home (I'm not too often).*
> *—New York, #2*

Its utility to him has become an article of "belief," as it has to this woman too:

Be interested in what is going on in the world. Television can be a great help—it takes the silence away and can also be informative.
—Woman, 81, 16

And it has one further virtue that shouldn't be overlooked:

Television can take the place of more expensive entertainment.
—Woman, 85, 13

Others turn to almost as ubiquitous a diversion to take up the slack of nighttimes. It's undoubtedly mindless gaping at TV that prompts this woman to scold,

Read—*shut off the TV for a while!*
—Woman, 75, 2

Some survivors simply revel in the pleasures of books:

Noel: *I like solitude. I think I've read about three hundred books in the last two years. Voluminous books, I mean—history, usually. And I can sit and read for four hours, and it doesn't bother me.*
—New York, #2

I read everything I can get my hands on, including the Scriptures. I like poetry and that, too, helps.
—Woman, 59, 3

For Jean, the printed page is a charm against loneliness:

I am an omnivorous reader so I am never, never lonely.
—New York, #1

And this woman reads to enhance all the other endeavors in her life:

Build a library that will furnish interesting material for the rest of your life: books and magazines that emphasize your hobbies and interests—cooking, crafts, weaving, knitting, crocheting, gardening, pets, health.
—Woman, 85, 13

And when she says "the rest of your life," she's not exaggerating:

My books and files of magazines saved since my husband died are pushing me out of the house—(until I "get time" to read them).

When it comes to the written word, you can of course be on the giving as well as the receiving end. In the previous section, we saw how some use letter-writing as alternative to talking face-to-face. And a certain kind of writing can give you a format for talking to yourself:

Talk about your feelings to a friend or anyone that wants to listen. Sometimes even writing about them helps.

—*Man, 59, 2*

Talk to friends and relatives, especially your children. Write down your feelings.

—*Woman, 69, 10*

This woman recounts how she wrote her feelings "out" as well as down—with the same two-fold benefit often ascribed to talking about them:

I wrote out the ways I missed my husband and added to it as I thought of more. Somehow this kept these losses from tumbling around in my head and was at the same time an appreciation of what he was to me.

—*Woman, 69, 2*

In the Epilogue (page 490) we'll hear from one woman who solaced herself by composing "letters" to her departed husband. The suggestion that you keep a journal has become a fixture in books about grief, and some of our survivors repeat it:

I would encourage the new widow/widower to begin a personal journal at once, even if it's just for brief entries. As time passes and loneliness and depression hang on, it's encouraging to be able to look back a few months or a year to see that progress has been made, despite setbacks.

—*Woman, 74, 4*

So writing about the events of your day—and a journal is literally a "daybook"—may be one more way to see you safely through that more treacherous time, the night. We'll come to others as we go along. But the ones we've just glanced at apparently sufficed to draw

Richard back from the edge on which he was teetering and make him a reasonably contented night person once again:

All my friends, I don't find them in the gym or the library or the church, but at work. And they're nice people, but after work it's their way to have a few drinks, put the games on, and all that. But then I found each day I was going to the bar a little earlier, you know, a little too much of it. That was because of the loneliness. So I got out of that—I'm over it now. I'm still uptight, but now I have a few beers, go home and have supper, and I don't mind watching television, reading a good book. I'm reading four books right now. Whichever one I want to pick up, I just continue on. And I was always a night person anyway. I always worked nights, so I'm used to that. I don't find it too bad, really—thank God!

—*New York, #2*

Your Health: Eating and Exercising

Tending to the welfare of the soul is an easier proposition if you are seeing properly to that of the body also. It's a commonplace that this woman illuminates in one sentence:

Proper nutrition and good health make the world less gray.

—*Woman, 72, 5*

And here are the textbook reasons why survivors in particular must try to keep fit:

Try to keep up with healthful habits—nourishing food, rest, and especially physical activity. Loss of a spouse is the greatest stress one can experience (according to the "authorities"), so you have to try as hard as you can to counteract that stress with healthful habits. Often the spouse's death has come after an illness that has debilitated the caregiver too, which adds to the stress.

—*Woman, 72, 3*

Another confirms her last observation:

A spouse's long serious illness can affect one's health (I got an ulcer shortly after—which cured in a month's time).

—*Woman, 71, 4*

On the strength of such knowledge, Edith acted right away:

The first thing I did was to get a good physical.
                                                    —*Boston, #1*

This precaution paid off, for, as we saw in Chapter 2 (page 50), her mind was apparently playing tricks upon her body. Of course, one can become too concerned with one's health, and one woman explains how she's avoided becoming fruitlessly preoccupied with hers:

I'm blessed with health. So I don't make a business of studying Alzheimer's, cancer, diabetes, and heart ailments except to find some action I can take to reduce my worries about them.
                                                    —*Woman, 73, 9*

Taking action places demands upon a willpower that may feel too sapped to meet them—but nevertheless must:

You must take care of yourself—eat, exercise, etc., especially at the time you least care to. Because, believe it or not, you will go on living.
                                                    —*Woman, 53, 2*

Food is the most essential ingredient in that enterprise:

Take care of your health and eat wisely but well—take time to prepare a good meal for yourself every day, and enjoy it.
                                                    —*Woman, 84, 9*

Yet just eating at all—not to mention "well"—may seem beyond you if a lack of appetite for life has led to lack of appetite, period:

Don't avoid eating because you are lonesome—eat regular meals.
                                                    —*Woman, 83, 6*

Sorry, I have no advice for the 99 1/2% of the time I am alone. Empty, no feelings, no desire to eat.
                                                    —*Woman, 78, 12*

The sharing of food constitutes the most elemental of human social occasions, and the thought of a meal alone may make you cringe. But food—abetted by a little planning—can entice other people into your company:

Maintain good health habits—plan your meals and don't think you have to eat out each day. Be creative with your food; ask other friends to share and enjoy.

—Woman, 78, 12

Do not give up on cooking—keep planning meals and invite guests. I always try to bring someone home with me for Sunday dinner who might be lonely. It's only when you think of others rather than yourself that you find fulfillment.

—Woman, 72, 9

This woman even ministered to the sick with her skills at the stove:

I like to cook. I entertained a lot and made special foods for friends who were sick. I did a lot of reaching out to others.

—Woman, 66, 10

If that seems too ambitious at first, there are the major standbys for the solitary:

Late afternoons need some thought. I have a light, good book for the hour before supper and have my supper on a tray watching the news.

—Woman, 73, 15

While I eat my meals is when I do my letter-writing, almost a full-time job in itself.

—Woman, 77, 3

People often quail at dining alone in public, but it cheers this woman up:

A friend once told me a psychologist told her widowed father, who was depressed, to make a point to go out once a day for one meal. It works well.

—Woman, 73, 8

This woman marshals a whole battery of such tactics:

Yes, there is that terribly empty space left by the loss of a spouse—mealtimes especially. Eat out with friends, or, if you have a favorite place where the waitresses know you well, pick up a good book (reading is

*a great pastime). Go there and enjoy your book and meal in the sur-
roundings of others. At home, eat off a TV tray—yes, in front of the TV.*
—Woman, 72, 4

If the preliminaries bore you, you can take shortcuts with them:

Elizabeth: *You should have a microwave. An awful lot of people don't
know how to cook, and they can buy frozen things to put right into the
microwave.*
Q: *You mean women too?*
Elizabeth: *Sure, they can be lazy also.*
Syd: *You're looking at one who's lazy—I have a microwave.*
Elizabeth: *You enjoy it?*
Syd: *I enjoy it. I put in leftovers, everything.*
—Miami, #2

Men (as our moderator's question implies) may be struggling less
with laziness than with ignorance, but as Jean tartly declares, they get
no sympathy from her:

*A man always feels that only a woman could boil an egg for him or
only a woman could prepare a meal. I have met some bachelors,
elderly men, who cry, "I have no one to prepare any food for me!"
We have some very nice catering places where I live, and so I say to
them, "Why don't you go in and buy something there? You don't
have to cook. All you have to do is warm it up."*
—New York, #1

But others, of course, get a kick out of making things from scratch:

Peggy: *Do you like cooking? Do you bake?*
Ruth: *I bake. I cook. My refrigerator and freezer are always full. You
would never think that just one person lived in my house*
Peggy: *That's an important point for people who live alone: to have
a well-stocked larder, and freezer, in case—God forbid—you're sick.
You have food for a week or two.*
Ruth: *Yes, but I don't like to buy frozen food or prepared foods. I like
to know what's in the foods that I eat. And so I make it myself.*
Peggy: *And freeze it.*
—Miami, #2

And their company isn't limited to widows:

> *Prior to my wife's death I never cooked a meal or did a bit of shopping or laundry. I learned to do it all and often prepared a full dinner for six to eight people. I was complimented on becoming a gourmet cook, and I could return the favor to friends who had included me in their dinner parties.*
>
> —Man, 70, 6

Apart from the culinary satisfactions and the provisioning of yourself against the unexpected, such an ambitious tack makes going to the market a more challenging errand—and, as we'll see in Chapters 5 and 6, some survivors have transformed shopping for groceries from a chore into one of their more agreeable opportunities for off-the-cuff socializing.

The kitchen can be an arena for more than the preparation of meals. Look at how a lump of dough, in its travels toward becoming a loaf of bread, can take some side trips along the way—and how many people can value it when it gets to where it's going:

> *Ann: You know what else is good for frustration? Working with yeast dough.*
> *Yvette: Yeah, that's fun!*
> *Q: What do you do with that?*
> *Ann: Well, you know, you're punching, you're pulling—*
> *Yvette: You're kneading the dough.*
> *Ann: Sometimes you're upset about something, and one way of getting frustrations out is to punch it.*
> *Q: Right. Did you ever see, what's her name, the French chef?*
> *Ann: Julia Child?*
> *Q: Julia Child! She's such a big lady, and I saw her one day going, "Whop! Bang!"*
> *Ann: Takes the dough and slams it on the board. She says that releases all the gluten and stuff.*
> *Q: It also releases something for you?*
> *Ann: Right!*
> *Diane: And then you have a loaf of bread, huh?*
> *Ann: Well, I do it because my kids just love homemade bread, and if they buy a loaf and I'm there for dinner, one of them will say, "You know, Grandma, you didn't make this." And I say, "You rotten,*

spoiled kids!'' [laughter].
Yvette: *Little kids love to work with yeast dough, too.*
Marian: *Oh, do they!*
Mary: *Play-Doh, you buy Play-Doh, what a mess it makes.*
Yvette: *But you can buy real dough and make real bread. A three-year-old can't hurt yeast dough. They have a wonderful time.*
Marian: *Your hands are clean.*
Rose: *But it's all over the patio floor, though.*

—San Francisco

As we keep the calories coming in, we must somehow put them to work, and burning them up is generally considered more acceptable than converting them to flab:

Adjustment takes time and movement—don't sit on your duff. Physical movement, if health permits, is absolutely mandatory!
—Woman, 50, 4

I'd advise some mental and physical exertion *(not just stimulation) every day—out of the house. (I took on a five-year Bible-study course and spread six cubic yards of dirt on my lawn!)*
—Woman, 67, 4

This last woman has devised an engaging combination of intellectual and manual labor, but if you don't have the raw material on hand for the latter that she did, exercise is the alternative:

Move the muscles—walk, garden, exercise, if possible.
—Woman, 72, 2

Maintain or start an exercise program. Out-of-doors is best—long walks are wonderful!
—Woman, 65, 2

Observe that starting is one of the possibilities:

Being alone allows you to pursue interests that you may not have found time for when married. For example, I took dancing lessons (square dancing and ballroom dancing), and I bought a bicycle and ride two hours each day in the summer.
—Woman, 58, 4

> *Take up new interests, join an exercise class or other sporting activities (I have joined a bowling team).*
>
> *—Woman, 64, 2*

Like many professionals in the field, some survivors deem making exercise a routine part of the day more important than making it an especially strenuous one:

> *Maintain a* regular *physical therapy program.*
>
> *—Woman, 68, 2*

> *Exercise moderately and* consistently.
>
> *—Woman, 71, 7*

So you should find a slot in your schedule for it:
> *Make time for some exercise (mine is walking) to keep healthy.*
>
> *—Woman, 82, 4*

A "sports or physical fitness program" engaged the energies of 20% of our survey "sometimes" and 15% of them "often."

Your health, even though it is your original rationale, may not be all that profits from exercise:

> **Beulah:** *I walk now. I hadn't, but I do now.*
> **Lillian:** *How much do you walk a day?*
> **Beulah:** *At least two miles, sometimes three.*
> **Q:** *Where did you get that idea, Beulah?*
> **Beulah:** *Well, I had been having my blood pressure taken every week because it was so high. And I got a pamphlet that said, if you walk, it will help. And it did—it has lowered it, so I don't feel so full of stress. I belong to the Council on Aging in Brookline, and I go walking with them. You meet a lot of people, interesting people, walking.*
>
> *—Boston, #1*

If you believe, like this woman,

> *My health and my friends are my two greatest assets,*
>
> *—Woman, 71, 8*

then the pursuit of one may lead you to the other. You have a practical reason to scout for a partner:

Find someone to take long walks with.

                                                                —*Woman, 68, 3*

Or, as we've seen, you can sign on with a group. Like clubs, classes are praised as chances to meet people:

Classes in various exercise groups will keep one in trim—also friends may be found.

                                                                —*Woman, 76, 12*

Join a good fitness class or other group that opens up new friendships.
                                                                —*Woman, 78, 11*

This woman parlayed such a class into friendships that now extend far beyond it:

I wanted to do something different, but I didn't know what. I tried hiking, but that was lonely. The family YMCA was giving a class on healthy backs, and I was having a small problem with my back, so I took that class. There I met a retired teacher, and we became good friends.
   The YMCA at that time was just starting a program of swimnastics (exercise in the water), so my friend and I joined that too. Enrollment in that was slow, just six of us at the beginning. I really enjoyed it. The class has grown to over thirty-five now, and many are new friends. We go for coffee after class and chat. We have a Christmas dinner at a restaurant, a picnic in the summer. And to all our special activities we always invite the ones that for some reason or another can't continue with the class, and that way we keep in contact with them.
                                                                —*Woman, 74, 13*

Survivors also pay tribute to the powers of exercise to rejuvenate them psychologically:

Exercising my muscles helped clear my mind.
                                                                —*Woman, 72, 5*

Physical fitness in different forms became very important to me. It helped me mentally to know that I was doing everything possible to prevent anything from happening to me. And it was a good emotional outlet.
                                                                —*Woman, 55, 7*

Instead of putting an additional strain on your body's reserves, it may relieve one already there:

> *Exercise is the best medicine for depression. Walk, ride a bike, swim, whatever—do it. Depression is a new phenomenon to combat—a powerful drain of one's energy.*
>
> —*Woman, 64, 6*

Ann's workouts helped not only to reorient her toward the future but also to chase away some demons from the past:

> *Now, my suggestion is to find an outlet like aerobics. Or join a walking club. Any kind of exercise—where you can go every morning. It gives you a reason to get up—and a healthy reason. Because you feel like a million. Get out and be physically active, and then that slows* this *down [tapping head with fingers to indicate mental turmoil]. You don't grind over the past. The past is gone.*
>
> —*Miami, #2*

Unfortunately, not all of us are hale enough for aerobics. Some of the most enthusiastic endorsements of exercise in this section have come from people in their seventies. And the older we are, the more we'd like to think our years are what we make of them:

> *Forget your own age.*
>
> —*Woman, 74, 5*

But as another woman just a year younger sighs, they can inexorably slow us up:

> *Learn, however, that you cannot keep up the pace of ten years back.*
> —*Woman, 73, 6*

And physical afflictions can hobble us even further. They have whittled this woman's "exercise" down to taking breaks from her daily routine in order to rebuild her strength:

> *If you are tired or weak, rest ten or fifteen minutes—completely relax. Then go back to your task. It works, I know. Basically, I am very healthy for my age, but I do have some physical problems with painful side effects. So I have to take short rest periods—disgusting, but*

I have learned to live with it. Others have much greater problems.
                                                           —*Woman, 77, 3*

Despite her infirmities, she's clearly kept her spirit in good shape.

Pastimes: Solitary, Social, or Both

Eating and exercise necessarily center on the self, but the preceding section shows how people—circumstances permitting—can make either one as solitary or as social as their temperaments dictate. The same holds true of other activities that may not be as critical to one's physical survival, but are perhaps even more protective of one's emotional welfare:

Get involved—in groups if you're a group person, or with hobbies such as gardening, photography, or volunteer work.
                                                           —*Woman, 76, 13*

Hobbies are the most help—a hobby such as painting, gardening, or reading that you can pursue alone when you are alone. And hobbies such as sports or cards that you can pursue with friends.
                                                           —*Woman, 73, 12*

Both these woman distinguish pastimes that you undertake alone from those you engage in with others, and they classify gardening as one of the former. In the preceding section, several favored it as a means of exercise—and survivors also hail it for revitalizing them in other ways:

I love to garden! I planted trees, shrubs, flowers and worked long hours in the garden. This was good activity/exercise—it was physical, tangible, and satisfying. I nourished my body with food from my garden and nourished my soul with the beauty of my flowers. I would advise anyone who enjoys gardening to go for it.
                                                           —*Woman, 41, 2*

Under its influence, mental tensions can just dissolve:

When I tend to worry, I go out and exercise by gardening. Many worries disappear as I work.
                                                           —*Woman, 74, 7*

Rose: I think one of the most wonderful things you can do is work in the garden.
Yvette: Oh, the smell of growing plants!
Ann: It's creative.
Rose: Yes, it is creative, and it's very good for my nerves, I think. I love to garden when I'm frustrated and have nothing else to do. I'll go down; I'll work in the yard. That's what I was doing when Pat called me yesterday. And I said, "Oh, I won't have to work in the yard today."
—San Francisco

As much as she loves it, Rose looks at gardening as something to do when others, like Pat, are not around. And some view a hobby in strictly the same light, as filling up a space that has been left vacant, by a spouse or others:

I have been weaving for at least thirty-five years—I think everyone should have a hobby of some kind, and mine helped me when my children both went away to school at the same time.
—Woman, 87, 8

Sixty-two percent of our survey told us that they had a "hobby or craft," and to Ruth hers is a companion in itself:

A hobby is very, very important. You know, you're never alone and you're never bored if you are doing something that interests you. I like to knit—[fingering blouse] this is one of the things I made—I like to sew, I'm self-taught, through books. Last year I decided that, even though I'm a little too old for it, I would like to learn something else. I got books and learned how to quilt. And I made myself a very nice quilt. I enjoyed every minute I spent making that quilt.
—Miami, #2

If you don't derive the pleasure these survivors do from working in seclusion, others demonstrate how a hobby can also be a route out of isolation, as this woman does with

family and pedigree "research." This involves relationships with relatives far and near, across the continent.
—Woman, 77, 14

Like Marian with her afghans (page 172), this woman makes the products of her labor contribute to her social life by giving them away:

> *Find a hobby—I embroidered tablecloths for practically everyone.*
> *—Woman, 72, 4*

Other arts can supply similar outlets. Music, for example, can be solely for the pleasure of the listener or the player:

> **Richard:** *I love my stereo. I play my music, my particular music, and I can find happiness right in the house by myself.*
> **Noel:** *Me too. Living alone is a boon to me because my friends don't like my music. And I don't like theirs sometimes. I run the gamut. In the morning I can listen to country and western or classical.*
> **Richard:** *I still listen to the big bands.*
> **Lee:** *I fool around on the piano and the guitar.*
> **Noel:** *I play the guitar also.*
> **Lee:** *I play to two o'clock at night—makes time pass just like that [snapping fingers]!*
> *—New York, #1*

Or it can gratify a wider audience:

> *I play piano for two clubs here.*
> *—Woman, 82, 7*

> *Do not sit alone by yourself. Reach out to other people. If you have hobbies, interests, pursue them. I have musical abilities. I have always sung and played the piano, and I will continue because this is my release.*
> *—Woman, 53, 2*

From the context, it's a good guess the latter's release stems as much from performing for others as from playing for herself. Music-making can of course be a cooperative effort also:

> *I stay fairly active in music—ensemble playing.*
> *—Woman, 78, 11*

Our survey group was an artistic lot: 41% of them said that "writing, painting, or other creative pursuits" claimed some of their time. But even when these endeavors are unsuited to collaboration (how many great paintings have benefited from being created by more than one pair of hands?), they can be carried on in the company of someone else—also doing it on his or her own:

> *I "ran" for years—perhaps I still do, to some degree. I took up regular swimming and walking, photography—also painting weekends with friends (to escape the loneliness of weekends—terrible!).*
> —*Woman, 73, 8*

Likewise writing need not be an wholly lonely act:

> **Elaine:** *I do some song writing; I belong to a writer's group.*
> —*Los Angeles, #2*

> **Dorothy:** *I have a flair for writing and I do that. I've been writing short stories for years.*
> **Lee:** *Why don't you send them in to one of the magazines?*
> **Dorothy:** *They don't accept me. But my neighbors love them. They do.*
> —*Miami, #1*

So, you needn't be by yourself—literally or figuratively—even when what you're doing can only be done by you. At the opposite pole are the pastimes for which others are indispensable, like many sports and games:

> *I play bridge a lot. That keeps my mind active and allows me to see friends often.*
> —*Woman, 77, 4*

Bridge demands a group, a demand often satisfied through the group at its most formalized:

> *I enjoy bridge, so I joined four clubs altogether. Joined the university athletic club, which was one of the wisest things I did. I love to take friends there for lunch or dinner, especially those who do not belong.*
> —*Woman, 78, 4*

Retirement communities are hotbeds of club life:

Q: Anne, what's your typical day like?

Anne: Well, in the morning I get up, I make breakfast for both my sister and myself. Then we do whatever has to be done for the house, and I'm always out. I've got a bike and I use it more than anybody I know. And over the weekend I go to the dances. I love to dance. During the week I go bowling. I'm busy all the time. I don't have time to get bored.

Loretta: How about your activities in the clubs? She's all over the place. She pours the coffee, sees that we get refreshments.

Anne: Yes, my sister and I take care of it. We have services Friday night, and we have a happy hour afterwards. We serve goodies, like good cake, coffee, tea, or punch, whatever. And then when anybody has a special occasion, like a birthday or an anniversary, we have a decorated cake made and special items to go with it. So it makes life very, very interesting and keeps me out of mischief.

—Los Angeles, #1

A club may enlist you in a more-than-social capacity:

I accepted a position as president of the university's women's club. Although I had turned this down several times when my husband was alive, I felt this was the right time to accept. It's been rewarding and has put me in contact with many people.

—Woman, 67, 3

Survivors tend to insist, as they do about jobs, that you should hang on to any club memberships (or those in other social organizations):

Keep involved with church and social groups you've been involved with before your spouse's death.

—Woman, 67, 4

Maintain your memberships in groups you enjoy. Be an active member. Contribute in every way you can.

—Woman, 77, 13

Keep active in all your clubs. It's hard to get started again if you quit, thinking you'll go back later when you've adjusted. It's easier to meet people immediately, so they'll begin accepting you and your problems. And it's easier for them.

—Woman, 73, 5

In their purest form, as societies created for the purpose of socializing, clubs may repel many survivors who are smarting at their newly single status. We'll glance at several instances in the next chapter, but this woman reminds us that many clubs are affiliated by interests that transcend the merely social ones:

> **Betty:** *So many clubs now have themes—music, literature. So that you don't feel you're just walking in and looking for somebody to say, "Dance with me."*
>
> —*Los Angeles, #2*

But even these specialized clubs—garden clubs are another example—are inspired by the aim of translating an individual activity into a group one. And that's exactly what survivors value in them most, like this woman who prizes one out of the same motives she does her neighborhood:

> *I enjoy a book club where all the others are much younger, and communicative; and I live on a street where most families have young children.*
>
> —*Woman, 78, 11*

More of those we surveyed credited clubs with helping them adjust (55%) than they did hobbies and crafts (51%).

Finally, in talking about pastimes, some survivors say their ideal is to mix the solitary with the social:

> *I tried to keep some balance between going out and being alone.*
>
> —*Woman, 69, 2*

> *Take time to grieve. Don't feel that you must rush into society and "get on with your life." On the other hand, don't become a recluse, which leads to depression.*
>
> —*Woman, 68, 2*

Not everyone would agree, among them this woman perhaps, who is caught up in such a blizzard of group activities that reciting them practically leaves her breathless (and she does *not*, incidentally, live in a retirement community):

> Don't *sit in and wait. Get out and explore. Get into circulation. Take part in activities. Learn square dancing, play cards, bowl, walk*

or ride bikes with others, go to classes and meetings, play musical instruments, and have meals out. Join widows' and widowers' organizations. Become a Senior Grandmother/Grandpa for children's activities. Meet other lonelies. Take ballroom dancing. Go to Senior dances. Visit the Y at least two times a month.

—Woman, 72, 3

To some, such hyperactivity might seem to merit a dose of the ''quiet time'' discussed on page 172. This woman tempers the bustle of her days with it:

Helped to organize a Widowed Persons Service (AARP). Thirty-plus years of participation in the League of Women Voters are ongoing. Organizations—Audubon, NOW, Common Cause, etc.—keep one active. I read a lot, as always, and I have a knitting machine and a computer (thought I should not miss out on the coming things).

—Woman, 70, 8

But in the end, all that matters is what works for you, like this woman, who draws on different things for different ends and recognizes and cherishes what she receives from each:

Hobbies, crafts, writing, and much volunteer effort give me a sense of worth. My church, reading, gardening, and a little travel give me stamina and pleasure.

—Woman, 83, 17

Pets

By sharing life with a pet, we may be able to stake out a highly rewarding mid-ground between being alone and being with other people:

My 120-pound white German shepherd has been enormous good company.

—Woman, 57, 2

I've raised a Labrador puppy this past year. She is a real companion and so lovable.

—Woman, 73, 2

In any case never forget that pets are good company to love and be loved.

—Woman, 85, 13

They satisfy the simplest of yearnings for this woman:

> *We had dogs: I find it essential to have something alive in the house,*
> *even though they tie one down (luckily I can afford it).*
>
> —*Woman, 70, 4*

Some were continuing a tradition:

> *I find pets are wonderful. We had a dog and cats when my husband*
> *died. Seven years later I have two dogs and five cats. Each is an*
> *individual, and I love them all.*
>
> —*Woman, 70, 8*

Others were striking out into new territory:

> *After my husband's death, I acquired a dog, the first one that is mine*
> *alone to care for, and that has been a real plus for company, a feeling*
> *of security, and a sense of responsibility for another living being.*
>
> —*Woman, 68, 4*

Others concur that, besides offering company and the chance to give
love and have it reciprocated, pets bolster your self-esteem by making
it your duty to see to their survival as well as your own:

> *Have animals: they are a responsibility and need your care.*
>
> —*Woman, 72, 5*

To a woman with grown children, they are almost like younger ones
in that respect:

> *If you have no young children, get a pet for companionship and a*
> *sense of responsibility.*
>
> —*Woman, 55, 2*

A reminder of the children that he doesn't have induces John to
talk about the pets he does:

> *Q: Do you have any kids?*
> *John: No kids. I picked up two cats. I never liked cats before, but*
> *it's amazing how they make a difference, because they become more*
> *than animals. They take on a spirituality.*

Q: What made you think of cats?
John: *My wife.*
Q: She liked cats?
John: *Yes.*

—New York, #2

If his cats remind him of his wife, Noel's acquisition of his dog, on the other hand, appears to have been his first move to put the death—and perhaps the memories of his married life—behind him:

I knew it was going to happen, and therefore I became a little selfish about myself. I said, ''I'm just going to do what I have to do,'' and the first thing I did was get a little dog, a dachshund. I always wanted a dachshund. I take him all over with me. I take him to work (I publish a market letter); on trips, I will leave an assignment early to get home to see him. He's been a great companion. In fact I am having a birthday party for him this Sunday. His dog friends are going to come over and they're all going to wear hats. I got him a cake, and it will have ''Puppies, yes! Yuppies, no!''—or something—printed on it. And I'll just put it down in the backyard, and they'll all dive in.
—New York, #2

Noel delivers a veritable rhapsody on the benefits of pet ownership:

I think I love this dog as much as I ever loved anything in the world, including my wife and my daughter. It is the most loyal little animal and it gives me a lot of satisfaction. There was a study out that having pets helps your blood pressure stay down—incontrovertible facts, they did tests on it. So, I think the biggest thing I did was get somebody as a companion who gave me what I think people in this room wouldn't understand unless they had the same companionship. [to John] You said you had it with cats. It's important. It's like having a child to come home to, but it's not a child, and he takes care of himself.
Q: There's just fur to pat?
Noel: *He's smooth-haired.*
Richard: *They're always glad to see you. They don't hold grudges or anything.*
John: *Go home for a weekend and come back?—they hold grudges sometimes. They look at you, ''Where have you been?''*
Noel: *It's a great way to meet people, too. I see a lot of people in my*

neighborhood, older than myself, mostly widows, walking their dogs at seven-thirty in the morning. I found out that, walking my dog, people don't ask me what my name is, they'll say, "What's your dog's name?" I've met a lot of people whom I've invited to this gala party Sunday. It'll take me two days to prepare for this party, and I'm going to enjoy every minute of it. So I'm finding new things to do. I never would have thought of doing this five years ago or ten years ago, but I'm doing it now.

Here is fervent sincerity, no question; but, if his opening sentence brought you up short, so it did us. In his comparison of caring for a dog and for a child, he reveals that what he has sought—and apparently found—is an equivalent to human relationships without the messiness that is an inescapable part of them. In fact, he makes this quite clear in his friendly sparring with Al over the question of whether one dog is neatly interchangeable with another:

Noel: You know, if anything ever happened to my dog, I would the next day have another dachshund. Maybe it wouldn't be the same color, but I'd have another, the next day. You can't do that with people. And maybe I've become a little eccentric about it, but it gives me a good feeling. I have prepared for his death in advance—he's going to live on in this other animal.

Al: I think, Noel, you're going to be disappointed when the dog dies. I had one for eleven and a half years. You don't want to replace him.

Noel: Well, I know I'm going to do it, so it doesn't matter.

Al: You think so now. Let's hope it doesn't happen for a long time. O.O. McIntyre wrote a famous column, which is in all the anthologies, entitled "Don't Give Your Heart to a Dog to Break." And it's actually the truth. Once a dog that you have had for a long time goes, you don't go out the next day and get one. I would doubt that very much.

Noel: I'm a strong person that way. I say what I mean and I mean what I say.

Al: You've made up your mind now, but I wouldn't bet on it.

Who's being more human here about animals? We'll let you decide. For Noel, his dog has not only warded off loneliness but has tidied up death into an abstraction—so far. For others, it is not so simple, like this woman (who chides us in passing, correctly, for having omitted the subject on our questionnaire):

For me, it is a heartbreaking, lonely existence after almost forty years of friendship and thirty-five years of marriage to a bright, witty histor-ian. As two professionals, our goals were to travel together, con-verse, read, walk, laugh, and to be serious. After slightly more than two years, I am alone. I am 60, working on a master's in English and filling my hours with reading, writing, and research. I have a circle of life-long friends, female and male, who share my loss as their own. I have a young dog and a cat (you did not ask about pets). But to be alone is just that.

—Woman, 60, 2

Finances

So far, our survey of ways to keep busy has covered those that can afford you some pleasure in the doing of them. We'll now address a few that probably can't—unless you are predisposed by an MBA in finance or a legal practice in trusts and estates. But, before we start, let us stress again the caveat with which we opened this book: it does not purport to be an objective compilation of practical information, on this or any other topic. Here, as elsewhere, you'll hear stories volunteered by people chosen at random, necessarily subjective and sometimes spotty on a given issue—and emphatically not to be relied on as advice for your particular situation. But these stories may offer you starting points for seeking advice from other sources.

Most of us regard the humdrum management of our money as a nuisance—if we can exert the degree of control that "management" implies. But it can greet us as a nightmare if, like many survivors at first, we can't. Take one of those who couldn't and who equated survival itself with learning how to master money:

Adjusting to handling my finances after such a shock was most difficult. It is difficult to remember how I survived.

—Woman, 76, 4

Others back her up, reserving words for experiences like hers that they would use of the loss itself:

Learn early in marriage how to handle finances and manage a home. I believe that the shock of being unprepared to handle such matters can be almost as devastating as the loss.

—Woman, 76, 7

Not knowing how to handle money would be dreadfully frightening. Adding this ignorance to the trauma of being alone would be devastating.

—Woman, 67, 2

In Chapter 3, in reviewing the standard advice to refrain from spending or investing large sums, we saw how money could also transfix people in panic, regardless of their economic well-being. We'll examine such fears in a bit more detail here, with the goal of separating those that are merited from those that aren't. Books about grief bristle with tales of people—women especially, but men as well—wrestling grimly with their finances, and ours will be no exception. On the other hand, we encountered no one who reported not coming out on top eventually.

The widow who doesn't know how to write out a check, much less balance the book from which it came—it's a stereotype, but plenty of its representatives still apparently populate real life:

I was well versed on our finances and I think it is most helpful for a woman left alone. So many women seem to know nothing about checking accounts or how much money will be available and just flounder when all this is thrust upon them.

—Woman, 80, 18

I believe that to be able to adjust to the death of a spouse, both partners in a marriage should work together to learn to make decisions on financial matters. Both should know how to reconcile a checkbook and keep records of stocks and bonds, etc. Too many widows I know have never written a check.

—Woman, 76, 3

And the villain in these set pieces is usually the husband who has insisted on "doing everything" about the family finances, sometimes abetted by a wife eager to be babied:

Q: If you were going to be talking to people who are married today, what would you tell them?
Connie: I have plenty to tell them. I have friends who depend on their husbands for every little thing, checking, money, everything. It's bad, very bad. I know a schoolteacher whose husband did everything, and when he died she couldn't even make out a check. She had to ask her son

to do it. That to me is terrible. Get involved, do the same things together. Learn—they can't even read an insurance policy. I can't either, but I try. I give it a good going over, half the time I am missing things, but I'll ask. But when I see these women who are so dumb, it makes me mad!
Q: Why do you think it is important not to be so dumb?
Connie: Because then they are going to get shook up when he's gone. And you really do see them shook up!

—*New York, #1*

These comments may be accurate enough, but note how each finds the stereotype embodied elsewhere than in herself. True, others admit that they were among the company of "checkbook illiterates":

Isabel: I was about to say that, when Connie was talking about some people not knowing about checks, I never made out a check while my husband was alive. Somehow or other, it just worked out that way. But, after my husband died, I felt I had to take over and I was pretty capable at it.
Bea: You were younger.
Isabel: Yes, I was younger.
Bea: Age makes a difference.

—*New York, #1*

Edith: I never paid a bill. I never looked at a bill. [ironically] Why did I have to pay bills? And I never bothered with checks.
Lillian: You never bothered with the checks?
Edith: No, I just wrote them once in a while.
Lillian: But if you had a check that was to be deposited?
Edith: I didn't have to unless he gave me the deposit.

—*Boston, #1*

And the husband may indeed have been to blame. This woman tries to give hers the benefit of the doubt but can't muffle her resentment completely:

Frankly, a bit more communication between us in earlier times would have saved me much concern over financial management. Not that he thought me incapable or did not trust me—just that he was busy. I'm sure he didn't realize and thought everything was cared for.

—*Woman, 83, 17*

Connie is less charitable, for good reason:

> **Connie:** *When my husband died, I found he put his bankbook in his sister's name. So what do you do about that?*
> **Jean:** *He only had one bankbook?*
> **Connie:** *That's it.*
> **Bea:** *Boy, he was a nice guy!*
> —*New York, #1*

Fortunately, she'd had the foresight to open an account of her own.

The remarks about inequity made by these women may have sprung from similar experiences:

> *A lack of communication and honesty about finances can leave the survivor confused and overwhelmed.*
> —*Woman, 62, 2*

> *Have a good understanding with spouse about financial affairs—so that any arrangements are made by mutual agreement and on a fair, joint basis.*
> —*Woman, 80, 9*

Grievances like these (if that is what they are) may exacerbate the anger we observed in Chapter 2. Other women, however, concede their unpreparedness was as much their lapse as his:

> **Lillian:** *And it's very difficult because he handled all the finances, and I didn't know very much about them. He tried to show me some things, but I didn't quite get them. I used to work as a bookkeeper when I first got out of high school, but all these things were like . . . I still haven't got them all straightened out. So it really has your mind in a whirl.*
> —*Boston, #1*

> *My husband did not train me to be a widow. Perhaps I was lazy—it was so easy for him to take care of finances, and he liked doing it.*
> —*Woman, 86, 8*

And some fault themselves entirely:

> *Get involved in handling family finances. My husband handled our*

finances because I refused to take an interest. This became a tremendous problem when I had to take over.

—Woman, 66, 8

Mary and Rose discuss the perfectly understandable attitudes that may have underlain such a refusal:

Q: Do you have any advice for other women, either widowed or not, about finances?
Ann: Learn while you're married what's going on. So that, God forbid, whatever happens, you're not left just high and dry—"Where do I start?"
Mary: Women have a tendency—we're so busy with home and children, family and work, that we just don't think about those things. My husband insisted that I do, so I knew. But I really didn't have the interest in it.
Rose: Some women don't want to bother—"Oh, my husband will take care of all this." And then, when it's too late, they're out of luck.

—San Francisco

The latter sort, Sarah speculates, may have been indulging in the kind of denial—in advance of the fact—with which we've already become familiar:

I guess you do build a crippling dependency on your mate if you are the kind of person who tends to lean heavily on others. And I think many women do it because they have the illusion that nothing will ever interfere with their lives.

—New York, #1

But whatever the reasons for the indifference or passivity, women scarcely hold a monopoly on it:

Be acquainted with your financial situation before you lose your spouse.
—Man, 58, 3

Edna: Now, with me, I did everything as far as bills were concerned. My husband would say to me, "Here they are. I make the money, you see that it goes." And this is the way we lived. So I was able to take over. But my husband wouldn't have been.

—San Francisco

The consequences she predicts came true for Lee, who had delegated the bills to his wife:

> *Q: After your wife died, was there something that you had to learn how to do?*
> *Lee: Bills—I got into a jam with my accounts. It got so that I was sending the same bill to the telephone company twice. That's exactly what I was doing! It was then I realized what a job she had done.*
> —*New York, #2*

Ideally, the economics of marriage should be an arena in which husband and wife act as equals; in reality, the drudgery of the details may have cast one partner or the other into the role of specialist—perhaps to the more or less willing exclusion of the other.

The moral to all this? If you had been prepared for dealing with your finances, give thanks to your spouse, yourself, happenstance, or whatever else deserves the credit. If you weren't, don't waste time trying to figure out why. You may have been a victim of your times:

> *Rose: I worked in business myself, so I was okay after he died. I was able to take over—I knew how to write checks and things like that. I have friends that don't even know how to write a check. They're widows now, and their husbands did everything. And that's sad, really.*
> *Mary: I think that was our age group. I don't think that'll happen again.*
> —*San Francisco*

Or the times may have had nothing to do with it, as Evelyn insists when she rebuts similar generalizations from Edith:

> *Evelyn: A woman should know what is going on and share with her husband in the finances.*
> *Edith: But in our age group the men were in control.*
> *Evelyn: No, don't say that. I'm in your age group, and I was in as much control as he was. We always shared all our finance problems, and we had equal rights with the checkbook. We knew what was being paid and when. So I didn't have that problem. And both my daughter-in-law and my daughter know as much about their finances as the men do. And I don't believe men should be in full control—not because I don't trust them, but because I feel that a woman should know.*
> —*Boston, #1*

It's of no matter now, for finances are an enterprise in which a focus on the present and the future are essential. And—contrary to Rose's words earlier—it is not "too late" and you are not "out of luck." Actually, a mere 6% of our survey group complained of having had "a great deal" of difficulty in "handling household finances"; and only another 18% of having had "some" (the remainder: "little or none"). So your fear may be nothing more than that. As this woman declares with a touch of exasperation,

> *When one has become a widow, it is rather late to learn to handle finances. But I am amazed at how many elderly women feel overwhelmed at the thought of paying bills, keeping bank accounts, and making long-term financial plans.*
>
> —*Woman, 75, 19*

So as these two command, "Take charge"—even though you may need the help of others at first:

> *Take charge of your money. Seek financial help (not from relatives) before investing your insurance money. Do as much paperwork as you can before you see a lawyer, such as writing to claim benefits yourself and having the checks sent directly to you. You have lots of hours to fill. Lawyers charge by units of time, and all of this takes lots of time.*
>
> —*Woman, 58, 7*

> *Share in financial planning and decisions throughout your married life. If you don't have this expertise, get a lawyer you've known and trusted. Learn from him, but don't simply turn over management of your affairs to him. Take charge of your own finances, but get the best advice you can.*
>
> —*Woman, 67, 2*

If you are hesitant, see if you can't emulate this woman's matter-of-factness:

> *My "ever-loving" insisted that the term "indigent professor" is a redundancy—he was right. As I had little money, it behooved me to manage it well, so I gave myself a short course in finance.*
>
> —*Woman, 72, 6*

Or this one's pertinacity:

> *Be as informed as possible on all aspects of finances; be alert and check*
> *everything carefully; never be pressured into doing anything; give*
> *it much thought and research. If necessary, be willing to sacrifice*
> *reading for pleasure, socializing, traveling, etc., in order to succeed in*
> *handling your personal and business affairs. It will* pay big dividends.
> *—Woman, 77, 3*

Becoming initiated might have been easier beforehand, but the two major tasks remain the same:

> *The emotional trauma of losing one's spouse can be lessened when one*
> *knows not only what is left but also how to manage what is left.*
> *—Woman, 87, 5*

Taking charge of your money demands that you take stock of it before taking action about it. And if we are to assure ourselves of a financial roof over our heads, our blueprint—a budget—must start at the foundations:

> *Understand how to estimate your present estate and, after this educa-*
> *tion, decide how much money you have to live on. Then evaluate your*
> *expenses—see what is left for whatever!*
> *—Woman, 60, 5*

"What is left for whatever" of course refers to the margin by which your income exceeds your expenses—that final piece of information which is the goal of every hopeful budget-maker. But to obtain it we must backtrack to what is left at the outset—"your present estate," which may consist of everything from yourself (in the form of your earning power) to the portion of that literal estate that was just passed on to you—or will be, sooner or later.

What the people in our groups have to say about settling the latter has been reserved for the section following this one. If your spouse's estate has not yet been sorted out, you may not be aware of all the assets that it contains, although a complete inventory of them will be a necessary preliminary to their distribution. But you may be painfully conscious of one fact about those assets—they may currently be beyond your reach. This is perhaps the commonest reason why a death can visit a financial as well as an emotional emergency even upon survivors who were well off in their married lives. For example, the name or names in which your and your spouse's property (including money) were held may have already caused you inconvenience or even hardship:

My first advice might be to couples: while they both live, put securities and real estate in both *names. With everything in my spouse's name except for my Social Security and some government bonds, I couldn't touch anything to meet immediate death expenses. Fortunately I had saved a sizeable amount from my Social Security and the interest from the H bonds, so that I was able to pay all expenses and have enough for my needs until the estate lawyer convinced my bank that the dividend and interest checks are mine, even though only my spouse's name is on them.*

—*Woman, 78, 2*

Joint ownership saved some from being caught in such a bind:

We had a community property agreement, as well as his will, so it was not necessary to probate the will.

—*Woman, 77, 3*

Even though my husband died very suddenly without warning, everything was in order. This is important: everything was in both our names. Therefore no court or lawyers were needed.

—*Woman, 53, 2*

And so some give it a blanket endorsement:

Have everything joint—checking account, savings, etc.

—*Woman, 61, 11*

But, for legal or technical reasons (accounts which need the signatures of both parties for a transaction, for instance), ownership in common can leave assets in limbo for a time too, and not a few voiced thanks that they had funds of their own to fall back on:

A bank account or liquid funds in your name—not joint—will be a life-saver, yours, to cover all expenses until your husband's will goes through probate and his assets become accessible to you.

—*Woman, 70, 6*

Eleanor: Every attorney will advise you not to have everything together, to have separate accounts. Have whatever you want together, but there should be a certain amount of money that the man has in his name alone and the woman in her name alone. You never know what will hold up a will. So you should have something to hold on to for the time being. You never know who will . . . .

Rae: Take advantage?

Eleanor: Not take advantage, but some people might want to say something about the will.

Connie: But if everything is in joint, you still can go to the bank and take things out?

Eleanor: Not if somebody would notify the bank.

—New York, #1

As Eleanor goes on to relate, the vagaries of estate settlement are not all that can precipitate a cash-flow crisis right after the death. State laws may make it impossible to gain access for a while to a spouse's safe deposit box:

And they tell you your husband should have your papers in his vault and you should have all his papers in your vault.

Connie: Two vaults?

Eleanor: Two individual vaults, yes, that's what an attorney tells you to do. So that if anything happens, you have everything.

Bea: Because they put a seal on the vault if someone dies.

The documents that vault may be harboring are essential for applying for such entitlements as Social Security and VA benefits; this woman ticks off some of them with a weariness clearly born of experience:

Know where the papers are. You will need birth certificates, death certificates, marriage certificates, bank account information, insurance policies, property deeds, military separation papers, etc., etc., etc.

—Woman, 62, 2

As the same woman attests, insurance companies don't always settle claims instantaneously:

Have enough money available to carry you through at least four months. I was fortunate enough to have a bank account of my own which I was able to use for funeral, cemetery plot, and household expenses until the insurance company, lawyers, and TIAA-CREF got organized.

And credit, though much easier to come by than it was several decades ago (for women especially), still can't be had just for the asking:

Stress the importance of having credit cards available in own name.
—Woman, 60, 5

If your health insurance was in another name, getting it under yours may be proving a costly, cumbersome business, especially if you have dependent children:

Know status of health insurance—is it transferable to living spouse and at what rate?
—Woman, 60, 5

Hospitalization coverage presents the greatest financial fear for me. My three college-age children and I were covered for only three months after my husband's death. I got coverage through a community group at a cost of more than $2,000 a year. I recently changed jobs and am now teaching at a university which gives hospitalization benefits to part-time faculty, a real bonus.
—Woman, 59, 3

Some women say they went back to work more for the sake of the health coverage than for that of the salary. This one bemoans her inability to find a position like the one above:

With two dependent children, I feel I have to work for health insurance and other benefits. Best advice is to get a part-time job to keep your mind busy but leaving you free to look after your children. I would like to see all employers carry minors on insurances, so widows don't have to work full time and drive fifty miles a day to get to a job to provide these benefits.
—Woman, 50, 3

Others without children simply opt to take their chances about some eventualities. This woman, covered by both Medicare and a former employer's medical and dental plan, decided she had to forgo additional coverage, despite her misgivings:

Although I am in good physical condition, my one concern is what happens when and if a very serious prolonged illness should occur. Recently I contacted a Blue Cross representative about long-term health care ("Lasting Care," they call it), but all four plans presented appear expensive. I suppose going without is one way of solving the problem for oneself, especially when one lives alone as I do.

—*Woman, 73, 4*

Only 28% of those we questioned judged their health insurance to be "very good"—in contrast to the 65% who, like the woman above, rated it "adequate" or less than that.

If it's now too late to avert problems like these, you may want to make sure (as discussed in the next section) that they will not befall your own possible survivors, such as dependent children or parents. As for yourself, once any temporary difficulties have been resolved (perhaps with an allowance from the estate), you can get on with the business of determining how much you really have to spend:

Be knowledgeable about all the possible sources of an income—salary or pensions, savings, Social Security, investments, and other assets.

—*Woman, 70, 6*

Some are occasionally overlooked:

See about Social Security. I had no idea that at 60 I was eligible for it.

—*Woman, 62, 2*

Also unanticipated may be the possibility that some may dry up, like the Social Security income of this working woman's retired husband:

Know what is applicable to you regarding Social Security—i.e., widow's benefits not available until 60, and then reduced. Be aware of the years you are on your own!

—*Woman, 60, 5*

Even if the inflows of funds are adequate overall, they may be less frequent or less predictable in amount than before, something that this woman says obliged her to adopt a new perspective on money—and apparently on herself:

One of the major challenges is that of changing from a monthly salary mentality to a "periodic payout resource management" mentality. It may take a few years, but then you'll have the advantage of knowing yourself better than you ever have before.

—Woman, 65, 11

Or your support may be all-too-predictable:

Learn to live within the constraints of a fixed *income.*

—Woman, 72, 12

Then comes the other side of the ledger. A budget may only bring your expenses to heel, but at least it will prevent them from stealing up behind you:

I live on a yearly budget, by months, so big expenditures do not crowd up on me.

—Woman, 83, 17

Unfortunately, the big ones are usually those over which you can't exert much discretion, but for which you must plan nevertheless:

What are your fixed expenses—mortgage payments, insurance premiums, real estate taxes?

—Woman, 70, 6

And fixed expenses—unlike fixed incomes—have a nasty habit of belying their name. Inflation is often the same bugbear to survivors that it is to retirees—especially to those who are filling both of those roles at once (as 80% of our survey group were):

Understand what the nickel-and-dime accumulation of it all does— increases in the cost of living, increases in utilities, increases in real estate taxes (despite all the propaganda from "powers who want to attach and attack my purse").

—Woman, 60, 5

Such knowledge has drawn Kay into what she dubs the "bag-lady syndrome":

Kay: *I think living in Santa Monica has been giving me a bag-lady syndrome—I'm afraid of the future, about whether, economically, I'll*

be able to manage.
Q: Bag-lady syndrome?
Kay: You see so many people with all their possessions in shopping carts. And even though I am comfortably off, the future looks a little ominous for people on fixed incomes.
Q: Why? What do you see happening?
Kay: Well, even though there's rent control in Santa Monica, rent does go up every every year. Food, auto insurance—everything seems to be going up. I might be worried needlessly, but I do worry about it.
                                                            —Los Angeles, #2

How reasonable are fears like hers? Drawing up a budget and watching the results unfold have been a reassuring exercise for some:

I think when you first become a widow you worry about money, you are not sure at first if you will have enough to live on. I budgeted very carefully the first year to be sure I could pay my taxes and other household expenses. After that first year, when I saw that I could live on my income, I relaxed.
                                                            —Woman, 69, 9

The loss of a much-loved spouse is absolutely devastating. But I have good health, a positive outlook, and, after going through the death tax process, I found I could live as well as before. There is no doubt that a sufficient income plays a vital part in recovery of one's spirits and getting over grief.
                                                            —Woman, 67, 10

In fact, their experiences appear to have been shared by the majority of those we surveyed. As we noted in the last chapter (page 117), 74% reported an "overall financial situation" that was "about the same" or "better" than it was previously. The median income of the group in 1986 was $25,320, and almost one-third received $30,000 or more that year. Only 5% of them replied, "Not too well," when asked, "Considering both income and expenses, how well would you say you are managing?" About one-third apiece of the rest answered, "Very well," "Well," or "Adequately."

That doesn't mean that they were flinging dollar bills about like confetti. A handful, it's true, have the luxury of declaring themselves unabashed hedonists:

If you have any spare money, spend it on yourself. *Have as good a time as possible. Don't sacrifice for yourself to provide for children after your death.*

—Woman, 71, 5

But it's saving rather than spending, and for a much more sobering reason, that instigates this woman to relay the same message:

Don't lend money to struggling children. Save it for possible stays in nursing homes.

—Woman, 70, 4

To shield yourself against that and similar threats, insurance is another option, and probably a more cost-effective one:

Medicare takes care of some emergency health problems, but does not cover long illnesses. Have a good insurance supplement to do what Medicare does not. Also, it's good to have insurance for nursing home care in the event hospital care isn't all that you need.

—Woman, 74, 4

Many in our survey who take a conservative tack had learned to do so in their earlier financial lives:

I was fortunate in not having serious financial problems. We had always lived conservatively and saved as we could, my needs were simple, and my children were grown.

—Woman, 76, 12

A similar prudence has enabled another woman to run a small surplus, that guarantor of independence:

Get good financial advice—I used (as my husband indicated I should) Mellon Bank for the insurance trust. My portfolio is managed by Gardner & Creston—through E. F. Hutton—in a conservative way (at my direction). Through careful savings during our marriage, and after the bequests from my relatives, I am independent and still saving—a little.

—Woman, 87, 21

Others, however, who describe their abilities to ''save'' are clearly acting under some degree of compulsion, even though they may not be entirely convinced of its necessity:

> *I would love to take nice trips, but I know how one could cost as much or more than $2,000. So that is where I save—that amount goes a long way toward letting me do my little good deeds [parties, gifts for friends, etc.] through the year. I have not had any kind of trip since my husband's death. I watch my friends go and love to hear about their trips, but you must have priorities in your life. I try to save something every month because I don't know if I will need more down the road. It's too bad we can't know what we will need.*
> —*Woman, 73, 8*

She is saving reluctantly, cutting back on her literal journeys to provide for her financial one, and that puts her among the third of the survey group who acknowledged having "had to make adjustments in lifestyle" for purely financial reasons. Her sacrifice of travel was the second commonest, that of 22% of the group as a whole and exceeded only by the 26% who said they had to eliminate "extras" in general, like those mentioned by this woman:

> *If income is limited, cut down on gifts, especially birthdays and holidays. The family will understand.*
> —*Woman, 65, 3*

Smaller, but still sizeable, were the numbers of those who had to make concessions that cut closer to home. Nineteen percent dined out and entertained less, 18% spent less on clothes, and 10% scrimped on "basics such as utilities or household maintenance."

So some did discover their worries were warranted. Most appear to have come through whatever retrenchment was needed with equanimity:

> *It was necessary to cut expenditures and learn to do many things myself. I can and do save a little. I am content.*
> —*Woman, 83, 17*

But an unfortunate few recognized right away that they were in more critical straits. As others in the group are griping about bookkeeping headaches, Barbara bursts out with a question that, she reveals, applies to herself:

Not everybody owns a home, has money in the bank. Everyone here has been very fortunate from what I have been listening to. Everyone has been left financially secure, more or less. What about the person whose husband dies leaving her virtually penniless?

—*Boston, #1*

Not knowing how to handle money is much preferable to not having any to handle. Several said they were left marooned by a lack of life insurance:

My greatest anxiety was that my life insurance benefits were minimal.
—*Woman, 76, 20*

When I was widowed I was devastated not only by my husband's death, but by the terrible feeling of being desperately poor—of being left in poverty. For we had no life insurance—it had been cashed in so we could take some trips.
—*Woman, 71, 5*

And this woman doesn't disguise how angry she is at being left in the lurch:

If there is no family wealth or investment income, you can't have too much insurance with the nation's economy in its present inflated state. I know this is materialistic, but as one whose husband did not believe in insurance to support a "rich widow," I feel strongly about it.
—*Woman, NA, NA*

Others were faced with having to struggle on alone with a venture that puts the means of many couples to their biggest test:

My husband died unexpectedly the day spring vacation was to begin in 1979. At that time he had been under considerable stress. He was in the age group that was still required to retire at age 65 after the federal law passed to extend the mandatory retirement age to 70. And he worried about how we would manage financially on a reduced income, with a daughter just starting a three-year graduate school program and a son just finished college and thinking about graduate school. The problem was even more severe for me after his death.
—*Woman, 68, 8*

Yet she apparently overcame it, as did these two, despite a similar dearth of resources:

> *I only wished I had had more advice and counselling on investing for the future. I had two children under the age of 18 and one went on to college, which I financed.*
>
> —Woman, 52, 7

> *I was a young widow and not typical. My most difficult problem has been sending three children to college, since Reagan had changed the Social Security laws and only my oldest daughter received Social Security during college. This cost my children approximately $40,000 tax-free dollars, which is no small sum.*
>
> —Woman, 49, 8

How did they do it? All three had jobs and apparently used them to shoulder most of the burden, since only one (the first) reported having to make cutbacks. But sometimes cutting back is not feasible, or not enough, and then you may be forced to violate the most hallowed precept in personal finance:

> *Don't erode your capital!*
>
> —Woman, 60, 5

Almost 24% of those surveyed couldn't abide by this rule, since they confirmed having regularly drawn money from savings or sold securities or property just to meet current expenses. That's how this woman, who had between $30,000 and $35,000 to live on in 1986, eked out some truly lean years before then:

> *For the first nine years of widowhood, I lived on less than $8,000 a year—TIAA-CREF, Social Security, some teaching, and return on investments. Every once in a while I had to draw on that investment capital, and what I'd be doing now with a dwindling income, I don't know. However, a brother's death, settling a trust fund to me, has changed all this, and I now have freedom from financial worry. I am very lucky.*
>
> —Woman, 77, 15

As she concedes, she was counting on her luck, but risk-taking may be the only recourse in circumstances like hers. Borrowing is even more of a gamble because of the future obligations it creates, and we hear the usual strictures against it:

> *Q: What else do we need to know?*
> **Connie:** *If you have enough money—or if you don't have enough money: throw out your charge cards!*
> —New York, #1

But the practice of loaning money came into being *because* people don't always have enough money. And this woman, seasoned early in the uses of credit, draws the most important distinction between them:

> *My father arranged for me to use his credit account after my mother died when I was age 10. He explained it was a convenience—not an invitation to spend.*
> —Woman, 84, 23

Borrowing, like investing, entails risk, only here you are taking risks with a deficit rather than a surplus—which (as we'll shortly see about investing) some find palatable and some don't.

In the previous chapter (pages 98-108), we saw how survivors could be of two minds about advice and how nothing sharpened that ambivalence like money. Those who could turn to professionals in whom they had confidence urged doing so without reservation:

> *Make no hasty decisions and seek advice from a lawyer and an investment banker. I had both, and they were absolutely invaluable.*
> —Woman, 55, 17

> *I was blessed by a fine group of professionals to call on—a real estate man my husband had known and respected, and both a lawyer and an insurance man we had depended on for twenty-five years.*
> —Woman, 58, 3

Others were left groping about, aware of how much they needed help but at a loss as to how to find a trustworthy embodiment of it:

> *My toughest job was deciding who to go to for financial advice. We did not have an accountant. The attorney who drew up our wills and did other work for us had become a judge. So deciding on an accountant and attorney was very difficult for me.*
> —Woman, 67, 3

You may be in this dilemma even if you had expert assistance when married, as this woman did:

> *We were indeed fortunate in having a professional financial plan set up a few years before my husband's death. It's certainly helped me.*
> —Woman, 51, 2

That planner is apparently no longer on call, for the same woman goes on to name as her greatest need

> *a reliable, comfortable "support group" to assist in making financial decisions. To have ongoing evaluations of my financial situation. Do I have sufficient coverage for prolonged illness? Are my investments relatively safe for myself and my children?*

Broad counsel of this kind is the quest of many, like the woman who wishes she had

> *the help of a disinterested financial advisor to review individually one's entire situation in order to make good choices. One's broker does not know about tax impact; tax lawyer or accountant is not qualified to give investment advice; estate lawyer is not familiar with priorities, etc.*
> —Woman, 65, 3

Another seconds her observation that professionals can be the prisoners of their specialties—or worse:

> *My husband took care of all business including paying all bills and balancing my checkbook. One learns fast when it becomes necessary. Had it not been for a caring family and devoted daughter who was there at all times to help work out the necessary problems, I would have been in deep trouble.*
>
> *Now they do have financial advisors who are competent to help, but at that time there were only a few around the country who were actually certified financial planners, who weren't representing a brokerage firm, insurance company, etc. Even the bank trust officer could not answer our questions.*
> —Woman, 68, 9

She's right on at least one count. Across-the-board "financial planning," complete with practitioners who are "certified" or "chartered,'' has burgeoned from virtual non-existence a decade or so ago into a service now widely available and affordable to people in relatively modest circumstances. But this development hasn't eradicated the possibility that a self-styled ''planner'' or ''advisor'' (and unlike attorneys, CPAs, and stockbrokers, they don't need to be licensed to call themselves such) may have interests other than your own at the fore. And the potential mischief he or she could cause has spooked some survivors away from them all:

My widow friends and I are at a loss to know for sure whether we are handling our finances in the most efficient way. The answer probably would be to have a financial adviser. But since we are constantly being warned in the press and otherwise that many of them are out to bilk widows, we are on our guard against any such solution.

—Woman, 86, 10

They need not remain thwarted. As noted in our section on ''Resources,'' at least two professional organizations in the field can supply lists of planners in your area with specified credentials, along with information about how to make the best use of their services. And books for survivors that go into some detail about finances usually contain guidelines for engaging professionals like lawyers, bankers, and accountants. Finally, for matters that are not too arcane, you may want to become a professional yourself. Quite a few recommend informal study or formal lessons:

Get well acquainted with all types of resource materials in the nearest public library. Periodicals such as Consumer Reports *are important and money-saving when deciding upon many of one's purchases.*

—Woman, 69, 5

Learn how to keep organized accounts—daily, monthly and yearly. Take a course if necessary.

—Woman, 78, 12

The curriculum of the typical adult-education program includes at least a few offerings in money management.

Successful investing, that elusive compound of art, science, and luck, demands expertise on the part of you, someone else, or both, at least for the ''scientific'' aspect of it:

Become familiar with stocks and bonds, etc. (I never paid much attention to this aspect). I am now a member of an investment club and find it helpful.

—Woman, 64, 3

This woman, sent into unwilling retirement in 1979 by her university's age limit for its faculty, is pleased to report,

During the 1950s I became interested in the stock market and have continued to be active in investing in securities. I have an excellent account executive to advise me in such matters. I also have a son-in-law who owns his own real estate business. Thus my interest in both continues, and the largest percentage of my present income is derived from rentals and investment income.

—Woman, 73, 4

And this one waded into investing with an enthusiasm that increased as her immersion did:

A knowledge of stocks and bonds was my weak point. I knew what we had, but I had let him take care of them. So I took a "crash course." I subscribed to two different Kiplinger *Letters,* Changing Times *magazine, and bought copies of* Money *magazine's "Guides." All have helped me, and now I really study the prospectuses and company reports I receive. I know about the terminologies, the fees, etc. I also find it satisfying to check my portfolio against the holdings of TIAA-CREF—it makes me feel more comfortable to see most of mine listed among yours. I also listen to listen to Louis Rukeyser—"Wall Street Week"—each week.*

—Woman, 77, 3

Another woman could summon up no such zest, but she had a portfolio to tend and knew she needed a suitable stand-in:

I was lucky to have a friend who was trained in the financial field. He helped me get involved in investing. I'm still ignorant but have sense enough to retain an intelligent counselor. (My problem is that I'm not interested.)

—Woman, 71, 18

Still, there's no substitute for being interested as a safeguard for your money's welfare. Moreover, to that extent that investing—as opposed to simple saving—puts that money at risk, you need to supplement interest with nerve. And some can't muster it up, like Mary, who divulges how little she shared her self-taught husband's knack for playing the markets:

Q: All right now, what was the stupidest *thing you did?*
Mary: If you don't know what you're doing financially, about stocks and bonds and things like that, just don't mess with it. I tried it, and it was a fiasco. I think you have to know your limitations.
Q: So then you should have gotten somebody to advise you?
Mary: Well, yes. My husband had introduced me to his stockbroker and told me, "You go to him." So I did, and he said, "Oh, all I did was buy. Tom would get the Wall Street Journal *and he'd tell me what to buy for him. I was always amazed that he did so well."*
Rose: So he was no help to you. Didn't you learn anything from your husband? I did. He didn't like it. But I made a point of it.
Mary: Well, mine was just the opposite—he was the ruler of the house. And I was afraid, because all I could remember was the Depression and people jumping out of windows. Being property-poor and having no money and going without.

—San Francisco

Dogged by her Depression memories, she exemplifies what the jargon of finance terms "the risk-averse temperament," and it's an axiom of investing that you must gauge how much risk you can comfortably tolerate. On the evidence of the dialogue below, the most risk that Connie wants to run is that of tying up her funds in a bank CD for a stretch—but with the assurance that she'll recover them all at the end of that period. To Eleanor, CDs are just one in a spectrum of possibilities that embraces stocks and bonds, instruments that, blue-chip or not, place your principal in at least some degree of jeopardy:

Connie: My first venture into taking my money out of a savings account was putting it into a CD. When I started to save and had accumulated a bit, I would read the papers. And I noticed each bank had different interest rates, which at one time went up as high as twelve, thirteen percent. And that is when I really got a taste of how to work with my own money—which was never too much, but I did work it a little better than if it just stayed at a regular bank rate. But how did you do it?

Eleanor: How? Well, we didn't invest much in the stock market while I was married. But after I started working and I was more in contact with the business world, I opened up an account with a brokerage house. And I became interested in state housing bonds and treasury bonds. And CDs—at that time these were new things.
Connie: But you did that after your husband died?
Eleanor: All after my husband died.
—*New York, #1*

If survivors frown upon investing without good advice, they regard figuring your taxes without it to be absolute folly. Says one who hired a tax accountant:

Seek professional advice—$300 or $400 is worth the peace of mind.
—*Woman, 55, 2*

Those we questioned put giving the government its due—in the shape of "filing income and estate taxes"—as the task they most dreaded among five we presented them with, with 32% confessing to feeling "a great deal" of anxiety about it and 26% to "some." (Contrast this total of 58% to totals of 17% and 27% on dealing with issues you would think more intimidating—"whether or not to work" and "where to live.") And some of these anxieties were borne out:

My greatest area of ignorance was how the changes in the sources of my income would affect my taxes. I would have benefited from some warnings about withholdings from my annuity incomes and the laws governing tax payments. I'm still in trouble with Uncle Sam on these matters.
—*Woman, 57, 3*

What may have put her in his bad graces is one oversight often made by people with incomes from which not enough taxes are withheld:

Don't forget to pay estimated tax!
—*Woman, 70, 4*

So some who personally discharged all their other financial duties drew the line at taxes:

Be sure you know how to pay bills, balance checkbooks, and how to prepare figures to give a CPA for tax purposes, as my husband taught me to.

—Woman, 80, 16

Marguerite: I always paid the bills, I always did everything. But not the income tax—that was what he did. I got all the stuff out and totaled it all up, and then he put it on the forms. So that's the only thing I haven't done, and I still refuse to do it.
Q: How do you get it taken care of?
Marguerite: Well, the last time I went down to, what do they call them?
Ann: Block?
Marguerite: Yes, H&R Block.

—San Francisco

You may actually recoup more than you lay out:

If finances permit, get assistance with income taxes if these are complicated. It may save you more than the consultant's fee.
—Woman, 71, 9

And if any fee at all seems like too much, some tax-assistance services don't charge one, like the Tax-Aide centers staffed by volunteers and sponsored by the AARP (the IRS offers similar help—see ''Resources''):

I needed income-tax help. But this year I did my own and then had the AARP counselor check it. He said I had it OK.
—Woman, 62, 7

Those who do retain a preparer get the usual caution about dealing with professionals—don't simply abdicate to them:

Instead of just signing the income tax statement, study it and become familiar with it in case you are faced with having to fill it out yourself.
—Woman, 65, 9

With taxes, of course, there's always the more compelling reason for knowing what you are signing—you are as liable as the preparer for what is in that statement. And if you do have to fill it out yourself, you may not be all that bad at it:

The first year I asked my attorney if he would take care of my income tax return. But he doesn't do tax work, and said, "Do it yourself. You can do it better than anyone else." I thought, "That was what my husband would have told me." So I have taken care of of all my taxes.
—Woman, 77, 3

This woman is not satisfied simply with doing her own:

Take the H&R Block Tax Course to help yourself—and others (great for moonlighting—a seasonal skill!).
—Woman, 58, 2

Perhaps it's best to leave the subject of this section on an unmaterialistic note, with some traditional reminders that money can't buy the intangibles. Up to a point, everyone would agree with this woman (who calls herself "very well provided for"):

There is an old Scottish saying that "there is a great difference between fat sorrow and lean sorrow"—meaning that if a widow is left without money and maybe with several children, it can be a hard life indeed.
—Woman, 81, 16

But that difference does have its limits for another woman:

Fortunately I had no financial worries, but I did resent people insinuating that since I had none, his death would be easier to bear.
—Woman, 68, 2

And those in more modest circumstances may find an outlook like Sarah's not the worst way of adjusting to them. When the rest of the group is chatting wistfully about how nice a windfall would be, she interjects,

About winning the lottery, that doesn't interest me at all. I've built my life around my own resources, and I was always able to extract the most from the least. So poverty was never a threat even though I was not left with very much. I've always thought, "I'm not interested in the economic sweepstakes, give me the emotional sweepstakes!"
—New York, #1

Estates: Settling Your Spouse's and Planning Your Own

For most, it is a once-in-a-lifetime experience to see a spouse's estate go through society's machinery for dealing with it. And the process is therefore apt to present them with some of the most vexatious of their financial problems. Almost 84% of our survey said that their spouses had left a will, and 94% of those said that it was up-to-date. The exceptions do tell a few horror stories:

All would have gone better for me if my husband had had a current, up-to-date will. He died in an accident—a fire. There had been a previous marriage which was bitter, and there were children from that marriage who were vengeful.

He left all to them, through a will made during the first marriage. I was not in it. It took me much time to settle. The pressures from his former family were terrible, and my attorney's fees were horrendous.

—Woman, 41, 2

But even a document free of such flaws doesn't guarantee that things will go smoothly or that you will be able to secure what is rightfully yours right away. In the preceding section, we glanced at some of the typical financial snarl-ups that can catch up survivors right after the death. It may take them much longer to free themselves from the entanglements of a spouse's estate—so long that a weary fatalism may seem their only refuge:

Besides the sorrow, expect the first year after your spouse's death to be frustrating. You'll never understand the legal system, so don't try to fight it—just exist, and it will be all over in a year or so.

—Woman, 71, 4

However, we are not encouraging you to throw up your hands as she does. For one thing, you may not have that luxury if your spouse appointed you an executor or executrix, like this woman:

My husband's three grown children returned to their respective homes (distances away), and I was faced with all the settlement of an estate. Even though I had kept detailed records of all our financial and legal activities, it was still a time-consuming effort.

—Woman, 73, 4

Even if you aren't engaged in these duties, your informed participation may make it easier for you in the long run, according to one expert:

> *In my work as a legal assistant specializing in probate, I have seen too many spouses (and other heirs) who knew nothing about the legal procedures required to settle an estate and who did not ask questions and/or make an effort to find out what was necessary from an impartial source. Invariably, it was more costly—in time, money, and stress—to them than if they had been informed and assertive.*
> *—Woman, 54, 4*

Even at best, the process may seem to drag on forever:

> *Do not make any hasty decisions. Stay where you are. Clear up all necessary paperwork, which can take as much as a year—or a little longer—to complete.*
> *—Woman, 74, 4*

> *Be patient about settling your spouse's estate. Do one step at a time. It will eventually be completed.*
> *—Woman, 73, 9*

Which makes it all the more imperative to start the wheels grinding as soon as possible, if you can:

> *Take care of any estate business right away. Don't put it off. It has to be done, so do it right away.*
> *—Woman, 65, 11*

Expert advice, almost everyone agrees for once, is an essential:

> *I had a wonderful lawyer to advise me and handle the estate—capable, understanding, and honest.*
> *—Woman, 86, 8*

> *Get professional help in these matters:*
> *1. Estates and income taxes.*
> *2. Appraisal of real estate at time of death of spouse.*
> *3. How to probate will, if you do it yourself.*
> *4. Transferring title to all property—real estate stocks and*

bonds to your name—securing death notices.

—Woman, 78, 12

We hear an occasional old-fashioned denunciation of lawyers for avarice and duplicity, as we do from this vigorous exponent of do-it-yourself probate:

Bud: *I was never lonesome, but I was stupid. That's why I say, don't sign anything, don't do anything, don't even hire a lawyer. Just sit back and think. And I mean that in all sincerity, because half the time people hire lawyers who rob them to death on probates. And I'll tell you, any one of you in here can walk down and do a probate in a week. One week, it's that simple. It doesn't matter where in the United States you are, if you know how to do it.*
Virginia: *Tell them why you know that.*
Bud: *Well, that used to be part of my job.*

—Los Angeles, #1

And there are books available (see the Bibliography again), although as Rae caustically remarks, possessing one does not inevitably lead to reading or understanding it:

My daughter bought my husband a book, all about wills. I don't know if he read it or he didn't, but he made every mistake that the book tried to prevent.

—New York, #1

But it's the rare person who's been able to tackle it single-handedly, like this professor of business (and businesswoman):

I can truthfully say that without my knowledge and background as a business administration major, I would never have accomplished the settlement of an estate.

—Woman, 73, 4

And you do have certain defenses against being fleeced (although keep in mind that cheapest is not always synonymous with best, especially when the charge is by the hour):

When settling an estate, don't hesitate in shopping for a lawyer, as their fees vary greatly.

—Woman, 66, 8

Although 16% of those surveyed reported being "disappointed" by their "lawyer or accountant" in the course of settling the estate, 68% indicated that everyone from whom they'd sought help had come through.

Books on grief commonly point out that survivors can use a spouse's death as an occasion for planning for their own, and some of our people concur:

> **Edith:** *Another thing we did, we arranged for our graves and all of that, so I'm taken care of too. When I die, all they do is open the grave and put me under.*
> **Q:** *Is that something people should do?*
> **Rose:** *Yes, absolutely.*
> **Q:** *When should people think about that?*
> **Mary:** *Right now.*
> **Rose:** *Right after your husband dies, make a new will and do the whole bit.*
>
> —*San Francisco*

If you and your spouse failed to prevent your own affairs from being left in disarray, you can translate hindsight into foresight and keep the same from happening to your survivors, dependents especially:

> *Be sure* your *will and personal records are in order, so your children will have the least amount of difficulty possible in settling the estate at a time when decision-making is the most difficult.*
>
> —*Woman, 64, 6*

Making out a new will is not one of life's most agreeable occasions; and it had inspired "some" anxiety among 21% of our survey group and "a great deal" of it among 10%—scores topped only by their fears about taxes. The superstitious may feel they're hexing themselves:

> **Connie:** *It's a very funny feeling when you make out the will. You feel, "Oh my God, tomorrow somebody is going to die!" You need it, and of course it doesn't happen like that.*
>
> —*New York, #1*

And a badly drawn will is worse than none at all, as Rae learned after her husband's appointment of his siblings as trustees embroiled her in a wrangle worthy of a Victorian novel:

> *Jean: If they die intestate, then there is a lot of trouble. Even if you have very little, there should be a will.*
> *Q: Do you ladies agree with that?*
> *Rae: No. My husband did everything—I never even could sign a check. And when the will was made out, the trustees and the executors were his sister and brother.*
> *Bea: Trustees?*
> *Rae: Executors. And trustees—that's when you have a few dollars. He figured our children were young and they wouldn't know how to manage it. Now the executor is only until the estate is settled, but the trustees go on for life, and that is where my trouble came in. My children have gotten nothing so far, but when the estate was settled they got their share right away. And then each year, whatever profit there is, they share it. And it's in the hands of lawyers, it's in the hands of accountants, and—*
> *Jean: They are the ones that get the money.*
> *Rae: Yes, everybody is making something out of it! All these years! And the price goes up every couple of years—with the lawyer, with the accountant. Plus the trustees' fees.*
> *Sarah: Did you ever attempt to get a lawyer and challenge this whole arrangement?*
> *Rae: Oh we went to court, we did all kinds of things, we got nowhere. It was, "This is it!"*
>
> *—New York, #1*

A well-thought-out trust, however, could have worked as much to her benefit as this one has to her detriment, as could well-chosen executors:

> *Mine was a case of sudden death. Having a will was a blessing; it saved a lot of frustration. Good support can come from the executor of the will, and this selection should be made carefully.*
>
> *—Woman, 68, 8*

And so you may want to have family members collaborate with you, as this woman's husband had her do:

> *As time for retirement approached, we undertook an estate-planning*

effort that became a team *effort—attorney, CPA, husband and wife. This is the one biggest asset I had when widowed—a working relationship with persons vital to an orderly settlement of the estate. I knew, at least in part, what was being discussed, what records were available, and where they were.*

—Woman, 69, 4

And estate-planning can extend to matters you don't need a team to attend to:

The best advice, and the greatest help and reassurance I received, came from my husband, who prepared and explained to me a detailed listing of our resources, names of people to contact, provisions he was making for children's education, decisions and options I would need to make in case of his death or incapacity. He was in the prime of life as well as his career when he unexpectedly and suddenly died of a myocardial infarction. This piece of paper became my lifeline in the utter desolation his death brought us.

—Woman, 73, 26

We'll close by gratefully reproducing an impressively exhaustive model for such a piece of paper which one husband bequeathed to his wife, a replica of which she now has on file with her lawyer and the trust department of the bank she has chosen to administer her own estate:

At the time of my husband's death, the following information was most helpful to me—all written (copy kept at home; copy in safe deposit box):

I. Instructions to Follow When Deceased and Address and Telephone Numbers for:

1. Relatives
2. Attorney, accountant, physician, dentist, optometrist, minister, etc.
3. Banks; investment companies, if applicable
4. Social Security Administration
5. Retirement office, if applicable
6. Insurance companies (life, health, property, etc.)
7. Household accounts; credit card accounts
8. Location of safe deposit box keys

II. Inventory of Safe Deposit Box Contents (individual envelopes for each):
1. *Last will and testament*
2. *Insurance policies (life, health, property, etc.)*
3. *Certificate of title to auto*
4. *Authorized signature card for bank account (with or without right of survivorship)*
5. *Receipts for purchase and/or sale of securities (stocks, bonds, etc.)*
6. *Retirement contracts, if any*
7. *Real estate property (individual envelopes for each):*
   a. *Currently owned property*
   b. *Property sold on installment sale contracts, deed of trust/notes, etc.*

III. General Information (briefly stated in outline form):
1. *Safe deposit box number (location, authorized signature card, location of keys)*
2. *Social Security number (date of birth, place of birth, etc.)*
3. *Location of bank accounts and number of account, giving information regarding authorized signature card, direct deposits to account, etc.*
4. *Investment accounts (name, location, account no., etc.)*
5. *Insurance companies (name of company, policy number, address, etc.)*
6. *Church affiliation*
7. *Income tax returns (by whom prepared, address, telephone number)*

—Woman, 73, 4

Household Upkeep

Assuming you've decided to keep the house, keeping it going may be straining you physically, financially, or both. The strain may be compounded by the fact that your spouse did most or all of the work. Among the widows of men who viewed house maintenance and repair as a traditional male preserve, we encounter a stock figure to rival the woman who can't write a check—the one who can't change a light bulb:

Connie: *I am ashamed of these women. They sit in the chair and . . . [with a beseeching gesture], "Pick me up!"—that sort of attitude.*

Jean: You are absolutely right. I have known women that cannot put a bulb in when a light blows out. "Call the superintendent!" Their husbands had to do it.

—New York, #1

We glimpsed her counterpart earlier in the widower who is fumbling unhappily to learn the rudiments of such "women's work" as grocery shopping, cooking, and keeping clothes clean and in repair.

Women like Jean and Connie grant the stereotype no excuses:

Q: You change your light bulbs?
Jean: I sure do.
Connie: Of course. You get up on a ladder and you change it.
Jean: I hang draperies and do everything—I hung draperies from a nine-foot ceiling.
Connie: You have to learn.
Eleanor: Do you know that, a month after my husband died, I called up a store and got a six-foot ladder so I could do these things myself?

—New York, #1

Others are almost as nonchalant. As was the case with finances, some had always been proficient—often happily so:

Julia: My husband was not handy, but I used to do a lot of things around the house and I didn't mind. So it wasn't a big deal, it didn't bother me at all because I liked doing things. I really do.

—Boston, #2

Others acquired the proficiency with apparent ease, sometimes to their surprise:

Lil: My husband was very handy around the house, but he wouldn't do a thing unless I handed him the hammer and the nails and stayed right with him [laughter]. Then after, I'd look at the hammer and I'd say, "Well, I watched him. If he could do it, I can."

—Boston, #2

Daily chores are more time-consuming, as you are doing your own household jobs and have the added responsibility of those of your spouse, whether you do them yourself or hire them out. One does learn many new skills if you accept the challenge.

—Woman, 60, 3

Not everyone wants to or can seize the initiative so readily, however. In our survey group, 39% experienced "some" difficulty with the "repair and maintenance of car, house, etc.," among them this woman, who clearly shrinks from the whole business:

Very handy if a widow has the practical ability to handle minor house repairs, to maintain household appliances (preventive maintenance), to run lawn mowers, tractors, Rototillers and not be afraid of the challenge.

—Woman, 60, 5

And these two are among the 15% who reported having "a great deal" of trouble:

My spouse and I made joint decisions, so it has been very hard for me to make routine ones about car repairs, household maintenance, repairs, etc.—I find my acquaintances are reluctant even to tell me whom they hire for such things, so I have had to learn to rely on my own ability to make the decisions and live with the results.

—Woman, 61, 6

Having to cope with household maintenance problems is sometimes overwhelming and frustrating. Having the work done is the best solution, if you have the money. Otherwise I do what I can and ignore what I can't do.

Woman, 64, 3

Hers is a commonsense approach, but be on guard against letting a distaste for these demands lead you into ignoring them too much. Caring for the house does more than uphold its physical integrity and its aesthetic respectability:

Make home improvements, if possible. Keep the home in good shape— it's an investment.

—Woman, 61, 11

And as we are so often reminded, it's normally most people's biggest investment. But even if you don't hope to profit from it in that respect, it can carry an economic value of another sort:

> *The four-bedroom house and lawn are getting too much to take care of now. But with the house paid for, it would be hard to find a place to live as cheaply.*
>
> *—Woman, 66, 10*

Looking after the house may yield other rewards as well. The time it consumes may be a good thing:

> *Understand if you keep your house, you will be busier than ever—the inside work plus outside—not all bad! You don't have time to feel sorry for yourself.*
>
> *—Woman, 60, 5*

It can confer independence:

> *I bought a snowblower, so I don't have to wait for a man to plow me out. I run the mower some too.*
>
> *—Woman, 78, 4*

You may even be able to transform it into a social occasion:

> *Elect to have* young, qualified *people help with various household and professional projects. Pay them well and also enjoy their company! Better than attempting these things alone. Helps motivation!*
>
> *—Woman, 72, 7*

As with finances, if you don't have the skills, you may be able to pick them up formally through an adult-education program:

> *To widows: learn to change a tire, take classes in plumbing, electrical repair. Learn to read warranties, deal with repair persons. My pension goes mostly to the service of appliances, or the replacement of them.*
>
> *—Woman, 62, 7*

Or the skills may be nearby, yours just for the asking:

> *If you need help don't hesitate to ask a friend or neighbor. Mine have been eager to assist.*
>
> *—Woman, 60, 3*

We have arrived at a subject of considerable controversy—favors. Some say you shouldn't hang back:

> *Remain as independent as you can, but if you really need help, accept it gratefully and gracefully.*
>
> *—Woman, 76, 12*

> *Don't fret about people doing things for you—your turn will come to repay!*
>
> *—Woman, 62, 8*

Others are adamantly opposed:

> *Don't expect favors. If possible,* pay *for services you need such as heavy yardwork, home maintenance, etc.*
>
> *—Woman, 71, 3*

The most likely dispenser of the favors is what makes the topic such a touchy one:

> *I hire someone to do gardening and handyman tasks I can't manage, rather than appeal to friends' husbands, who don't need more of this sort of thing than they already have to do.*
>
> *—Woman, 68, 7*

Connie dismisses these scruples:

> **Connie:** *The other thing you can do is look for a neighbor to help you.*
> **Bea:** *No, I wouldn't ask a neighbor for help. A friend of mine resents the widows in the building asking her husband for help.*
> **Eleanor:** *I don't blame her. Even though I'm a widow.*
> **Bea:** *She says, "He is not a super."*
> **Eleanor:** *She is right.*
> **Connie:** *But I think that's silly.*
>
> *—New York, #1*

Sexual jealousy, as we'll see in the next chapter, may also be triggering the resentment Bea mentions, a possibility that flusters the innocent Marilyn:

God, I never thought about it that way [laughter]! I never knew how to put a nail in the wall or anything, so I'd go to my friend's husband and say, "Can you help me with this?" and he did.

—Boston, #1

If you are a widow, we'll leave it to you to decide how you want to negotiate this particular minefield. But if you do prefer to or must hire people in the home-repair trades, you may enjoy Loretta's ruse for smoking out the shadier ones:

Loretta: One time I was going to have a new roof put on. There was a man working around the neighborhood, and I said, "Would you like to look at my property and see how much it would cost for a roof?" "I'll be over tonight. When will your husband be home?" Well, I didn't think for a minute, and I said, "My husband's deceased." "Oh, you're a widow. Oh, we'll treat you fine."
Others: [in unison] Oh, yeah!
Loretta:"We'd love to help you." So I said, "OK, but I'll have to contact my son. You'll have to call him at his office." He said, "What's his number?" And I gave it to him and I said, "Incidentally, he's a lawyer." He says, "Oh, thank you very much, we'll call him right away." Never heard from him [laughter]! So to everybody that deals with me, I say, "You'll have to talk to my son. He's a lawyer."
Virginia: That's a good one!
Leonard: These gals are smart, aren't they?
Loretta: Incidentally, I can take my son off the hook. He's a patent lawyer.

—Los Angeles, #1

No reason why men with children who are lawyers can't use this gambit too.

Travel

We'll turn now to new experiences of a more enjoyable sort, even though the first—travel—may seem terrifying initially and may never regain the charms it had while you were part of a couple. Travel is sought out as a recreation precisely because of the new experiences it offers. Their newness is what makes them so intensely felt, an intensity that sharing them with a spouse can easily double. Without that fellow traveller, your delight in them may sour. For husband and wife, pitting themselves against the unknown can be an adventure; for only one, it may just be an ordeal:

> *I hesitate to travel long distances and have not taken any long trips since I have been alone, though my husband and I used to travel a lot.*
> —*Woman, 79, 2*

Traveling for pleasure was one of the uses of their leisure that our survey group said they had cut back most sharply. Those who traveled "often" had dropped from 35% to 23% and those who did so "seldom or never" had risen correspondingly from 12% to 23%. As we saw in "Finances," newly tight budgets account for some of the fall-off, as this woman corroborates:

> *Fortunately, I have the funds to travel extensively, which I throughly enjoy.*
> —*Woman, 60, 6*

But, even for those with the money, two fears may make travel unpalatable—first, that of having to go off on your own, and second, that of having to come back:

> **Catherine:** *I'd like to be able to travel alone, with groups.*
> **Q:** *You can't? Why?*
> **Catherine:** *I don't know. I guess something holds me back because my husband and I always went every place, all over the world together, and now I can't seem to do it or want to do it.*
> —*Miami, #1*

> **Lil:** *I took I don't know how many trips, and it was just the same—it was worse!—when you had to come back and start all over again.*
> —*Boston, #2*

Of course, some say they were never encumbered by such qualms:

> **Marilyn:** *We did a great deal of traveling, traveled the world. And I didn't stop. I just kept on doing it, either with friends or alone. And I'm glad I did. I think that's important too, to just keep on doing the things that you would have done together.*
> —*Boston, #2*

Travel—get away (best of all!). Do things with friends or by yourself.
                                              —Woman, 69, 4

Travel is also helpful—a trip to the Orient was a fine adventure.
                                              —Woman, 52, 2

And a few launched themselves right back into it, with happy results:

If you can afford it, travel. Three months after my husband died, one of my professional friends insisted I go with her (and a group) for three weeks in China. I had to give a paper! That shook me out of my doldrums in a hurry. Since then, I have taken at least one trip out of the country every year—most often with professional colleagues and seeing how others in world care for their old, sick, psychiatrically ill people. If you haven't already guessed, I'm a mental-health worker.
                                              —Woman, 64, 6

I decided a tour, someplace I'd never been, might help me. I took the trip and came back with new perspectives. I hadn't recovered, not forgotten, but I did have something else to think about.
                                              —Woman, 83, 15

Others found it a struggle even when it proved worthwhile:

I had no desire to travel, but relatives and kind friends in different parts of the country invited me to visit, and eventually I went. The necessary planning, preparation, and memories afterwards helped me.
                                              —Woman, 70, 2

And others eventually found it a struggle worth giving up:

Elaine: I'm tired of traveling alone. I've had it. I've taken some very lovely trips, but I don't like to go and just sit around a pool and lie about my income [laughter].
Q: What do you mean?
Elaine: Well, "You have fourteen apartments?—I happen to have thirty-two." "You get $100,000 a year?—I get $300,000."
Q: Are you talking about men?
Elaine: No, women—you know, how wealthy they are. In fact I want to go to a place where there is a program of some kind, where there is a discussion, where they offer me something that is worthwhile going

to. I've taken a Semester at Sea and that sort of thing. But there comes a time when you figure, "Well, it's been very nice, but traveling alone again? Forget it!" And, that's what happens. You start . . . petering down.

—*Los Angeles, #2*

If it is in fact such a battle, why fight, especially over a matter so purely discretionary? Despite her sarcasm and her professed resignation to "petering down," there's a note of reluctance in Elaine's voice. "Wanderlust" didn't gain its name for nothing, and travel holds a huge allure for many of us:

Ann: *Ever since I was knee-high to a puppy, I would lie in front of the fireplace and read and read. And I used to say to myself, "One day I would like to travel and see what goes on in the world and how other people in other cultures live." Some of it, a little of it, I've done. But not enough.*
Q: *Any place in particular, places?*
Ann: *No, I'd just like to take a pin and stick it in a map and say, "That's where I'm going."*

—*San Francisco*

Travel grants us a license to ramble outside the psychological as well as the literal boundaries of our homebound lives:

Molly: *On a trip, sometimes people will talk to strangers more readily and more honestly than they will to someone they know very well. For some reason, we hesitate to bare our souls, so to speak, to our next-door neighbor. But you'll run into a complete stranger you just met on a bus, on a cruise, somewhere, and you'll talk a blue streak, and it's so good!*

—*Miami, #1*

For these reasons, many survivors view travel as one of the ultimate tests. It represents getting out of the house on the grandest scale, a perilous reconciliation of the urge to escape and the necessity of returning:

Travel! *Wonderful—and it brings you friends. It is also* running away. *You have to come home to the awful nothingness eventually. But it is worth the pain.*

—*Woman, 70, 4*

For Molly, traveling is as elemental and inescapable as "keeping busy":

It was hard to go on a bus trip—we used to go places on the bus. And I'd say, "Oh my God, I'll never get on that bus." The lady said, "Come on, I'll show you. You're going to go, Molly, you're going to go." I remember going up the steps, oh it was awful at first. But then when I got in and met people, you know—you don't forget, but you get used to doing those things alone. If you want to go, you have to go by yourself, and it's hard.

Q: It's hard, but what does it give you when you do it?

Molly: It makes me feel good.

Q: If you didn't do it, what would happen?

Molly: Well, I don't know, but I do it, I keep going, I keep busy and do everything I want to do now. Very busy, it's the only thing to do.

—Boston, #1

Gladys finds it just as arduous—but again is pleased to tally up the same incremental gains from her efforts that Molly does:

I'd like to go on big trips, but there's no one to go with. But on a couple of little trips, I found—"Gee, I am laughing. Gee, I am a little stronger. Let me see if I can go home and do that too." And I got home and I fell apart—because I wanted to keep on going. And I wish I could. I have a neighbor who is gone ninety-nine percent of the time, and this has been her life. I don't agree with that, but I think you can run away. There's no doubt it's still there, but you can resolve enough of it, you can put it in another place and then come back to it. And I think when you come back to it each time, you're a little bit stronger and a little bit happier. I'm going on a retreat this weekend. I'm going on a psychological retreat, meditation and psychology. I'm trying everything and I'm trying to get away. I only wish that I had enough places to go.

—Los Angeles, #2

Her contention that she is constructively yielding to the impulse to flee is echoed by others:

I have also found travel helpful, especially during the anniversary season one year after my husband's death, when even the weather reminded me of him.

—Woman, 68, 7

We encountered several others who used it as a means of exorcising the pain of anniversaries or holidays:

> **Frieda:** *Every New Year's Eve I go away on a cruise. I don't want to feel bad up in my own apartment—that's murder on New Year's Eve. So I just go away.*
>
> —*Miami, #1*

In the Epilogue (page 486), Pat unfolds an account of how she vanquished the specter of the first anniversary of the death by doing the same.

Like Gladys, those who dread traveling alone may be able to call on aid from one resource close at hand—their friends:

> *I went to Santa Fe to the opera and I went with three other women. Two of us each shared a room. The woman I was with didn't know the others, but I knew all three of them. It was my first trip, and they'd been through quite a bit with me. And we had a* wonderful *time—we were like kids.*
>
> —*Los Angeles, #2*

Friends supply the spark that some consider essential to making the whole experience catch fire:

> **Rose:** *I don't like to travel alone. I like to have a partner with me.*
> **Diane:** *Me too. I've got to have somebody with me.*
> **Rose:** *My grandkids say, "Grandma, you're so outgoing, why can't you travel alone?"*
> **Ann:** *When I see something beautiful, I need someone that I can poke and say, "Isn't that magnificent?"*
>
> —*San Francisco*

Enlisting such companions may require overcoming a certain initial reserve on your part and theirs:

> **Edna:** *When I first started traveling, I had three women friends. They were all either divorced or had lost their husbands by death. And I told them I had planned this trip on my two weeks of vacation, and I asked them to go with me, to share expenses and just for the companionship. "Oh, I couldn't do that, and you can't either." And I said, "Well, that's just what you* think." *When I was a child and I told my mother, "I*

can't do that, Ma," she'd say, "There isn't such a word in the dictionary. You go get the dictionary. You find it." I couldn't find "can't," and I still can't find "can't."

—*San Francisco*

But after enough practice, you and they may become as supremely casual about it as Sharkey and her circle:

Q: Where do you like to go?
Sharkey: *Anywhere. Somebody will call me up and say, "Well, Sharkey, do you want to go here?" or, "You want to go there?" I say, "Sure." Next week I'm going to Portugal and Spain.*

—*Boston, #1*

Relatives can sometimes play the same role:

Edna: *And I keep traveling as much as I can, but not alone. My brother died five years ago, so my sister-in-law and I travel. We just came back from Australia [pronounced "Aus-try-lia"—laughter]. Five weeks; a hard trip. We went through Australia and New Zealand; ended up in Fiji and Honolulu.*
Q: Did you learn to speak "Strylian"?
Edna: *Well, I have a very good friend I met in England, and she was from Australia. And I said, "When you get to San Francisco, call me up." She did. She stayed a whole month. Beware of the Australians. That's what they're going to do. They're so far from home when they travel, they stay. But, anyway, she always used to say, "You come down and see me." Well, this was a tour, but we spent a day with her; she lives in Adelaide.*

—*San Francisco*

Family, if properly compliant, can facilitate getting around in other ways too:

Since my daughter lives abroad, her residence has provided an additional excuse for travel—as has my son's profession as an adventure-travel specialist.

—*Woman, 73, 12*

Traveling with friends is a recourse generally confined to women:

Jean: *When you travel to foreign countries you see groups of women,*

but you never see groups of men.
Eleanor: First of all, three-quarters of them are dead.
Jean: Once in a while you will see two men traveling, but you see vast hordes of women.
Bea: And if you see two men, they are homosexuals.
Sarah: That's not the inevitable conclusion.
Bea: Well, that's what they say.

—New York, #1

But later in the session, Jean is obviously in earnest about what she advocates to a male friend who had just lost a wife:

I said, "Get to know as many single men as you can and go away on vacations with them. It doesn't have to be an expensive vacation, it could be a short vacation, make as many friends as you can, and keep yourself busy doing the things that you love to do."

And there is one further possibility:

Q: Does anybody here ever go with a friend? You said you go with someone.
Fay: Yes, I went with a friend. I went to Vegas recently. It's a new friend, and he keeps saying, "We laughed for three days." We were so compatible! We had the greatest time!

—Los Angeles, #2

Of course, being at close quarters on the road can begin to chafe, and trips can undo some friendships as quickly as it can create others:

Edna: I have taken tours, and I've been by myself, and I've made friends that way.
Rose: I think that's wonderful, just to pick up and go. Of course, you can go with a lemon, too. I traveled with a couple of my friends—and we didn't like each other afterwards [laughter].
Ann: You know, that happens. Your very close friends go and when you're close together like this . . . [rubs fists together].

—San Francisco

Edna goes on to outline one preventive measure:

I've taken cruises by myself and got a single cabin, and they've always said, "Don't you want a double cabin?" I said, "No. I'm going to be five days on that boat, and I'll be quite frank with you, at times I have a rotten disposition. And I don't want anybody around me to bother me. So I'll take a single room." And I always do and I've enjoyed every one of those cruises. I've met people and have had glorious times on them. But, as I say, when I wanted to be alone, I went to my cabin and I was alone.

For those who can't recruit friends, organized journeys may offer a suitable compromise between being alone and having company. Cruises strike exactly the right balance for some:

Betty: I find that ships are the answer because you're never alone. You're at a big table. There's lots of activity, and you get to mingle. And while it hurts lots of times not to be able to share some of the things, I say, "Well, I'm so lucky to be able to experience this," and I've always had a great time. I've done a lot of traveling since I've lost my husband. It took a little while to get started. But I go.
—Los Angeles, #2

Just the community of interest can be enough to put you at your ease:

Ida: I just came back from a trip with a group, and I tell you, there were a lot of prominent people there, and it doesn't make any difference. When you go on a trip, everyone has the same thing in common: they went to have a good time. Whether you're single or married, it makes no difference.
—Miami, #1

And if in the course of your travels you've alienated friends, groups give you an excellent chance to replenish your supply of them:

Frieda: When my husband was alive, we used to take trips on our own. We'd lay out our itinerary and go. Now, alone, I wouldn't dare to do it. So I go with groups and I have met some lovely people. I go without knowing a soul and come back with a bunch of friends.
—Miami, #1

Not unexpectedly, group excursions organized for educational purposes often win the approval of current or former teachers:

Travel, if you can. "Elderhostel" is a great place to go to learn—you keep up with subjects you're interested in and meet new people.
                                                                    —Woman, 73, 6

I find Smithsonian and other such tours that have an instructive level, like seminars, suit me well. University tours with a special emphasis (art history, literature, for example) are also excellent.
                                                                    —Woman, 68, 7

Others favoring groups point out that the drawbacks of solitary journeys are not merely social:

I hesitate to travel alone—always so expensive for single passage on tours that are listed.
                                                                    —Woman, 67, 3

And others remind us that travel need not consume large amounts of money—or time:

Frieda: *Go away on a trip even if it's only for a week.*
Dorothy: *Even for three days, for a weekend, with somebody.*
                                                                    —Miami, #1

Connie: *A group of four of us travels together, and we don't take long trips. Most of them are short—five-day trips. We are going on to New England for the fall foliage.*
Bea: *Where are you off to?*
Connie: *Vermont, New Hampshire, Massachusetts. It's just a break. It's not expensive. But it's a break in your life.*
Bea: *We went to Cape Cod last year the same way. A few of us. It was nice.*
Connie: *You don't have to spend thousands of dollars to go away for five days or a weekend.*
                                                                    —New York, #1

Finally, for some, travel is not only a collection of new experiences but a new experience in itself, the exercise of a new found freedom:

Rose: *I think after your husband dies you want to do things that you didn't do before. You're limited a lot—not that you didn't love your*

husband, don't misunderstand me—and there are things you've always
wanted to do. And I found I wanted to travel, because Tom didn't care
too much about it. We did a little, but he was a worker—he loved to work.
—San Francisco

And 81-year-old Edna's yen to travel repudiated society's attempts
to pigeonhole her into its preconceptions about widowhood:

I will never forget the telephone call I got from my sister-in-law. She
said to me, "Well, after all, you've got to make up your mind now.
You're a widow and you are a fifth wheel and, wherever you go, you're
going to be the odd one."
Rose: *Oh, how awful!*
Mary: *That's terrible!*
Clara: *What a horrible thing to say!*
Edna: *Well, I'm part Irish, and that got it up. I guess that's when I*
started fighting. I decided I was going to take a trip. And everybody
said, "Well, you can't." I said, "I'm going!" So I did—started
traveling by myself. I had a new car and I just set off.
—San Francisco

She provided her family with an itinerary and phoned them faithfully
every night—but she doesn't disguise the relish with which she
thumbed her nose at some of their other concerns:

When I took the first trip and went to Canada for two weeks by myself,
I had a nephew who even told me, "You cannot stop on the highway and
get out of the car. It's dangerous!" And I just looked at him. Then I
came back and I showed him my pictures, and one was of where I
was going out towards the big mountain in Washington. It was
raining cats and dogs, and nothing but trees on each side of me. And
I saw this truck coming. So I pulled over to the side and parked, got
out of my car, and stood there until I could get the picture. The truck
driver waved at me, and I climbed back in the car and on I went.

And she "just looked at" her aunt in the same spirit too:

When I left, my son said, "You call now when you get to Aunt Mabel's."
I said, "Yes, I will." But I got into Long Beach and I saw a sign that said
"Catalina Island." And I thought, "That's something I always wanted
to see." So I made reservations on the boat to go there the next day. I
got to my aunt's two days later at one o'clock. And the greeting she

gave me as I walked in the door! She said, "Where have you been?" I just looked at her. I said, "Have you ever been to Catalina Island, Auntie?" She said, "You haven't changed. As a child you always had to see what was on the other side of the mountain." And I did, and that's what I'm still doing—because the only thing that keeps me going is gasoline!

Education

Journeys of another sort—from offhand jaunts to major expeditions—were undertaken by many who interpreted "keep busy" as a charge to the intellect:

Keep your mind busy. A person left to himself will lose it all.
—Woman, 57, 5

The important thing is to keep active, maintain an open mind with a lot of interest in things around you, keep intellectually active, too.
—Woman, 73, 4

For some that means nothing more than staying abreast of current events, remaining interesting by keeping interested:

Keep up on newspaper, local activities—stay interesting.
—Man, 61, 3

Keep yourself interested in all of life. Be aware of what is going on all over the world as well as at home and next door.
—Woman, 73, 11

But others nursed larger ambitions:

Take up a challenging study—learn a language or how to play the piano.
—Woman, 71, 11

Keep busy! I earned a second M.A. and am almost through with a doctorate—all since my husband died, and all while working full-time.
—Woman, 64, 8

Forty percent of our survey group were "attending a formal or informal education program," almost a third of them "regularly."

Courses for adults that did not lead to formal credentials like a degree proved the most popular:

> **Emily:** *I go to psychology classes three times a week. I don't think I need it, but I go there for the companionship and I like it.*
> **Syd:** *And it's an exchange of ideas.*
> **Q:** *How did you get to this psychology class?*
> **Emily:** *Oh, it's in the newspaper, and one friend will tell another and so forth.*
>
> *—Miami, #2*

Mental stimulation and social diversion—these are the twin reasons why many consider these programs to be such a productive use of their time:

> **Ida:** *Those free lectures and courses that you get from the different schools and the library, all those places, keep you going. Instead of sitting home and wondering, "Am I am going shopping at Macy's today or Loehmann's?"—you go spend an hour and a half there, and you come home enriched.*
>
> *—Miami, #2*

That's not to say, as she later explains, that even a course in psychology can't also have exact practical applications:

> **Ida:** *I was having trouble with a daughter-in-law—no matter how sweet I was to her, I somehow always rubbed her the wrong way. When I went to that free psychology course that Helen Rose gave—*
> **Peggy:** *Oh, I know her.*
> **Ida:** *She is fantastic, and I never missed a class. I opened my mouth all the time to ask questions until finally people said, "You're monopolizing the class!" I didn't care. I came there to learn, to air my problems, and it really helped me with my daughter-in-law, that course.*

As was mentioned earlier in this chapter, finance can often be on the menu, and so can sports:

> *Take as many courses as possible, on finances particularly, and anything else that interests you.*
>
> *—Woman, 65, 2*

Learn a new skill—both educational and a fun, recreation-type activity. I learned to play tennis through a tennis program in the community, also skiing, and joined a biking club. Also, courses in a local community college.

—Woman, 61, 12

Or you may be able to learn new things to do around the house—perhaps, like this woman, without even leaving it:

Obtain cable or satellite television for access to good *programs on the educational and inspirational networks. These are* so *rewarding during winter months, enabling one to "attend classes" on painting, sewing, cooking, home repair, gardening, history, etc.*

—Woman, 80, 4

Some seek out settings that cater expressly to older people:

Betty: I have found something quite wonderful here in Santa Monica, a college for seniors called Emeritus, which is an offshoot of Santa Monica College. And I have met many people in my courses because we have things in common. At the same time it's exciting, we're learning something.

—Los Angeles, #2

A well-known coordinator of services like these is Elderhostel, the nonprofit umbrella organization (mentioned in passing in the previous section) that enables people aged 60 and older to travel to universities and other sites here and abroad to take courses there (see "Resources"). Senior-citizen centers also typically sponsor educational events, and several survivors remark on how this purpose can humanize the uncongenial atmosphere that they say prevails at gatherings held for a purely social purpose:

Fay: I've gone a couple of times to these senior clubs—
Gladys: Oh, and it can be devastating!
Fay: I walked in there and I looked around and I said, "What am I doing here?" It wasn't my cup of tea.
Gladys: Well, it isn't mine either, Fay, but I go. I have been to several "singles" things. Hated it! Hated it!
Betty: That's why I find it much more satisfactory, when you want senior groups, to take courses. There you have people who are compat-

ible and learning something in common. And I never walk into the senior social clubs.

Gladys: *I've taken ten courses, and I haven't met anyone at a course group.*

Betty: *That's a matter of luck. Have you met anybody at the other groups, the social groups?*

Gladys: *No, I haven't.*

Betty: *With courses, at least you're learning something, you're growing inside.*

—Los Angeles, #2

Others, however—just as old—enjoy how going back to school can surround them with the young:

Take a class with younger people. Be a part of the fun—they can add a lot of joy to your life.

—Woman, 73, 8

Edith: *I went back to school full-time, post-graduate work, and that was the greatest thing in the world. The kids there were so alive and so laid back, and nothing bothered them: "This is life and accept it."*

—Boston, #1

Courses may let you hone old skills and talents to a new sharpness. Pat did—and look at the ripples it sent out into her social world at large:

I think it's important to find out what you were good at when you were younger and maybe pursue that. When it happened to me, my son said, "Mom, you used to like art" (I was a pen-and-inker). He said, "You haven't done anything like that for years. Why don't you try it?" He knew I wasn't a joiner, I don't like that. Maybe I'm selfish, but I don't even like volunteer work—I'm kind of a loner. So I joined the Americus College art class. It was wonderful. There were a lot of widows there and women with illnesses. But it was an ego-booster, and we made all kinds of things. And it's funny. I've sent out maybe two dozen Christmas cards, and from the ones that I bought, I got Christmas cards in reply. But from the ones that I drew, I got telephone calls.

—Los Angeles, #2

Or you may venture into areas for which you've never had the leisure, like this woman, who made them an avenue to an even bigger intellectual enterprise:

> *My way of coping involved getting busy with volunteer activities in libraries, art museums, etc., and taking courses I had never had time for when I was teaching. These activities tided me through the most difficult period; since then, I've turned to writing and have a first book coming out in the spring.*
>
> *—Woman, 68, 7*

And of course what you learn may be a useful adjunct to a job, paid or volunteer:

> *Even went back to college and got my MBA. Haven't done anything with that, but it does come in handy in all the volunteer jobs in which I am now involved.*
>
> *—Woman, 63, 11*

Learning may exert a powerful pull on you if your career, like hers, lay in teaching. Here is someone who joined what sounds like a model experiment (see ''Resources'') in letting you gladly do both in retirement:

> *Seek an occupation or interest that will deflect your thoughts from yourself. I have chosen a new field of study (history) somewhat related to my old field of specialization (languages and literatures) and frequently lecture on subjects in this field. The organization, the ''Institute for Retired Professionals'' sponsored by the New School for Social Research in New York, has been of great help to me by enabling me to pursue these studies. It offers opportunities to participate in study groups in a great variety of fields, and, above all, to meet people similarly placed as myself, two or three times a week. My own experience is shared by some 600 to 700 members of this particularly well-conceived rallying place for Senior Citizens, especially those among them who are widowed and lonely.*
>
> *—Woman, 85, 8*

And here is the other end of the spectrum of possibilities—Ann, who never finished college. We left her toward the end of the last chapter (page 142) after she had moved unhappily to California for the sake of her disabled husband's health and was trapped in an isolation so profound that her only companion was the dial tone in her phone. Then, suddenly, it was as if she had rediscovered her ability to act as an independent human being:

> *My husband could not do anything, and I was home with him, and it was a matter of constant running back and forth to the doctors, to the hospital emergency room. It was really a very bad time. After five years of it, the doctor said, "If you don't get out of the house, you're going to go bananas." I asked, "How can I go away? What if something happens while I'm away from home?" And he said, "It's going to happen whether you're there or not."*
>
> *And so one day I happened to come down to the lobby of our building, and there was a stack of schedules for classes at Chabot Community College. I picked one up and said, "Hmm." I had been taking all kinds of courses during a lifetime, but never for credit. I said, "Hm, maybe this is my lifesaver."*
>
> *So I called, and they said I had to come out. and pick up an application. I ran out, I picked it up, and I said, "I'll fill it out tomorrow, I'll send it in." And then I said to myself, "No, if you wait until tomorrow, you're not going to do it." I sat down right away, quick, filled it out, and the first thing the next morning, while my husband was still in bed, I ran over to Chabot and turned it in. They called me and I started school—two days a week, two and a half hours.*
>
> —San Francisco

That burst of decisiveness was richly rewarded—then and afterward:

> *I graduated from Chabot College about nine months after my husband died and I knew that, up there in his heavenly abode, it was a beautiful sunny day, he was looking down and he was smiling and he was saying "Great!" And from there—and this was my lifesaver—I went to Mills College and I got my degree. When everybody was sitting around, you know, when it was time to retire and do nothing, I got my degree!*
>
> *And really, I'm very proud of myself—because I did something because I wanted to do it. And my friends used to say, "Why are you doing this to yourself? Why are you beating your brains out? Why are you working so hard?" Because, I swear to you, it was not easy. And when I used to complain to my kids, my son would laugh and say, "You know, Mom, nobody ever promised you a rose garden, and you knew it was going to be tough. But it was something that you wanted to do."*

She then proceeded to get a job, something we turn to next.

A New Job: Paid or Volunteer

We have already heard survivors (both in Chapter 3—pages 118-122—and at the start of this one) elaborate on the truth of this axiom:

> *As my spouse said, "Your professional activity now is like insurance payments for a time you might have to live alone."*
>
> —*Woman, 69, 2*

But what about those who for one reason or another weren't carrying such coverage, whether in the form of a profession, a business, or just some sort of regular employment, gainful or otherwise? Quite a few were able to compensate:

> *I found the most comfort in working very hard at new jobs which required learning new skills (at first in "operations" at a TV station, later in dealing with students at a university as Intern Coordinator).*
>
> —*Woman, 68, 19*

Some managed with surprising speed:

> *I would advise a widow of suitable age to find voluntary or paid employment within four to six months after her spouse's death. New associations, a sense of being needed, a new avenue of respect—all help in the adjustment.*
>
> —*Woman, 75, 24*

Almost a quarter of a century later, she reports she's still drawing down a salary.

Another woman let only two months elapse:

> *I had to keep myself busy, and I decided after two months of widowhood to go to my local college and take courses enabling me to get a part-time job. It reopened enormous benefits—the friends, luncheons, etc.*
>
> —*Woman, 58, 8*

Her need to return to school for training, however, points up the hurdles that finding work (especially paid work) can put in the way of many survivors (especially women). Age may be one, as this woman sighs:

> *Work would be a great comfort if I were younger.*
>
> —Woman, 85, 18

Peggy wonders how she would handle widowhood if she had to face it today:

> *Of course when you're on in years and you lose your mate, it's very difficult to go out and get a job. If it had happened to me at this age now, I don't know how I would cope. But, when I was a young woman, the job was the answer to everything.*
>
> —Miami, #2

Regardless of age, many women may be stymied by having chosen homemaking as a career, although this was an obstacle Frieda shoved vigorously aside:

> *Too many in our generation didn't go into business. We stayed home and raised children. When our children grew up and left and our husbands died, we were left with nothing. Nothing to do but sit home and brood, and that's very bad. You've got to keep busy, you've got to do something. Go to work. Here I'm going to be 80 years old, I just retired three years ago, and I would be working today if my boss hadn't taken in a partner that I could not get along with. And he still wants me to come back to work.*
>
> —Miami, #1

The search may be a time-consuming affair even for those who aren't hampered by the stresses of being a survivor:

> *I was lucky to find a job about three months before my spouse's death. (It took six months to find a job.)*
>
> —Woman, 50, 3

Seeking a job can bruise one's self-esteem as much as finding one can be a salve to it. That was brought home to this woman, who nevertheless is determined to renew the efforts that were thwarted by a mastectomy shortly after her husband died:

> *Before this surgery, I had planned to find a job. At 55, in a college*

town, it is very difficult to find a job. It is an ego-bursting experience.
But I find it necessary to continue looking. I think a job will give me
a feeling of self-worth—pride in doing more than I am now.

—Woman, 55, 2

Despite these impediments, over a third of those surveyed logged
some time in paid employment after their spouses' deaths, and half of
this third had not been working when their spouses had died. This
woman, acting under grave financial duress, was among the latter:

Mine was not the usual widowhood experience. I was widowed with-
out warning at 43 with four sons 2 to 16 to educate, with only Social
Security and group life insurance for income (because of my hus-
band's uninsurability). So I had a desperate need for money. We had
just moved to a new university, far from old friends, so I was living
in an unfamiliar town with no close friends or relatives nearby.

I had never held a job before my husband's death, but the new
university where he had been a professor offered me a position. At
the cost of long hours, hard work, and incredible anxiety I succeeded
in building a twenty-three-year career.

—Woman, 68, 25

For those going into the job market for the first time or returning to
it, some books on grief contain virtual inventories of job-hunting
strategies, techniques, and aids, which of course include other books
solely devoted to job-hunting (see Bibliography). Here, we'll simply
set down the experiences of those who tried and succeeded. For
Isabel, it was much less nerve-wracking than it was for the woman
above—she likens it to ''going back to school'' in the broader sense:

I found that, as soon as my husband died, I started to look for a posi-
tion, though I hadn't worked all the time I was married. And I found
that getting engrossed in trying to work out something for myself and
to make a living almost had the effect of, well, going back to school.
It was good for me—put me in the business world, with new people,
away from the home, away from everything I had before. Because
my husband died a young man, he was about 50. And all my friends
had their husbands. So I felt I had to make a new life [pause]. Which
I did.

—New York, #1

This woman also made ''a new life'' pivot upon a new job:

Carve out "a new life." For financial and nonfinancial reasons I got a job that I find challenging, demanding, and rewarding. I have been working for a New York state senator for eighteen years. After three years of full-time, year-round work, I opted for session work for six months of the year. That is ideal. I have wonderful "new" friends at the capital and attend receptions and political functions. The six months I have off, I spend traveling and renewing my "old" friendships.
—Woman, 76, 20

As we've seen before, the payoffs of work can go far beyond the pay. Little more than a quarter of those in paid employment after their spouse's death said that they were motivated by ''mostly financial'' considerations; for another quarter it was ''mostly nonfinancial'' and for half ''a combination.'' Just human contact—nothing as ambitious as ''friendship''—was what made Loretta's job most precious to her, even though it was economic necessity that impelled her into it:

Loretta: I just went out to work.
Q: How old were you?
Loretta: When my husband died? Forty-nine and holding.
Q: Why did you go back to work?
Loretta: Well, I had a brand-new car, and we still had a mortgage on the home. The first thing I did was to sell the car, because I couldn't make payments on the car and the house. Then I went out to work, and it was a wonderful experience. I worked in the mall ten years until I retired and came to Leisure World.
Q: What did it give you, aside from the money?
Loretta: Well, it inspired you. You meet people and you don't think of yourself. You just went out and worked and met people. And being with the public—my job was always with the public—it just felt good. Just like now.
—Los Angeles, #1

Besides enlivening their days, work eases the nights of several:

I found working very helpful. Living alone, if your days are full, you are not as lonely at night.
—Woman, 71, 19

If you have meaningful work to do—and this includes volunteer work—you are fortunate because it can not only absorb you while you are at it but lets you return somewhat refreshed to your loneliness.
                                                                                                    —Woman, 72, 3

And it wards off self-pity and the allied evils:

Either work full time, part time—or volunteer. I am busier than I ever was before, and there is very little time left for feeling sorry for myself.
                                                                                                    —Woman, 69, 18

Were I not employed, I feel my answers to the questionnaire might be quite different. I am constantly active, too busy to be depressed.
                                                                                                    —Woman, 67, 2

Self-pity and depression can both be side effects of self-contempt, which the accountability inherent in any job can do wonders to neutralize:

I would suggest that some regular job either paid or volunteer be undertaken very soon, not necessarily for the money, but because one ought to feel needed and be responsible for—and to—someone as soon as possible.
                                                                                                    —Woman, 81, 12

The subject of how she went back to work lures Isabel into some outright boasting:

It was great, just getting dressed and out—I was very capable, I always took care of myself, I didn't look for others to do things for me.
                                                                                                    —New York, #1

And if you are one or the other of those compulsive characters—the workaholic or the perfectionist—a job can be something in which to exult:

Work!—more than you can ever get done. I am a worker—known as a "workaholic." I like to work; I am accustomed to working; I am the happiest when I am working. IT IS MY SALVATION.
                                                                                                    —Woman, 77, 3

Frieda: I worked until two or three years ago. I'd go back tomorrow, and my boss wants me back—at my age! Ever since I was a little kid, whatever I did had to be better than anybody else could do. If it was something I couldn't do well, I didn't bother with it at all.
Dorothy: You're a perfectionist.
Frieda: Yes!
Dorothy: That's terrible!
Frieda: No! I say the same to youngsters today, when they tell me, "Oh, in Florida they don't pay decent salaries, you only get paid like that in New York." I say, "If you're the best at your job, you're going to get paid as well here as you will anywhere." I was—and I was an old woman. Because I knew what I was doing, and my boss knew it.
—Miami, #1

If you are having trouble landing a full-fledged brand-new position, you can resort to some shortcuts. You can return to a previous line of work:

I returned to the University to renew my teaching certificate and obtained a job. Both my new husband and I believe our teaching helped in our rehabilitation (he was widowed also).
—Woman, 63, 22

If you lack the time or energy for full-time labor, you may be able to cut a job down to a suitable size:

I had no children at home at the time I was widowed. Taking a part-time position as a school librarian (my former profession) in a new environment was just great for me. I met new people and formed new friendships.
—Woman, 66, 10

Or you can pyramid part-time positions, like this woman, for whom time and energy were clearly not scarcities:

Keep very busy. I took two part-time jobs in addition to my regular one.
—Woman, 61, 12

Temporary-help agencies are often a ready source of such situations, although often, as with part-time work in general, the hours you must put in are not all that's diminished:

Keep busy—ideal would be a part-time job paying real *money.*
—*Woman, 60, 5*

But hourly compensation isn't the only possible arrangement:

Helping a friend who has her own tour company with group tours has been my light at the end of the tunnel. I am not paid a salary, but all of my expenses are paid. And this has given me an opportunity to travel and acquire some lovely new friends—many of whom are in my situation.
—*Woman, 59, 3*

And you may not need to leave home to get to the workplace:

Margaret: *I don't belong to any clubs, but I do work for the Associated Schools, I help them with their mailing lists. But I do that at home and earn money doing it. I'm very contented.*
—*Miami, #2*

Finally, as we've been hearing all along, an alternative to paid work is available:

I realize that I am fortunate to have rather special and meaningful work that I can still do at the age of 80—a freelance artist, designing, illustrating, and often writing books on botany. But I think that everyone can keep himself busy with some kind of serious occupation—there is always very useful volunteer work for retired people to do. It is the only way to escape the doldrums.
—*Woman, 80, 5*

This woman's friends seem to have left the doldrums behind:

Volunteer! I don't do as much as I feel I should and would like to, but my best role models (some much *older than I and in ill health) give hours of loving community service.*
—*Woman, 62, 12*

Age also posed no barrier to this woman; on the contrary, she feels rejuvenated:

My advice to widows is to work with and for others *in a capacity that gives you pleasure and a sense of fulfillment. Since my retirement in 1979 I have been active in volunteering—in creating educational programs in the public school in University City and working for "Probation and Parole" as a volunteer. I feel valued and fulfilled, and I feel that I am creating a place for myself which is satisfying and rewarding. I am 87 years old and feel much younger.*

—Woman, 87, 16

Like her, many turn to volunteering in retirement as a substitute for their old jobs:

I was fortunate in having a part-time position at the time of my husband's death and found the activity and contacts good for my morale. When I retired five years ago, I took up several volunteer activities (I had done volunteer work before).

—Woman, 75, 19

After a retirement-related move, being a volunteer helped ground this woman in her new community:

Continuing work on a part-time basis was very helpful for me. I am now retired and have moved away to be close to my sister and brother-in-law in another state, where doing work at a local hospital gives me a purpose in life.

—Woman, 73, 12

Many former teachers find volunteering an ideal way to prolong the pleasures of their vocation into retirement:

Kaye: One thing I find very important is to be around young children. So I volunteered with the Board of Education to teach reading. My first pupils were two brothers who didn't know when a sentence ended. They didn't even know what punctuation marks were. And they finished up with library cards! It was such a wonderful experience that I'm thinking seriously of starting again.

Q: Where did you do that?

Kaye: In the library. I didn't want to do it at my home, especially with what's going on with molestation [referring to a child-abuse case]—I'm being very practical.

Q: Do the schools have any programs like that now?

Elaine: Yes, they need teachers' assistants.

Margaret: In Michigan, they have a grandmothers' program in a

school where my husband's Auntie—who is, I think, 90—works with
children.

—*Los Angeles, #2*

Volunteering demands more of some than working for pay ever
did:

Someone who is not working should volunteer for church, Grey Bears,
senior citizen center, etc., and become very active. I now have time
to use my business experience as church financial secretary and am
very active in A.A.U.W., volunteer at local museum, am project man-
ager of an art study group and President of local Daughters of Ameri-
can Revolution. I've never been so busy even when I worked.

—*Woman, 76, 8*

"Community service and/or political activity" was named as a
pastime "often" pursued by 19% of the survey group and "sometimes" by another 24%. They cite the same benefits as those with
paid jobs do:

Volunteer—*in whatever field gives you pleasure. This is a super way*
to make friends and feel needed.

—*Woman, 75, 2*

Keep busy. I work at Moody Keswick Bible Conference in St. Peters-
burg thirteen weeks (January-April) as a hostess. I don't have time to
think of myself—just try to please our guests.

—*Woman, 60, 3*

I found doing volunteer work (hospital library and gift shop and tak-
ing blood pressures for the American Heart Association) a release
from depression—and it gives me a feeling of self-worth.

—*Woman, 78, 5*

The Epilogue opens with an impressive instance of the powers just
described.

But volunteer work often carries with it a dimension that paid jobs
usually lack:

Get involved in volunteer work. You will then be with people. Most important, you get great satisfaction, knowing that you have helped others less fortunate.

—Woman, 68, 10

Find a place to serve.

—Woman, 79, 20

This woman had found such a place in her career and has rediscovered it in her retirement:

I find volunteer work interesting (meeting new people) and challenging (learning a new type of work and service to others). As a teacher, I was a public servant to children. Now, with hospital volunteer work, I enjoy being a servant to adults.

—Woman, 67, 3

For these two, it is a servitude that liberates them from the confines of the self:

"Doing good." There's nothing better. Certainly most women want to serve some larger purpose than self-indulgence. I'm in a book club, a writing club, assist in an adult scripture course, am a volunteer at a nursing home, help support a young divorcee. (Worse than being widowed, I think!)

—Woman, 70, 4

My advice? Remember all the good times and pluses—don't become a "poor widow woman" expecting special consideration, but look around and find a way to make some contribution to your community.

—Woman, 76, 10

The possibilities range from immersing oneself in the past to agitating for political and social change:

I serve as treasurer of the County Historical Society and contribute local historical and genealogical articles for publication.

—Woman, 75, 7

I became active in community organizations which advocate security, housing, and health coverage for vulnerable citizens, young and old.

—Woman, 59, 2

Some gravitated toward what they already knew:

> *For people with time on their hands, volunteer. Choose services that you enjoy doing and can do without a lot of training time.*
>
> —*Woman, 78, 2*

> *My husband was an artist, and we both were interested in art; so naturally I turn to the art museum to work wherever they need me. I have friends who are enjoying the hours they spend as volunteers in the library, the hospital, working with foreign students, helping people learn to speak English. The list is endless and offers many exciting opportunities for helping others.*
>
> —*Woman, 74, 4*

Others exploited their chances to get into something new:

> *Volunteer in some field you are interested in or would like to know.*
>
> —*Woman, 64, 2*

> *If you don't have outside hobbies and interests, force yourself to develop them. Volunteer!*
>
> —*Woman, 70, 8*

And one activity has a way of proliferating into many:

> *The first few months after my husband's death I was devastated—ill, lonely, and bored. But upon the loving advice of my children, I volunteered for service at the local hospital. Gradually this work became all-absorbing, I made many new friends, I felt useful again, and later I was asked to take on more and more leadership roles. My days are now filled with many interesting tasks.*
>
> *This volunteer work led me to take a more active role in my church and in other civic organizations. Now I serve on three governing boards in my city. I say this modestly, for such activities have meant much more to me than to them. In summary, I would urge all widows and widowers to become active in some organization—health care, church, conservancy, tutoring, school, hospice—and your personal rewards will be many.*
>
> —*Woman, 72, 4*

This is not to say that every volunteer job is a picnic. Taking

pleasure in the task is a must, but, as Peggy illustrates, that pleasure
can run deeper than the superficial sort:

> *I have worked for the last four years as a volunteer with the mental
> health association, in a school right here in the area. I am what they call
> a "Listener" for children who have problems. One day a week I see
> about seven children. And they come to me, and some talk and some
> don't. You have to work awfully hard to get them to open up and tell
> you about the problem.*
>
> *Q: Why are you doing this?*
>
> *Peggy: I do it because it makes me feel that I am worthwhile—I'm
> serving a purpose.*
>
> *Ann: Right. But I have to be around happy faces. I take on another
> person's sorrows.*
>
> *Peggy: This is not a happy thing I do.*
>
> —Miami, #2

Although securing a paid position is usually harder, obtaining a
satisfactory volunteer one may also entail some persistence—and
perhaps the overcoming of some reluctance:

> *Gladys: I have been looking, but I felt like I was chasing my tail. My
> volunteer work is fund-raising for an organization. But I have a need
> to help people and I haven't been able to fill that need.*
>
> *Kaye: There's a local number for your senator's office, and you can
> call up and ask them what there is or tell them what you need.*
>
> *Gladys: And then they tell you to call somebody else. Like I called
> three or four organizations, and I'm not being negative. As my
> psychologist says, "Don't say you can't." But I have called—and
> then they all send me to a bad neighborhood. Well, I don't want to
> go to a bad neighborhood.*
>
> *Fay: Have you tried the RSVP office in Santa Monica?*
>
> *Gladys: RSVP? I don't know that.*
>
> *Fay: The senior volunteer program. They have a lot of different
> volunteer jobs to do, like assisting children in the classrooms.*
>
> *Gladys: But I'm not in Santa Monica, I'm in West LA, so I won't
> know what's going on—*
>
> *Fay: If you sign up with them, you get this little booklet each month that
> lists all the different volunteer positions that are open.*

Kaye: You would be good for answering phones when KCPT has their drive.
Gladys: Well, that's once a year.
Kaye: Yes, I know, but multiply that with other things, and before you know it, you have things to look forward to.
—Los Angeles, #2

If not "negative," Gladys is unquestionably ambivalent, because she raises every possible objection she can. Perhaps, in spite of her obvious interest, she is still shying away from making the commitment that even the simplest volunteer job demands. And of course volunteering requires giving up as well as giving—forgoing the opportunity to make some money, although Hannah was one of the rare people who are able to have it both ways:

I also had been a volunteer at Mt. Sinai, and when my husband died, they called up and said, "You know, life must go on. Can you come back?" I said, "Yes, but I cannot afford to be a volunteer." And I was one of the few they took in and made a paid worker. I was very, very fortunate. I had a position there for about fourteen years, and for those years it was my life. And I got such an education there! Because, on weekends, I was the only one that spoke Yiddish. It was fractured, but I understood them and I made myself understood. And the stories I heard were hair-raising.
—Miami, #2

And this woman, presumably an expert, describes how volunteering can apparently be a springboard to paying work:

Find a genuine outlet for your abilities and interests through activities that stimulate and compel an awareness of the needs of others. My work today is as director of the Retired Senior Volunteer Program in our county, which means I'm always helping others over 60 find meaningful ways to spend their hours in selfless service. Over five hundred of these persons during fifteen years have returned to paid employment because of a renewed sense of self gained through the right assignment.
—Woman, 80, 25

While many say they cannot get their fill of volunteering, a few, it must be admitted, groused about having had a surfeit of it:

Yvette: I volunteered for everything. And I would advise widows not to do it, because I'm still trying to get out of some of it. I just jumped into everything. My husband had been ill, going downhill for two years, and I was very much tied down and couldn't go any place. So I was free. And I got into too many things.

—San Francisco

At first I volunteered for everything—just to keep busy. Church, Meals on Wheels, Operation Santa Claus, Hospital Guild, Widowed Persons, Salvation Army, packing baskets for Thanksgiving and Christmas. Then it got to be too much. I found I was just running to keep busy. You can sometimes be more lonely with people.

—Woman, 74, 3

Some tell you in particular to beware of "work" that counterfeits the real thing:

Failing a paying job, volunteer work—not make-work—can be useful as therapy.

—Woman, 62, 8

Always have a positive purpose in everything you do. Just "busywork" will not accomplish anything—grief and sorrow will creep through.

—Woman, 77, 3

And as this woman, a physician, reminds us, you can expect too much of even the most meaningful job:

From personal experience, all I can say is that work is a good diversion, but certainly not a cure.

—Woman, 66, 3

The volunteer activities that most keenly gratify many seem to be those that re-create family relationships:

Elaine: I'm in the UCLA host-family program—when foreign students come in, you become an extended family. UCLA keeps lists of those you might be interested in and calls you and says, "I have a student coming from Japan or China or India," or whatever.
Gladys: Do they stay with you?
Elaine: No, they do not stay with me. However, it becomes an extended

family relationship. And I always ask for a family with children, because, with children, you become sort of the grandma. It's a very interesting cultural and social exchange. I've had students from various parts of the world.

Gladys: *What do you do for them?*

Elaine: *First off, when they come in, some of them don't speak English very well. So I invite them to my home for dinner and we talk. You see, before that, you correspond and see what their needs are. Then you take them down to UCLA and show them where to register, where the Health Building is, where to market, where to bank, you help them with housing. You become an extended family, and you observe their birthdays, holidays—their holidays are not the same as ours many times.*

Gladys: *What do you do for transportation?*

Elaine: *Well, I drive. And of course most of them end up with a car if they're here for any length of time, particularly if they have a family. I usually ask for someone with a family. I've had single people, but it becomes difficult unless you have single people to introduce them to.*

—Los Angeles, #2

We've seen people derive the same sort of satisfaction from working with young children, and Fay acts as surrogate family for the elderly:

Fay: *I do telephone reassurance in a program.*

Q: *What's that?*

Fay: *You call the homebound people who are alone. They look forward to the call, someone to talk to. They don't have family.*

—Los Angeles, #2

Marguerite, who at 75 has been tending a an 85-year-old cousin crippled by a foot ailment, was spurred to do so by the dissolving of the dependencies within her immediate family, the result of maturation as well as death; and her daughter has set out to emulate her:

I think you're only happy when you're helping somebody else. I mean, really, seriously happy. Because now my kids don't need me. My youngest grandchild just started at UC at Davis, and his sister's already there. And my daughter, who is now in her mid-40s, decided it was too much for her, losing all of them—because she always had a family of kids in her house. So now she's going to school to get her master's in social work. And that's the way it goes.

—San Francisco

Nora seizes on this thought and wonders whether the inability to do what Marguerite is doing can't shorten our own lives:

Nora: Do you think the key is to be needed? It seems we are all expressing the same thing.

Marguerite: That's it! If there is a need, yes, if you can do this volunteer work.

Nora: I think all this comes from having been needed in your family, bringing them up, and all at once the need is no longer there. You miss your kids, you miss your husband, and nobody seems to need you. I seem to be getting this picture from other senior citizens like me—not anybody wanting you, really needing you. I think that's what makes us pass on, too, sometimes—a lack of involvement with others.

Just as the family lets us triumph biologically over death, so helping others may let us do the equivalent within our extended family at its largest:

We can all try to behave like responsible people. We live together in a world where we all know death in some form or another. It gives us common understanding. We can build on that and honor our lost one(s) by helping each other.

—Woman, 70, 14

Nora thinks so too. We ended Chapter 2 with her farewell promise to her husband (page 87), and we'll resume her story here:

We were the old-fashioned type. My husband did not want me to work, not for money, so I did most of my working in the community—PTA, church—where I did nothing but drama. You weren't supposed to do that at my age, you know. You didn't do theater in our community, in the black community, if you were to be considered the best sort. But that is what I was born to do and I did it—at the PTA, with the mothers, with the students, until my kids grew up.

And when they were grown up and married, then I went for it. I am the founder and executive director of the Black Repertory Group. I'm sure that you've been reading about us over the years. And all of those years I spent working, trying to get that building up, and it's up now. You can pass there now and close your eyes and you think it's a dream, but it's there. We'll be opening it Sunday. And our minister asked, "Well, Nora, how did you get to be such a strong matriarch?"—or whatever. I said, "I knew that if I hadn't done it, He wasn't going to let me in those Pearly Gates when I got there" [laughter].

—San Francisco

She then reflects on another reason for her tenacity:

So that's it. I don't think I'm going to stop, though—it's impossible now to stop being busy. I don't think I deserve all the praise that I get now from the community or what have you. I really don't. It's just something you have to do. I'm sure all of you know that there's something you have *to do. You know, you can't just wait to die. You're going to have to keep on doing it, till all at once—here comes The Guy! He's gonna come and getcha. I don't think we need to sit and wait for him. Let* him *find* us *somewhere. That's what I think about being a widow.*

Chapter 5

Being with Others: "It Helps You and Them"

Ruth: When you become a widow you get out of the mainstream of life for a while. Sometimes you're pushed out and sometimes you get out on your own. You want the time to think over what you're going to do, let yourself mend a little for what went on before. And then you have to get back again. That's the hardest part. You don't know how. That's where you need a lot of help.

—*Miami, #2*

We closed the last chapter with some thoughts from survivors about helping others. In this one they're talking about help for yourself, in particular the emotional sustenance given to you—or denied you—by others as you go through the process of reordering your relations with them. As Ruth suggests, for many that process seems to take the shape of a withdrawal and then a re-engagement. Many survivors are utterly unprepared for how dramatically the death can alter their relations with the living, especially with those who matter most—family and friends. Perhaps you are the one to initiate these changes, "getting out on your own." Perhaps others do it for you, and—in one of the commonest and cruelest realizations of many survivors—you are "pushed out." In either case, you may need this prescription:

Get back into the flow of life; being with others helps!

—*Woman, 64, 2*

That help should theoretically be within close reach:

No one can know exactly what you are feeling, but relatives and friends can be a tremendous help in overcoming some of the loneliness. They also help to get you out and into the mainstream again.

—*Woman, 82, 3*

Their aid, moreover, should work to the advantage of both parties:

Let your friends and family help. It helps them and you.

—*Woman, 55, 3*

You especially, of course. These two claim it was what pulled them through:

I have found that, without family and friends, I would not have been able to make it.

—*Woman, 63, 2*

The shared grief and love of children, relatives, and friends is crucial to survival, especially in the first year.

—*Woman, 71, 9*

And to many survivors, that support was given without stint:

Ellen: *If you are in fortunate circumstances, every hand is out to you in compassion and help. And I had a lot of that, a lot of help, and I think that sustains you and carries you through.*

—*Boston, #2*

Indeed, some never had to leave the mainstream at all:

In my case friends and relatives rallied to my support 100% of their own volition. I cannot stress enough the importance of close friendships and strong family ties.

—*Woman, 78, 5*

In their social world, their interconnectedness with others never unravels:

I have a large and supportive family and understanding friends. From them I got all those things that one needs to sustain one of life's greatest losses. And I will in turn provide support for others in this network as they may need it.

—*Woman, 59, 3*

And for some without family to call upon, friends alone were enough to pick up the slack:

> *People our age do not have parents who serve as a support group. It is the friends of thirty years who are family. Often doing things for new and old friends takes the place and fills the need of "doing" for the lost spouse and children who have left home.*
>
> *—Woman, 57, 2*

At best the aid offered by family and friends transcends companionship and moral support, valuable as they are. If the crux of coming to terms with loss—as we'll argue in Chapter 7—is gaining a new sense of the continuity of time and our place in it, then others can help in ways of which they aren't even conscious:

> *Allow family and close friends to help you in beginning to look forward to new challenges while holding close to memories.*
>
> *—Woman, 68, 20*

This may grant you a new perspective on those people as well. Some sturdily maintain that old relationships have stayed exactly as they were:

> *Remember your kids are still your kids and your friends are still your friends.*
>
> *—Woman, 72, 7*

But others are surprised and pleased that they are beginning to see them from a new and perhaps a more discerning angle:

> *A friend told me that the loss of my husband, in time, would allow me to be more perceptive as to my children and friends and my relationship with them. This has been true for me. I am now able to "see" relationships in a very different light. This gift has helped me deepen old friendships and start new ones. I still have a long way to go.*
>
> *—Woman, 63, 3*

So some were able to obey this simple directive right away:

> *Let your friends and relatives help you. Most of them are only a phone call away and looking for a way to help, if you let them know*

what you need.

—Woman, 82, 3

But for one reason or another, others can't pick up that phone. Some, as we'll see in detail soon enough, lay the blame elsewhere:

You lose a lot of friends and relatives from whom you would expect support.

—Woman, 68, 2

To others, however, the cause seems to lie within themselves, leaving them to puzzle their way out of this paradox:

And when I most felt in need of help, I found myself least able to seek it.

—Woman, 57, 3

The ambivalence with which many people greet their need for practical advice, which we examined in Chapter 3, multiplies tenfold when the need is for emotional support. We can become mired in fears that range from a terror of rejection to a dread of dependency. Elaine didn't banish the latter without a struggle:

I'm supposed to be the strong one in the family. If anybody needs anything, they come to me. But you have to learn that, just as you like to help someone, someone else may like to help you. And if you've been a very independent person all your life, it's very difficult to change.

—Los Angeles, #2

So difficult was it for Sylvia that she had to turn to help of the professional variety (the subject with which we'll close this chapter):

Q: You've found a psychologist. OK. What brought you to that, and how is that going? Would you recommend it to other people?
Sylvia: Yes, absolutely—to anyone who is more of an introvert, who finds it difficult to go outside of herself to other people. It helped me to deal with it.
Q: How do you go about finding one? Ask your doctor?
Sylvia: I went to this psychologist because my daughter had just gotten her Ph.D. and had said, "Syl, do you want me to take time off from work and come home? Or are you going to get some help [laughter]?" Well,

*needless to say, Daughter doesn't have to come running home to
Mama—because Mama's always taken care of everybody else.*

*So I went, and he interviewed me. We sat there and we talked, and
he asked, "Why are you here?" And I said, "I'm not really sure why.
My daughter seems to think that perhaps I could use a little help."
And he said, "Do you want me to help you?" I said, "I beg your
pardon?" He said, "Well, you have to decide you want help and
you want me to help you. And then I have to decide if I want to accept
you." And I looked at this man as though he were out of his head.
He said, "So, first things first. Do you want me to try to help you?"
And I said, "Are you willing to accept me?" He said, "Uh-uh, first
things first." And I want you to know I almost choked on it. But that
was the beginning. I had to say, "I need help and I want you to help
me." And then he said, "Yes, I will take you on."*

　　　　　　　　　　　　　　　　　　　　　　　—Los Angeles, #2

She then tells how she did in fact choke on confiding it to her
friends earlier:

Q: Can you share why that's so hard to say?

Sylvia: Because I'm not accustomed to saying I need help.

Q: I see some nodding heads.

*Sylvia: I find it easier to stay in the house and, perhaps, have people
say, "Oh, she's become so aloof," or, "She doesn't seem to care,"
you know, rather than to admit—*

Sara: You're used to giving rather than getting.

*Sylvia: I'm used to people coming to me. I'm not used to going to
other people. Everyone said, "Syl, if you need anything at all, please
call, please call, please call." But I'd say, "Yeah, after a while, they
haven't been calling so much." Or "They haven't called at all." Or
whatever. But [pointing to herself] it was me—Sylvia never lifted
the phone. I wouldn't even have had to say I needed help. If I had
called, if they'd heard my voice, they would have been there. So I found
it hard to accept, but it is true, I have to take responsibility for some
of these things that we are talking about.*

Her words are suffused with the uneasy mix of emotions that may be
stirred up by the prospect of "going outside of yourself," especially
for a self-styled introvert. Besides risking your independence, you are
courting the possibility, no matter how slim, of a rebuff. Perhaps it
was a fear of the latter more than the former that was edging her into

self-pity by whispering to her that her failure to take action was really the fault of others.

So take heed of Sylvia's example as we watch friends and families who seem to fall short of expectations. Some indeed do so, but others may be reacting to your reluctance to take the lead. By holding back you may be retreating:

> *Having been married over fifty years and with an established family, I am conscious of the fine line between independence and dependence, and I think the answer is very honest communication. The temptation to withdraw is very strong, especially at first, when everything is new and strange and frightening and yet is so unreal. My most important advice is to keep the lines open with family and friends and accept the loving support that is offered.*
> *—Woman, 79, 6*

This woman assures you,

> *Don't panic. There are many people waiting to help you.*
> *—Woman, 70, 4*

But they may just keep on waiting unless you make your wants known:

> Actively *seek help from relatives and friends. Too many well-meaning people say, "Call me if you need me," without specifically offering anything. The widow/er must* ASK.
> *—Woman, 67, 10*

A hazard naturally accompanies such a willingness to ask: that you'll get some evasive or inept answers back—or no answers at all. This chapter will present some cases which may convince you that the side for the negative wins hands-down in the debate over how open you should be. (Chapter 1—pages 18-22). But we'll see opennness lavishly reciprocated too. And even the most reserved of survivors may not be able to escape being subjected to sympathy that strikes them as awkward or just plain obtuse—like formal condolences that go awry.

Condolences

''Condoling'' literally means ''grieving with,'' but attempts at it are notorious for flying wide of the mark:

> *Participation in a widows' group would have been most helpful if there had been one available nearby. Just being with people who have gone through the same is comforting. Friends try to help with ''I know what you're going through . . . .'' But they really don't if they haven't lost a loved one.*
>
> *—Woman, 71, 6*

Books on grief rank that sentiment high on their lists of the favorites of maladroit comforters, along with two others at which Sylvia lashes out in the Prologue (pages 7-8)—''Be strong! and ''How well you're handling it!'' Some react by valuing only the sympathy, no matter how commonplace, of someone with the same credentials as their own:

> *One of the best things that were said to me was in a note from another widow: ''You won't always feel this bad. Time will dull the ache.''*
>
> *—Woman, 82, 24*

Lil fled into the company of other widows precisely because it gave her a refuge from *any* expressions of concern from those who weren't survivors:

> *I had a friend who lost her husband and she said, ''Why don't you join one of these widows' and widowers' clubs?'' And I did—just to have a social occasion when you get away from the family and friends. They'd all say, ''Gee, I feel so sorry, how are you making out?'' And then you'd feel worse when you got home.*
>
> *—Boston, #2*

What galls her in particular seems to be pity—a variety of sympathy that, with its overtones of detachment, strikes many survivors as degrading, more suitable for beggars than the bereaved.

We'll hear more about the pros and cons of associating primarily with other survivors, but we should point out that hard-and-fast rules no more govern condolences than they do any other corner of our subject. Fear, and the strain of trying to place an extreme human experience in a safe social contēxt, lead many more people to bungle attempts at fellow feeling than callousness does. In trying to convey how they really feel, they may know how mechanical they sound—as this woman did in responding to them:

> *To get through the early days and weeks, I rehearsed again and again saying many of the things I knew I would have to say to people, until some of the pain was gone and I had at least a semblance of control.*
>
> —Woman, 68, 8

Some survivors do draw strength from the ceremony of exchanging condolences, as this man did, despite some twinges of exasperation:

> *I found it personally therapeutic to answer with short notes the hundreds of messages of consolation I received after her death. (Of course, it was* also *a grind and a bore.)*
>
> —Man, 67, 2

And if a message strikes you as especially ill-conceived or heavy-handed, bear in mind that it may have scored with someone else. Here is a woman who's told "How well you're handling it!"—and who positively glows:

> *I have received so much encouragement and so many expressions of faith from a multitude of supporters. They did not dwell on my sorrow and grief—they freely expressed their confidence, without exception, in my ability to accept my loss and carry on. Not just at the moment—it is still going on. "We are so proud of you—we knew you would do it," in every letter and note.*
>
> —Woman, 77, 3

Words never spoken, moreover, may do far more damage than words misguided:

> *Educate friends and associates to keep the deceased's name current. To never hear anyone mention the name makes it seem he or she never existed. Nothing can be more cruel for the widowed.*
>
> —Woman, 64, 6

Books on grief bear her out and contend that the most effective consolation can come from people who simply share their memories of the spouse with the survivor. In Chapter 7, we'll look more closely at how memories may evolve from hurtful to helping. Although Lee found hers hard to face at first, Frieda plunged right into hers on her own when her friends hung back:

> **Frieda:** *A lot of my friends used to be afraid to speak to me about Arthur, and I would speak to them about him because it made it much easier for me. To this day, I feel as though Arthur is in the next room, because I think of him constantly and I speak of him constantly.*
> **Lee:** *Later on, it's easier, but not when it happens. When it happens, you choke up when you mention the name.*
> **Frieda:** *Yes, but I was still speaking of him. And a friend would start talking and then hesitate.*
> **Lee:** *Yes, because they feel strange. . . .*
> **Frieda:** *But I would speak. I would mention his name.*
> **Lee:** *I think your memories are too fresh when it first happens, and that's why you can't say anything.*
> **Frieda:** *I think it's the thing that got me out of it.*
>
> —*Miami, #1*

Frieda's conviction that she was rescued by her own volubility brings us back again to the reputation of talk itself as a survivor's best restorative—and to the corollary that the best condolers may be those who keep quiet much of the time:

> *If possible, take a trusted friend with you in the journey from your own seeming death back to life. Talking seems to help, and people will follow your lead.*
>
> —*Woman, 69, 2*

> *Tensions build up, and talking is good. Let ''up'' friends help. A good listener is very helpful; advisers or ''downers''—no.*
>
> —*Woman, 66, 21*

Lee, who we just saw was loath to utter her husband's name, nevertheless stresses how much talking did for her—and for someone else:

> *I think you need someone to talk to—someone who will listen and not give you any answers because there aren't any answers. Just someone to listen, so you can get all the little things that you think about out into words.*

Two years after my husband died, in the complex that we lived in, there was a man whose wife died very suddenly. She was not really a friend, but, of all the people in the complex, he called me and said he thought I was the only one who could understand what he was going through. He came to my apartment, and he talked for about three and a half hours. I didn't have very much to say, just let him get all the things off his chest.

—Miami, #1

And she ratifies the standard wisdom about improving our interior well-being—that we can do it best by bringing what is *in* there *out*:

Thinking of something and saying it out loud are two different things. When you get your thoughts really out into words, it's better for you than just thinking them. That's why everyone needs somebody that they can talk to. It's not easy for the listener, really, but it does you an awful lot of good—more than anything else, I think.

Of course, the patience of even the most receptive listener can be exhausted faster than you'd like, and so perhaps these cautions are in order:

Be prepared for some family members and friends to feel you should be adjusted to widowhood after just a few months.

—Woman, 64, 3

Don't expect to "get over" this in a matter of weeks or wonder why you're not "on top" as soon as people seem to expect you to be.

—Woman, 55, 2

In fact, getting over it, as we'll see in Chapter 7, may never come to pass at all (getting on top of it is another matter). In any event, this woman didn't hesitate to set such friends straight:

It takes time to get over the grief, and do not let your friends tell you differently, because they have not been through it. It took me three years before I snapped back to normal.

—Woman, 69, 8

But if you level with your friends like that, be aware also that you may be making unreasonable demands on them:

Don't expect others to continue mourning as you do; they have their own lives to get on with.

—Woman, 72, 3

Don't expect your family and friends to turn their life upside down for a long time, just because yours has been.

—Woman, 45, 2

Finally, regardless of whether condolences helped or hurt you, you can console yourself with the thought that you can now turn that experience entirely to the benefit of others:

Remember how you felt and the kind things others did for you that made you feel better, and do these for others when their time comes. Also, avoid saying the things that many say when somebody dies—that you didn't like to hear and were not helpful to you.

—Woman, 62, 3

Family

An adage holds that happy families are all alike, whereas unhappy families are each unhappy in its own way. Perhaps we have two examples here:

After a very good marriage, the loss was devastating. It was probably easier for me to adjust because my family all lived around me. I have three grown children and three grandchildren. We were always a close-knit family and still are; also my mother, sister, and brothers live close by. If it weren't for my children, grandchildren, mother, brothers, and sister, I might have had a very difficult time adjusting.

—Woman, 62, 4

Marilyn: *I have an added problem—my mother lives downstairs from me and, as I said, my father died six months afterwards. My daughter and my father had a very special relationship. My father was stone deaf, but he could hear my daughter when she whispered, it was really incredible. Losing him on top of losing her father did a terrible job on her. And my mother is a very outspoken woman and would say things to this man I was dating. When he would come in the house, I would think, "Oh my God, she is going to do it again!"*

So I had both of them to cope with and sometimes I would just lose it all and I'd say, "Leave me alone!" I would actually start screaming—

and it's not like me—and I'd say, "Please leave me alone, let me get on with my life. You're stifling me, you're killing me actually, leave me alone!" And it's hard, because then they start crying and then you feel, "Oh God, what have I done?"

So it's very hard, there are so many things that are hard when you lose someone, so many things go wrong . . . afterward.

—*Boston, #2*

In placid generalities, the first woman tells how four generations are cooperating to buoy her up; in anguished details, Marilyn recounts how mother and daughter seem to be conspiring to drag her down.

You might object that some obvious special factors are producing the friction in Marilyn's household. The impact of her father's death on all of them has of course compounded that of her husband's; her friendship with a man has keyed up tensions not only with her mother but probably with her daughter as well (more about this in the next chapter); and—maybe the worst irritant, in your view—she's living with her relatives instead of just having them close by. All these ingredients obviously exacerbate the situation. But the mournful bafflement with which Marilyn surveys it and her response to it—and she is perhaps the most self-aware and self-possessed person in a group full of people with these qualities—may be rooted in an exceedingly simple fact. Happy or unhappy, families can be as variable and unpredictable as individual human beings. And she's certainly right about the consequences: instead of strengthening an understanding we thought we'd reached with these central figures in our lives, the death of a spouse can subvert it deeply.

This section will scan a few of the ways things can "go wrong . . . afterward"—and go right as well. But once more, the usual proviso: no universals and no absolutes. Marilyn's woes may appear to vindicate the byword of a good many survivors:

Never move in with any relative or child.

—*Woman, 76, 8*

It's gospel among some who otherwise thrive in being around them:

Visiting my children several times a year, and traveling with them sometimes, has helped. I would never want to live full-time with any of them. I don't mind living alone.

—Woman, 77, 4

Living near (not with) family and grandchildren, I enjoy all the children's sports, games, school projects, etc.

—Woman, 72, 9

Others with more mixed feelings wince at the idea of even being near, much less with:

Ruth: *I have one son in Alaska and one in California. When my husband died, they expected me to pick myself up and go—*
Peggy: *Come live with them?*
Ruth: *Out to California to be near them. I said, "No, this is where my home is. You want to see me? You're very welcome, I love you. But here is where I live."*
Peggy: *Well, I ended up with one in Dallas and the other in California. So it's a twice-a-year deal: I go there once, they come here once, we talk on the telephone every week. I don't think that's any ideal for a normal relationship between parents and children.*
Ruth: *In some ways it's much easier on you.*
Peggy: *Sure it is. I don't know what's going on there that's bad. They only tell me the nice things.*
Ruth: *Every time I go out there, I feel that if I were living close by, I'd always be butting in and saying things that I shouldn't.*
Peggy: *You can get into trouble that way, talking out of turn.*
Ruth: *I know, but when I feel myself ready to say something, I just stop, because I figure, "Well, I'll be going home next week, let's keep it this way."*

—Miami, #2

And much as she hates living alone, Hannah, who has been at loggerheads with a daughter for years, is appalled by the thought of having to live with her and her family:

So far I've never come to them for help. I'm not a kid. But I would never live *with them. Never!*

—Miami, #2

It's not anathema to others, though, if only for sanctuary during the initial shock:

> **Lil:** *I used to get up in the morning and say, "This is a bad dream, it never happened," till my daughter said, "You can't stay there by your-self, you've got to go live with me." And I stayed with her six months and said, "What am I doing here? I want to go home." Wouldn't you?*
>
> *—Boston, #2*

This woman gratefully let relatives come to her:

> *I had excellent support from my family. A cousin stayed with me for three months. My sister and two children stayed with me for over a year. The house was always full, and lots of conversation helped the days pass.*
>
> *—Woman, 59, 12*

Quite a few traded a life alone for sharing quarters with relatives, even at the price of some domestic disarray and discord:

> **Margaret:** *First my son came down from up North to live with me. Then my ex-daughter-in-law died, and her husband really didn't want my grandson living with him—it was interfering with his life. And he just dumped him on our doorstep last April. So I've got my son and my grandson, and my house is a mess [laughing]. They've never really settled in. But I guess that's the way I've always lived—in a turmoil. I don't know if it will ever stop. It beats being lonely, though, because I'm a mother hen—I just like to do for others.*
>
> *—Los Angeles, #2*

> *A niece who had lived with us since she was three years old (we had no children of our own) came home after I had lived alone for two years, bringing her husband and two teenage daughters with plans to add to the house and live separately. The wing did not materialize, and we are crowded—two strong-minded women under one roof. The situation is not ideal but better than living alone, and I am content to put up with inconveniences to stay in our home on a 140-acre farm. Things don't stay as shipshape as I'd like, but it's a challenge. I could write a book that would be unbelievable. But enough!—I'm sure you get the picture.*
>
> *—Woman, 86, 8*

Some adapted quite easily. Besides flourishing among the rest of her progeny, this woman has apparently settled into harmonious housekeeping with a son:

> *My four children and their spouses have been supportive in every way. I know, without them, I would have had to ask for assistance in all business matters. My single son and I enjoy sharing the expense and upkeep of a house together, and this makes it possible for me to continue my "life profession" of being a homemaker. My married children, their spouses, and grandchildren visit frequently, and I visit them. We all enjoy cultural and recreational activities together.*
>
> *—Woman, 69, 2*

Syd is furnishing a home to a daughter and son-in-law in their retirement:

> *I was married fifty four and a half years, and it was a very happy marriage. We had one child. My daughter and I, we've always been friends—we consider each other our best friends. And she has a husband who is not only a son-in-law to me but a son. Now they're retiring, they're coming to live with me in the home where I've been alone for the past four years.*
>
> *—Miami, #2*

This man's feat is one that folklore deems impossible:

> *Her widowed mother lives with me, and we support each other psychologically to an extent.*
>
> *—Man, 68, 2*

And, lest you assume these ventures succeeded because the survivors all apparently stayed on their home turf and therefore retained some measure of command, here is one who didn't:

> **Margaret:** *My daughter and my son, who lived in Florida, said, "Retire early and come down." So I retired at 64 instead of 65, and now I live with my son and daughter-in-law. Very pleasantly. My daughter-in-law is a gem! I have two granddaughters, 15 and 12. My daughter is married and lives around the corner on the next block. She has two little boys. And the strange thing is, my son and daughter were both adopted as babies. And my daughter's two little boys were adopted!—they're brothers.*

Peggy: *That is a nice story.*
Margaret: *And I live for my family.*

—Miami, #2

Chapter 3 (page 143) contains several instances of those who moved in with siblings, with equally agreeable results.

These stories and the ones to follow often demonstrate the unstartling truth that our ability to live with family afterward, emotionally if not literally, may depend very largely on how we've lived with them before:

> *I don't think anything helps much except the support of your children. If you had an exceptionally happy marriage (as I did), time is about the only relief you get other than loving, thoughtful care by your children—which can only result if you had a loving, caring relationship with them prior to widowhood.*
>
> *—Woman, 68, 4*

> *I know the wholeness of our family of four and the oneness of our marital relationship were prime factors in my recovery. I knew Robert Frost's "dashes of pain" that could unexpectedly destroy me, but I also knew my husband believed in my ability to cope.*
>
> *—Woman, 80, 25*

The happy marriage cited by Syd on the previous page clearly helped forge her friendship with her daughter and son-in-law; and Margaret's "adoption" by her children seems inevitable, given familial instincts so strong that they've led to a chain of actual adoptions.

At the other extreme, the Hannah who vows "Never!" to the notion of moving in with her daughter traces their estrangement at least as far back as the death of her husband:

> *Q: We've heard stories from some of you about things that happened between you and the kids. Do you have children?*
> *Hannah: Yes, I have two.*
> *Q: How old were they?*
> *Hannah: At that time, my son was 30, and my daughter was 18.*
> *Q: And what kinds of things happened?*
> *Hannah: Well, my daughter resented his death very, very greatly because they were very close. And strangely enough, although I re-*

spected my mother, I was very close to my own father too. And we are going through a very . . . "difficult" (shall we say?) period right now, even though my husband's been gone a very long time.
Q: *How old is she now?*
Hannah: *Forty-two.*

—*Miami, #2*

And the antagonism was apparently raised to its current pitch by an event eight years ago:

Our relationship became almost intolerable after her brother died. Because she was also very close to him. And my guess is she felt. "Now I'm alone and I don't want to be responsible for what might or might not happen to my mother."

Although she skirts the specifics, her guarded remarks do illustrate how bad blood can get worse, decade by decade and death by death. And perhaps generation by generation too. One is tempted to speculate whether the daughter might not be re-enacting a scenario her mother laid down for her: a closeness to male relatives that breeds a hostility to the female ones who may be perceived as competitors.

Of course, family relationships need not always proceed with such inexorability (if that's what it is), and we'll see some cases that don't. But if we're not helpless captives of our families and the past we've shared with them, both exercise an influence on us—benign or baleful—that is second to none. Their power is often most concentrated in those rituals by which we mark time's passing, usually in company with family: holidays and anniversaries. Survivors agree that these occasions can loom up as some of the grimmest trials of the first year—and perhaps every year after that.

For most people, holidays and birthdays are not the simple-mindedly joyous sprees in celebration of the present that those who merchandise them would often like us to believe. Instead, they are more like a crucible for feelings about the past and the future, in which the good and the bad melt together. The major holidays draw us back into our personal pasts as surely as they do to the events in various collective pasts to which all but one pay homage—and even New Year's Eve bids us sing "Auld Lang Syne" even as we look forward. But the other holidays are forward-looking too—we commemorate the past in order to keep that past alive for the future. This of course is exactly what makes these days the bane of so many survivors.

All the pain of Lee's loss crystallized about Thanksgiving:

> *Thanksgiving dinner—oh God, I used to suffer through that! This last one, I suffered through it. I said to the kids, "If you have somewhere to go, you all go ahead because I might have someplace else to go." Then I was invited to the church dinner, and I went, and everybody was there with their wives, and I wasn't with anybody. And I had to believe, like, what's the use I'm there? It was getting on me. I didn't have a partner! My own partner was gone!*
>
> —*New York, #2*

His statement that he "used to" suffer through it is belied by what happened at "this last one." He fended off his family but tried to recapture some of the former spirit of the day anyway—with a wrenching lack of success. His dilemma may be shared by many others whose need to solemnize the occasion impels them to make it a social one:

> *Be sure you are not alone on special days, e.g., spouse's birthday, Christmas, Thanksgiving, wedding anniversary.*
>
> —*Woman, 66, 6*

Many do count successfully for that company on family, on some of its more outlying members in Al's case:

> *Q: I hate to mention this, but Thanksgiving is coming up.*
> *Noel: That's the tough part, Thanksgiving. More than Christmas.*
> *Q: Really?*
> *Tom: Fortunately I come from a large family, and I always make it a point to spend holidays with family. If I had to spend them alone or with relative strangers, I would feel bad. But being with family helps a lot.*
> *Al: I agree absolutely. I am fortunate to be invited by my family, my cousins, to spend Thanksgiving Day and Christmas with them, and it is a great help. I would rather not spend a holiday alone—it's not the greatest thing in the world.*
>
> —*New York, #2*

And friends sometimes step forward to fill a family's traditional holiday role:

Richard: My friends are very good. I'm always invited on holidays to different people's homes. As a matter of fact, some of them overdo it. They feel sorry for me, you know.

— *New York, #2*

So some try to carry the past forward into the present on holidays, and those responsible for families of their own may feel particularly committed to doing so:

If there are children at home, continue the traditions you may have established—where you go for Thanksgiving, Christmas, summer vacations, etc.

— *Woman, 73, 9*

But a mood of constraint may have replaced a festivity that once was more unfeigned:

Smile—it becomes a habit, and people like to be with happy people. Make a determined effort to concentrate on the good memories on holidays, and all family and friends will relax.

— *Woman, 56, 2*

And some therefore enjoin us to jettison the past:

Do not dwell on memories of holidays—create a new way to celebrate. Do not feel guilty about not maintaining old ways of celebrating.

— *Woman, 68, 2*

Quite a few take outright flight from the old ways, like the Frieda whom we saw in the last chapter (page 237) boarding a cruise ship as New Year's Eve was bearing down on her. Lee tells her that she wasn't fazed by that prospect but that other days drove her to distance herself not only from the familiar but from family as well.

I didn't go away on New Year's Eve, because New Year's Eve means nothing to me. It's just another night. But when it came to the anniversary of my husband's death, or a holiday which the family spent together, I used to run away. I used to go away for the week-end. My kids were really upset with me. I said, "I can't control it. And rather than stay with you and feel down and make you feel sorry for me, I'm just going to get away." I did that for three years. And it helped, because when you get involved with something else, you don't have time to think of yourself.

—Miami, #1

Pat (Epilogue, page 486) also reveals how such tactics got her through the day that has no tincture of good to it—the anniversary of the death.

Lee and Pat kept their families at arm's length as a temporary measure. Noel also chooses to spend holidays among strangers, but with a much more radical aim in mind:

I found out Thanksgiving can be a pleasant affair even though you don't have relatives or your wife around. Last year I met some people at Judson Memorial Church in the Village. I am not a religious person, but I used to sing in the choir there years ago. I met this girl who had just gotten here from Indiana. She was about six feet tall and must have weighed three hundred and fifty pounds, and nobody ever thinks to invite anybody like that out. And I invited her over for Thanksgiving dinner, and I said, "Do you have anybody else you want to bring?" These were complete strangers, and we had a great time. We had the fireplace going, I had my little dog there. And this year I intend to do the same. Or else call up one of the city services and have a family come down. There are plenty of people around who have no place to go, and you can find a new family that way, I think. And they're not really your family, which is good, because you are not beholden to them.

—New York, #2

Spurring on his extraordinarily venturesome attempt to create a new family for himself is a profound alienation from the old. Or so it appears, as he explains,

They are your friends. I have a lot of good friends. I've never been pushed aside by my friends. My relatives, yes, but not my friends. I differentiate between them. You choose your friends, you're stuck with your relatives. That's the way I feel about it.

Later on, he discloses that he may have done as much "pushing aside" as his relatives—and may have meted out the same treatment to some of his friends too:

I think if you hang out with your relatives and people who have gone

through this with you, you're making one damn big mistake, because all you're doing is reliving everything. It always comes up in conversation, and it doesn't do you any good. You remember Christmas thirteen years ago when you were all together up in the Adirondacks, and things like that. I don't want to hear that. So I sort of disassociated myself from my family—which I wasn't that close to—and found new friends. And my credo now is, if I don't feel comfortable in a relationship, even in a conversation with somebody—again, my own selfishness—if I don't feel comfortable with them, I'm usually not going to see them again. So my coterie of friends has become smaller but more intense.

Note how memories of Christmas symbolize what he finds disagreeable about being among his family. Well, has he shed the past as decisively as he believes? Let's see:

Most of my friends are younger than I am, twenty, thirty years younger than I am, and I did that purposely because I didn't want to be . . . it helps me. I teach them, I tell them all about history, about World War II and the Depression I grew up in, and it's a process of educating other people. But they are interested in me as a new friend.

He's simply reliving another history he feels more comfortable with—whether out of an admitted selfishness or a justifiable sense of self-preservation we can't of course easily judge.

With Noel, we have arrived at the opposite extreme—we've gone from those who discover their best friends in family to those who feel they must make a family out of entirely new friends. In fact, a running debate unfolds over the question of who is the better—family or friends:

Stay close to members of your family. Although friends are very helpful and sympathetic, they cannot take the place of your brothers and sisters and other close relatives. Only they can know the utter loneliness you are suffering.

—Woman, 88, 2

Richard: *As he said [nodding to Noel], relatives do have their own life to lead, and they have kids. I don't go to them that much anyway, I never did, really, except around the holidays. But thank God for my friends.*

—New York, #2

> *My children and their families are my best friends. It was that way before my spouse passed away. Friends are nice, but family is essential.*
> *—Woman, 67, 3*

> *Continue to cherish, nourish, and cultivate your friends. It will help you let your children go.*
> *—Woman, 62, 12*

And of course there are the lucky ones who can embrace both of the sides:

> *Friends* are so important. They really need you as much as you need them. (*This certainly includes family.)*
> *—Woman, 65, 2*

> *You survive and carry on with help from all sides. Children and friends are your most wonderful assets.*
> *—Woman, 77, 22*

> *My children were my chief source of comfort, but many friends also rallied to my support by invitations and various attempts to distract me from my grief.*
> *—Man, 67, 2*

In the next several sections we'll see how variously people get on with the different varieties of family, and then we'll proceed to the different varieties of friends.

Grown Children

Of the 87% of those in our survey who were mothers and fathers, most—78%—had children older than 25, an age we may be inclined to categorize as "grown," if only because those children are usually no longer economically dependent on us. And we've already seen some grown children who've become comfortable equals with their parents in other respects as well. But the old dependencies die hard, and some survivors implore us not to try to perpetuate them:

> *Don't impose your feelings or beliefs upon your children.*
> *—Woman, 76, 10*

Above all, don't try to run your offspring's lives. Just be good friends, help them when needed, and enjoy your grandchildren.
                                                    —*Woman, 81, 16*

Like Ruth, who bit her lip rather than "talk out of turn" (page 279), you may need to muzzle yourself sometimes:

Attention to one's family is very helpful. Remember to be loving, never critical.
                                                    —*Woman, 76, 12*

Stay in communication with your children. If they are adults, do not try to run their lives, even if you disagree with what they do. Offer advice only when asked.
                                                    —*Woman, 74, 11*

You may be obliged to let their needs take precedence over yours:

If you have a family, stay as close to them as they *want.*
                                                    —*Woman, 75, 10*

And they may prefer to stay aloof, like the son and his wife who Gladys feels "have somewhat abandoned me" (Prologue, page 9).

She appears to be atypical, however. Ninety-one percent of the survey group with children 18 or older said they spoke to those children personally or by phone at least once a month, with 39% doing so weekly and another 35% almost every day. Only 6% reported seeing them "less often" than before the death, compared to 36% who reported the opposite. So closeness rather than distance seems the emotional norm. Moreover, when it comes to meddling in the lives of family, the survivor may not necessarily be the one at fault:

Listen to your children's wishes for you, but do not be swayed by them too easily—think things through carefully.
                                                    —*Woman, 78, 4*

Don't let friends or relatives (especially children) dictate to you what activity is—or is not—proper for someone of your age or sex to engage in.
                                                    —*Woman, 71, 10*

And even those who may not want to control your behavior may become somewhat obsessive about monitoring it:

> **Edna:** *There were times I would take off and run from my children because they had to know every minute what I was doing. And if I went anywhere, I had to report in.*
> —San Francisco

Their itch to interfere, like that of the survivor, may spring from the best of motives, but a contest of wills may also be at work:

> **Lillian:** *I have two children. They have been wonderful, but sometimes they are so good and they want to do so many things and do it their own way that I have to put my foot down.*
> —Boston, #1

It's a stock observation about families with grown children that a balance of power prevails in every one and that it must be renegotiated periodically. And some of our survivors support its truth, although they may describe outcomes that are more like a see-saw than a state of equilibrium. This struggle is especially likely when the children try to wield something of the same authority over a parent—especially a newly vulnerable one—that the parent once wielded over them.

Nora wittily sums up the results of that attempt to turn the tables:

> *When my husband passed on, I had five sisters and brothers. Every year, one of them left me. At the end of five years there wasn't a single one left. Only me, and I was the youngest. And everyone always said, "Well, you've got your kids." I don't know if you feel this way, but I'd say, "I don't have my kids; my kids got* me" *[laughter].*
> —San Francisco

She goes on to capture some of the complexities that may impel grown children to domineer. As with younger ones (coming up next), fear for themselves may still be the wellspring. Although Nora describes her children as "too protective," their anxiety clearly seeps out of an unease about their own vulnerability as well as hers, one that her illness (not to mention the disappearance of the rest of her generation) has heightened:

Nora: I was quite ill this winter and spring, and my oldest daughter kept saying, "Mama, you're going to have to get up because we're not through depending on you yet" [laughter].
Marguerite: Scared out of their wits if anything should happen!
Nora: Yeah, but if they'd just leave me alone and stop worrying about Mama—"You're doing too much," and so forth. As I explained to them, "When I need you, I'll call you. I'll let you know. But right now I'm busy" [laughter]. They're too protective. They're constantly on you, you know.

So the ideal for a survivor like her is this:

My children are a great source of pleasure and comfort who do not tell me what to do.
                                                                —Woman, 71, 18

And many give identical instructions about how to realize it:

Keep in close contact with your children and grandchildren, but don't be dependent on them.
                                                                —Woman, 82, 22

Keep in touch with children and grandchildren but remain as independent as possible.
                                                                —Woman, 72, 7

Friends were most important. My children were supportive and loving, but I did not want to make an adjustment dependent on them.
                                                                —Woman, 73, 8

Stay close to your children, but don't be a dependent nuisance.
                                                                —Woman, 69, 2

Just as your children fought to win their autonomy from you, you must fight to prevent the surrender of yours to them, for the sake of both sides:

Lil: It is very, very easy to give up. But if you do, then you are a problem for your children, they feel bad, they'll worry about you and everything, and gosh knows they have enough problems.
                                                                —Boston, #2

The same applies when *they* threaten to become problems for *you*:

> *It's important to remain an individual, even when faced with the problem of a daughter and granddaughters going through a perilous divorce. I moved to be near them, but I'm still my own person.*
>
> —Woman, 68, 5

The trick for many, like the last woman, lies in balancing closeness and distance. It's not within the power or inclination of everyone, naturally. This woman, bedridden from a stroke and almost blind, can't escape near-total dependence on someone and has had the good fortune to find that person in a son:

> *My son, a devout Catholic like me, took care of my husband before his death and takes very good care of me, sharing his love, time, and resources to comfort me. He cooks and keeps all the order in the household, hired a nurse's aide to care for me during the day while he is at work, and reads newspapers and books to me to keep me informed of the world's affairs.*
>
> —Woman, 73, 4

At the opposite extreme, this woman is all distance, flintily so:

> *Don't let your children make you feel guilty. Be your own person. They are due nothing. Stay in your own place with your own life. If they are adults and doing poorly and could use financial help,* don't, *unless you are very wealthy. You owe them nothing.*
>
> —Woman, 48, 2

This man sees his only "a few times a year"—and is content with that frequency:

> *Don't get too involved in your children's lives.*
>
> —Man, 58, 3

But, much more commonly, able-bodied parents are repressing a wish for closeness that could infringe on their offspring's obligations to their own families:

> *I try not to rely on my children. We love each other very much, but I also*

realize that they have their own spouses and children to care for.
—Woman, 70, 4

My children have been wonderful, but I realize they must be allowed
to live their lives and I must remember I cannot totally rely on them. I
must do things for and by myself, so I don't become a burden to them.
—Woman, 60, 5

A parent's undue demands upon a child can inculcate guilt just as
surely as a child's upon a parent:

Those with children should not depend on them, nor make them feel
guilty.
—Woman, 48, 7

Many parents discovered that, by increasing distance, they increased nearness:

The stronger you are, the more help you receive.
—Woman, 67, 11

This paradox hails straight from the debate over how open to be
(pages 18-22):

My children were very supportive. The more evidence one gives of
being able to be independent, the more support one gets from chil-
dren, family, and friends. Do any moaning in private! Pride yourself
on being strong.
—Woman, 69, 6

What these parents shrink from most is "burdening" a child with
their needs, whether those needs are relatively trifling or potentially
all-encompassing:

Do not become dependent on children. They will seek your company
more often when they are not burdened with being responsible for all of
your entertainment.
—Woman, 62, 4

Connie: *You can't hook onto your children.*

Isabel: No, but they're there. You know they are there.
Connie: They're there, but if you show them you are independent, they love you more.
Isabel: That's right.
Connie: Because they don't want to burdened. I had plenty of burdens, but they never felt them. I would gripe to myself, but I wouldn't gripe to them.
Sarah: Also a child can't help but resent it if you've mortgaged your own independence to theirs. No child wants to feel that you are living through them.
                                                                    —New York, #1

By setting the example, you can lend them strength:

Jean: It is very important, when a person becomes a widow or a widower, not to throw the whole burden of sorrow on their children—
Bea: Oh, I think you shouldn't throw any of it.
Jean: But to make yourself the kind of person—that was my goal—that your children would be proud of. Not to just hang on them, but to be busy, so busy that they'll be very proud of you.
Sarah: If you are capable of bearing up and making the adjustment, it would serve as the inspiration for them to do the same.
                                                                    —New York, #1

And, like Mary, you may be able to sound out the valedictory wisdom of many books on child rearing—that releasing your hold for good only binds them to you more tightly:

Mary: I was, I have to admit, a very possessive mother. I wish I weren't. It's wrong. I've read somewhere that, if you let them go, you'll really have them when they come back.
Ann: Right. You have to learn when to cut that umbilical cord.
Mary: Yeah, I had to learn that the hard way. But my daughter lives in Portland, and it's such fun to have her say, "Oh, Mother, you've got to come up!" You know, she wants me. I should have stock in the airline!
                                                                    —San Francisco

Some adherents of independence reveal that what they're really seeking is interdependence:

Try not to depend completely on your children for your emotional support. They always need your support.

—*Woman, 69, 9*

Stay close to your own family—by letters, surprise fun cards, and phone calls. Visit them occasionally but not too often. Seek their advice when needed. Help them when they need help.

—*Woman, 76, 6*

In the aftershock of the death, only being depended upon could restore Marguerite to a sense of her old self:

I was a zombie, just a zombie, because it had been very sudden. And the only thing that really brought me out, the only time I was happy for the first year—or was even myself—was when I'd be helping my family out. Because my son-in-law was in very bad health for five years, and my daughter had two children. And when she needed me—and I was needed—that was the only time I could say I was really happy.

—*San Francisco*

This woman's appointment of herself as an organizer could strike her family as an intrusion—but because of the self-reliance that fires it, we suspect that it's entirely welcome:

Do not retire from life, but take the initiative in planning activities for yourself, your grown children and their families, and your friends. Strike out in new directions. (I have applied for, accepted, and commenced a job for this summer in Yellowstone Park.) I have organized two campouts for my children and their families—and feel we remain close because of these. Also, because I am taking responsibility for myself, my children do not need to worry about me.

—*Woman, 68, 2*

So far, we've mostly seen survivors who have felt the need to redefine their relationships with grown children after the death—a project that entails deliberation and restraint:

Get involved in things outside the home. Keep in contact with family and friends, but do not rely solely on them to keep you occupied.

—*Woman, 61, 5*

Perhaps it's well to close by returning to those enviable parents who've made the transition almost effortlessly:

> *If you have a loving child who is free to spend a lot of time with you, as I have, it is easy.*
>
> —Woman, NA, NA

Far from veering away from the risks of overmuch "reliance," some court them recklessly—and apparently without ill effect:

> *My three daughters and their families are wonderful. The oldest is a doctor at an eastern university, married and a son 10. I talk to her by phone twice a week. I moved from our home of forty-one years to my present home to be near the other two. They live within five miles of me, two sons-in-law, and three granddaughters. Both girls are teachers. I see them most every day or hear from them by phone. I am welcome at their homes at any time, we enjoy lunches together. I sew for the little girls and babysit when convenient.*
>
> —Woman, 75, 6

Loretta cheerfully abdicated to her son when it came to deciding where to live:

> *I didn't know anything about Leisure World. And my son was trans-ferred here in '76, and he called me and said, "Would you like to come to California?" And I said, "Sure—I'm coming for a visit." He said, "No, I'd like to know if you'd like to live here." I said, "Well, find me something where it's not a lot of work," and he said, "OK." Somebody told him about Leisure World in Laguna, so he went down there. And he said, "That's not for my mother." They ride horses, and it's real sporty, real ritzy, dressed-up and everything. And more expensive. Then somebody told him about Leisure World here. And he came down, and he picked out a place and paid a deposit and paid for the moving.*
>
> —Los Angeles, #1

This woman preserves with a daughter some of the pursuits she enjoyed with her husband:

> *My husband and I were very interested in doing things together. So I've tried to continue these special projects with the help of a very interested and understanding daughter. I am so very lucky.*
>
> —Woman, 80, 8

As we've seen, people blessed with this kind of "luck" regard their children as friends foremost, like this woman, who had become such with hers before the death:

The most help came from a close-knit family of three children and their families. My husband and I had made a point of cultivating our adult children as friends. They stood with me, and we supported each other.
—Woman, 63, 2

Sarah's friendship with her daughter evolved afterwards, with only a little accommodation on her part, as she notes with typical wryness:

My daughter and I reinforce each other as much as possible. She was very attached to her father; and after that, instead of being mother and daughter we became best friends in a way, although I recognize she is entitled to her own life and even thought that I was entitled to mine after a while.
—New York, #1

So valuable do some consider this bond between the generations that they urge those without it to find a substitute:

If your adult child or children live in another state, develop a strong friendship with an "adopted" young adult.
—Woman, 73, 3

Finally, Marilyn and Fran performed one further service for their unmarried children that friends traditionally can—fixing them up with a date:

Q: Fran, do you remember anything that you used to help yourself after your husband died?
Fran: Well, my son is very close with me, he kept me going, doing things—we started going on trips together. And I guess we will still do those things, unless he gets married. Which I hope would happen—I would like him to have his own life, I can't expect him to be with me. But there's nobody out there.
Marilyn: How old is your son?
Fran: Thirty-one. And he can't find the right girl.
Marilyn: [laughing] I'll talk to you later.
Judy:[aside] She has a 29-year-old daughter [laughter].

Marilyn: *I have a* wonderful *girl!*

—Boston, #2

Young Children

Although the small emergency Mary and her son surmounted may have lasted for only a week or so, their story delineates in miniature the kind of crisis that descends upon many survivors with younger children for a much longer time. The president of her son's college called to give her his sympathy and to ask after her son, who had the lead part in a play:

> *He said, "Do you know we have a big problem? There's no under-study. And your son hasn't been here for rehearsals." My son said, "I don't want to talk to him, leave me alone!" He was in shock too. He was saying, "I can't do it—I've forgotten the part." So I realized I had to do something. He had the book, and we went to the backyard, and now I know every last line in* The Lady's Not for Burning. *I didn't know what the entire play was about, and I'm sure the neighbors must have thought we were crazy. But we did it, and it got me out of myself completely. I was so concerned with him. And he was wonderful! Everyone thought he was great.*
>
> *—San Francisco*

If you still had children in your care at the time of the death, some details here may jog your memory: the slightly delayed realization, for example, that their shock may be as great as yours (something it may take others to apprise you of fully) and that it may jolt them, like you, out of the roles expected of them with just as much attendant fear and anger. And you may have responded as she did—taking charge instinctively and authoritatively—and, in doing so, may also have found that it helps you as much as them.

The needs of children can recharge people like Mary with a sense of purpose at the very time when death may have drained it from the rest of their existence:

> *I don't think I gave much thought at the time to the task of "adjustment." My children, two of whom were still in school, needed me, and I tried to be available for them. There was an immediate requirement that I find full-time employment, and the demands of my new job required both time and energy. I felt there were lives to be lived and that I must*

get on with meeting my obligations.
—Woman, 68, 19

"There were lives to be lived"—the fact that she can use the plural rather than the singular plainly makes all the difference. That and the knowledge that those other lives obligate you:

I wasn't left alone. I still had responsibility for my children.
—Woman, 71, 21

At the time of our survey, none of the parents in our group had any very young children (under the age of 6); and only 2% had any between the ages of 6 and 17. But those who did have children at these ages at the time of the death generally gave thanks for it:

Try not to feel sorry for yourself. In my case, I lost my husband at a fairly early age, when I had a 12-year-old son to raise. Having him and being concerned that I make as good a life as possible for him gave me a purpose.
—Woman, 64, 16

When my husband died, I still had a 15-year-old daughter at home. I was not employed at the time, and our daily routine was much the same for the three years she remained in high school. Evenings were very lonesome, but my concern for her outweighed my self-pity.
—Woman, 62, 7

A younger woman, one who can still use the present tense, bolsters their recollections of how such concern helps banish self-pity:

Quit feeling sorry for yourself and get on with living. It's easier sometimes for those of us with small children and urgent responsibilities because we do not have the luxury of being depressed. It helps because you have to move on.
—Woman, 49, 3

Younger children can allow you much more of a chance than older ones to get out of yourself by entering into their lives:

These are the thoughts of someone who was widowed at a relatively young age with two small children: immerse yourself in their activities.
—Woman, 59, 17

And Anne's children came to the rescue of sanity itself:

> *Well, when my husband passed away, it was a rough situation with me. I was 35, and the children were young—they were 5 and 6 years old. I couldn't go to work because if I did, I would have to have someone in to take care of them. I lived in Pittsburgh at the time, and employment wasn't that good, and whatever I'd make would not be enough to pay for someone. So I took care of my chidren. And if it wasn't for them, I would have landed in the booby hatch, because I was really out of it, I wasn't really alive.*
>
> *Q: How was it that the kids kept you out of the booby hatch? I've heard that before.*
>
> *Anne: Well, because I had to take them here, take them there. One was in kindergarten, and one was in first grade, and I used to pick them up at school. It would keep me busy doing things for them. Otherwise, I'd really go out of my head.*
>
> *—Los Angeles, #1*

Not only children as young as hers inspired such gratitude:

> *I might well have considered not living, had I not had three young adult children not yet established in their own lives, and two of whom still needed help in completing their college educations.*
>
> *—Woman, 57, 3*

Guiding children through college or graduate school had been a major undertaking for many of the parents in our survey—and was one still among the 7% who had children between the ages of 18 and 24:

> *I also derived much comfort and pleasure from my three children— seeing them through college and out into the world. They have done well, too. One has a Ph.D. and is a university professor, another is a doctoral candidate at Columbia.*
>
> *—Woman, 68, 19*

"Seeing them through" may of course involve more than mere observation, as absorbing as watching a child's story unfold may be. In their previous comments on finances and jobs, we saw how a child's college education presented many survivors with their toughest economic test. But providing for children at any age can be a battle:

> *I became a widow twenty-three years ago at age 40 with two small children. Our only income at the time was Social Security and TIAA-CREF. Not much, but I made the decision to stay home and care for the girls, as the illness was long and hard on them. Even with much economizing after five years, I could not manage on the income and went back to work—eight years at a part-time job paying minimal wages and these last ten years with good pay and full benefits.*
>
> —*Woman, 63, 23*

All survivors caring for children under the age of 18, by the way, should be aware that regardless of their means, they probably qualify for Social Security benefits.

Many swore not to let a preoccupation with themselves deprive their children of their remaining parent:

> *I had two children to educate twenty-five years ago, and I was determined they wouldn't ever feel like a burden or have to cope with a mother only half alive.*
>
> —*Woman, 80, 25*

> *My 14-year-old son was excellent company and very courageous, but he needed me very much at that time, and I was forced to carry on in a normal way. I was determined that his life would be normal, not shadowed. And I think I have succeeded.*
>
> —*Woman, 47, 3*

Convictions like these commonly animate parents—widows especially—to resolve to be strong or be brave for the sake of their offspring:

> *Try not to feel sorry for yourself. Having four children helped a lot; I wanted to be courageous for them.*
>
> —*Woman, 58, 3*

> *I not only have to cope with my loss, but have to be strong for my children, especially for my youngest child, who was only fourteen when she lost her father.*
>
> —*Woman, 45, 3*

For Connie this kind of emotional strength stretches physical stamina to its limits:

When my first husband died, I had three kids—not children, I should say, my daughter was twenty-one. And it was hard because the year before I had had a stroke. But I said, "I can't get sick. I just have to accept it, because no one is going to take care of my kids but me." So I have a lot of strength. I can just handle it—I might collapse at the end, but I just don't let anybody else take charge.

—Boston, #1

Lil is equally obdurate about not getting sick, but she appears to have something other than physical illness in mind:

You have to pick up the pieces, you can't be sick and let your children worry about you. It happened so suddenly, my younger son went right to pieces, but I said, "I can't let them see me like that."

—Boston, #2

And her fear of letting them see something in her that they shouldn't brings us up against some hard questions. How much should you try to conceal your own feelings for the sake of the children? And which feelings in particular should you not show?

This is an issue that taxes the authors of many books about grief, including some devoted exclusively to the topic of how parents can best help younger children handle their loss. (There are other books addressed directly to children of various ages, and even a few to children and parents both—see the Bibliography.) For Lil above, it is unthinkable to reveal to her children that she has suffered enough emotional damage to leave her "in pieces" like her son; she is, after all, the one who "picks up the pieces." Does her kind of fortitude spare her children or deny them? Again, the same answer: it hinges on the individual. And here the individual is not only you but one or more others engaged in one of the trickiest of all human endeavors—attaining adulthood.

Ideally, you may have been able to strike the balance recommended by this woman:

Help children to grieve with you. They hurt as much as you do—even older children, teens and 20s! Don't try to be "brave" in their presence because it would be false. But also don't tell them they have to help father/mother as a replacement. It is too much responsibility for a child to assume.

—Woman, 73, 9

She is describing, after all, the crux of all parent-child relationships: reconciling intimacy and authority. Too much of one may draw them too near; too much of the other may drive them away, perhaps for good. Virtually no one seems to dispute her warning against encouraging a child to step into the missing parent's place. Some among our group rued that they had:

> *Judy: My oldest son was only 11, and he decided he was going to take over, he was the man of the house. And that was bad. He did cooking when I went to work, made sure the other kids were dressed nicely and off to school, because I had to leave about twenty minutes before they did, and—I don't know, it was good in some ways, but in other ways I depended on him almost like he was the father. When they had to do homework and I was too tired, he would help, because he was smart. "I'll do it, Ma"—that type of a kid. And he just wanted to learn how to cook, to do a load of laundry. It's not that it hurt him, believe me, it didn't, because his wife thanks me for it now. But he really took this seriously, and then the first time that I ever brought someone home . . . hmmm . . . that wasn't too pleasant at all.*
>
> *—Boston, #2*

Her words evoke a cry of recognition from Marilyn, who capitulated to a daughter in just the same way and with just the same consequences— an explosive reaction when she started dating again (more of both their stories begins on pages 442-43 of the next chapter):

> *Marilyn: I did the same thing! I let her take care of me that first year, she did everything. And that was a mistake, a very big mistake, because she became the boss, right? And then this person came in the house, and now she was not top dog anymore, and it bothered her.*
> *Julia: Is she an only child?*
> *Marilyn: Yes.*
> *Judy: She doesn't want to lose you.*
> *Marilyn: And I didn't have to let her do it. I just thought, "Well, maybe this will help her cope." But it was wrong.*

You may have no practical alternative to delegating a much larger share of the domestic chores to your children. But it's critical not to relinquish your prerogatives as a parent at the same time. Ruth may have pulled the trick off—at least, she mentions none of the repercussions that Judy does:

> *I treated both my boys when they were home as though they were my daughters, too. They both know how to cook, they both can iron a shirt. They can sew. If a button comes off, they don't ask their wives to put it back on, they know how. They know all these things. My daughters-in-law love me for that! And I think it's just as important for a woman to know how to balance a checkbook.*
>
> —*Miami, #2*

Letting a child appropriate too much responsibility after the death, however, is not the only way you can unwittingly upset the disciplinary order of a household:

> **Marlene:** *It's been seven years. My husband committed suicide, and I still had three children at home and I think I was letting them get away with too many things because they lost their dad. I was too easygoing. It took about four years before I ever went out. I did everything for them. They went and played soccer and football and they didn't think about me. And I woke up and said, "Boy, they're going to be gone one day, and I'm going to still be here by myself." So I had to change, a real big change. And so I started going out. I joined bowling, and I went to PWP meetings.*
> **Q:** *Everybody know what PWP is?*
> **Grace:** *Parents Without Partners.*
>
> —*Miami, #1*

Redressing her overindulgence (which the suicide may have made unavoidable) sparked some face-offs:

> *At first it was difficult. They'd say to me, "Well, you can't change us." "Oh, yes, I can! If I can change, you can!"*

And she is still warding off the occasional counterattack:

> *I've learned plenty from them since my husband's been gone. They're at a difficult age, especially the girls—it's harder for them. The twins are 16, and they've been giving it to me. I mean, I set the rules down, and they always think I should get called on my own rules. But I tell them, "I'm over 21."*

Whether Marlene believes she succeeded in changing her children, she doesn't say, but others are frank about failing. Ann blames her college-age daughter's orneriness entirely on a selfish refusal to acknowledge how illness and death transformed their finances:

> *Age has no bearing on maturing emotionally, no bearing whatsoever. In my case, we had been so very well off, and then trying to save the life of our other child took everything we had. My husband died immediately after that. I was used to money, and I was left flat on my ass financially—it's not funny, baby. And I had a daughter who was a spoiled brat, who had everything her heart desired, and suddenly. . . . She never did accept the fact that her father was dead and the money wasn't going to roll in anymore, that there was no provider. And when I'd say, "Honey, I can't do that, I don't have the money," she'd yell, "I don't want to hear about it!" And she would stomp out of the house.*
>
> —Miami, #2

Peggy's story of how relations with her daughter deteriorated over the years presents a less one-sided—and even more somber—picture. The child was apparently simmering with animosity as her freedom of action narrowed and her mother's widened:

> *My daughter was 11 when her father died. We didn't get along. She was a "key kid"—because I was going to work. You know how they'd refer to "key kids" because of the things they'd wear around the neck with the key on it? I don't think you could do it in this day and age, but, years back, it wasn't as dangerous to let a kid come into the house by herself.*
>
> *We had tremendous friction as she grew older. When she became a teenager, when she was 16, it was unbearable. I attributed it primarily to the fact that suddenly I became the boss in the household. And I hadn't been before—I'm not a clinging vine or anything of that nature, but my husband was the man of the house, and he made all the primary decisions. Suddenly I'm writing the checks and doling out the money. And I think part of it was resentment: you know, Daddy isn't here anymore, and I was bringing home the bacon. Suddenly I'm in charge of everything, and she's taking orders from me.*
>
> —Miami, #2

That key may have been a literal yoke around the daughter's neck, but she wasn't the only one chafing at the new state of affairs:

Oh, Mama paid for everything, that was all right—thank God I had the wherewithal! I didn't want to deprive her of any of the things that children who had two parents were having. You know, like the Sweet Sixteen party, she had one like everybody else. Fortunately, between what was left to me by my husband and my income from my job, I was able to supply her all these things.

Given the feelings of both, it's hardly a surprise that the daughter jumped at the chance to translate the emotional distance between them into a geographic fact—and that the mother acquiesced readily:

She was a very good student, so she was accepted wherever she applied. And when the time came to select a college, she couldn't seem to get far enough away. And you know what? I didn't fight it. I feel very sorry now that I didn't. We were living in New York at the time, and she came home and said, "I think I'd like to go to Berkeley." And I laughingly said, "California! Well, can't you get any further away than that?" We laughed about it, but I welcomed the thought of her going that far away because we were getting along so badly. We were at each other's throats constantly. And she'd been very close with her father. More so than she had been with me, you see. Sometimes fathers and daughters are that way—closer than with the mother.

Shades of Hannah and her daughter (page 282)—as Peggy herself exclaims later when she hears their story ("What I talked about before! So you know what I mean!"). But what if Peggy *had* tried to "fight" her daughter's decision? The outcome for both might have been far worse than the uneasy truce that eventually ensued:

Peggy: That was where she went and, I have news for you, she has never come back [murmurs of dismay]. She is now 39 years old—
Syd: You haven't seen her?
Peggy: Oh, sure, we're good friends. But she fell madly in love with California, and I think the distance lent a lot of enchantment to her. And she has never come back.
Elizabeth: She came back to visit you?
Peggy: Oh, she's here all the time. No, I don't mean we never visit. As a matter of fact, I'm going out there on Tuesday. But when she graduated from the university there, she went to law school. She's a very successful practicing attorney out there in San Jose. Unmarried—

if that has any bearing on the fact that she lost her father, I don't know. There may be some psychological connection, but I'm not smart enough to figure that one out. And . . . I'm sorry, I'm sorry about the fact that I allowed the friction to separate us and to put that distance between us. You see a child twice a year, that's hardly a mother-daughter relationship. We talk on the telephone every week, yes, but even that is hardly a decent relationship.

Ruth: Peggy, remember that even people who live close to each other don't see each other every day.

Peggy: I blame myself, you know, I was so glad when she said "California."

Ruth: You did the right thing if that's what she wanted.

Peggy: You know—"Get off my back and let me live!"

Her last words are probably truest to the daughter's feelings, as her lament that ''she has never come back'' no doubt is to her own. But a will to believe otherwise lingers in ''Oh, sure, we're good friends'' and ''Oh, she's here all the time.''

If any motif recurs in these portraits of parents contending with their children, it is the inability of each party to grieve with the other in a way that works, whether the parents have granted the children too much latitude (like Judy, Marilyn, or Marlene) or too little (like Peggy, perhaps). And often what symbolizes this failure are words unspoken or, if spoken, unheeded, as by Ann's daughter: ''I don't want to hear about it!'' Marilyn knows, for example, that her daughter isn't badgering her out of simple truculence:

The worst of it was—my daughter had terrible guilt. You know how kids are always fighting with their parents. Well, she had words with him that morning, and she never got to say she was sorry. And it really did a job on her. I think it still is. I don't think she has totally gotten over it, because she still mentions it. And now she has this fear every time I go out. You know—"Drive carefully, be careful." It is driving me crazy, but it is making me feel bad for her.

—Boston, #2

At least Marilyn is listening, but how fully is she responding? ''I don't think she has totally gotten over it'' sounds more like a guess on her part than a fact they've established together. Maybe that is why her daughter, although now almost 30, seems locked into behavior characteristic of much younger children. For example, she may be prey to the aftereffects of the well-known "I wish you were dead" syndrome that can bedevil young children who've been at odds with the parent they lost. They utter the wish (in so many words), see it realized, and hold themselves to blame, literally so if they are construing cause and effect with the naivete of the very young. Her anxiety for her mother's safety may also mirror that of younger children caught up in a dread that the remaining parent will vanish too.

Similar worries may be drawing Marlene's children to trespass into what she considers private territory:

> *It's been very difficult with the children, because they want to know where you're going, what you're going to do, and what time you're coming home.*
>
> *—Miami, #1*

But she's convinced she knows how children can best alleviate stresses like these when those stresses do build up—talking about them, even if not to her:

> **Marlene:** *I've always told my children, "If you can't talk to me or one of your sisters, find a friend. And if you have anything that you want to talk about, talk!" My son, who is 18 now, never was one to talk to me, but he could talk to my oldest daughter. I would say, "As long as you can find somebody to talk to, it's better than to keep it inside of you. The worst thing is keeping it inside you."*
> **Catherine:** *My children never talked about their father. They never could bring it out into the open.*
> **Marlene:** *That's why you should have done it.*

It's hard to quarrel with her reprimand to Catherine for allowing her children to retreat into such an inscrutable silence. Virginia likewise couldn't, or wouldn't, break through the wall her children erected:

> **Virginia:** *It was hard in one way because my boys would never talk about it. To this day they haven't mentioned it.*
> **Q:** *How old were they?*
> **Virginia:** *Nine, 13, and 15.*
>
> *—Boston, #2*

Children as mute as hers may be responding to the silence of a parent who is being so "strong" as to make them ashamed of their own feelings—or of a parent may have mistakenly judged them too young to grasp the fact of the death. Melba expresses the conventional view:

> *My daughter was 10 years old, and of course it hit her too. The boys were little, they were tiny, and they didn't understand the whole thing. But she and I, we really had a time going through it together. But we made it.*
> *—Miami, #2*

But some have argued persuasively that even the "tiny" are quite cognizant, in their own way, of what has happened and that you ignore it to their harm.

The twentieth century has of course exalted the ideal of "communication," of "sharing" feelings with "openness" and "honesty," into a colossal banality, especially by insinuating that it can be effortlessly achieved. But it is unquestionably what a surviving parent should strive for above all in enabling younger children to come to terms with the other parent's death. As Marlene asserts above, and as another woman postulates below, the parent may not be the only path to that goal:

> *My children were 16 and 19 when their father died. I wish there were support groups for the kids in all different age groups. They were hurting but had no groups for them to attend and get it all out like I was able to do.*
> *—Woman, 43, 2*

As a matter of fact, groups like those she calls for are fairly widespread, often sponsored by the public schools. But, since your children came into being out of the will of you and your spouse to see to it that "life goes on," no one may be fitter than yourself to instruct them in this fact:

> *Remember, if you have children, they too are grieving. Encourage them to share their feelings and remind them their parent lives on within them. This feeling of continuity of life (perhaps) is helpful to some.*
> *—Woman, 64, 6*

That parenthetical "perhaps" is astute, because you can't do justice to the continuity of life without reflecting on what is no longer a part of it:

> *Barbara: When my grandchild was born, I felt so happy but sad that my husband would never see the child. And there's sadness in the different stages in what the children do. And graduations are always sad . . . weddings.*
> *Edith: But you have to think of all the good things.*
> *Barbara: True, but I think those are things that make you sad.*
> —*Boston, #1*

And if the right words fail to come at the big solemnizations, then perhaps less momentous occasions may bring them forth, as they apparently did for this woman, who made an unpretentious sacrament of a small household task:

> *Do something your spouse did: bake the cookies your wife did; or sand and paint the kitchen window you wanted your husband to do. You feel close to her or him, and in conquering something you haven't ever done, you feel you aren't helpless. This is even more so if you have small children and let them "help" you. Give them something to try, and something they will feel good about too, if they can remember how Daddy or Mom did that thing.*
> —*Woman, 61, 2*

Grandchildren

Most of those with grandchildren rejoice in them, sometimes in identical words:

> *I have sixteen grandchildren who have helped* fill the void *in my life.*
> —*Woman, 62, 3*

> *Involve yourself in lives of children and grandchildren. I can't stand all nineteen of our grandchildren at once—so I take only a few at a time. If I hold them on my lap, hug and kiss them, it helps fill the void some.*
> —*Woman, 59, 3*

They serve many of the same ends that young children of your own might:

If you have grandchildren, baby-sit them—they will make you feel so much better. A child can make you forget your sorrow.

—*Woman, 60, 4*

But as a grandparent, you are usually liberated from the responsibilities that fence in a parent, and you can use that freedom to achieve a standing with them that a parent cannot:

My suggestion for trying to accept widowhood is to get involved in helping young people to realize their own possibilities. They need someone to listen to their dreams and give them encouragement. I try to be a friend to each grandchild, and their friends as well, by just listening to them and encouraging them.

—*Woman, 78, 2*

In turn, they may be able to respond with a disarming directness, unencumbered by the hesitations that might inhibit them with a parent:

Lillian: *One daughter lives in Framingham, and she teaches and she has a 10-year-old girl, who was walking down the corridor in my building one day a couple of weeks ago. And all of a sudden I hear, "Grandma, your head up and your shoulders back!" And I thought, "How right she is"—because I hate that slouched look that I can have. And so now whenever I start to walk two steps, I think of what Jamie said: "Head up and shoulders back!"*

—*Boston, #1*

Increasing life expectancies have made it more likely that many—women especially—will get to know a fourth generation:

Hannah: *Grandchildren are a great joy to me, because they are all grown. One is 30, one is 26. The 30-year-old has two babies, so I'm a great-grandmother. They're adorable, but not for me anymore. Two and a half years old? And 5 months? You have to have eyes all over.*

—*Miami, #2*

Some may share her discomfiture with one of the traditional functions of grandparents, serving as unpaid babysitter. This woman doesn't find it onerous:

If there are grandchildren, give their parents a break and mind the children when requested.

—Woman, 73, 9

But some parents issue the request so regularly that books on grief have been obliged to warn grandparents against becoming exploited labor. On the other hand, some thrive so much in being grandparental that supply can't keep up with demand:

Margaret: *I had children that rushed to my side. My grandchildren are with me just every moment. And foster children—somebody always wants a new mama, a new grandma. I have so many I can't count them, and they love me just like my own. I am so lucky!*

—Los Angeles, #2

Margaret seems to have recruited so many additions to her grandchildren that she can barely tell them apart. You may scarcely want your life as flooded with kids as hers is, and, by taking in foster children, she's assuming a parental as well as a grandparental charge. But as we noted in the last chapter (pages 255-263), volunteer jobs can afford less strenuous opportunities to grandparents who want to enlarge their boundaries beyond the immediate family-—or to non-grandparents who are curious to know what it's like to be one.

Parents

At the same time as we are reordering our relationships with the generations in front of us, we may need to do the same with the generation behind us—and that may not be a matter left as much to our discretion:

Helping care for two ill, elderly parents two hundred miles away occupies much of my time at present.

—Woman, 61, 6

My 81-year-old mother broke her hips two years ago and has been with me since, and my preoccupation with her has not allowed me a lot of solitude.

—Woman, 60, 3

Just as the increases in longevity during the latter half of this century have bestowed more time upon us to watch grandchildren grow, so they've granted our parents more scope in which to age.

For some, the one fact is as welcome as the other:

My 90-year-old mother lived with us and is a continuing help.
—Woman, 58, 2

Mother is 90 years of age. I have been blessed with her support, sometimes critical.
—Woman, 69, 6

More often the support must come from the opposite direction:

If you have an aging parent who is alone and needs help, give it generously.
—Woman, 64, 9

Some who did as she directs found the motto of this chapter vindicated:

I helped my aging parents most every weekend. Doing for others seemed to help me.
—Woman, 61, 12

But it was wearing down others whose parents were in graver straits:

I am almost 65 and taking care of my 90-year-old blind invalid mother in her house, and that is no life.
—Woman, 65, 23

At present widowhood is the least of my problems. I have no brothers or sisters, and both of my aging parents are in the hospital. Their poor health is a great concern. Also it interferes with any thought of a social life.
—Woman, 63, 6

The erosion may of course be more than social and emotional:

About a year and a half after my husband's death I had to take on the financial responsibility of having my folks (father, 87, and stepmother, 74) live in a residential home. About six months ago I moved them close to me. By this time my stepmother needed skilled nursing care (in a nursing home), and I kept my father in my home. In April I had to put him in the nursing home too. Then in May I lost both of them—one week apart.

It was most difficult to see my financial resources depleted so rapidly. The residential home costs for the two of them were running about $2,800 monthly. The nursing-home care for my stepmother was $1,525 monthly, which did not include pharmacy charges, doctors, etc.

In trying to honor my father and stepmother, and also care for my teenage son, insurance was a critical problem. I feel I have enough life insurance, but health insurance is still a bugaboo for me. How much supplemental health insurance and what kind—hospitalization, protection against long-term illness, or what? I don't know what TIAA-CREF could do to address this problem, but it surely is one that needs to be dealt with by widows/widowers.

—Woman, 57, 3

Her matter-of-fact account of how she tried to honor those who raised her certainly does high honor to her, especially given that she was still raising others in her turn—a doubly draining situation that arises from the interplay between longer life spans, improved medical technology, and the preference of more women to postpone having children until their late 30s and early 40s. And we can answer her question about us. TIAA phased out its limited business in standard major medical policies in 1989, but it has recently begun to offer insurance against the costs of exactly the sort of long-term care she was providing, both at home and within institutions. People now working for or retired from public and private nonprofit educational institutions can purchase this new coverage for themselves and their spouses, as well as for their parents and parents-in-law.

The dependency of aging parents upon their adult children for care—physical, financial, or both—was one of the most disturbing social trends to emerge during the 1970s and 80s, when the children often had no choice between either shouldering round-the-clock responsibility or consigning the parents to institutions, usually for keeps. Many in the 1990s will not be forced to the latter extreme until their parents' condition—rather than their own—makes it genuinely unavoidable, thanks to the increasing availability of services to help them stave such an action off. These services range from those that aid you in maintaining relatives at home (theirs or yours), like Meals-on-Wheels and visits from home health workers, to those that give you a break from it, like adult day-care centers and residential "respite" programs that will take your relatives in for temporary stays. The growing incidence of disabling chronic diseases like Alzheimer's has conferred a near-professional status on the caregivers who must bear those diseases' brunt. They now may have recourse to everything from training programs to support groups (see "Resources"), not to mention a slew of books (see Bibliography).

One traditional goal of the professional, however, is likely to elude them: detachment. Ministering to someone you love who is in an irreversible decline is one of the most emotionally rending experiences life has to offer, and it may be made especially poignant if that person is a parent who is now as dependent on you as you were upon him or her in your infancy. And that dependency may not be a particularly docile one, as those tending the sufferers of Alzheimer's know well. In fact, the "dependency" even of parents who are not impaired physically or mentally may be just as imperious. As in the case of some survivors with grown children, the old habits of command and obedience can still be well-entrenched. Mary compares herself to a schoolgirl seeking the teacher's permission to leave the room:

> *I have to raise my hand when I'm not going to be home at night. For heaven's sake [to Marilyn], you're talking about* your *mother! Mine is close to 90. I am going away for a weekend, and I told her the other day, "I am going away next month with the group from Harvard." She said, "You're going to be gone for a* month!" *I said, "No, just for two nights."*
> *Angela: Does she have somebody that lives with her to take care of her?*
> *Mary: Well, I'm upstairs, and she is downstairs.*
> *Q: But when you are away, is there somebody nearby she can call on?*
> *Mary: Well, my sister lives close by, but she just wants me there. But she depends on me too much. Now, [to Marilyn] you can go off on a trip—*
> *Marilyn: No, I have the same thing with my mother downstairs too. In the beginning I stayed home, but then I said, "No, this is not right."*
> *Mary: That's why I'm going away next month.*
> *Marilyn: It's not right to let people . . .*

Angela: Govern your life.
Marilyn: Exactly, it sounds cold and heartless, but it's not.
Angela: They become dependent.

—*Boston, #2*

As they do, so may you—into a spiral that can needlessly constrict the lives of all involved. Marilyn has resisted it, but her declaration of independence is under constant challenge not only by mother but daughter as well:

My mother is 91, but she doesn't look it or act it. She's a very healthy woman. She has crippling arthritis, and she can't walk. But other than that, she doesn't have a thing wrong with her. She has all her faculties, and she is just as alert as anyone in this room. But she doesn't want me or my daughter to be far. And unfortunately, my daughter caters to her too much. My daughter is very special. It's very rare to find a young person today taking care of a grandmother as compassionately as she takes care of her. But again, I wish she weren't like that, I would rather she have her own life.
Angela: You said she doesn't have any boyfriends.
Marilyn: Even if she did, when she goes out, she does what she is always telling me—"Did you give Gran the telephone number? Always leave the telephone for Gran, this is very, very important."

Who's more dependent on whom here? So many needs have become interlocked that any easy answer would defy their intricacy.

Siblings

In taking leave of family, it's worth pausing over the good words that some have for siblings. As members of your own generation, they may have the most appreciation for what you are going through and the surest touch for easing it:

Keep close contacts with your siblings—they were and are the ones I can depend on.

—*Woman, 87, 21*

Having a sister nearby to "flee" to when desperation set in was especially helpful early in my widowhood.

—*Woman, 62, 13*

Irene's brother, and her sisters-in-law, were the first people she turned to:

> *Q: They called you up, they told you of his death. So what did you do next?*
>
> *Irene: Well, it was a quarter past four in the morning, and I was really beside myself. About five-thirty I called my brother because I couldn't hold out any longer. And I woke them up and I told them about it—my brother and his wife—and I called up my husband's sisters about six o'clock and I told them about it. And one of them came over and stayed with me for about ten days, and that was very good.*
>
> —Boston, #1

Sarah does have a cautionary tale about a sister who kept on calling, too often for her brother's good or for her own:

> *She was incapable of making a telephone call to anyone except her brother. It seemed the only strong tie that remained in her life was her brother, and in a way she ruined his marriage too. She would call his home twenty times a day to hear the sound of his voice. Which was terribly resented.*
>
> —New York, #1

But Raymond, at the opposite extreme, withdrew into what he called a "trance" —until (much as he'd like to take the credit himself) a brother apparently broke its grip on him:

> *Raymond: Finally I decided that, rather than get sick, I better take hold of myself and that's what I did.*
>
> *Q: How did you do it?*
>
> *Raymond: Well, we had such a beautiful life together that I remember all the memories. That's it.*
>
> *Q: I'm just wondering. You said you thought you needed to get hold of yourself. Did you do anything special? You remembered the memories. Did you do anything else?*
>
> *Raymond: No . . . first thing, my brother gave me a lecture, and then he and I took a trip for six months. When we came back, I was all right.*
>
> *Q: How long after your wife died did you do that?*
>
> *Raymond: Oh, approximately a year and a half.*
>
> —New York, #2

This sort of intervention may reflect a lifelong pattern of one sibling watching out for another, like the one who fetched Sylvia to her present home in a retirement community:

Well, I'll tell you what brought me in: my brother took me by the hair of the head. He lives in Mutual 5. You probably know Art Gillespie, everybody does. And with him growling at me constantly and me living in Downey by myself in a great big house, where he thought it wasn't safe, and him living here, where it was—well, he just wore me down, let's face it, because he's always been like that. He's been my crutch all my life.

—Los Angeles, #1

In-Laws

In-laws serve well as a bridge to friends because they occupy a middle ground between them and family. Like friends, they are unhampered by the traditional obligations that rope the members of a family together. And so their reactions can be quite as unpredictable as those of friends.

Some in-laws lived up to their cartoon reputations as ogres of self-concern (a reputation which may owe something to the fact that we can displace onto them the resentments we don't as readily like to own up to about our own families). Ann's cut her dead, by her account:

I have found that family isn't always there for you. You take in-laws: when my husband died after twenty-three years of marriage—forget about me, there was a child—there were uncles, there were aunts, there were cousins. Right? Not one of them gave a damn *whether we were still alive or dead. I never even received a sympathy card when I lost my husband, believe it or not. And when my daughter got married, I was the one who walked her down the aisle because there was no one from the family there to do it.*

—Miami, #2

Evelyn also confesses to the error of having trusted in-laws to be "the family":

I was always one of the family—until my husband died. He had five sisters, and he was the baby, the only boy. His sisters idolized him and, when he died, they were very angry. Being a professional, my husband helped the other members of the family in everything. We were very close, and everything that was done, we did for the family. And now, it's just like . . . I might as well be dead also. I asked one of my sisters-in-law, "Why is your hurt more than mine?" She said to me, "Well, another husband you can get, another brother we can never get."

Sharkey: *That's stupid, that's sad, that's ridiculous.*

Evelyn: *And I have nothing to do with them now.*

Q: *Let me go back to that for just a second. How did you feel when they said that to you?*

Evelyn: *Angry. Angry, because that was not so. I mean if I ever did meet somebody, he could never take my husband's place, never.*

—Boston, #1

Her anger, at least, seems well founded. But, as usual, someone can counter one story with its opposite:

Beulah: *But then again—you know how Evelyn was kind of an outcast from her family? My husband's family were absolutely wonderful to me. They appreciated me, all the care and loving he got over the years. We're still in touch. They're a great help.*

—Boston, #1

For Pat, the two families had become practically one:

He had one remaining sister left, and when my son called her in Elkhart, she cried, and she said "Now I'm the last limb on the tree." But she took care of everything, the Mass and the funeral arrangements. She was the last Tucker, and she just died three weeks ago, and it's like losing a sister.

—Los Angeles, #2

And this woman's testimony about the in-law of a sibling may redeem the credit of the lawyers we besmirched earlier (page 232):

My attorney is my sister's brother-in-law, and he's my guardian angel. To him goes the credit for my handling all of the estate work myself; he assured me I could do it as well, or better, than anyone else. He calls me often, as does his wife—always ready and willing to listen.

—Woman, 77, 3

Friends

Take the problem that unites all survivors:

> *You have to get out with people. It seems you are different, as every-*
> *one has someone. That's the hardest part—being alone, eating alone.*
> *—Woman, 61, 6*

Apply this solution:

> **Fay:** *I can go into a movie alone, I can go into a restaurant alone.*
> **Sara:** *I can travel alone.*
> **Margaret:** *I can, too. You have to learn to go alone.*
> **Elaine:** *I traveled alone when I was younger. But, you see, there is*
> *something lacking. So you've seen the movie—there is nobody to dis-*
> *cuss it with.*
> **Q:** *Does she have any options? Does she have to go alone?*
> **Gladys:** *Go with a friend.*
> *—Los Angeles, #2*

And let Sarah append this homily on the subject:

> *Even one good friend would be a great solace. I mean, any feeling of*
> *aloneness can be appeased by the right kind of companionship. And*
> *if you've lived long enough, and if you haven't been a hermit, you*
> *must have made certain friendships. And get around a little bit. You*
> *may not have a very dynamic incentive to get around at the beginning,*
> *but you have to command yourself to do it.*
> *—New York, #1*

How nice if it were this simple! Both Gladys and Sarah are right,
but, in the halting words of the first woman quoted, the sense that
"you are different" is of course *the* hardest part for a great many. It
may be the most blighting for those who lost someone in addition to
a "mate" or "partner":

> *The first two years of my widowhood were very difficult for me, I was*
> *not living, just existing. My husband and I had been very close, we*
> *did just about everything together, he was also my best friend.*
> *—Woman, 63, 8*

Richard: In the beginning I did a little more drinking than I usually did. I was sort of lost, you know. I've got a lot of friends and all, but none close like my wife, and I think I went out looking for that.
—New York, #2

But even those who were admittedly on more distant terms may feel that each is the lone exception to the reputed rule that "everyone has someone":

My husband left me in pretty fair financial shape, but I feel very lonely and deprived. Although he was not a great companion, I did feel secure—and taken care of.
—Woman, 68, 3

This woman was among the 17% in our survey who answered "no" when asked if they "see any close friends on a regular basis." So, although the security she longs for is clearly a combination of the social and emotional, she's not been able to find a facsimile of it in society at large.

In fact, what may make you feel in limbo is that you *are* different:

Being alone is so very different than being part of a couple. Like yourself.
—Woman, 69, 3

Even with your self-esteem intact, you may rediscover some of the dread that being found "different" by playmates or classmates holds for the child or adolescent. Socially, you have become a new species. And nowhere are you likely to come upon more divergent reactions to that change than with friends, who can express how they feel much more freely than can family. Ann speaks for many when she depicts her old social life in ruins, with a wholly new one to be constructed from scratch (though most don't seek a wholly new setting for it too):

When you are living with a husband, your status is entirely different. And then suddenly you are bereaved, and you are one. *Something happens to people after that. They're afraid of you, the women are afraid of you. They're afraid they're going to lose their husbands. They're afraid that they might have to pick up the tab for you some-*

times, just to be decent, you know what I mean? They just don't want to have much to do with you. And you'll find that friendships—the strongest friendships—are no more.

You see your chances of starting new in another town, in another state, where most people don't know anything about your past. And if you're the kind that doesn't weep—you know what I mean?—you will make new friends, they'll mean much more to you than family ever would. Because family feels you're a burden once you have lost your mate. And I have made friends all over the world. You can't hold on to anything, it's impossible. But it's good to have them as you go through life, and you learn something from each and every one of them.
—Los Angeles, #2

But Elizabeth immediately, and ebulliently, retorts that she inspired no such fear in her friends:

My husband has been dead twenty-two years, and my daughter was 12 when he died. I said to her, "Honey, we're in this together. We both loved your daddy, we miss him, but life has to go on. We cannot live yesterday, we have to live today and tomorrow." I would tell everybody that you cannot live in the past, you have to go on. And as far as my friends go, I still have the same friends I had before he died. They've always been right with me, they've always included me in everything. I mean, hell, who would be afraid of me? They all love me! I don't mean to sound conceited, but they do. They call me up, and the husbands call me and ask me out with the wives and all.
—Miami, #2

You can see more of this knack for rallying her friends around her in our concluding glimpse of her in the Epilogue (page 491), throwing a party in honor of her new washer-dryer.

Jean and Eleanor also square off on the question of how to deal with what is perhaps the most awkward legacy of a survivor's former life—those friends who are still married:

Jean: You have to start a whole new life with people who are single. It cannot be with the old married friends anymore. If they have a husband, you can't socialize with them. They think that you have ulterior motives. They do when you are young. Or even when you are older. If the husband is driving and they have to say, "Pick up So-and-so," they resent it.

Eleanor: When my husband died, everybody that I knew was married, and I had nobody else to turn to, and I was very young. And I never lost a friend. I have kept my married friends an entire lifetime.
Jean: But, actually, you are always friendlier with the woman—
Eleanor: I am friendly with both because our husbands were friends. After I lost my husband, the first time a couple invited me to their home, I said, "I don't want to go." Then I said, "But I cannot be alone forever," and I went. When I got there, I thought I would die because everyone was there with husbands. While I was there, I was very nice. When I got home and opened my door, I was hysterical! But nobody knew it. And I felt I had to go on, and I've kept these married friends to this day.

—New York, #1

New friends, old friends, couples and singles: the rest of this section reveals how they gave cause to survivors to swear by them—or at them. Not, of course, that everyone is as polarized as Ann and Elizabeth or Jean and Eleanor—and even they are not diametrically opposed to one another. They all seem agreed, for example, that winning or keeping friends demands concealing their grief, a theory by no means accepted by everyone. Ann freely concedes that she is overstating the propensity of couples to fling survivors aside:

There are the exceptions—understand that I'm generalizing. There are those who do, and there are those who don't.

More important, although Eleanor retains old friendships, note how she must *re*construct them to a degree—thus "starting new" in a fashion that may be even more arduous than Jean's or Ann's, because she must work with the past instead of discarding it. And Elizabeth's determination straightaway "to live today and tomorrow" may be what ultimately won her the fidelity of her friends from the past.

So this woman's warning may pertain just as much to those who cleave to old friends as to those who don't:

Accept the fact that there will be changes in your social life.
—Woman, 82, 22

More of those in our survey said that their social lives had picked up (40%) rather than slowed down (34%)—with the fewest (26%) saying those lives remained "about the same." Whatever your case, you may need to take action. The death may have put old friendships into a suspended state which may cost you as much pains to reanimate as beginning afresh. Either way, you will be reaching out, a gesture that may make you wince as if you were flexing a sprained muscle:

> *Do things to keep old friends and to increase the number of unattached women friends—even when reaching out is hard.*
>
> —*Woman, 67, 8*

> *Reaching out when you are hurting badly is difficult, but for me the effort has helped. I have friends of all ages, some thirty years younger and some twenty years older.*
>
> —*Woman, 62, 2*

In any case, whether you make the overtures to old friends, new friends, or both, you'll be heeding an imperative that's hard to ignore, the one that Eleanor awoke to: "I cannot be alone forever."

Old Friends

Many are shaken when the death of a spouse ushers in the same revelation that other forms of personal misfortune are proverbially supposed to:

> *At this time one knows who true friends are; some of mine were wonderful and still are.*
>
> —*Woman, 74, 9*

> *While some friends stick, most will turn out to have been colleagues rather than friends.*
>
> —*Woman, 66, 3*

> *Richard: I found out that some of my close friends weren't close enough. They had things to do, and . . . [with a wave of the hand] forget it! I got over that.*
>
> —*New York, #2*

These two responses—hosannas for those who stay loyal and maledictions for those who don't—are often voiced together:

> *This may sound cynical, but I have come to use the word "friend" very*

sparingly. I have found most are acquaintances rather than friends. I do have such a friend fortunately. She has been willing to listen (without judgmental comment) whenever I had to talk out my problems and feelings and is always next door when I need her. I am grateful for that.
                                                                    —*Woman, 61, 6*

Some, usually women, had grudges to bear toward those who may have been better friends with the spouse:

Forget about HIS friends, you'll never see them again!
                                                                    —*Woman, 62, 7*

Simple inaccessibility may be the reason if those friendships were forged in the spouse's working life:

Never had much of a social life except where my husband's work was involved. Now it is very limited.
                                                                    —*Woman, 58, 3*

I was educated in the same general field as my husband and participated in his career in an informal way, and I miss the contacts with the men with whom he worked. I find myself in an excessively feminine social life and miss the meaningful conversation that I was a part of.
                                                                    —*Woman, 68, 3*

As this woman points out, however, such friendships may not be the ones you should care most about sustaining:

Accept all forms of support, but begin to realize which is being given because the friends were basically his (and therefore in subtle ways keeping you attached to your spouse, and placing you, essentially, in a fantasy world) and which comes from people who are ready to transfer their concern, attention, and interests to you.
                                                                    —*Woman, 59, 2*

All old friendships, after all, must be reconfigured as she describes if they are to stay in proper working order. And some apparently had no old friends they valued who couldn't make the shift:

I had to keep myself busy, and my friends were a tremendous help.
                                                                    —*Woman, 58, 8*

Thank goodness my husband and I always cultivated friends and acquaintances. Friends and family and my faith in God saw me through.
                                                           —Woman, 72, 3

This woman's friends apparently gladly smoothed her passage through a trying time:

About two months after my husband's death I realized I needed a change of scene, so I went back to the state where we had lived before retirement and spent three weeks with two couples who had been our closest friends. They were loving and supportive, but not smothering.
                                                           —Woman, 76, 4

Almost half of the 83% we surveyed who reported regular contact with close friends said they see still see old friends about as often as they do new ones, with almost another third saying that the old were more frequent companions than the new. This woman feels obliged to enclose "old" in quotation marks, presumably to dispel any imputation that it means superannuated:

Continue your "old" friendships and club affiliations and keep in touch with family and relatives.
                                                           —Woman, 76, 20

Past and present coexisted well for this woman too:

My husband's old friends and golfing companions were most kind and liked to talk about him. I felt he was not forgotten. I appreciated their remembering and mentioning him in an unself-conscious way.
                                                           —Woman, 82, 5

Marguerite kept some old friendships glowing among the embers of old flames:

I go out a lot and I go out at night. Maybe a friend will just take me to a movie. I have one five years younger than me. He used to be a boyfriend; now we're just the greatest friends. I can't tell you how many of my old boyfriends keep in contact with me, always remember my birthday, for instance.
                                                           —Los Angeles, #2

Old friends proceeded to re-engage this woman in their lives so significantly and yet so deftly as to leave her a bit mystified—but hugely appreciative:

> *Strangely enough, the most helpful of my friends were those who asked me to play bridge frequently (and shortly after his death) or asked me to go for short trips. I've always enjoyed traveling and I travel more often now. I realize more and more that old friends are the best friends.*
> *—Woman, 68, 2*

Old friendships, simply by embodying the past, can be imbued with pain as well as pleasure:

> *Share with your children and friends the past and present—it is a great outlet and helps you feel better. Even though it hurts, keep up with the friends you shared.*
> *—Woman, 69, 9*

The hurt, moreover, may be mutual, and as this woman cautions, you should take care not to let your grief interfere with theirs:

> *Talk to friends, but don't overdo in the grief department, as friends are supportive for a normal time, but tend to become uncomfortable if it's overdone. One must realize they, too, are suffering a loss—that of a good friend. So one must begin early on to recall the good times, and all the good things, and be thankful for these, and there's comfort in sharing—hopefully in a happy frame of mind.*
> *—Woman, 68, 4*

We've heard from the likes of her before, of course—the centrist party on the question of how open you should be. By now, we know the extremist positions too: to be unabashedly confessional or sternly tight-lipped.

The course you adopt will depend, again, on them and you—specifically (and with old friends possibly more than with anyone) on the degree that they feel comfortable about giving help and you about receiving it:

> *Just try to be a reasonably happy, well-adjusted person—interesting to be with; and do your grieving on your own time. Love and support*

others, and their love will support you.

—Woman, 69, 2

It is not easy to make the adjustment. It can't be done overnight. But one finds that there are always people who are concerned and want to help in any way they can. Friends will listen—talk to them. Don't be afraid to let them know of your emotions.

—Woman, 75, 3

In any event, be attuned to the possibility that the 49-year-old woman reminds us of on pages 487-88 of the Epilogue: that wrongly "relying on others to make things better" can estrange you from yourself as much as it can from them.

For some, niceties like these pale before the sheer effort needed to maintain old friendships. In their social lives, they adhere to a creed that is the equivalent to "get out of the house"—"never say no":

My advice to a widow or widower is to accept all the offers of help that might be extended to them by close friends. Do not hesitate to attend social events because you are alone.

—Man, 70, 6

Like "get out of the house," this admonition is often couched in the language of self-compulsion:

Q: Does it ever occur to anybody here that you don't feel like going some place you've been invited to?
Gladys: *Very often.*
Sylvia: *Sure.*
Sara: *A lot of times.*
Gladys: *But I make myself go. I never say no to anything.*
Elaine: *Anything—I'll go to it!*
Margaret: *I never say no to anything.*
Noreen: *I don't do it unless I really want to.*
Elaine: *You have to* learn *to want to.*

—Los Angeles, #2

If such a spirit occasionally snares you into some absurdities, that's a price worth paying:

A neighbor advised that I should accept every invitation I could possibly handle. On the strength of that, I had the occasion to see a Japanese comedy with no subtitles. Nonetheless, forcing oneself out has proved useful. "Among God's best gifts to us are the people who love us."

—*Woman, 53, 2*

So set the excuses aside:

Friends have been so good to call or want me to go somewhere. I go and find that housework will wait.

—*Woman, 67, 3*

Accept invitations to mixed *gatherings, even when you feel like the "extra" woman.*

—*Woman, 79, 20*

Accept invitations whenever possible. Assume those who ask you really want you.

—*Woman, 77, 13*

If you don't, those who ask may make an equally erroneous assumption in their turn:

Don't refuse social invitations. As much as you don't want to go, force yourself. If you don't, you lose contact with old friends.

—*Woman, 61, 8*

Try to see old friends and, if health permits, never say no when they want to include you in their plans. If you always say no, they will finally stop asking.

—*Woman, 67, 6*

Just saying yes, of course, isn't the end of it. Part of the time, you must still take the lead, regardless of how truncated your new role may seem:

One has to accept that this is a couple-oriented society; hence it behooves widows to join in activities and to keep in the mainstream. If I make the effort to entertain here—dinner, slide shows, bridge, etc.—I find that I am entertained also.

—*Woman, 76, 20*

Entertain friends—do not hesitate because you are a ''single.''
—*Woman, 80, NA*

The outgoingness of these two may have something to do with the fact that both report they are doing ''well''—and that the latter has remarried. In any event, taking the initiative may be the only way to convert those who were friends of the both of you to friends of yourself alone:

Make sure you have social engagements lined up for weekends. In other words, accept invitations and also extend them. Even the former associates of your husband will rally.
—*Woman, 72, 8*

By shrinking back, you may be lapsing into selfishness, as well as self-pity:

Initiate seeing friends and invite them to your home—especially couples. Reciprocate—don't expect others to do everything for you while you grieve and do nothing in return.
—*Woman, 69, 4*

Being sociable means putting the welfare of the group ahead of the individual—and that, ironically, means putting yourself forward. And don't be taken aback if you must *over*extend yourself somewhat:

Be sociable. If people invite you for dinner, invite them back. Have parties on your own. Don't expect people to feel sorry for you, and don't wait to be invited to things. Take the initiative and entertain as you may have before widowhood—maybe even more.
—*Woman, 61, 12*

My advice to other widows and widowers would be always to do your part and maybe a little more than your part. When my married friends invite me to dinner or take me to lunch, I don't wait very long until I repay them. I entertain both of them for their entertaining me once. I also give them little surprise gifts—a book, a box of candy, or cookies I make when their children come to visit. I don't brag, but they love me, and I'm always in demand. I do the same with my single friends. Even people with a lot of money like to be remembered for their kindness. Many widows think they have this coming to them.
—*Woman, 73, 8*

By thinking the opposite, she continues, she has transformed entertaining into an entertainment for herself:

> *I have many friends—couples we went to college with, and I also have a lot of widowed friends. They won't let me stay home, so I'm on the go constantly. I still belong to bridge clubs, study clubs, and a couples' dinner club, which by now has six widows and two widowers. I volunteer to do things, and I take my turn to entertain—I am older than many of the members, but it's a game I play. It makes me feel good.*

For Syd also, reciprocity lies less in any tally of deeds done tit for tat than in the attitude that has made those deeds come naturally:

> **Emily:** *Continue with your friends, keep your friendships going.*
> **Q:** *How do you do that when people drop you? How do you handle it?*
> **Emily:** *I'm not in that situation.*
> **Q:** *But some people are facing that, so what would you advise them?*
> **Ruth:** *You have to invite, too.*
> **Elizabeth:** *Absolutely, it's a two-way street.*
> **Syd:** *I'll tell you what. In order to have friends, you have to* be *a friend. And people that* are *friends* have *friends. I have a multitude of friends. I can't handle any more.*
>
> —*Miami, #2*

To which Ann mutters darkly, "It doesn't work that way every time." We earlier heard her grounds for saying so (page 321)—and they did not reveal her to be someone who could not necessarily "*be* a friend." It was just that, with old friends, she was at an impasse. Unfortunately, her words find echoes among almost as many survivors as the ones we've just finished hearing from. For those others, somehow the deeds do not bear fruit, the effort is not repaid, the right attitude avails nothing. And they must deliver themselves of Ann's dour RIP: "The strongest friendships are no more."

For survivors like her, new friends must come to the rescue, but, before we turn to that topic in the next section, it's worth looking further at why *all* the old friendships can seem to fail—and, if that's the case with you, whether you can't reconcile yourself to it. We'll start with this question: who is rejecting whom in these cases? And "rejection" is not too strong a word. Witness how fiercely this woman slams the door on her past:

> *Do not expect to continue your social life with previous friends; it's impossible. Plan to establish a new life for yourself—new friends, new activities, probably new surroundings.*
>
> *—Woman, 67, 10*

Not everyone is as vigorous, and apparently unremorseful, about obliterating the old as she and Ann are, but even they may be recoiling from having been shunned first. And others don't conceal that they were haunted by the shame of being outcasts, at least for a while. This woman remembers how stung she was by

> *the feeling of loss of "position." I was a college professor's wife for thirty years, and all of a sudden that distinction is gone. I was immediately excluded from private social gatherings of college friends, I suppose because I was the numerically odd person. After a time of feeling hurt and rejected, I have sought new acquaintances in other circles and have practically no connection with the college community.*
>
> *—Woman, 61, 6*

Nothing ignites eloquence like being forsaken:

> *I feel that I have lost my line of communication to people that we knew only mutually. It's like being in a room without windows.*
>
> *—Woman, 64, 2*

This woman sounds the knell of her isolation in long, doleful "o's":

> *Being a widow is a very lonely business. Old friends fade away. A lone older woman is a social liability.*
>
> *—Woman, 77, 15*

A liability, that is, to those who still possess the asset of a husband or wife. And they may have comprised practically all of your friends. These two were bitter enough about theirs to convict the whole lot of hypocrisy:

> *Do not rely on so-called old friends—they will abandon you. You will be considered to be a "fifth wheel" at any of their social functions. You will not receive as many invitations as before. The only people who*

*will be of help and comfort to you are other widows or widowers
who are in the same boat.*

—Woman, 70, 4

*The hardest thing for me was so-called friends who never telephoned or
visited after my husband's death. My job and the wonderful people I
worked with saved me. I realized that I had to make new and* sincere
friends on my own, which I did.

—Woman, 73, 17

And it's not only women who are nursing a sense of betrayal:

Raymond: *Most of your friends push you aside when you are by your-
self because they're husband and wife and you are—you might as
well say you're single. They want no part of you, and don't let any-
body tell you anything different!*
Q: *Really. Has anybody had a different experience?*
Al: *I haven't found it that way.*
Murray: *I haven't either.*
Noel: *I found it the opposite. I mean, I have some relatives—*
Raymond: *I'm not talking about relatives, we're talking about friends!
No, they don't want you around! You can't tell me that—because
they're husband and wife and they go dancing, and you're only in
the way. Unless you've got a girlfriend with you.*
Al: *I'm going to go to some friends right from here.*
Raymond: *[with an overall snort of disbelief]: Ahhh!*

—New York, #2

Although Ray has identified one generally applicable reason why
he's been shouldered aside, the vehemence with which he overrides
Al and Noel lends weight to this woman's apprehension that you will
blame those friends—or yourself—exclusively:

*I think the worst shock for widows is being dropped from the social
lists of many, and I would suggest talking this over with others, so as
not to take it too personally.*

—Woman, 56, 9

The "too" is a key qualification, for how can those who have
experienced it *not* take it personally to some degree? But one reason

comes to the fore again and again: the almost unthinking proneness of the still-married to ostracize the newly single (that word Ray finds so distasteful). The phenomenon has been surfacing throughout this section, of course; but we've largely been emphasizing what survivors have done to counteract it. We'll hear now, and hear loudly, from those who could not.

Many put it into this nutshell:

> *It is a "couples' world" and the loss of a spouse in whom to confide and share life's joys makes the adjustment to single life as difficult as it is lonely.*
>
> *—Woman, 64, 6*

> *Realize that life may change drastically—e.g., professional associations will probably dwindle, and in the case of widows social engagements may diminish (it's a couples' world!).*
>
> *—Woman, 61, 9*

This "truth" is propounded with everything from philosophical shrugs to cries of consternation. The cruelties of it stagger this woman, who, widowed a mere three years, can't help calling old friends "ours" rather than "mine":

> *Our former married friends have deserted me. They call on the phone— and then tell me that they are on their way out with other* couples. *They see friends of ours of long standing but don't consider that I might like to see old friends. In other words, they're* couple-*oriented.*
>
> *—Woman, 65, 3*

This woman has had four more years to collect herself and is still transfixed by nostalgia:

> *At times, I feel it is a world of couples and often contemplate how much different and better it would be if my husband were still with me.*
>
> *—Woman, 71, 7*

Likewise for another who has had double her time:

> *Am still quite lonely—my married friends whom we saw as couples dropped me like a hot potato.*
>
> *—Woman, 82, 14*

To survivors like these, this discovery heralds the single biggest transformation, and often the most unexpected, that the death brings about:

> *My lifestyle, I find, has changed completely upon my husband's death. I miss being with couples socially.*
>
> —*Woman, 81, 2*

And even those who've salvaged something of the past can't look backward without the same longing:

> *Adjustment is easier if you can accept that it is a couples' world and you will no longer be included. This has been very difficult for me because not only have I lost my husband but also the close contact with dear friends (couples) who include me occasionally now, but whom I no longer see on a regular basis.*
>
> —*Woman, 59, 3*

> *Socially it's a couples' world. A widow's social life takes a deep plunge, and I miss dreadfully the conversations with mixed couples. I find, if I want to be invited out, I must do some entertaining myself and try to have people in for a meal at least once a week—couples as well as singles. It's not easy without a host's help, but it can be done. I find it's your friends who help you with your day-to-day problems and see you through your crises.*
>
> —*Woman, 78, 8*

For some, though, the strain of being "the odd one"—a social as well as numerical anomaly—just proves too much:

> **Lil:** *Afterwards, I broke away from my friends who had their husbands, because, whenever I was asked anywhere by them, I was . . . well, the odd one.*
>
> —*Boston, #2*

The fact that you are now only one may carry this consequence:

> *It's a lonesome life—if you go visiting, you're always a loner.*
>
> —*Woman, 71, 4*

Add a couple and that makes three, a number so unpalatable to this woman she prefers to be one again:

> *I find that my good friends are always there, but, as time flies (six years ago, G. died), they check me out but do not think of me as before. Three's a crowd—I feel that saying is true. Really, I don't care to go to old familiar places. I do my thing often by myself—I can cope with no New Year's party, no Super Bowl party.*
>
> *—Woman, 69, 6*

Worse yet, add two couples and you get five, a sum that gives rise to the ubiquitous metaphor of the spare tire:

> **Edna:** *As the saying goes, I felt very much like the fifth wheel. Because all my friends were my husband's too, and everything that we did was together. And I was just gradually dropped out of their organization, you might say. I don't think I have—I know I don't have—one married friend left. They're widows.*
>
> *—San Francisco*

> *Widows and widowers should not feel bad when they are a fifth wheel, they should learn to live with it. It is a fact those you socialized with as a couple will for the most part become very scarce. It is almost like starting over.*
>
> *—Woman, 48, 7*

It's as if the death had declared them aliens in a country they'd come to regard as their native land:

> *You are no longer a "couple" and don't feel comfortable with the old bridge and dinner groups.*
>
> *—Woman, 71, 3*

> *As a widow I see decidedly less couple-friends. My life no longer fits in.*
> *—Woman, 80, 5*

Gladys quite literally could not fit in—save with one sterling exception:

> *I know I'm single, but when a married couple drives up and you jump in the backseat . . . [grimacing]. I went through that with my mother, I went through that with my mother-in-law, and now here I am—some-*

times very dressed up, going to the country club, and I'm in the backseat! It gets to you [clenching fists]. But I do know one married couple, and, bless them, when I go to open the back door, she says, "What are you doing? Get in the front seat with us." I say, "There isn't enough room." She says, "There's always room for you." And all I can say is, "God bless her!"

Elaine: *You have one good friend there!*

Gladys: *I don't see her that often, but she is a woman who has compassion. That's compassion!*

—Los Angeles, #2

Elaine was subtly made unwelcome by her group of theater-going friends—and none of the generosity she had shown other couples was extended to her now:

We used to have theater tickets with a group, and, if we couldn't go, we'd call somebody and say, "Here are our tickets. We can't go tonight." And after my husband died, one of our dear friends called me and said, "Do you want to subscribe to the theater again with us." And I said, "I'd love to. But, you know, I wouldn't want to meet you at the theater. Can I meet you in Westwood, or somewhere, and we can go together?" "Well . . . I don't know. Sometimes we may go out to dinner, we may do this, we may do that." And the upshot was that I didn't subscribe. And nobody called me and said, "Well, come on along with us."

—Los Angeles, #2

If they had, she might then have run afoul of one of the most seemingly petty but often very sticky practicalities that lie in wait for the odd one out—"paying your way." We saw Ann speculating that she was shut out by friends who in part were "afraid that they might have to pick up the tab for you sometimes, just to be decent," and Jean conjures up the same image of the husband digging into his pockets and grumbling to himself—and afterwards to someone else:

First of all, when it comes to the money problem, how do you pay your way? You know, that's embarrassing. Because how do you say, "Please take this for my dinner or please take this for my theater"? The first time, they'll say, "Oh, no!" But then they'll say to their wives, "How long do you think I'll take your friend along?"

—New York, #1

Betty advances this solution:

> *Well, it's a little embarrassing when there's a man in the group and he insists on paying. The best way to repay I have found is to try to reciprocate by acting as a hostess.*
>
> *—Los Angeles, #2*

But as Connie observes, entertaining at home somehow doesn't compensate for the times when you are going out with couples:

> *You cannot keep up with these married people if you want to go places. If you want to go places—if you are just visiting socially, to someone's house for dinner, that's a different story. No, to go* out *you really have to go with your friends, where you share and pay your own way.*
>
> *—New York, #1*

Fay, Gladys, and Elaine have gained a footing of this sort with married friends, but it takes constant jockeying to maintain it:

> *Fay: I have friends I've known for many years, and then when this happened, I made it clearly understood right away: "When we go out to dinner, I'm going to pay my own way. Otherwise I can't go with you." And that's how it's been. I feel better about it, and I think they do, too.*
> *Gladys: Yeah, well there are times when the husband will say, "Tonight you are our guest."*
> *Elaine: Oh sure, it's just that I wouldn't want to feel that I am dependent. Sometimes my friends will say, "No way!" And then other times we'll walk into the restaurant, and I'll give the waiter my charge card and say, "Put it on there." Or I just happen to have two extra tickets for the theater. You* can *reciprocate. It depends on with whom. There are the givers and the takers.*
>
> *—Los Angeles, #2*

But ultimately the fifth-wheel syndrome has these women stumped:

> *Connie: Single, we know that you pay your own way. But what if you go out with couples?*
> *Ida: One solution would be to get theater tickets and let them pay for the dinner. You pay for the tickets.*
> *Connie: How could you pay for the four people and they pay for one dinner? $40.00 a ticket!*

Bea: [resignedly] It happens once . . . and that's about it.
Connie: Exactly, and then you go your own way.
Isabel: I have never gone to a restaurant with two of my friends and their husbands.
Connie: That's what I mean.
Sara: Friendships get less and less.

—*New York, #1*

Little obstacles like these, however, can scarcely explain why even lifelong attachments should shrivel up:

Ruth: My best friend—we grew up together, came to New York together—she came around once or twice with her husband. After that, she didn't know me.
Elizabeth: It stopped?
Ruth: It stopped. For no reason! You see, her husband was my first boyfriend, as it happened. Then we drifted apart. When we got to know each other again, he was married to her, I was married to my husband, and we lived within a block of each other. So we became friends again and all those years we were friends—until my husband died. There wasn't a weekend that we weren't together. Not a weekend! We went on vacations. All the time.
Q: After he died what happened?
Ruth: I think once or twice they came to the house, and then she'd phone me once in a while, but never inviting me.
Elizabeth: Did you ever call her?
Ruth: Yes. She lived not far from me, and I even stopped off to see her one day.

—*Miami, #2*

"For no reason" doesn't satisfy the many who want to plumb deeper (and it's surprising Ruth doesn't, given that the husband was once her "boyfriend"). A few take society at large to task:

Old married friends who were important to me just disappeared. Today's world has little continuity to cling to in times of stress. Society is just beginning to address itself to singleness and aloneness. I was prepared in all the logical ways to be independent, but had little preparation for the emotional impact.

—*Woman, 56, 2*

One finds oneself abandoned on a lonely planet, and one gets little support from society.

                                                                    —Woman, 60, 2

This woman seems to spy some complicity on the part of particular institutions:

There are many of us who find that couples don't want us. Universities drop the spouse (wife in this case).

                                                                    —Woman, 75, 3

Much more commonly blamed by women in particular, though, is the psychology of the individual, specifically that of the wife:

Edna: I belong to a singles' club, and the only men there now are the husbands of the women who have gotten married.
Ann: They look daggers at you if you look at their husbands.
Edna: Like one man on the trip said, "You ladies better be nice to me—I'm the endangered species" [laughter].

                                                                    —San Francisco

The next chapter contains more such vignettes of female jealousy—and male complacency. Both come in for some typically raucous derision from Frieda:

I have found that, when I came along, married couples shied away, no matter where I have moved. They're afraid we single women are going to steal their "bargains" [laughter]. Who wants 'em? It's true—who wants those bargains? They're half-dead, most of them [laughter]. I'm old but I'm still alive.

                                                                    —Miami, #1

But not all find it so easy to scoff. Sexual jealousy, like all jealousy, may be emotion misplaced, but it's enough to make this woman think twice about being mistaken for a "bargain-hunter":

For myself, I avoid being with friends when the husband is present, or asking his help, so I am not accused of "husband-stealing."

                                                                    —Woman, 62, 5

This one advises you to get the property owner's permission first or face a charge of trespassing:

> *Consult your female married friends before you ask the husband for advice or assistance with your problems.*
> —Woman, 73, 3

But jealousy can make him turn against you too. Judy explains how— to the momentary confusion of our moderator, who assumes Judy refers to the conventional opposition:

> **Judy:** *Their husbands told my friends, "I don't want you going out with her, she is a swinging single"—as if we were out to pick up somebody! This is the honest-to-God truth! I wasn't too bad when I was younger—as my son says, "a foxy chick." Anyway, the husbands didn't want the wives even to go out for coffee with me. I could be . . . the merry widow, I guess. They were afraid I was going to lead their wives astray—and I wasn't even dating at the time. And that makes you even more sad because you figure, these were really close friends, you hung around with these couples all your married life! I even went to school with some of them.*
> **Q:** *Did that happen to anybody else? That the wives said, "You better not hang out with my husband"?*
> **Judy:** *It wasn't the wives. It was the husbands that didn't want their wives to go out with me, because I might put ideas in their heads.*
> **Q:** *Did anyone else run into that?*
> **Julia:** *No, but I've heard about it.*
> —Boston, #2

Jealousy plainly has a hand in making husbands like these close ranks with their wives. But what about husbands who couldn't care less whom the wives associate with? As long, that is, as those single women don't infringe on *their* lives:

> **Gladys:** *I've had a friend for many years, and her husband really doesn't want single women around. And there are so many among her friends. He says, "Go out and have lunch with them, do whatever you want. But not with me." Can't stand us.*
> —Los Angeles, #2

Here we may have entered a further dimension in the couples' world—the fear of death. And not exclusively on the part of couples, of course. That fear may have been at the bottom of the complaint that this woman scribbled next to her "no" when asked if she sees any close friends:

> *Friends, neighbors—even relatives—shy away from you.*
> —Woman, 73, 4

Mary seems to have sensed what already might be stealing over the husbands and wives alike in her group; and after acting to forestall it, she had her intuition confirmed by the most honest of those friends:

> *Somebody said something about a "fifth wheel." Can we go back to that a minute? We belonged to a couples' bridge club. There were six couples, and every month we'd be at a different home. We had three card tables in my living room, and we had a buffet dinner and everything. Well, my husband was the first one to go out of this world, and when he did, my very best friend said, "Mary, you're still coming. We'll get somebody else for you. We'll get another widow. I know a widow who'll come." I said, "God bless you, Lilly, no, it's a couples' club." And I quit. Because I couldn't—it would be nice later, but I wasn't going to go right away. And sure enough, she said, "Mary, you were so right. They didn't want you." You know, she didn't say it that way—she said it kindly. But what it came down to was that all the men there were my husband's age; these were all married women and they could put themselves in my place. And I think the men too were afraid of their own mortality.*
> —San Francisco

Then she goes on to report the ironic denouement. The friends that may have been driven away by intimations of mortality were eventually brought back by their actual encounters with it, each diminished by one:

> *They didn't want me around to remind them, you know. But it really took me years to get over it, and . . . .*
> **Ann:** *It hurts.*
> **Mary:** *It hurts. But, you know, it's funny, three of them are widows now.*
> **Ann:** *So now you have four! Now you have a bridge table!*

Mary: Yes, we have the Irish Mafia: McGarry, McCusker, O'Brien. [laughter]. We play bridge. And we each put a quarter in, and last time I won it. High stakes! My son was home over the weekend, and I said, "Tom, today is my bridge group." He says, "I'm going to get the heck out of here before that Irish Mafia comes."

She's made the passage from one social landscape to another—but only as her friends did too. The knowledge that "there but for the grace . . . " may not invariably make people turn aside:

Marilyn: My friends kept me with them, and I didn't feel like a third party, I really didn't. In fact one of my friends took my loss very, very much to heart and changed her whole lifestyle. Because she realized suddenly, "My God, this could happen to me!" And I've never seen anything like it, we were all amazed. She did a complete about-face, and it really did make a difference in her life. That's a curious thing. Very curious.

—Boston, #2

She's right to be bemused—such a flowering of empathy is rare indeed. Most aren't capable of it until fate forces the same experience on them:

Edna: I know someone who had a very close friend. They had been friends since they were very young girls and, when she became a widow, she wanted to go to see her, down South somewhere where she was living. And the girl asked her not to come. She said, "I'm working nights, and I just don't like to have you be here alone with my husband." Then she lost her husband and she wanted to come up here. And Ruth was saying, "Now the shoe is on the other foot!"
Ann: Nice story!

—San Francisco

Like them, you may find it hard to repress a certain vengeful relish when you hear of a similar reversal of fortune. One friend of Gladys is now penitent "too late":

I was at someone's home for dinner one night, and one woman whom I knew was there and her husband wasn't. And I figured, it's tax time (he's an accountant), he's probably busy. A couple of months later I was

at another affair and again I saw her alone, and then I inquired. I was informed, and so I went over and I extended my condolences. I told her, "I didn't know your husband had died." She said, "You know, we had a friend whose husband died. We took her out to dinner . . . once. Now I know what we should have done and didn't." But then it's too late.
—Los Angeles, #2

But suppose she had done "the right thing"—would that have assured her of repayment when her turn came? Again we hear from Gladys:

I have another friend who lost her husband, and every single night she was with my husband and myself. Every single night, even when we went out as much as we could, she was always asked. Well, the tables have turned. She's developed a different kind of a life . . . [with a wave of dismissal] whatever. It's not reciprocal.
Elaine: *Very rough.*
—Los Angeles, #2

If these stories yield one lesson, it's that, where couples are concerned, you'd best abandon pat expectations about how they or you will behave. But if certain patterns start emerging, recognize them for what they are—something "natural":

You and your husband may have had many friends and acquaintances because of his professional position. After his death you may feel embittered at how few of them continue on the same level of intimacy, but be glad if you have some who do. Socializing is no longer easy and natural without a spouse.
—Woman, 68, 25

Rancor—or self-reproach—will impede your efforts either to keep old friends or to resign yourself to their loss:

Seek new interests and people whenever possible, and try not to wend away from close old friends. Couples tend to socialize with couples after a while, so don't be hurt. It doesn't mean they do not want you . . . open your door with hospitality to all you can. Don't wait until they invite you. Be a tiny *bit* aggressive *on this score.*
—Woman, 73, 9

I do not expect to be included in couples' activities and so am rarely offended.

—Woman, 62, 7

Retain old friendships if it feels comfortable, but don't feel guilty if your contact decreases. Do make new friends.

—Woman, 54, 3

Ideally, to understand is to forgive, as Elizabeth did when tutoring a newly widowed friend in "the way of the world":

Within twelve months of my husband's death, hers passed away. I gave her a lot of sympathy, and I went with her everywhere. After a few months she called and asked, "Have you heard from the So-and-sos?" I said, "Well, once in a while I call her or she calls me." "Do you know that they haven't called me? They haven't been near me?" I said, "Well, why are you different than I was?" "What do you mean?" "This is exactly what you did to me. But I don't hold it against you. I understood. In fact, I was flattered that you would think that your husband would be interested in me." And that's where it ended. I still see her, I never parted friendship with her. But I let her know that what others did to her, she had done to me. And she shouldn't be angry because that's the way of the world.

—Miami, #2

New Friends

To be newly valued for yourself alone—that, as we've seen, has been the reward sought by survivors from old and new friends alike. It's time to listen to those who unhesitatingly give the edge to the new, at best in the same mood of acceptance we have just witnessed:

The wisest advice I could give is to accept the fact that your circle of long-time friends will change dramatically. It is a couples' world, and it is natural and normal that in most cases their lifestyle will be entirely different than yours is now. It is not that they have deserted you—it is that you are "one" now instead of a "couple." It is very important that you make new friends that share common interests with you. You can be alone without being lonely!!!

—Woman, 60, 3

This woman also evolved from the phantom remnant of a "two" to a real "one":

> *Many old friends abandoned me after my husband's death, seeming not to see the remaining half of a couple. But new friends took their place, seeing me as a whole, not a half. I felt restored to a whole person through meeting people who never knew my husband; this fact gave me a lot of courage and hope. My advice is to work, keep very busy and productive, make many new friends, and of course keep in touch with old ones if they are helpful.*
>
> *—Woman, 71, 24*

And this one, despite having old friends who *were* helpful, likewise prefers the company of those untrammeled by any memories of "the other half":

> *My friends were very supportive, but I found it easier to join groups who had not known my husband.*
>
> *—Woman, 63, 11*

Among those we surveyed who saw close friends regularly, more than one in five—21%—reported they saw the new more than the old.

Acquiring new friends in no way demands that you divest yourself of the old—we've already seen ample proof to the contrary. But if old friends find something wanting in you, it may occur to you that the converse is true. Gladys seems to have sensibly decided that if her more casual married friends saw her as half a couple, there was no reason not to respond in the same spirit:

> *I've been invited to people's homes, and I've also been invited out to dinner. And these are peripheral friends; they're not people that are really close, that I see often. And a couple of weeks ago I gave a luncheon, and I invited only the women—because I thought that was the best way.*
>
> *—Los Angeles, #2*

Contrast them with Elaine's new friends who—couples though they may be—appreciate her just for herself:

> *A lot of my friends, couples who I thought were dear friends, gradually*

*they dropped away. With some of the new friends that I have made,
married couples, you're accepted differently. You are accepted as a
single, as a widow, and the relationship is entirely different. You can go
out with them—not all the time, but there are times when you can.*

—*Los Angeles, #2*

Her outlook on herself may have undergone as much of a shift as
her friendships have. We may be watching the same change at work
in this woman:

*Seek out new friends (single people that will be in similar situations).
Stay in touch with old friends, but they will not be as apt to do the same
activities you may want to do now.*

—*Woman, 51, 2*

Her preferences, not theirs, are what govern her. That difference may
be what separates these two, affronted alike by the insults a couples'
world has dealt them:

*We feel alone, left out!!! We used to be active socially with mixed
groups—families with husbands. Now you feel separated from this
social life and forced to go places, to travel, with women friends. On
tours, all over the world, of the forty-four passengers on the bus, you see
only two or three who have husbands.*

—*Woman, NA, NA*

*Do not expect much from your friends. As a widow you become a second-
class citizen. You are not included in social activities by your married-
couple friends. Making new single friends helped me a lot. I traveled
with them.*

—*Woman, 79, 20*

To one, traveling on her own is just another of her grievances; to the
other it's a way out of them. If you lack the incentive for doing the
new, new friends may propel you into it—and prevent you from
drifting into self-pity:

*It is essential that one sees old friends but also makes new friends
who are stimulating and increase one's interests in new exploits. Do
not feel sorry for yourself—learn to laugh!!!*

—*Woman, NA, NA*

Some crossed the line quite deliberately, after a dwindling cohort of old friends signalled the need for a hard-headed self-appraisal:

The observation of one widow is true, I think: the first year, all your married friends continue to include you in their social affairs. The second year there is less of this. By the third year a small nucleus remains. You better decide how you can get involved with other groups of widows or singles or couples, whichever you prefer.
—Woman, 84, 23

This woman recommends a similar stock-taking, without necessarily restricting the answers to other people:

I believe survivors should realize that singles move in somewhat different circles than couples. This should be simply accepted. Then sort out the things that one enjoys the most and find the outlets which best serve single status.
—Woman, 65, 3

And indeed this woman has gravitated toward outlets that are more solitary than social:

Many of my friends have become widows. No matter what their husband's profession (most were executives), they now discover they have been, basically, relegated to a women's world. Your social life changes drastically. Your contact with couples will fall off dramatically. Books and music became extremely important in my life.
—Woman, 81, 6

But more commonly you are urged to move further outside yourself than deeper within:

If it seems your couple friends are forgetting or you feel you might be imposing by accepting invitations from them, get with the singles (I prefer that word to widow or widower). They can be very supportive.
—Woman, 74, 4

Don't get depressed when couples drop you from their couples' social activities and you become more widow-, or female-, oriented. Broaden your contacts and activities.
—Woman, 78, 12

Two of the last three, you'll notice, seem resigned to having their world of singles be a single-sex one—something that troubles other women deeply. We'll encounter more about this shortly, when we hear widows on the topic of being with their own kind. Men don't seem bothered by the equivalent phenomenon—perhaps because it doesn't exist. The causes for its absence could range from the far-fewer widowers (in our survey, as in life at large) who are around to voice complaints about it, to one of the consequences of that fact: widowers find it much easier to remarry and have their membership in the club of couples reinstated. Something like the latter clearly preoccupies the only man in our survey who expressed any thoughts on the subject:

> *Seek friends (partners) who have had the same experience. Cherish the memory of the departed spouse, but also be ready to develop friendships with other people (including the opposite sex), especially with the ones with the same or similar experience.*
> —*Man, 63, 3*

Widows rather than widowers are on his mind, perhaps because, among other things, he may be seeking to replace someone who had created his social milieu for him:

> **Gladys:** *It's the woman who is the focal point, who is the pivot, who says, "Let's take Gladys out." I don't think the husband thinks of it.*
> —*Los Angeles, #2*

> *The women sometimes are at a loss as to the finances of the family. But then the men who have had their wives arrange their social lives are just as much at a loss.*
> —*Woman, 59, 3*

Despite all the contemporary glibness about male bonding, men without women still tend to be more ingrained loners than women without men.

In the next chapter we'll see more of such motives in the relations between the sexes. Here, we're focussing on new *friendships*—and some women's style of marriage has made those essential if they are now to enjoy *any* social life:

My husband and I were so close throughout our lives we felt we didn't need anyone else besides our children. He and I did everything together. I would suggest to others to make many other friends through life, if possible.

—Woman, 75, 5

Cultivate friends who are not necessarily your spouse's. We did everything together. He enjoyed his home life, so we didn't socialize much. Therefore, I don't do much socializing since he's been gone.

—Woman, 72, 6

I wish we had not led such a closed life together; this habit of retreating into ourselves made it difficult for me to reach out to others after his passing.

—Woman, 68, 3

This woman had to start from nothing too, but she succeeded:

Because my husband and I spent a great deal of time pursuing interests away from our hometown, and because we were both quiet people, we lacked the kind of close, supportive friends that I was to need after his death. I had to develop a whole new world to survive in.

—Woman, 56, 2

How? Most likely by dint of that grubby little word that keeps bobbing up in this book—effort:

Do not go into seclusion. It takes tremendous effort to force yourself to attend functions alone, but there is at least an opportunity to meet others in similar situations.

—Woman, 62, 4

Once again, we are exhorted to knuckle down to it sooner rather than later:

Get involved with something. The longer you are alone and uninvolved, the harder it will be to get out and make friends—and you will need to make new friends.

—Woman, 69, 3

And that may be draining:

Keep close to old friends. Make new friends to do things with (this is not so easy—one has to take the initiative—don't wait for them to come to you).

—*Woman, 81, 16*

Friends will help, but you can't predict which ones will—and which will just vanish. So you have to be open to new friendships, and that takes effort that you may feel you lack energy for. But it's worth pushing yourself—and besides, life can seem pretty empty if you just sit back and think about your loss.

—*Woman, 62, 2*

For Gladys, "never say no"—despite the anxieties aroused by "exposing yourself"—applies as much to her chances for carving out the new as it does to patching up the old:

Well, apropos of what Fay said—"I won't go if I don't think I'm going to like the people who'll be there"—I have a friend who believes that you have to . . . expose yourself. You never know where you are going to meet someone. It could be a man or a woman, whoever can give you what you need or want, or nurture you. We don't know whether meeting someone here today might not develop into something socially. And if someone says, "Look, I have a brother-in-law who is a widower and I'd like you to meet him," you never know. It can drive you crazy because you are forever exposing yourself. But you have to do it.

—*Los Angeles, #2*

Her perseverance has borne fruit—bit by bit, through give-and-take, and notwithstanding the occasional spasm of boredom:

Q: You say you've made a network of friends. Where do you meet these people?
Gladys: Well, a friend of mine gave a luncheon. She's been a widow for many years, and we hadn't been in contact that much. But she had a big luncheon, and I met two women there that I became friendly with. But I have also given of myself. This one woman had surgery a few months ago, and I spent three nights with her, and she hasn't forgotten me for it. I'm going over there tonight, and I've met someone through her, and she's invited me to a certain movie tomorrow. Sometimes I get very tired of women and only women. But I'm on the phone constantly. At night I come home and sit with the phone, and I have a network I call and say,

"What are you doing?" And I try to plan my week.
                                        —*Los Angeles, #2*

Families helped some through the transition from old to new friends. This woman appears to be still using her family—along with her church—as a refuge from a previous social life:

Felt awkward about social situations—church parties, department parties at my husband's college, etc. Found most comfort in family and church relationships. Grateful for a large family who stay close by.
                                        —*Woman, 58, 4*

Isabel, however, has reemerged from a similar respite with her family, though it has taken her quite a while:

My sister and brother-in-law were very, very good to me, exceptionally good to me. They included me in their weekly functions, which was wonderful for me. And then it reached a stage where I had to make a break and go out on my own.
Q: Why did you feel that, Isabel?
Isabel: Because I felt that it wasn't fair to them to be with them every weekend.
Q: When did you get this feeling you should make a break?
Isabel: I started about a few years after my husband's death. I started to belong to a beach club, and then I met lots of people like me, single people. It took a little time, but I made a life and I have these friends who are very good for me.
                                        —*New York, #1*

On the other hand, one can overrate the difficulties, too. Ida makes an effort wherever people are gathered together—but selectively, not compulsively:

Q: Ida, earlier you were saying, "Get around a bit." What did you mean by that?
Ida: Well, go to places where other people congregate and see if they are friendly, if they are congenial. You latch on to those that appeal to you. Ignore the rest, because in large gatherings there are bound to be people that are not your sort, with whom you have nothing in common. But at least try, even if you have been a loner, make an effort.
                                        —*New York, #1*

In the last chapter, we reviewed a parade of new pursuits that can bring new friends in their train: paying jobs, volunteer ones, classes, clubs, group travel. But some saw new friends as the object of the exercise from the start:

> *Make new friends—a good way for me was by doing a lot of volunteer work in an Eldercare home, in a Women's Center, in an art gallery, in a hospital.*
>
> *—Woman, 79, 11*

Fay's synagogue does double duty as a social club, for men as well as women:

> *You could meet men in temple. At temples they have all kinds of activities—for older people. You meet and you talk and you make friends, men and women both. So if you're a man, you don't have to be lost if you want to be active. They have a breakfast program and a lunch program, and in between there are arts and crafts, whatever you want to do—play cards, dance.*
>
> *—New York, #1*

Jean maneuvers her way with aplomb through shoals on which many others have run aground—a weekend for singles at a resort. And she succeeds partly because she won't be deflected by preconceptions about the friends she ought to bring away from it:

> *Jean: I go up there once a year.*
> *Rae: How many men up there compared to the women?*
> *Jean: Quite a few men.*
> *Ida: I don't think you have to travel to country places. Senior centers offer this.*
> *Jean: But I like to take a vacation up there; it is very pleasant. It's an entirely different atmosphere. And I have made some very nice friends there. You should not take a negative attitude on that. You don't have to go up there looking for a boyfriend. You go up there to make friends.*
> *Rae: Do you keep these friends? Or are they just for when you're there?*
> *Jean: No, I've kept them. Many friends. As a matter of fact, I met a Canadian lady who was sitting at my table, I thought she was a lovely person. She said, "When you get to Toronto, look me up," and I said, "Same here when you come to New York." I have been to her home on*

vacation, she's been to mine, and we call each other at least once a month.

—*New York, #1*

Apart from these organized occasions for sociability, many survivors have become adept at exploiting the chinks that may open up in such mundane little routines as shopping:

Dorothy: *In the supermarket, I find friends. When I have to stand on a line, I don't get impatient, I always find somebody to talk to. Many times I come home with phone numbers.*
Marlene*: They could be just as lonely as you are.*
Frieda: *I talk to everybody. If I'm coming down in a building, in an elevator for two minutes, I'll talk to them.*

—*Miami, #1*

Not everyone is up to being so chatty—in fact, the more reserved may dismiss Frieda as downright pushy. But, as this woman implies, perhaps some of that reserve is more self-isolating than self-protective:

Widowhood is not going to change someone's basic personality, but perhaps one can cultivate one's more gregarious aspects.

—*Woman, 62, 12*

Marlene needs no rake or hoe to work in that particular garden:

When I'm in the grocery store, somebody talks to me, I talk to them. And I enjoy talking to people because that's the only way you're going to meet somebody, really. No matter where you are, you just get to know who you can talk to. It's something about the other person, maybe, that makes you want to talk to them.

—*Miami, #1*

This sixth sense may fail her every now and then, and she does have an adolescent daughter writhing in self-consciousness about how free and easy she is. But Marlene's ironic retort is well-aimed:

I'm friendly to everybody, I have always been that way. But one of the twins has this attitude—she cannot stand *it! I say, ''You mean you're going around in life until you* really *know somebody before you're going to talk to them?''*

For those getting on in years, there's one more reason to go recruiting as she does—the gaps in the ranks of your old friends may not have been left there by their own volition:

Make new friends as older friends pass on and your circle of them becomes smaller.
—*Woman, 80, 12*

Make friends among younger persons—aging and retirement result in the loss of many one's own age.
—*Woman, 76, 15*

Otherwise, some say, your social world stands to become fossilized:

Keep in contact with a whole range of people—young through oldsters. Stay out of senior citizen groups—except to join only when you want to participate in a selected activity.
—*Woman, 60, 5*

The same variety keeps physical as well as mental atrophy at bay for this woman, in part because her younger friends *don't* make allowances for her age:

Keep a wide range of friends if you can. You need peers who share your experience and time frame, but you need young friends, too, who expect you to keep on trucking and don't take your arthritis into consideration.
—*Woman, 62, 12*

The ages of this woman's dinner companions span more than half a century:

Build a network of friends—of all ages. Last week I went to dinner one night with co-workers in their 20s and 30s. The next night I had dinner with my neighbor who is 80.
—*Woman, 58, 3*

Her *husband's* job gave this woman a link to her juniors:

At times "when a door closes, a window opens." His students were so broken up by the death of their teacher that I requested they all sit with me at the funeral service, as I felt they needed my support. They visited me every evening for quite a while, and by now, sixteen years later, they have become my dearest friends—"my boys," as I call them.

—Woman, 81, 16

The younger your friends are in relation to you, however, the less your chance of having this in common: knowing what it is like to outlive a spouse. And that brings us to the final segment of this section, friendships with other survivors, the bond that meant the most for some:

In widowhood the most comforting friends are those in similar situations. I see more of new friends than old.

—Woman, 80, 11

For me, widowed friends offered the most support and help.

—Woman, 77, 6

For a few others, they are the *only* friends that matter:

Friends help, but only if they have experienced the same loss.

—Woman, 79, 8

Only people who went through the same as oneself can really understand it fully.

—Woman, 61, 6

Fellow survivors may have come to anchor the social worlds even of those whose old friends haven't drifted away:

Friends and neighbors are very helpful and kind. I am especially fortunate to have a new friend and neighbor, recently widowed. We have much in common. We can share our problems, sad times and happy times, we enjoy the same hobbies and shopping together. Most important—we are always close by to be helpful when we are needed in any way.

—Woman, 69, 2

Old friends still help by including me. However, I found accepting invitations to group weekly outings helped me to circulate again and to make new friends. Widowed people were the most *comforting. Also, I now have a special widower friend who makes life easier just by being there.*

—*Woman, 65, 8*

The lives of others have coalesced solely about their own kind:

Syd: My friends right now are all widows, and we have a lot in common, we play cards, we go out to dinner, to the pool, and we have a community center which I belong to. And so you make your own life.

—*Miami, #2*

Bea: I live in a big apartment house, with quite a few widows. So we get together, we seem to be compatible. Also I belong to a beach club in Brooklyn. And that's how we spend our days—go to the movies once in a while, play mah-jong, you know, all of that stuff.

—*New York, #1*

"All of that stuff" bespeaks a settled routine, as securely and sedately organized as that of any clique of couples. Those who can't fit into one scheme of things have devised a not-uncommon solution—creating an entirely separate alternative for themselves:

Team up with other widows, widowers, singles, to attend concerts, lectures, go out to dinner, etc.

—*Woman, 79, 12*

To some, it was almost as if they had stumbled into a "widows' world," a universe parallel to that of the couples:

I didn't realize how many widows are out there in life until I became one myself, and I now have several friends in that group.

—*Woman, 55, 2*

In spite of all you do, you will still miss your spouse. But remember you're not alone—there are thousands just like you. Call one—invite her (or him) over for lunch. Or go out—it can even be dutch treat. But don't *withdraw from the world.*

—*Woman, 73, 8*

A complementary "widowers' world," as we noted earlier, doesn't exist, and that may be why these women have banded together for the long haul:

> *Through church and social contacts we have developed a group of widows who travel together, go to concerts together, eat together a couple times a week, and generally see that no one of us feels lonesome. We are all realistic about what the next ten-plus years may bring healthwise and have planned to cope through the retirement communities available to us.*
>
> *—Woman, 77, 20*

Your counterparts may bring along two essential ingredients for a social life that your married friends may lack—the inclination and the time:

> *Though family members and friends can be supportive and most helpful, they have their own lives to live. It is other widows and widowers who have the time and interest in travel or other activities which make adjustment easier.*
>
> *—Woman, 67, 2*

Others chime in with the same word—it's easier:

> *It is very true, that old saying "you can be alone in a crowd"—especially when the "crowd" is mostly couples. I feel very sad when leaving such events. It is easier to go with other widows.*
>
> *—Woman, 64, 3*

> ***Laura:*** *I went out with a lot more couples back then. And now I just go mostly with singles. I do go with couples, but, as Lee says, I feel more comfortable with women who are in my own position. Because we just sort of do what we want, say what we want. I think it's easier.*
>
> *—Miami, #1*

The emotional logic of such companionship—the freedom to "say what we want"—is clearly assuming an importance equal to mere logistics—the ability to "do what we want."

For this woman, the practicalities of survivorship merge into the greater release of "just talking about it":

One does get comfort from those who had the same experience. My neighbor lost her husband the year before my husband died, and she did help me quite a bit. In handling estate matters and also just talking about it.

— *Woman, 62, 3*

It can be a genuinely two-sided conversation:

Find a friend who is also a widow. Another widow is more ready to share her experiences of grief with you in exchange for hearing yours.

— *Woman, 80, 3*

And you're not as liable to be hamstrung by taboos, as this woman suggests in noting why she prefers to "see new friends more":

Faculty friends are more afraid of death and talking about it than church/nurse friends.

— *Woman, 70, 4*

Another prizes the same forthrightness about the same facts:

"Old" friends could help by just calling to see how you're doing and showing they care, but it is surprising how they act like widowhood is catching. I was helped more by people I never knew before who had cared for my husband at home—two nurses and a physiotherapist whose sister had committed suicide.

— *Woman, 58, 3*

In fact, this woman rules out those who have only known losses of another type:

There is a natural rapport with others who are widowed (not divorced). Sharing this experience (in or out of a group) is part of the healing process.

— *Woman, 60, 20*

Sarah is offhand about the sense of solidarity that underpins the rapport:

After a while you make friends with other women in the same situation and develop a kind of sisterhood, I suppose.

— *New York, #1*

But others were startled by the ways it could manifest itself. Members of the sisterhood came out of nowhere to console Lillian even before her husband died, when he was lingering on in a New York City hospital after an unsuccessful cancer operation:

> *He only lived about five weeks afterwards, but I was there every day. And in this particular hospital, you couldn't stay with him all day—you had to leave for a few hours in the afternoon. And I would go over to Riverside Drive and sit on a bench and I'd cry and I'd cry. And people would come over to me, mostly women, and they'd say, "Well, what's your problem? What's the trouble?" And they'd tell me their stories.*
>
> —*Los Angeles, #1*

The aid this virtual stranger tendered came unbidden:

> *I found that, after the funeral, etc., and living alone, and so scared, the kindness I remembered most was another widow checking up on me for several weeks by phone to just talk. She was someone I had never met, although her second husband knew mine.*
>
> —*Woman, 65, 8*

Elaine cemented a lasting alliance with another widow in exactly the same fashion—again "before we ever met":

> *When I made a reservation for that weekend, I was crying because it was the first time since my marriage that I was going away alone. And about an hour later, I got a call back from the young lady I talked to. She said, "I've arranged for you to have a room for yourself." And I was quite touched by that, because I knew we were supposed to go two in a room.*
>
> *Then she said, "I have something else to tell you. After you called, another woman called and she broke down, just like you did. She told me that she, too, was a widow. I wanted to give her your phone number, but I hesitated. But I did tell her about you and I took her number. So if you care to call, go ahead."*
>
> *I did, and we became good friends. It was six months, at least six months, before we ever met, but every day we spent between forty-five minutes and an hour on the telephone. And when we did meet later, we started going away together. It was great for both of us to have somebody to talk to.*
>
> —*Los Angeles, #2*

True, there is a minority opinion about the desirability of consorting with your fellow sufferers:

> DON'T *get tied up with other widows, so that couples can't include you. Entertain couples.*
>
> > *—Woman, 67, 16*

And even some who no longer care about staying in the good graces of their married friends are leery of admitting survivors to the company of those they've found as substitutes, as this woman says with an edge in her voice:

> *Try to seek out new friends—many former friends are not interested in half of a couple. Others "in the same boat" are easier to be with, but this does become tedious.*
>
> > *—Woman, 57, NA*

Far from beckoning Ann on, the chance to share similar stories makes her turn her back:

> ***Ann:*** *I have one suggestion, if I may. Don't hobnob with widows if you're a widow.*
> ***Q:*** *Oh—why?*
> ***Ann:*** *Find people who are single for other reasons. There are women who have never been married and who are up in years. Then there are divorcees. They have different types of experiences. In other words—*
> ***Ruth:*** *Diversify!*
> ***Ann:*** *Diversify, don't run with your own breed, your own crowd, get a little bit away from it. The less you are among people who have had terrible experiences, the happier you will be.*
>
> > *—Miami, #2*

Some, although not rejecting all survivors, discriminate between those they judge are bearing up well and those who aren't:

> *If the widow has coped well herself, her advice and friendship are invaluable. But others who still seem to be adjusting after long years have had little time for my grief.*
>
> > *—Woman, 65, 2*

Groups of widowed people may be a help or a hindrance, depending on the people. Those who find activities are fine; those who spend their time talking about their former spouse, details of last illness, hardships since the death, are to be avoided.

—*Woman, 71, 5*

The same range of opinion emerges in the commentary on the last subject of this chapter—counselling. That word may repel you if it evokes an image of the experts taking you, the hapless novice, briskly into their custody and spooning into you large doses of one received doctrine or another—a caricature, of course, for counselling cannot work outside of a genuinely reciprocal context. But fraternizing with those like yourself may engage you (among other things) in getting—and giving—"counselling," with exactly the same benefits that others realize from the more formalized brand.

Staving off self-pity, for one:

I think getting with other widows (which I did not do for three or four years) is most supportive. It gave me a less self-centered attitude, finally.

—*Woman, 65, 21*

Learning to be open to help, for another:

My friend's husband died a year before Bob died, and her letters were probably the best help during the first months. She said, "Be angry, be hurt, be honest. Grief is natural and grieving goes through a process." She told me the way it was, and I'm most grateful to her. "Face it—Bob's gone—your life goes on."

—*Woman, 59, 2*

And ultimately being able to help in turn:

Comfort someone else. Expend your pent-up love on another lonely, grieving person.

—*Woman, 75, 3*

Comforting other friends who are widows through their difficult time gives one strength and a realization of how far you have come in facing your loss.

—*Woman, 72, 11*

As this woman acknowledges,

> *I don't think that you can be of use to everyone you know who loses a spouse—unless you're very special. But do reach out to anyone you feel simpatico with.*
>
> —*Woman, 62, 12*

And this one seems to have pulled off exactly that:

> *The most difficult adjustment is the loneliness. Reach out to others when they experience this loss. It helps you and them also. I reached out to a widow a year ago, and we have become very close friends. She has more strength and self-confidence, now that she has had to assume full responsibility for herself. She is doing an excellent job.*
>
> —*Woman, 67, 3*

A hint of the expert's pride in the novice's progress may be sneaking into her words here—a reminder that at least some authority must be assumed if one is to counsel others successfully. But between friend and friend that authority may of course be a much subtler affair than between counsellor and subject—especially if the latter is officially patient or client. And getting help of the non-"professional" variety, from your equals, may require that you defer to another type of authority—that of the group. Some find that not their style:

> *Your married friends drift away from you, but that is to be understood because you are now a single person. I became friends with several widows, and that companionship helped, as I am not a joiner of different groups.*
>
> —*Woman, 74, 12*

One's friendships, however, may constitute more than an assortment of scattered individuals:

> *I was the first widow in our social group. I was alone four months, and I went crazy with loneliness until I heard a golf buddy had lost her husband. She became a friend, and we went everywhere together. We met two others—new widows—and now the four of us are a close group.*
>
> —*Woman, 61, 6*

She progressed from the individual to the group, and of course you may prefer to do likewise. But, as an invitation to the skeptical to read on, we'll hear from one who did the reverse, with equal success:

> *I did not know any widows, widowers, or single people, only our friends and co-workers who were still all couples. My doctor suggested a singles group that had a variety of people—widowed, divorced, and separated adults—which he heard about from one of his patients. I looked into it, became involved, and through it made many new friends.*
>
> *These new friends have become an important part of my new life. We have many things in common, have many of the same problems, and do many things together. Meeting them was my salvation.*
>
> —Woman, 63, 8

Counselling

To many survivors, "counselling" stands for what Catherine rather delicately terms "that kind of help":

> **Catherine:** *First, I had to go to the doctor. Oh . . . I just had a nervous breakdown. There were so many things that I couldn't do afterwards! For some reason, I've always been a sort of an aggressive person, but I just went to pieces and I needed that kind of help. But, in the two years, I've gotten over most of the things that were wrong with me. I'm getting over it, you'd be surprised. It's not too bad.*
> **Ida:** *Say, "Thank God."*
> **Catherine:** *Oh, I do, I do. Are you kidding?*
> **Ida:** *Because there are so many people worse off.*
> **Frieda:** *First, we all need psychiatric care. Then you cool off.*
>
> —Miami, #1

Frieda may not be far off the mark, but hers is decidedly the minority view. While not restricting counsellors to professionals handling emergencies, most are inclined to regard them as fallbacks, people to whom you resort when being with others isn't delivering the help it should—or when you simply haven't found others to be with:

> *Find someone who listens; this person does not have to be a counsellor, although it is a good idea to seek one out if regular friends are not enough.*
>
> —Woman, 48, 2

Talk with other widows/widowers who can understand your feelings of sadness, anger, loneliness, loss of sharing and closeness. If this is not possible—a therapist.

—*Woman, 64, 3*

Noel believes that only special situations call for counselling:

I think the circumstances are the main thing. When my mother passed away, she was 42, but she had been sick for nine years, and it almost came as a relief to my father. And I don't think either of us needed counselling. But if it's a sudden thing, if something happens—bang—like an airplane disaster or a car crash or stroke, when it hits you where you're not expecting it, like John said, I think counselling is almost mandatory.

—*New York, #1*

For some it's a last-ditch measure to avert a breakdown:

Try to comfort others who are widowed, but avoid those who constantly feel sorry for themselves. Suggest counselling to the latter. When "the weight of coping" gets unbearable, seek professional counsel instead of discussing it with friends.

—*Woman, 69, 3*

In her eyes, the counsellor inhabits a preserve cut off from the realm of ordinary social life. The same line is drawn by others, who congratulate themselves on not having had to cross it:

I am from a very close-knit family (one brother, two sisters). One of the sisters is my twin, who had lost her husband just eight months before I did. I found them all to be the most support—and probably why I needed no outside support.

—*Woman, 71, 6*

I found that I received all the support I needed from my children and a few close relatives, who were always there when I needed help with situations that were too difficult to handle alone.

—*Woman, 74, 12*

And even some counsellors seem to pride themselves on having been able to forgo the ministrations of their own kind:

I did not seek counselling because I am a counsellor and know the grieving process and that what I was feeling was normal, if very painful. I did seek out a couple of other widows and a couple of colleagues when I was desperate to talk.

—Woman, 57, 3

Since I am a professional counsellor—therapist—my opinions are perhaps both personal and generalized. I found talking with friends about my feelings and about my husband—about how much I missed him—very helpful. I think that I did not seek professional help partly because several of these friends were colleagues of my husband who valued him and loved him also.

—Woman, 73, 8

About their own cases they may have been correct (the words of the last woman certainly seem to attest to that). And they undoubtedly speak for many more who share their outlook. But some countervailing opinion is definitely in order:

Assistance from recently widowed friends (or a widowed persons service) is invaluable.

—Woman, 75, 8

Seek out others who will listen to you without giving advice or becoming uncomfortable listening. These people are out there! It can be a professional mental health worker, minister, friend, relative.

—Woman, 64, 6

Don't try to avoid the grieving process—it is necessary to go through it. Don't be ashamed to grieve openly, find at least one person you can discuss all your feelings with. A friend who has been widowed can be very useful in helping. Or seek professional counselling and/or a support group.

—Woman, 64, 2

Observe how all three mention counsellors of different types in the same breath they do family and friends, as if they were almost interchangeable. But this woman sees in the former a necessary corrective to the good intentions of the latter:

Join a support group. Don't let your friends keep you so busy you don't

have time to sit down and really accept and understand your situation.
　　　　　　　　　　　　　　　　　　　　　　　—Woman, 63, 15

Pat decided likewise after it dawned on her that there is little point in having someone to talk to if he or she doesn't understand what you're saying:

And then I joined this support group. I wasn't going to rely on my one son in Santa Monica, even though he was calling every day. Because he was listening to me, but he wasn't hearing what I was trying to tell him, you know. He thought I was losing my mind, some of the things I was saying, and I probably was.
　　　　　　　　　　　　　　　　　　　　　　　—Los Angeles, #2

Sylvia was afraid even to speak to her children:

Q: What were you looking for?
Sylvia: *Just other people to talk to, somebody to share with. I have children, but I always felt that people came to me for support, that I couldn't do it the other way. So I didn't feel I could say anything to them because they'd worry about me. They'd get scared.*
　　　　　　　　　　　　　　　　　　　　　　　—Los Angeles, #2

At the other extreme, a group may have unchained this woman from the kind of dependency we were warned of earlier:

Don't try to live through your children. Join a support group and get out and do things.
　　　　　　　　　　　　　　　　　　　　　　　—Woman, 63, 3

And here is a counsellor who suggests he may have been guilty of a little hubris:

Very difficult to give advice, since each individual's starting point and resources are so very different. I am a male, *so that makes a big difference. I have had experience in the helping professions, and I am familiar with the stages of grief. So that's a difference. Nevertheless, I discovered, after almost a year, that I* could *have used professional counselling—and had trouble finding it. My wife and I were exceedingly close—and I had difficulty "letting go."*
　　　　　　　　　　　　　　　　　　　　　　　—Man, 68, 2

Granted, only a small slice of our group—11%—had availed themselves of "professional counselling to help deal with grief." And, of the rest, only 11% believed it would have done them good, as opposed to 57% who said "no" and 32% who were uncertain. "Rather find my own way," jotted down one next to her checkoff of "no" (woman, 87, 2); and another agrees:

> *I felt I could handle my own grief in my own way and adjust sooner, so I did not participate in any therapy sessions. To me they would only prolong the adjustment.*
>
> *—Woman, 68, 3*

This woman did give them a try—and came to the same conclusion:

> *I found that support groups didn't help much, because I had to work things out myself anyway.*
>
> *—Woman, 80, 5*

But going "my own way" held a different outcome for others:

> *I wish I'd had counselling within a few weeks—privately or in a group. I deeply regret becoming a workaholic and a bit reclusive.*
>
> *—Woman, 61, 7*

> *I would advise widows and widowers to seek more psychological aid. I wish I had—from the church or psychologists. Not to do so causes possible unnecessary grieving or feeling guilty, even though you may really know you did all you could. You may feel, also, that your spouse had not been very appreciative of your often superhuman efforts. In my case, I had no children to talk to, and only two much older sisters with whom I could communicate by phone. They lived hundreds of miles away. I had to "talk to myself," so to speak, but it made my health degenerate.*
>
> *—Woman, 82, 11*

Another woman seems on the verge of a similar realization. Next to her acknowledgment on her questionnaire that counselling might have helped, she writes, "I still have my problems after eight years, but I try to keep it to myself." And her long essay, briskly cheerful in spots, meanders to this melancholy standstill:

I feel I am really depressed inside, and I can't help it. I feel I don't have anything to look forward to. I do have a lovely daughter, son-in-law (an attorney), and a grandson who is 28 and an M.D. and a 16-year-old granddaughter. But sometimes I feel so all alone in my own family. I try to be very independent and not to show how I really feel about being a widow.

I haven't written about this before, so I didn't realize all this would come out of me. I hope it is a little bit of help to you. Nobody knows *I feel blue because I don't show it.*

—*Woman, 73, 8*

Some say the danger of getting bogged down in your emotions like this is best met by speedy intervention:

If professional help seems necessary, by all means seek it out as soon as possible.

—*Woman, 71, 24*

Let others help you—talk it over with family and friends and seek a support group after a few months. Seek immediate counselling if you feel it is necessary.

—*Woman, 49, 3*

Nor need you feel *in extremis* before you do. Although this woman apparently wasn't facing an emergency, she wishes she hadn't been so dilatory:

I went to a widow/widower group about ten months after my husband's death. I should have started earlier. I was well on the road to recovering at that point, but could have used the group early on.

—*Woman, 55, 7*

And this one, who portrayed herself earlier as "in a fog and very frightened" the first year, appears to have gotten on top of things, but could have used a boost in doing so:

My advice for other widows is to try to get some professional help. I decided to return to work after nineteen years, and, with the annuity checks I receive, I run the household the best I can. I do admit I find it difficult working, running a home, and trying to help my daughters make decisions pertaining to college. We try to talk it out and see what's

best. Both are good students and have received some scholarships. But sometimes I think that, if I had sought professional help, I could have coped much better not only with loneliness but almost everything.
—Woman, 53, 2

Her mention of her daughters reminds us that counselling may not profit you alone:

Professional help in dealing with the death of a spouse is one of the best things I did for myself and my family. To understand why you have certain feelings and that they are a normal part of grief is a great mental relief.
—Woman, 45, 2

This woman brought the family along:

Counselling was/is very helpful. I received a great deal of support from a bereavement group at a local hospital. I also saw a psychologist on a private basis—with my children, who were 15 and 13 at the time.
—Woman, 41, 2

Another's children eventually joined her and a counsellor in resolving an unsettling "paradox"—that becoming a grandmother on the heels of becoming a widow exacerbated her grief instead of tempering it:

Grieve however long it takes and pay enough attention to the psyche. I wish I had been encouraged to see a therapist soon after my husband's death, because my family of young adults were difficult to grieve with. My only daughter's first baby was born just one month after my spouse's death—very upsetting and difficult for me to deal with. This caused me much anxiety until the strange paradoxes were explained to me by an excellent therapist after a relatively few sessions—bringing us all together for the final one.
—Woman, 62, 3

Even if others don't participate with you, counselling may benefit them indirectly by giving you a less parochial and self-involved slant on them:

Seek counselling to talk about your children, your friends, and how you're coping after your spouse's death.

—Woman, 38, 2

If you think counselling might work for you (and if you've read this far, you've probably formed an opinion), you have quite a wealth of choice, an abundance of which many survivors still aren't fully cognizant:

Tom: I believe many aren't aware that there is specialized *counselling on the subject or even that there is any counselling at all. And it's too bad, because a lot of people don't know which way to turn in a situation like this.*

—New York, #2

In fact, some have made a specialty of helping survivors locate the right match for their needs:

The Widowed Persons Service is a big help—didn't have this organization when I first was widowed. For the past six years now, I have been on the Board of WPS and am also a counsellor.

—Woman, 79, 11

The nonprofit Widowed Persons Service, founded by the American Association of Retired Persons, is now the country's most extensive umbrella organization for survivors. As noted in ''Resources,'' it can refer you to various counselling programs in your area—or even help you to organize one—as well as pass on information about such matters as managing your finances and finding a job.

Of course other purveyors of counsel have been in business for centuries:

John: I am not overly religious, but I was raised a Catholic. And, to my surprise, I got a lot of solace from talking to a parish priest. The only thing that occurred to me after having seen a counsellor was that he was younger than I and his contact with this experience was zilch. You know, it was all intellectualizing. This priest had seen people die every other day.

—New York, #2

As Sylvia complains in the Prologue (page 7), not every representative of organized religion is up to conducting you through a catharsis. But when Nora hit bottom, a clergyman enabled her to make it a turning point:

> *Nora: If it's possible to enjoy being a widow, I think I am. I'm not too sad, the way I was.*
> *Q: Were you in the beginning?*
> *Nora: Yes.*
> *Q: What did you do about it?*
> *Nora: I couldn't find anything. I couldn't talk to my friends. We had husband-wife friends, and I didn't feel that I fitted in any more with them. I kind of shied away from them. So I found a minister. Not my regular one. I found another minister that I could sit down and talk with. That was several months or so afterwards. I needed help—somehow I felt I wasn't going to make it. So twelve o'clock at night I called this minister, and he told me to come over to his office the next morning. I guess he thought maybe fifteen minutes, half an hour or so. But we sat there and talked about two hours, just talking. It all came out then. After that, I started building back.*
> —San Francisco

In addition to this long-accustomed role of providing consolation in private, houses of worship have increasingly been sponsoring collective forms of it:

> *Angela: In our parish, we started a widow's club. And I think the reason why it has been successful all these years is, it's more or less a spiritual thing. We have our fun, but we go to mass one Saturday a month and we put our husbands' names in a box. And then we pick out the name of somebody else's husband, and we think about him, pray for him. And these women are so interested in each other, it's a beautiful thing to see.*
> —San Francisco

Church or temple can serve as a purely nonsectarian meeting ground as well:

> *Q: Noreen, you said that you had gone to a support group. Why did you do that?*
> *Noreen: Well, I was caring for my elderly mother and that's how I got*

involved. But it's a mixed group, and they talk about everything and do everything, and I just think they're a bunch of wonderful people.
Q: How did you find them?
Noreen: Through a neighbor of mine. It's on 11th Street and Washington in Santa Monica at that little—I think it's a Lutheran church, I'm not sure. They meet on the first and third Fridays of the month. And they're just gorgeous—because everybody's trying to help each other.
Betty: There are quite a number of groups like that.
Q: Did you ever go to any of them?
Betty: I used to. There's a widow's group that meets in one of the temples. And—like here—most people would tell their story, and when you have the same tragedy in common, you hang on to each other, there's a feeling, you know? And then you ask, "What are we doing now to cope with this?" That is the important thing.
Q: Do they ever touch on that in those meetings?
Noreen: Yes, yes. They bring psychologists in and other speakers.
—Los Angeles, #2

All of the three groups described, you'll notice, seem driven more by consensus than individual leaders and animated by an easygoing tolerance for the diverse needs of their members—ranging from the "spiritual" to "fun"—that doesn't smack of anything dogmatic or rigidly programmatic. Nevertheless, such support can buttress this woman's deepest conviction:

> *The most important is your faith in God. No matter how bad it gets, if you continue your faith and the Holy Spirit dwells in you, God will walk with you all the way. It may not be easy, but you won't walk alone. Investigate support groups—this is also very important. You need a good support group wherever you might be.*
—Woman, 59, 3

In addition to these local and largely informal efforts, several nationwide networks for survivors have evolved under religious auspices, most notably the nondenominational THEOS and the NAIM Conference for Catholics (once more, see "Resources"), which are avenues to a service midway between traditional pastoral counselling and more modern therapy.

My advice would be not to "go it alone." Although I relied heavily on

*our children, I also often turned to professional persons in our church.
Differing from most churches today, this did not involve individuals
trained in psychology but those trained spiritually to meet the human
need. I also know from friends that support groups of all kinds are
available today through hospitals and other agencies.*

—*Woman, 63, 2*

Her concluding aside is correct, and prominent among the other
agencies are those alternatives to acute-care hospitals for treating the
terminally ill:

A hospice bereavement group was very helpful.

—*Woman, 57, 3*

*I took a bereavement course through Caritas—a hospice-type organi-
zation that had helped me through two years of caring for my husband
at home.*

—*Woman, 74, 3*

In fact, the resources have multiplied so much that those who nurse
some suspicions about the self-interest of "the helping professions"
may see a virtual "grief industry" at work. But better profusion than
scarcity, even if it does complicate the decision-making.

If you sense that counselling might be to your benefit but have had
no prior acquaintance with it, you may face one conundrum in
particular: will you be better served by an individual (and therefore
most likely a professional of some sort) or by a group (which will
presumably include some lay people like yourself)? We've already
seen how some survivors found one route much more to their liking
than the other—and how others were able to travel comfortably via
both. Your preference may depend as much on your personality as on
the problems you want to address. This woman's instinct is to rely on
the expert:

*Had I had any emotional problems at the time of my husband's death,
I would not have tried group therapy—I have some skepticism about
that. I would have gone to a psychiatrist for a one-on-one discussion.*

—*Woman, 84, 23*

"Skepticism" wells up here too, but from a different spring:

Al: I personally can't see going to a counsellor who, despite his or her experience in psychology or psychiatry or the like, is still a stranger to me. As Noel said, if you acquire friends who are sympathetic to your point of view, I think that would be much more helpful than going to a stranger who is dissociated not only from your past experience but from your likes and dislikes.

Noel: It's not even necessary to tell these friends what you went through.

Richard: Yes, absolutely. I don't believe in psychiatrists, I don't have faith in them.

Noel: They can't get into my head. I went to a marriage counsellor once with my wife and that turned me off completely.

—New York, #2

The opposed parties above are speculating, of course (and over Noel's words there seems to hover the image of the counsellor as a would-be witch doctor), but those who can speak with more authority are sometimes just as divided. What proclaims itself to Al, Noel, and Richard as aloofness and even arrogance may impress others as precisely the detachment and dispassion they expect the true professional to personify:

For me, professional help from a skilled psychoanalyst was the best way to work through the grief—the "support group" method would not be useful to me, though I know some are best helped this way.

—Woman, 67, 8

I felt I was not handling my grief very well, so I sought counsel from a psychiatrist. A few sessions with this professional person helped considerably.

—Woman, 81, 20

Dorothy has logged more than just a few:

Dorothy: I've been going for years. She's a psychologist and she turned my life around. And when I don't go for a week, I say, "Boy, I need a fix."

—Miami, #1

And if you fail to settle into a rapport with the first person you consult, you can heed the standard adage about engaging professionals—shop around:

> **Gladys:** *When my son said, "Mother, you've got to go get help," I went to two or three different ones before I found what I think might be better. I went to a psychiatrist who didn't work out and to a psychologist—a woman—who didn't work out. Because they all thought I was going to be just* perfect *[with a sweep of the arm] in a very short time. I wasn't getting "perfect"; I wasn't even getting "good." But now I'm seeing another psychologist, and it's very interesting, in my estimation.*
> —*Los Angeles, #2*

What piques that interest in her new counsellor, and thus her amenability to help, is their shared belief that we can't navigate in the present until we do some deep dredging into the past—a doctrine that underlies many traditional schools of individual therapy but that, as she mentions below, has been set aside by some more recent ones intent on quicker results. But she is not demanding quicker results:

> *When I went to him, he evaluated me, and as he did, I realized that many of the problems I have today do not stem from today. They stem from early childhood. And I've gone to seminars where they say that they don't believe in going back, they believe in moving right on from now. But I found that was not good for me—I am still living with what happened then. I was a lonely young woman for obvious reasons, and I'm a lonely old woman for obvious reasons. But I was a lonely child for not-so-obvious reasons. And these are things I have to overcome.*

She sets off on her quest, however, with an independent mind as well as an open one, not kowtowing to his expertise (nor subscribing to his jargon):

> *I was with him today, and he said to me, "You know, this is one of the first days you haven't cried." I said, "Well, I have to go to a group and I don't want to ruin my makeup." He said, "You see, you do have that wonderful sense of humor. Let's go on from here." And now we're at a point where he says he's letting me "ventilate" rather than get into "insight." I said, "What does* that *mean? He said, "Well, for the time being, I think it's better for you to just come here and tell me all of what's going on." I feel like it's a lot of nonsense. But maybe it's going to mean something, I don't know.*

Those who prefer to work with just one person, however, may be looking for aid of a more expeditious and perhaps more immediately practical kind:

> *See a counsellor* in your age category, *one old enough to have some experience in surviving an experience of widowhood—one who knows* step by step *what you do about insurance, Social Security, etc. I think having someone from a widows' group calling on you* consistently *and working with you* individually *would be a wonderful help.*
>
> —*Woman, 71, 5*

She is describing the "widow-to-widow" model of counselling which grew in part out of a pilot program of that name in Boston in 1967 and has since been duplicated all over the country. AARP's Widowed Persons' Service, which started as a national extension of the model, can tell you about programs in your locality. Edith was recruited into one after she became a widow the first time around; when her second husband died, she confesses—in a testimonial to the indispensability of a second party—that she tried and failed to be her own counsellor:

> *I have lost two husbands—the first when I was very young. Many years later, when I was married again and had a child, I was approached and asked if I would join HELP WIDOWS. I had nothing to do, and I'm always a volunteer, so I did. It was especially for new widows, on a one-to-one basis. And they trained us: where to go for Social Security if you had children, how to get in touch with banks, a variety of things widows have to know. So I had* had *the experience. But when it came to myself—smarty Edith couldn't get it together. You just can't cope immediately.*
>
> —*Boston, #1*

In theory, it should be an easy step from programs of the sort Edith joined to the ones that these women did:

> *Join a grief recovery or other support group within the twenty-four-month period following spouse's death.*
>
> —*Woman, 52, 3*

> *Join a widows' or widowers' group for spiritual strength, for the social*

contact, and friends who understand.
                                                            —*Woman, 71, 4*

But many who acquiesce fully in the one-on-one resist the thought of having that other "one" supplanted by "some." It's worth marshalling their reasons—because (as should be no surprise now) every single one is contested by someone else's opinion. As to who's right? Once more, we'll let you judge.

Some were stricken by the very fear groups are intended to counter:

Can't get up the courage to go to the meetings alone.
                                                            —*Woman, 61, 6*

But many groups encourage the timorous to bring along friends or relatives, as Catherine is doing:

My daughter goes also, with me, as a support person, and really, it's been good for her too.
Q: How does it help her?
Catherine: It helps her to realize, just like me, that life is short and there are other people who are worse off.
                                                            —*Miami, #1*

Once there, this woman chafed at the company of others like herself:

I feel that the grieving experience is one's own, and while others have found support groups necessary and helpful, I did not. In fact, I resented being pushed into social circles composed primarily of other widows.
                                                            —*Woman, 65, 3*

What makes her edge away, of course, is exactly what reels others in:

Seek the help of a widows' support group. Those who are in the same boat are more understanding and provide the best advice and most comfort—they are willing listeners. You find you are not alone.
                                                            —*Woman, 67, 2*

Nor must the group itself be a narrowly focussed one. Marlene, for example, enjoyed Parents Without Partners for the heterogeneity of both its members and their problems:

It was about all different subjects—meeting somebody, sex, everything that you could think of. Of course there are all different age groups in PWP. You have young, divorced, you have widows.

—*Miami, #1*

This woman wonders whether groups don't tend to protract the pain:

I am familiar with support groups for the widowed, and they are wonderful for those who may need them. I feel that they may prolong the grief process and cause people to focus on the past, although I know people deal with grief in an individual way and these groups serve some people well.

—*Woman, 59, 3*

In fact, these two say theirs got them giggling again:

I'm in a group of "widowed and orphaned" women who try hard to keep the proper amount of silliness and humor in our lives.

—*Woman, 57, 2*

Join a widow's support group. I still attend the local Family Service-sponsored group over twenty months later. We meet once a month, and now we can laugh and smile again.

—*Woman, 72, 2*

This man warns us to watch out for an overindulgence in sackcloth-and-ashes:

Have some kind of support group, but make sure it's a positive one. Some groups seem to want to wallow in sadness instead of getting on with their lives.

—*Man, 58, 3*

But again and again others give groups the credit for arresting a slide into self-pity:

Join a widow-widower club. You can't feel sorry for yourself when you see fifty other people in the same circumstances, many not as well off or prepared as you are.

—*Woman, 73, 5*

Attending just once was enough to leave Evelyn feeling chastened:

There are groups, outreach groups, and I went to one meeting of one for widows given through Emerson Hospital. It was very enlightening: there were all age groups, and we sat around a circle, and everybody told their stories.

And what helped me was that I met two young girls, very young. One, who had a six-month-old child, lost her husband when he was 29 years old. And the other also had a child, a 6-year-old, and she was pregnant with her second. Her husband dropped dead playing tennis. Due to the shock, she gave birth to the baby very shortly afterwards—almost full-term. But it had a heart problem and also died within three days.

I said to myself, ''Well, I'm not so bad off. You know, how can I feel sorry for myself when both my children are married, they're out of college, and it's just me that I have to worry about? At least God gave me so many years, whereas these people were cheated altogether.''
                                                              —Boston, #1

Lee believes a group would only have aggravated her guilt:

Everyone goes through the same guilt, the same feelings that you could have done this when he was alive and you could have done that. And I don't think there's any answer because, for every person, you have to find your own way. What's good for one may not be good for another. I couldn't go to a support group. I think I would feel worse.
                                                              —Miami, #1

This woman, however, reports that she didn't go and regrets it:

A support group would lessen the feelings of guilt over the inability to ''save'' the spouse and all the other thoughts that assail the survivor. Knowing these are common feelings would ease the burden, if not the pain.
                                                              —Woman, 70, 8

Guilt, of course, dwells on and in the past; and this woman bridles at how one group seemed bent on getting rid of the past entirely:

My church started a widows' luncheon group where the general consensus of opinion was to forget your mate. When you have been

married for fifty-five years, you don't want to forget your partner.
                                                    —Woman, 79, 4

But a similar group allowed Virginia to look forward without forgetting:

I'm a Catholic, and my church has a Singles Club. I think it's good to join a club like that.
Loretta: *NAIM was like that, too—for singles.*
Q: *If you were to advise other people to join a club like that, what would you tell them they would get out of it?*
Virginia: *Well, you learn what they've all experienced, just like we have here. And it makes you look forward to things—they have a lot of trips that we would go on. It just takes you out of your sorrow, and you start living again. I was with my husband that whole year [before he died] day and night, and it was sad. And you don't forget a person when you've lived with him thirty-eight years. But I felt, "Well, now I have to make a new life."*
                                                    —Los Angeles, #1

Like Virginia, this woman was with her husband day and night during his final illness (which also lasted a year). And when she saw those she judged not as faithful compounding their "disloyalty" afterwards, she bristled:

I only attended one session of a grief group because all the women were seeking one thing—a husband to replace the one they had lost. None had nursed their husbands but kept them in the hospital, etc.
                                                    —Woman, 58, 3

Marlene detected the same ulterior motive in many men:

I had one girlfriend, we went together—she was divorced and I was a widow. A lot of the guys, I found, are looking for mothers for their children. They still have children, and they're looking just for a mother for the child—which is the wrong way to go about it.
                                                    —Miami, #1

But others don't appear to agree:

Joining a widow/widower support group was helpful. In fact, I met a widower and remarried.

> *—Woman, 52, 2*

I met my present husband at a widowed persons' support group. We were married fourteen months later.

> *—Woman, 61, 5*

This woman decrees the resumption of romance to be one of a group's legitimate objectives:

> *I found getting into a widow/widowers support group was the best thing I could have done. Being able to talk to someone who has been through it was very comforting. Also, I could start socializing with the group without feeling like a fifth wheel with couple-friends. I also started to date a widower from the group about eight months post-widowhood. Nothing has come of the dating except to make me feel like a person again—a reason to get up in the morning and to try and look my best.*
> *—Woman, 43, 2*

If dating did that for her, it scarcely deserves to be styled as little more than "nothing." As we saw in Chapter 3, a reason to get up in the morning can elevate "just existing" into "living." Dorothy tells Molly how a group led her through a similar progression of experiences to a similar reorientation—the willingness to make plans once again:

> *I'd like to speak to Molly. I see you're very sad and I know how you feel. When did your husband die?*
> **Molly:** *Four years ago. He was killed. He was never sick a day in his life.*
> **Dorothy:** *He was killed? Well, that's a very hard thing to overcome in your mind. But, when my husband died—he went suddenly, in my arms practically—I was berserk. The only thing that helped me—it saved my life—was going to groups for grieving. When I found other people there and they'd talk, I saw that I wasn't alone in the world—other people had known it. It gave me a little consolation. Then I made so many friends, and I'm still friends with them. And little by little, I won't say that I'm walking on air . . . , but I've got a lot of plans and, in the daytime at least, I'm occupied.*
> *—Miami, #1*

Some of the participants in our own groups—to our surprise as much as theirs—were also galvanized by the discovery that they weren't alone in the world. One of our discussion groups, for example, drew exclusively on the residents of a rather tightly knit retirement community, and quite a few of those in our group knew each other. But Edwin said most of them had always conspired to observe a certain tactful silence:

> *I always felt that the whole 10,000 of us, we've gone through the same thing. Most of us are widows or widowers, and I figure they don't want to recall their troubles and don't want to listen to yours. So I just never mention it.*
>
> —*Los Angeles, #1*

And yet when our group broke the conspiracy, some of its perpetrators pronounced themselves relieved:

> **Sylvia:** *Now I can identify with all of you because of all that you've been through. I thought it was only me.*
> **Lillian:** *Yes, because, living in Leisure World, we think it's only fun. We laugh and we joke. Nobody ever knows the other man's background.*
> **Q:** *You guys haven't talked about this before?*
> **Others:** *[in chorus] No.*
> **Q:** *How does it feel for you to be talking about it?*
> **Irene:** *It feels good.*
> **Lillian:** *You can understand the feelings of each and every one.*
> **Gil:** *Better than talking to yourself in the mirror. Ever done that? That's what I've done.*

Our groups, to be sure, didn't buck everybody up. Mary's reenacted a previous one that had inflamed her anguish instead of mollifying it:

> **Mary:** *[in tears] I lost my son, that's what makes me feel bad. Not to bore everybody. He died jogging.*
> **Others:** *[In dismay] Jogging, jogging?*
> **Mary:** *He was 28. He died a year after my husband. I went to talk with people who were trying to get help for things like that. And I came out like my head was going to burst. One woman was there whose son had been stabbed—I'd seen her picture in the paper. But I couldn't talk about it. It was too much.*

Q: Have you ever talked to anybody about it?
Mary: I tried. This reminds me of things like that.

—*Boston, #2*

Nevertheless, she laments her isolation, and a group (she did come to ours, after all) may yet offer her the most feasible escape from it. So it seems to Marilyn, who practically orders her into one:

Q: Mary, you said that you don't have a chance to meet people. Does anybody have any ideas that might be helpful to Mary? You guys know the area.
Marilyn: Don't they have church functions? I know there is one group, I read about it in the paper—where do you live?
Mary: Arlington. I just go to mass on Sundays or Saturdays.
Marilyn: There is a church in Medford and they have something for widows and widowers. I guess it's like a support group, but it's more than that too. It's a place to talk to other people. And it's good to do it. Don't not do it. Don't think you don't have to or you don't want to. Make *yourself do it.*

Edwin suffered a double loss strikingly like Mary's, and it bound him to Bud, whose wife had died of a brain tumor around that time:

Edwin: My wife died of cancer in 1982, and a year prior to that—I don't care much to talk about it—my oldest son was murdered.
Others: Oh, how awful!
Bud: It proved one thing, that sympathy creates companionship.
Sylvia: Or misery loves company.
Q: Why do you say that, Bud?
Bud: Well, we sought each other out. Because, after a traumatic experience, right away you associate with people who've had experiences similar to yours. You seem to be closer to them.

—*Los Angeles, #1*

"Misery loves company" and "sympathy creates companionship" delimit rather neatly the two contrasting functions that a group can perform, preferably at the same time. First, letting us huddle together with others over what unites us in the past:

John: There are a lot of things running around inside of people with experiences like that long after the experience is over. A number of my friends were in Vietnam, and a lot of them sought help when they got back. It wasn't a question that they were drug addicts or crazy or anything like that. But these guys had gone through some very tough experiences. And it was funny to see a guy 6' 3" with tattoos sitting down in a sort of sensitivity group, but they really found it helpful in coping with that sort of thing, violent death all the time.

—New York, #2

And second, giving us escorts as we launch ourselves into the future:

Pat: In my widow-to-widow support group, I have made the best friend I've had in my life—and that includes my maid of honor when I got married.

Q: Where did you find this group? How did you hear about it?

Pat: Through Santa Monica City College.

Gladys: I know it! Who did you have? What was her name?

Pat: Phyllis.

Gladys: I went to the same one, but I didn't meet anyone I cared to be with.

Pat: We had had about three meetings, and the subject for that day was whether there was something you've been wishing you could do but were afraid to. Well, all of us were afraid to start in the group! I know I was. I didn't want to go, I thought I'd cry all the time. Anyway, when my turn came to talk, I said, "I just wish that I could get back to entertaining. I never used to have a lot of people over, but I'd like at least to prepare a nice dinner. But I can't do it. I don't know one wine from another, so I don't know what to buy. And I'm afraid I'll collapse in the kitchen."

There was this little girl sitting next to me. She's a good twenty years younger—I'm in my 70s and she's in her 50s. She raised her hand—we had to raise our hands if we wanted to talk—and she said, "I would just love to help you." And she was sincere about it. From then on we became very close. She's just adorable. We've taken trips together. If I'm leaving her house, she says, "Call me when you get home." I do the same thing. I do not feel alone—if something's bothering me, I call her, and she does the same with me.

Gladys: Isn't that interesting? I was so disappointed! There wasn't one woman that I had an affinity to. I was in the wrong group.

—Los Angeles, #2

Although Gladys reminds us that you can come away completely empty-handed, Pat and her friend have collected what many consider the best bonus a group can offer—the chance to repay in kind the debt of being helped:

> *To be able to cope with a loss of a spouse,* keeping busy *is the key.* Helping others *is wonderful, too. We are not alone in our grief—being an advocate for the less fortunate is most gratifying. Seek out others in support groups—your community has them, I'm sure!*
> —*Woman, 68, 3*

Some don't like incurring this debt in the first place, and we opened this chapter with a few people who, receptive as they may have been to giving help, were resistant to getting it. And the notion that a group might supply help may harden that resistance—but without diminishing the receptivity:

> *For myself I would not want to seek comfort from a group or from others who had suffered the same loss; but I would be happy to help anyone who might need such comfort or companionship, if I could.*
> —*Woman, 69, 6*

Toward the end of the last chapter, we saw how many survivors vented this impulse in formal volunteer work. But "help others" runs like a drumroll through all sorts of contexts. Although we didn't tabulate its frequency, as a dictum "help others" almost rivals "keep busy," often as an essential corollary to it:

> *Adjustments, I believe, are much easier if one looks around, finds people less fortunate, and attempts to help them. Keeping busy in this way is real therapy. We all need each other.*
> —*Woman, 74, 17*

In helping others we have arrived at a school of therapy endorsed by virtually everyone.

We encounter the same sentiments over and over, almost like a currency that circulates among all survivors:

> *I have offered my support to many of my friends who have since lost their*

husbands, and that is therapeutic too.

—*Woman, 69, 9*

The first year after my husband died, I worked as a volunteer in our town nursing home. This was very therapeutic, working with people less fortunate than I. It made me count my blessings instead of indulging in self-pity.

—*Woman, 60, 6*

It led this woman to enumerate hers:

Helping others is a good way to be glad for your own blessings. You have to believe the glass is half full rather than half empty.

—*Woman, 64, 7*

It gave this woman the same kind of lift:

Whenever I get depressed, I make a point of doing something for some one less fortunate than myself; it helps the morale.

—*Woman, 77, 5*

These two insist that doing something *with* others jibes best with doing it *for* them:

Be thoughtful and helpful to others. Do not always stay on the receiving line. Invite people to your home; suggest doing things with them—or for them. Do comfort others in their bereavement. Your understanding of their grief will mean so much to them . . . and to you.

—*Woman, 77, 13*

Doing something every day for someone else gives you less time to think about yourself. There are so many people who are so worse off than yourself—so concentrate on serving others. Every single person has some outstanding talent that could be shared.

—*Woman, 70 5*

The same sense of mission is shared by this pair, who both command, "Don't wait":

I have reached out to others, not waiting for them to come to me. I touch base with some of the homebound members of my church frequently.

When a friend or church member dies, I feel that I have a special ministry to the family because I have experienced what they are experiencing.

—Woman, 68, 3

Never sit down and wait for sympathy and attention to come to you. Immediately start giving that to others who are in need of it. Your happiness will return to you tenfold! Never let an opportunity pass when you can send a note or card, on special occasions, for special accomplishments, always your sympathy in their time of need and just to let them know you are thinking about them. That is my "hobby," while I eat, and I keep the postman busy carrying mine out and the many, many I get coming in.

—Woman, 77, 3

And these two instruct us to incorporate helping others into every day's routine:

Help other people at least once a day. Talk daily to a friend or someone you may feel is lonely.

—Woman, 76, 10

Help others. Let no day end without a small, unsung kindness to someone.

—Woman, 73, 18

Stagnation within the self may be the alternative:

Don't brood and retreat into yourself. Help others who need you!!

—Woman, 70, 5

Knowing that you matter is one of the most flattering revelations the world can vouchsafe you; and efforts to better someone else's lot may bring it forth much faster than efforts to better your own:

Do something, anything, to make yourself feel wanted, needed, appreciated.

—Woman, 54, 3

That quest has become so central to Lee's routine as to push diversions like his guitar and piano and nights out—beguiling as they may be—to the periphery:

> *I have a brother-in-law. He's 82, he lives around the corner. I go shop for him, and I go back and forth to see how he's doing; and I help my daughter a lot. I have my music. Then I go out occasionally to dinner. And that seems to take up all my time. I don't have time to think about myself anymore. It really helped me a lot, by trying to help—helping to take care of people.*
>
> —*New York, #2*

Survivors like Lee seem to personify the enhanced appreciation of human interdependence that survivorship is traditionally said to endow us with. To the extent he really doesn't have time to think about himself, his life has literally become selfless; but, as he's well aware, it's one that also caters to his deepest self-interest. In the conventional calculus, if the happiness of others is our end, we may need to trade off some of our own for theirs:

> *And try to make not only yourself happy, but try to give of yourself to make other people happy.*
>
> —*Woman, 65, 2*

But to Mary, as to Lee, the two go hand in hand:

> *Mary: I was a beautician and, despite my age, I'm still a beautician.*
> *Q: I've been admiring your hair.*
> *Mary: But instead of working in a shop I help out my friends. I go to the homes of shut-in people who can't get out to get their hair done. I think, "Well, if I didn't do their hair, I can just imagine how they would look!" And it makes me so happy to do it. Just this last week, I did a lady that had Parkinson's disease. A helper and her sister held her up to the sink so she could bend her head over, and then I cut her and gave her a permanent. By the time the permanent was finished, she was too ill to have it set. So we put her to bed, and then I came back two days later and set it. And she was so happy!*
>
> —*San Francisco*

What might depress others in this scenario—a woman so housebound and debilitated having her hair done, and that in such painfully slow stages—elates Mary precisely because it seems to have the same effect on her "client." So partaking of another's sorrow, far from being a lugubrious business, may actually cheer us up:

> *Keep active mentally and physically. Helping others is perhaps one of the most healing activities. Giving an emotional boost to another grief-stricken person can help you to heal. That way, you share their unhappiness and diminish your own.*
>
> —*Woman, 66, 26*

Compassion is most often what is said to motivate such a communion:

> *Help others less fortunate—showing compassion.*
>
> —*Woman, 78, 4*

It has convinced this woman that she's part of a chain—of those who have experienced what befell her, and those who haven't yet but who will:

> *Now I find that I must help others who will suffer the loss of a loved one. I have a circle of lifelong friends, female and male, and I have come to understand how they share my loss as their own. And I have resolved to be helpful and compassionate to others who will at some time or other be in the same emotional shock of loss that I was.*
>
> —*Woman, 61, 2*

But the root meaning of "compassion" goes beyond "suffering with" to "feeling with," pure and simple:

> *Relate to others; help others; sympathize with them in time of sorrow; rejoice with them in times of joy.*
>
> —*Man, 73, 5*

And as this woman observes, it's this kind of fellow-feeling that undergirds the ultimate in support groups—civilization:

> *My advice to others to cope would be to instill a feeling of love and compassion in their children, and to be a part of a real community—church, friends, relations, neighborhood—which is the building-block of civilization. Without it, what is money, status, and fame worth? I was the daughter of a millionaire, I should know.*
>
> —*Woman, 73, 4*

Chapter 6

Starting Anew with the Opposite Sex: "Alone at the Dance"

Q: Anyway, getting back to your questions about men's groups, what do you think they said?

Marlene: *You tell us.*

Q: Pretty much what you say. That they had the same feelings. They were very emotional and they had not been widowed all that long, most of them a year and a half, two years. A lot of them missed their wives a lot. Didn't want to start up again. Didn't want to get remarried. Does that surprise you?

Others: *No.*

Ida: *The same way as women, the same thing.*

Dorothy: *What did they say about the women they take out?*

Q: They were afraid, too.

Dorothy: *They don't even want to, I'll bet.*

—Miami, #1

Rehearsed above are some themes that will run throughout this chapter: the reluctance of men and women alike to entertain not only the notion of remarrying but even that of dating; and an unquenchable curiosity about how the other sex is faring on these fronts—a curiosity springing from all the usual human longings. No surprises here. In every sexual relationship, fear and desire contest with each other. Marriage is such a civilizing institution because it can allay or even banish the fear without eliminating the desire—with luck, even heightening it. But now, as in so many other areas of life, the fear comes flooding back. Or the desire just seems to ebb away.

We'll start with those who are hanging back for one or the other of these reasons before we go on to those who, for better or worse, have let the opposite sex reenter their emotional lives. Throughout

391

this chapter, by the way, you'll hear from the discussion groups more often than from the survey. The reason is not hard to divine: a subject almost irresistibly elicited in a group (especially in groups of one sex) is not one on which individuals responding to a questionnaire are likely to expound at length—especially when that questionnaire respected what we assumed would be the natural reticence of many by not raising the topic. We skirted it only with a question about current marital status, which yielded totals of more than 93% "widowed," 6% "married," and barely 1% "separated or divorced."

That question drew a mild reprimand from a woman who replaced our categorization with hers:

> *I'm single (the "widowed" label is inappropriate after a while).*
> —*Woman, 60, 20*

Quite a few, however, would dispute her.

"I Still Feel Married"

Twinges of guilt, at the very least, are likely to afflict every survivor who begins dealing with the opposite sex in admittedly sexual terms:

> **Grace:** *Especially when I first dated, it was so, so hard to do it. I felt that I shouldn't be going out. In fact, I went to a drive-in theater one time with this fellow, and there, parked right next to me, was somebody that I knew from my deceased husband's family. And I actually hid myself so they would not see that I was dating already.*
> —*Miami, #1*

Sylvia has come all the way to the brink of remarriage without ridding herself of a similar embarrassment:

> **Sylvia:** *There is a man in my life now, a very nice man.*
> **A:** *You're lucky!*
> **Sylvia:** *Yes, I am. And it's two years after my husband passed away, and he is a widower. There is talk of getting married. I'm not sure whether I care to or not. It almost seems that it's not right. It's almost like acknowledging that you're having an affair.*
> —*Los Angeles, #2*

In search of a reason, she describes how distasteful it was to realize, just recently, that she was "single":

Talking about sex is something I have never been comfortable with. I'm from a large family, and while we are very close, sex was never discussed with my sisters and brothers. I was taking a class at UCLA with a bunch of friends. The ages ran from very young, to me and people a little older than me. And they were talking very, very personally. And someone said, "It's all right if we talk this way because, after all, we're single." Now that was two years after my husband died, and it was strange—it was like being hit in the stomach. I always acknowledged I was the widow, but I never thought of myself as single.

And some never will:

For those who can accept the marriage as over and are able to seek another to share their life, perhaps they are better off. For some, the relationship was too special—so they just continue to work toward accepting loneliness.

—*Woman, 64, 6*

Her refusal to "accept the marriage as over" lands her in a lot of company:

I might add, I am not interested in widowers. This town is full of them. My widow friends think the way I think also—they aren't interested in getting married. I prefer to remain single—I had the best husband in the world, and so much happiness. I'm sure not all marriages are like ours was for so many years.

—*Woman, 73, 8*

I miss my husband more and more as each year passes, and I hear the same from other widows who had wonderful marriages. Some widows who have not had good first marriages, they marry again. I personally will never meet one as good and wonderful as my Paul. And, if I did remarry, it would not be fair to the man, as I would probably always be comparing them. I still feel married to Paul even though I am considered single. This may not help you, but it's the way I feel.

—*Woman, 75, 10*

Such fealty to the dead may seem quaint to those who consider themselves transformed by one Sexual Revolution or the other, but an impressive number of survivors pledge themselves to it—if not forever, then for a good long stretch:

> *In the first years—five approximately—I didn't join in singles groups. I needed time to grieve and thought it a disrespect to my husband to participate in anything but non-sexual activities.*
>
> *—Woman, 61, 12*

Even being friends with men has lost its allure for this woman, though she doesn't lack candidates:

> *Have not really felt the need to go out and meet men friends, although I do meet some through my weaving guild.*
>
> *—Woman, 87, 8*

This woman sounds as if she may be content to abide permanently with only her memories of her husband—as lover as well as friend:

> *My husband and I had spent thirty-five years together. We were very happy and very close as lovers and friends. I am so thankful I have lovely memories to cling to.*
>
> *—Woman, 59, 5*

She has left unspoken the commonest premise by which survivors forgo not only the prospect of remarriage but also of a renewal of romance—that you'll never find anything to "replace" what you've lost:

> *The only way to survive is keep busy and mingle with friends. It is the greatest shock of a lifetime, after living with an interesting, charming, and intelligent partner for forty-nine years. No one could replace him, and he is still part of my life in every way.*
>
> *—Woman, 87, 13*

In fact, if your spouse is such a force in your life, searching for a substitute is beside the point.

For some, a spouse lives on metaphorically, in the practical or moral lessons he or she has imparted:

Recognizing the importance of my husband in my life—the guidelines he set, the values he chose—was of enormous help to me after I recovered (slowly) from the initial shock. He is still with me in these ways.
—*Woman, 66, 16*

But for others, that presence is both more intimate and more pervasive:

If it was a long and beautiful marriage, as in my case, live on in the same way you did before, so that the one who has gone is still around in spirit to give you the strength for the daily struggle or joy.
—*Woman, 87, 6*

And for a handful, a spouse seems literally still around:

Since I do not feel the "essence" of my husband to have left me (nor did I eight years ago at the moment he dropped dead), I did not grieve.
—*Woman, 76, 8*

The departed has entered a trouble-free state, but my belief is that they don't desert us entirely. I feel that I'm comforted and made to feel more secure by a "presence" or an aura, if you will, of the departed. I welcome this feeling. "No man is an island . . . ."
—*Woman, 68, 4*

The last two may strike you as extreme cases, but what they're experiencing is clearly of a totally different order from the hallucinations, observed in Chapter 2, that sometimes beset those in the early stages of grief. This woman also senses something equally tangible around her and rebukes those who might question her level-headedness:

Since we had always been very close due to an (I think) unusually understanding relationship, I still feel as if he were always near me (and I do not belong to any cult).
—*Woman, NA, NA*

Melding the past and the present is perhaps the major task of grief, or so we'll contend in the next chapter. And keeping a spouse as vivid in the mind as this is one way to do it. Is it necessarily bad—or "maladaptive," in the jargon of the behavioral sciences? We don't presume to say because we don't presume to know. Here we're only hazarding that it may severely inhibit the resumption of new relationships and may even foreclose them altogether.

If the memory of your spouse commands so strong a loyalty, you probably have one person to answer to besides yourself:

> *Don't ever give up, as your spouse would have wanted you to carry on and live a full life. Enjoy every day and be happy with your family. Am very lonesome and miss my spouse more than anyone knows, but we were very happy and had a good life together.*
>
> *—Woman, 67, 3*

Doing what your spouse would have wanted—it's the star by which survivors like these usually sail by, and it seems almost always to be a benign one, leading them toward self-fulfillment and not self-denial:

> *When my husband died, I felt that I should go on living my life to the fullest. I think this is what he would have wanted me to do.*
>
> *—Woman, 68, 3*

> *Enjoy life—that's what your spouse would want you to do. Go to dances, shows, bus rides with other single people. Life is what you make of it. Just like my husband would say: one day at a time, but enjoy what you can.*
>
> *—Woman, 65, 5*

Ironically, but probably inevitably, those who are respecting these hypothetical wishes balk at the one instruction their spouses may actually have left behind:

> *He had wanted me to remarry as soon as possible. But I never met a widower that was anything like him, and I always doubted I could love anyone as devotedly as I had him.*
>
> *—Woman, 84, 23*

To someone like her, the notion of remarrying must be tantamount to bigamy. Any suitors for Beulah's hand seem fated to remain figments, purely speculative inhabitants of the mind:

While he always said to me, "I don't want you to be alone; I think you ought to marry again," I would never do it. Because I could never, ever find a man that was as nice and as good. He had the qualities of a Boy Scout [smiling], all the things a Boy Scout should be—you know, reverent and honorable and conscientious, always of good cheer, whatever, he had them all. There is just nobody, in my mind, who could possibly measure up to that.

—Boston, #1

Sharkey tells Beulah how she recoiled when her terminally ill husband urged her to start laying the groundwork for remarriage:

That's what my husband used to say, the same thing, "You're not going to be alone, you're going to get married again." I would get so angry with him! I said, "Don't say that!" "No," he said, "I want you to get married. I don't even mind if you go out now." Saying that to me—I felt so bad, I didn't want to talk about it.

—Boston, #1

Nor did her repugnance fade after he died, when she listened to the same entreaties from a friend:

My friend, her husband died shortly after my husband. A few months later she was dating somebody. She said, "Shark, you've got to make a new life for yourself." I said, "Well, I'm not interested—I can't forget." She said, "Well, he would have wanted you to." But I just can't.

If you share her conviction that you "just can't," how reasonable is it? Ida casts a cold eye on many who would elevate the departed to sainthood:

Why is it I know of many families where the husband and wife lived a hell of a life together, a miserable life all the years, and as soon as the mate dies, he or she becomes a god? They become immortalized—"My husband was the most wonderful man in the world!" Now, I've seen one woman in particular—when you passed her door, the whole hallway shook, they were at each other's throats so. The minute he died, she was ready to jump in the grave.

—Miami, #2

No such leaps for her. She instructs other widows to emulate what she presumes their spouses would wish for *themselves* had cases been reversed—and those wishes are decidedly un-Boy-Scout-like:

> *Ida: I would tell them it's all over, you cannot live in the past, if it were vice versa your mate would go on living just the same. If it were a man, he'd lose no time in picking up where he left off [laughter].*
> *Ann: Oh, sarcastic!*
> *Ida: I picked up where I left off and always kept busy and never felt sorry for myself, because I wasn't jumping in the grave. Because I always looked at it—if it was reversed, what my husband would have done. First, he would have been smiling and smiling [laughter]—*
> *Ann: He probably would have had somebody lined up ten years ago!*
> *Ida: Yes, and he would have asked the lady out for dinner—now that he could "afford it"!*

As entertaining as this fantasy may be, it's very likely the product of a none-too-tranquil union. It contains also the first in a series of sexual stereotypes that will parade through this chapter. As usual, the caricature doesn't belie the real-life face entirely. This man, with a touch of brusquely "masculine" asperity, makes a powerful case for men and women alike against letting the supposed desires of the dead usurp those of the living:

> *Realize that your spouse is dead and gone and can no longer be a part of your life. Get involved with other people socially. Pursue and develop your own interests. Don't linger on the thought of what you have lost, but instead concentrate on how you can make the most of the rest of your life. If your marriage was a good one and you enjoyed it, think about getting married again. Nothing you do can possibly make any difference to your dead spouse, so don't behave as you think he or she might have wanted you to, but instead do what you think is best for* your *future. It's* your *life, and no one else is going to live it for you.*
> *I remarried, we live part of the week in her condominium and part of the week in my house in a more rural area.*
> *—Man, 69, 2*

These male ears, however, would be deaf to his logic:

When my wife passed away, we were a few months from our fortieth wedding anniversary. We had many, many happy times together. She died in 1982, and I still miss her very much. I find comfort in the memories of those years, and I try to keep busy and live the kind of life that I know she would approve. I have been told that I'm fairly handsome, but I have no plan or desire to remarry.
—Man, 76, 6

Lee is somewhat more receptive, but other loyalties still intervene:

After your wife passes away, you seem to have a block to keep you from remarrying. It's as if . . . you want to get married, but you have her on your mind. You have that allegiance, that feeling you can't get rid of.
—New York, #2

And, to this man's allegiance, the death made no difference whatever:

When Lila died in 1984, we had been married almost twenty-eight years. Essentially half my life had been with her. When our thirtieth anniversary occurred in 1986, I pledged never to leave her, and that we would be together, as we hoped thirty years earlier, from here to eternity.
—Man, 57, 3

So for many, the marriage will endure until the end. Diane acknowledges that her continuing love for her husband locks out the competition—not only from her own life but also from the lives which the two of them brought into the world:

I had a friend in the church who dated me. He really wanted to get married, but I just couldn't put him in the place of my husband, to think of him coming into my house or me going into his. He said, "You're still in love with your husband." And this was ten years after. I said, "I know I am. I'm still in love with him. And I can't share." I just didn't feel that I could share my life, my children, my grandchildren, with another man.
—San Francisco

"I Couldn't Care Less"

Q: How do you feel about remarriage? One person here has done it.
Angela: I think it's wonderful.
Lil: Yes, but she is so young.

Q: What does that have to do with it?
Ellen: It is such a lonesome life alone when you're as young as she is.
Q: What about when you are older?
Ellen: Well, it's lonesome too, the nights are long, I hate the winter coming.
Q: What do you do about that?
Ellen: I read, I like antiques and I finish furniture, and I keep busy.
Q:The rest of you were saying something like that, the nights are long, you don't like winter. Has anybody done anything about meeting men?
Ellen: I couldn't care less.

—Boston, #2

"I couldn't care less" can state the truth. Or it can be a classic piece of bravado—not infrequently heard on the playground—which tries to conceal that you couldn't care *more*. We didn't make out which was the case for Ellen, for she didn't rise to the question our moderator then put to the group:

Q: Well, I'm going to tell you what a widow said to another bunch of ladies in this room. To the women who said, "I couldn't care less," she said, "I don't believe you!" Come on, is this really true, you really don't want to meet anybody?

That earlier exchange had gone like this:

Beulah: I never considered it.
Edith: I don't believe it!
Beulah: You don't?
Edith: Yes, if I scratch every one of you deep enough, I'll find you're going to get married if you have the opportunity [laughter]. It's the divorced women that are afraid, because of what they went through. Most widows want to get married.

—Boston, #1

On the evidence of the previous section, Edith's last observation may be overstated, but it's hard to contest her argument that at least some of the indifference may be simulated. A startling example cropped up in our survey, when a woman who opened her essay with this sentiment,

I am not interested in remarrying or having an affair or relationship with someone else . . .

closed it shortly afterward with this:

I long to have someone really care about me—not just in a social or friendly capacity, but to be a wife who is deeply loved.
— *Woman, 67, 3*

Like many survivors who haven't yet put themselves to the test at all, she tends to equate resuming sexual relations with the vastly more momentous decision to remarry. But perhaps she has illumined what makes her feelings about both so contradictory. We must give love in order to get it, and, to be "deeply loved," we must invest far more emotional capital than we do to reap a return from love's other enterprises, whether they be a pet, a volunteer job, friends, or even family. That—it's hardly news—can be a deeply scary proposition.

The very idea of merely dating again can make survivors panic like adolescents—even more so if they have been accustomed to decades of sexual security within a marriage. When we "go out," we're not just doing it in the literal sense. We are going outside the safer confines of our lives on the gamble that someone else will do the same in turn. No venture can put our self-esteem in more jeopardy than that. Marilyn had to summon up every ounce of her fortitude, and Julia flatly declares she's just not up to it:

Marilyn: I went to dances.
Q: Where did you hear about them?
Marilyn: I saw them advertised in the paper, and I thought, "I've got to do it." It was terrible the first time. If you haven't dated for twenty-five years, it's a very hard thing to do—go out and cope with a lot of the men that are out there today.
Q: Julia, have you heard of these dances too?
Julia: Yes, I've heard of them.
Q: Did you ever go to any of them?
Julia: No, I'm not really such a great dancer. I wouldn't be in the mood to meet someone. I really wouldn't. I like friends and I like to mingle. But I don't think I would like to go out with anyone.
— *Boston, #2*

The dance floor. It's the second-most-elemental meeting ground of the sexes, and we'll see several little dramas played out there—tragedies or farces, according to the perspective of the protagonist. It takes guts for anyone to attend a singles dance on the strength of a newspaper ad. Unlike Julia, however, Catherine does enjoy dancing, and she's in a comfortable haunt where she knows the music and has some of her family with her. Yet she's immobilized in a way she can't seem to fathom when a man offers her his arm:

> *I sometimes go down to a small bar with my daughter and son-in-law. I go for the music—they have a band there. I sit at the bar and have a cranberry juice or something. And if any man comes over and asks me to dance—now I want to tell you, I love to dance, but you couldn't drag me out of this chair! The chair and everything would go with me. I can't get up. I don't understand it.*
>
> *—Miami, #1*

"Going out" may exemplify getting out of the house at its most frightening, and many had to battle the instinct to run right back:

> *Q: Has anybody else gone out again?*
> *Lil: Oh, yes.*
> *Q: Was it a hard thing for you to do?*
> *Lil: First, I wanted to come right home. The first time I said, "Oh, what am I doing here? I'm crazy!"*
>
> *—Boston, #2*

Lil at least made it through the first time, but Molly "went home" even before that:

> *Q: Molly, where are you on all this? Are you dating? Has it occurred to you?*
> *Lydia: No, I haven't gone out once in the four years. And I had a lot of chances. For instance, my friends gave me an introduction to a man, a blind date, and he called me and he wanted to come up, and I wouldn't let him.*
> *Frieda: Why?*
> *Lydia: I wanted to see what he looked like. So we made an appointment to meet at the Drugworld, outside the entrance. I got dressed and I went over there and I walked through a different door so he wouldn't see me.*

I took a good look at him—he was standing there reading the paper. But my heart didn't tell me to go over to him, and I kept on walking, I went home. I couldn't, I just couldn't.

—Miami, #1

She's met with a barrage of exhortations, of a sort we've heard already:

Frieda: *If you're going to listen to your heart, then you're going to be alone for the rest of your life. Four years, honey, you have to let go.*
Laura: *You have to go once. You have to push yourself. And then, once you go, you'll go again.*
Lydia: *I was married fifty-five years.*
Frieda: *Honey, it doesn't matter if you were married 105 years. Unfortunately your husband has gone. You're not. You have to keep living.*
Lydia: *I just can't think that way.*

Marilyn couldn't "think that way" either—at first:

I had decided I was never going to go out again—and that was it! And I was wrong, I found that out the hard way. I think it is extremely important to find male companionship, companionship. And that saved me, it really did.

—Boston, #1

Her salvation sprang not from her own perseverance but that of her friends:

I was forced into going out with other men by my friends, literally forced. The girls in my office were always introducing me, everywhere they took me. And, oh God, I was so rude—"I don't even want to meet you, leave me alone!"

And when she at last let her guard down, the past stubbornly kept intruding into the present:

I finally did meet someone, and it made a difference—a tremendous difference. I kept calling him by my husband's name. I did! It was awful, I could have died every time it happened, but it's just a natural thing.

Despite slips like these (and she's right, they're very common), his presence enabled her to face the future with something like confidence for the first time:

> *But he was very understanding. And it turned my life around, because I was now over this terrible time of "Gee, why did it happen to me? What's going to happen to me?" It was the turning point and from then on it was a lot easier.*

How nice if every survivor could tell a similar tale of emancipation! But many of those who can't are convinced they don't want to; and what makes Marilyn's story so instructive is that, for a while, she counted herself among them. So if "I couldn't care less" has been your credo, you may want to test it. Has the desire really died? If it hasn't, then what is it a desire *for*? Many of those we've heard so far talk of dating as if it were the immediate prelude to walking up the aisle—or something even more unthinkable:

> *Peggy: Nobody mentioned the word dating. Is that a naughty word?*
> *Ruth: I never dated, and I've been widow for fourteen years.*
> *Peggy: You never! You've never?*
> *Ruth: Never, never!*
> *Peggy: That's very interesting because, over twenty-nine years, I dated a lot.*
> *Ruth: I'd known my husband from the time I was 17. And I'll tell you the truth, to think of going to bed with a strange man. . . .*
> *Peggy: I'm not talking about beds; I'm talking about going out to dinner.*
>
> *—Miami, #2*

And when Ruth protests that even the latter has become a long-lost art for her, Peggy ticks off all the ways it need not be:

> *Ruth: Or even going out, you lose the touch. You lose the touch of talking on general subjects.*
> *Peggy: No, it's rekindled, it really is. To go to dinner with someone, go out for coffee with him, go for walks, go for a movie—there's nothing wrong with that.*

So perhaps it's time to draw some distinctions:

Dorothy: I'm not looking for romance. I just look at it, "Maybe you'll find a friend." That's what I would like, just a friend.
Frieda: I don't mean you have to go to bed with them, no. Not unless you want to. There's nothing wrong with that either, if you want it.

—*Miami, #1*

Evelyn: I would like a companion, but I don't think I'd want to get married again—that's a different thing altogether.

—*Boston, #1*

Murray: I've decided that I had one good spouse, and I'm not going to get married any more. I do have some friends who are widows, but I've made up my mind: I don't want to get entangled any more.
Q: Lee?
Lee: Well, I don't think it's really written for me to get married again. Because I don't think I'd make another a good partner. Like the gentleman there, I think I'm happy to stay just as I am at this point in my life.

—*New York, #2*

A better idea of what you want may bring into better focus what you're afraid of—such as a would-be lover if your quest is for a friend or a would-be husband or wife if it is for a lover. At best, you may be able to bring desires and fears into trim as neatly as this couple, who seem to have learned how each can "go home" happily:

I went so far as to join a travel club and through it found a widowed gentleman. We share all expenses equally when traveling. Neither of us needs a meal ticket, just happy companionship. We both value our privacy and solitude and keep our two homes. Neither of us are eager to remarry. We have a great time together but are willing to go home when the party is over.

—*Woman, 73, 7*

Companionship: "Platonic" and That Other Kind

This woman (coincidentally of the same age and number of years widowed as the one just quoted) now knows what she wants—and it's what she has let pass her by so far:

When my husband died, for some time I still felt so married to him that, when other men showed some slight interest in me, I didn't notice it at the time. But now, although I'm not eager for marriage, I would very much enjoy knowing a man whom I could phone or who would phone me now and then, to suggest we go to a show, explore the countryside, walk a beach, take a class together, or have a meal together—a good friend. It's the male companionship I miss. So I would advise widows to graciously welcome male attention whenever it appears.

—*Woman, 73, 7*

"Companionship," as the excerpts at the end of the previous section bear out, can span a good many degrees of intimacy. How far does it extend in her case? She doesn't specify. But another clearly prefers a togetherness unclouded by overtly sexual overtones (although she allows a hug that might bring her to the borderline):

Male companionship—even platonic—especially platonic—can be helpful. Good conversation with a man is a change of pace—a nice hug can go a long way too!

—*Woman, 57, NA*

In this section, we'll give precedence to survivors who seek contact with the opposite sex mainly—and sometimes solely—to gratify social needs rather than physical ones. But that doesn't mean the physical can't happily (and now and then unhappily) infiltrate some otherwise platonic understandings.

This woman means to keep men an indispensable part of her life, but a chaste one:

I have not remarried and have no desire to do so. However, I do have a number of friends who are males and whose company I enjoy. Some are the husbands of friends. Some divorced, some widowed, and some single. Most knew my husband. I treasure these friendships. I do not want to live in an all-female world.

—*Woman, 74, 15*

Rose shared her wish, and she also had it granted as a legacy of her married life:

Q: Is it hard or easy to meet men? Has anybody met any?
Rose: I have. I've been very lucky, I have to admit it. I belong to B'nai Brith—I'm Jewish—and my husband was president three times

*and he knew so many people. And one of our past presidents, a
lady, passed away just six months after he did. She had come to see
me when my husband died, and I knew her husband. That's how you
meet people—through people. And I went with him for quite a while.
We'd go to Marin and walk and just air our brains out! And that's what
really helped me through all the tragedies I had [the deaths of all
her brothers and sisters around the same time as her husband's].*

—San Francisco

We'll see several instances when a communion between the bereaved
like theirs is consummated in marriage. But Rose is content to stop
well short of that:

Rose: And he moved to Los Angeles, which was fine.
Ann: Dirty pig!
*Rose: No, I hadn't planned on marrying him. He was a good date,
but that was it.*

If the past can't furnish you with friends like these, you may be
able to acquire them from other friends through word of mouth:

*Dorothy: Where do you find these people? Dig them up from under a
rock?*
*Lee: The safest way is through an introduction. If somebody knows
someone and they put you together, most likely they know something
about him, and so it isn't a total stranger.*

—Miami, #1

But later Lee relates how, even among her mother's generation, an
introduction is no safeguard against sneak attacks—even as she
asserts that many men, like many women, may be in search of nothing
more than talk:

*My mother is 22 years older than I am. And do you know what she
said to me after someone introduced her to someone? "First they
take you out to dinner and then they want to take you to bed!" I
said, "Mom, it doesn't always work that way." She said, "Well,
what do you do?" I said, "Keep your legs crossed"—you know, kidding with her. But a lot of people want to go out for companionship,
to talk to someone. The same thing with a man as it is with a woman.
And you'd be surprised—you find things to talk about.*

—Miami, #1

When introductions are lacking, your own talk may serve in their stead:

> **Frieda:** *I've never had anybody introduce me to anybody.*
> **Dorothy:** *How do you meet people?*
> **Frieda:** *I have a big mouth.*

(Yes, and we'll hear more from it in just a minute.) You can sharpen your verbal skills at the usual pick-up spots, which need not be as highly-pressured as the dance floor:

> **Rae:** *I go to museums, I talk to people. There are men that are there alone, you talk to them. Sometimes something develops—they take your number or you take theirs.*
>
> *—New York, #1*

The same developments may unfold in more homely settings:

> **Fay:** *Zsa Zsa Gabor says, "Wear your diamonds to the supermarket, because you never know who you're going to meet."*
>
> *—Los Angeles, #2*

Jean lectured a male friend who, she says, was "really incapacitated" when it came to shopping and cooking:

> *I said, "Learn to do the things that you have to do by yourself. Walk into supermarkets and talk to people. Women like it very much when you ask them, 'How do you cook this?' or 'How do you prepare that?'" I know I've been approached by men there who say, "What do you do with this piece of meat?" And I'll tell them, "Do you live alone?—this is a simple way to do it." And I've met many men this way.*
>
> *—New York, #1*

Lee's repertoire of recipes is in heavy demand:

> *The woman does the shopping, does the cleaning, does the cooking, and the man usually does nothing. And when they're left alone, they don't know how to shop. They ask you how to cook something. Just the other day, I had somebody call me up for a recipe.*
>
> *—Miami, #1*

Frieda and Dorothy give mixed reviews of their exploits in the produce department:

> **Frieda:** *And they tell me the best place to find a husband, in case you're interested, ladies, is in the supermarket.*
> **Marlene:** *Right.*
> **Dorothy:** *Find out what he's buying?*
> **Frieda:** *No, he's going to ask you. I've had gentlemen talk to me.*
> **Dorothy:** *I've asked them if this is a good cantaloupe, and he looks like he doesn't even know what a cantaloupe is.*
> **Frieda:** *Well, how do you expect him to know?*
> **Dorothy:** *Maybe he likes tomatoes?*
>
> *—Miami, #1*

Dorothy envies the supposedly greater freedom with which men can seize on these opportunities, but Frieda boasts that she routinely makes the first advances:

> **Dorothy:** *Men don't have the same problems we do. If they meet a woman, they can go up and say hello.*
> **Catherine:** *Some of them can, and some of them can't.*
> **Frieda:** *Honey, many a time I've sat in a mall, like this, where there's a bench, and a man will sit down and take his newspapers out and I'll look over at him: "What time is it, please?" And we'll start talking.*
> **Dorothy:** *What if he asks this question: "Aren't you wearing a wristwatch?"*
> **Frieda:** *"It isn't working. It's a lousy watch. It's a Timex."*
> **Marlene:** *She's got all the answers.*

Frieda insists she's in the market for a friend, not a husband:

> **Frieda:** *But there are always men wandering around a shopping center.*
> **Dorothy:** *Their wives threw them out of the house. That's why they're wandering around.*
> **Lee:** *Some of them could be married, and they're shopping around.*
> **Frieda:** *I'm not looking to get married. I'm looking for people to talk to.*
> **Lee:** *You get in trouble that way.*
> **Frieda:** *Where? Where? When I say to a man, "What time is it?" I'm not looking for him to take me to the courthouse.*

But all the puns and innuendos—and the preoccupations with marriage—betray that occasions like these have a sexual fillip that lift them above a workaday transaction like buying groceries. They've become flirtations. And a flirtation is a negotiation. Once it's in motion, you and the other party must be in at least tacit agreement about how far you want it to go.

Frieda, for example, welcomes some physical contact:

> *Frieda: I don't want to get married, but I do want the friendship of a man. I want to go to dinner with a man, go to a movie with him. I can't sit and hold hands with a woman!*
> *Marlene: That's for sure.*
> *Frieda: I prefer the friendship of men to that of women. I find that they're more sincere.*
>
> —*Miami, #1*

But "friendship" it strictly is, and she spells out the rules to every potential paramour who reaches the traditional threshold:

> *Frieda: When I meet a man, I tell it to him right away: "I'm looking for a friend, not a lover. If you can take me to my door at night and kiss me good night and leave, fine, we're going to get along. Otherwise, forget it."*
> *Dorothy: This is a revelation to me. I like that lady! I think you're very smart.*

What rouses Dorothy's admiration is the memory of how flustered she was when it came time to say good night:

> *Dorothy: I'd like to ask a question. What do you do when somebody makes a pass? I date very rarely, because I don't really care that much. I think I want somebody in, but then I shy off. Once I was polite and I said, "Would you like to come in?" I don't know why I did that. Now, when the old crock—pardon the expression—made a pass at me, . . . I almost threw him out the door!*
> *Frieda: No, don't throw him out! Say, "Thank you."*
> *Dorothy: Oh, I wouldn't say that.*
> *Frieda: You're still attractive! Say, "Thank you."*
> *Dorothy: "Thank you"? Then what do you do?*

Frieda: Nothing. You kiss him on the cheek and say, "Good night, buddy, I'll see you tomorrow."

But Dorothy refuses to go even that far:

Dorothy: I don't want to kiss him.
Frieda: If you don't want to kiss him, then you shouldn't have gone out with him in the first place.
Dorothy: I didn't know *him in the first place*
Frieda: If you hadn't thought he was nice, you wouldn't have gone out. If he's that nice, a kiss on the cheek won't hurt. It's not catching.

Lee (whom we'll come upon at the end of this chapter revelling in the success of her remarriage) seconds Frieda's opinion, and posits that taking a chance with someone you don't know is the only way to "give yourself a chance":

Yes, give them a little kiss, make them happy. You have to get to know somebody, you don't know whether you're going to like him. I think, once you're widowed, you have that attitude of—"Nothing! I'm just going out for the evening." But you've got to give yourself a chance.

Dorothy is unpersuaded, and she later thinks she discerns exactly what is making Catherine so squeamish when Frieda tries to coax Catherine into dancing again:

Frieda: If you get up once and do it, you will enjoy it.
Catherine: Well, I don't know what it is, but I just can't.
Dorothy: She doesn't like the physical contact. I'm not saying any more, but that's it.
Marlene: Exactly. Doesn't want to be that close to a man.
Catherine: He has to have his hands on me to dance.

So some "platonic" relationships are more platonic than others. The most innocuous tokens of intimacy between the sexes—a good night kiss in a doorway or the clasp of a dancing partner's hand—are enough to unnerve Dorothy and Catherine. Should they have tried to make it clearer to the men in their lives? Again, we don't pretend to have an answer, except to postulate that perhaps they must first make it clearer to themselves. Sarah would encourage older men looking for lady friends to go to senior centers:

> *If they are 60 or over, they can join a senior center. And they will certainly meet women because there are hardly any men in these groups. They will be flooded with invitations—perhaps for just companionship. I guess there are women who can be aggressive, but on the average an invitation from a woman might be for a home-cooked dinner or watching television together.*
>
> *—New York, #1*

How explicit about that should the invitation be? Dorothy shrinks back from even extending one, but note how the "fear of rejection" has become all snarled up with fear of the opposite:

> **Dorothy:** *You see these commercials: "Pick up someone, you're a new woman." I can't! The fear of rejection would devastate me. I can't be rejected.*
> **Q:** *What's that commercial about?*
> **Dorothy:** *You know, "Nowadays, if you want to get to know a man, call him up and invite him over for some wine."*
> **Q:** *That's the product?*
> **Dorothy:** *Yes—"I've got a bottle of wine, come on over."*
> **Grace:** *And you* can *do that today.*
> **Dorothy:** *I know I can't go do it. It all works out beautifully on television. But I invite him over and ask him into the house—and I was in trouble!*
>
> *—Miami, #1*

Perhaps a less open-ended overture would let her master both of these fears. To hear Frieda tell it, if she'd been in Dorothy's place she would have practically issued her date a written protocol for the event. Nevertheless Frieda has apparently maintained purely friendly relations with one man for half a century, regardless of the ups and downs in his romantic life:

> *I have a friend whom I met with his wife about forty-five years ago. We were together at least once or twice a week. The three of us. Then Edna became ill, she got multiple sclerosis. And for a while she would*

still go with Al and me. We'd go to brunch almost every Saturday. Then she became housebound. To make a long story short, it's now fifty years, he has remarried, but now he and his wife are separated. And he and I are still friends. Just friends after all of these years! Sometimes it's hard to believe that there's such a thing as a platonic friendship. I usually don't believe it either, but with Al and me, that's exactly what it is.

—Miami, #1

And what of the Als of this world? On the strength of testimony like Frieda's, they must exist. But if there were any among our survey or discussion groups, they chose to stay mum—which is why you've heard only women's voices in this section so far. Richard and Tom *might* be describing platonic liaisons:

Richard: *The way it is now, with this lady I go with, everything's fine. We have dinner together, we both enjoy a lot of the same things, we like to read, love to take walks, drive down to the Seaport for something to eat. And that helps me a lot.*

Tom: *My situation is pretty much like Richard's, where I don't intend to get married again but I do have lady friends who enjoy the same things I do, travel and restaurants and theatre and things like that. So socially I get around town pretty well, and it seems to quell any depressive tendency.*

—New York, #2

But of course the surest way a man can call down the curse of sissihood on himself is to admit that he prefers female company but isn't interested in sex. And so it's little wonder that the only male advocate of the "platonic" (as a precaution against AIDS) is misusing the word:

Roger: *The only solution is a one-on-one relationship for both people who have been tested, with the understanding that it is going to continue as a platonic relationship.*

Q: *Platonic? So no sex?*

Roger: *Well, no, pardon me, I used the wrong word. No, without marriage.*

—New York, #2

On now to more who think as he does.

Barracudas and Peacocks: Sex versus Sex

> *Sarah: A woman I met on vacation recently told me about a couple she knew who were very comfortable together. They had worked out an arrangement. They didn't see each other during the week because they could fill their daily lives without that; they didn't feel the pressure of loneliness then. Weekends seem to emphasize the feeling of needing someone. So during the week they sort of kept their distance, but they spent every weekend together. One was 81, and the other was 85—*
> *Ida: Chippies!*
> *Connie: More power to them!*
> *Sarah: They found it the most comforting and most comfortable arrangement they could make.*
> *—New York, #1*

Sarah then lets loose the question that is no doubt pent up in every mind in the room:

> *Sarah: People ask me whether the arrangement was just for companionship or whether these two in their 80s were having sex. I said, "I don't know, it never occurred to me to ask." But I too have privately speculated on whether . . .*
> *Eleanor: Now, if they were good friends of yours, you would just say, "Are you having sex [laughter]?"*

Even the sturdiest of friendships might not tolerate such an inquiry, but if it did, a yes would win a burst of approval from these two:

> *Find a good sex partner, it doesn't have to be love. Enjoy! Be happy.*
> *—Woman, 63, 3*

> *Allow yourself a new relationship, if it comes along. Life can have many wonderful situations again.*
> *—Woman, 73, 9*

But it's best not to assume that "wonderful situations"—a phrase which seems to fit the serene weekends Sarah describes—will amble peacefully into your life of their own accord. You must set off in search of them. And, as you do, many survivors warn, be prepared to do battle, don't underrate your opponents, and keep a sharp eye out for ambushes on the march.

The essence of courtship is competition, in more ways than one. We must win over someone from the opposite sex and must often win out against rivals among our own sex as we do. The fish and the fowl in this section's title (an admittedly outlandish pairing, but more on that later) symbolize the two sides in the conventional brand of romantic warfare. And we'll watch them fighting some spirited engagements. But we'll also see (in this section and the next) how antagonists can emerge from quarters where you least expect them—and how they can take the shape of abstractions as well as people.

Time, for example. To this man, time is pure potential:

You are still alive and have a lifetime to live. Your life and future are up to you alone. Your love for the deceased can continue for the rest of your life. However, there is a capability for another love in addition.
—Man, 61, 3

But if time can fulfill that capability, it can also frustrate it. You may think it too soon for another love. Or you may think it too late. Women in particular are prey to such doubts, and, since they make up the majority of our contributors and our readers, we'll hear them out before we do the men.

When her therapist ventured that enough time had gone by, Frieda erupted:

My husband died very suddenly in a hotel in Atlantic City when I was 35. And I went wacko to the point where, after about five or six months, I knew I needed help or I was going to wind up somewhere I didn't want to be. So I went to a psychiatrist in Miami Beach that somebody recommended. I'd go to him, and I'd talk and talk. And he would listen. Then he said, "There are two things I want you to do." I said, "What's that?" "I want you go to work." "But I don't need to work." "I know you don't, but I want you to go to work." I said to him, "What else?" "I want you to go to bed with a man." I looked at him. My husband wasn't dead six months! He said, "Now, I want you to listen to me!" I paid him his money and said, "Go to hell!" And I walked out.
—Miami, #1

And when she next encountered him, doctor's orders remained cheerfully unobeyed:

A while later, I was walking on Lincoln Road, and he comes along in the other direction with his nurse and another couple. As we got next to each other, he said, "Did you fill that prescription I gave you?" Wait till you hear the answer! I said, "No, I haven't found a pharmacist I would trust" [laughter]. Well, he burst out laughing, and I am certain that the people with him must have asked, "What's this all about?"

Frieda makes it plain she took umbrage not at what he said but at when he said it:

Q: Now, is that ever good advice?
Frieda: To go to bed with someone? Sure—but not that soon!

As Chapter 3 suggests, such a refusal to trust anyone else so soon afterwards may be founded on a healthy self-distrust. But others who are biding their time also keep open the possibility of a change of heart:

A widower friend has asked me out. I went once. Really not interested—yet!
—Woman, 72, 2

Barbara: Enough time hasn't gone by yet for me to think about someone else. Another two or three years, I might feel completely different.
—Boston, #1

This woman, alas, discovered that she had let time get the better of her:

I had a chance to remarry, but the timing was wrong. I am now widowed more than three years. If I had met that man now, I would have kept him as a friend. But after he tried for a year to persuade me, I told him to find someone else—I was still grieving very much. He finally left town and got married. I now realize he was a good person and I liked him —respected him. I would advise people to keep other people warm—you never know!
—Woman, 75, 4

Too little time is not what inhibits other women, but rather something that seems like a surplus of it—their ages:

Lee: If you're young enough to enjoy sex, then you want to make sure you're not stuck with someone who isn't right for you.
Ida: It's secondary, though, at this stage in life.
Q: Ladies, hold on. You don't want to have sex?
Marlene: No, no.
Dorothy: That's for kids.
Molly: We're not teenagers.

—*Miami, #1*

But when Mary suggests that we may be heading into obsolescence by the fifth or sixth decade, Marilyn refutes her with an example from the seventh:

Mary: After you reach 55 or 60, I think you're out of the swim, so to speak.
Marilyn: That's not true because my mother-in-law was 70 and had been a widow for quite a while. And when she met a man, it really was the greatest thing that ever happened to her. She became such a happy, active woman. I think that age has nothing to do with it. I don't believe in age for anything.

—*Boston, #2*

Jean introduces a woman who wasn't out of the swim in her 90s:

A friend just returned from a vacation at a camp for senior citizens in Connecticut. And she met a woman there who was 94 years old. A woman in exuberant health who swam around the lake every day in cold water. Most of the younger people couldn't. This woman brought a boyfriend up there, he was 75. They shared the same room.
Ida: A younger man, no less!
Sarah: Was he as capable as her . . . I mean . . . ?
Jean: I don't know what took place in the privacy of their room, but my friend said the entire camp was aghast at how brazen she was to bring him along.

—*New York, #1*

Sometimes the older generation delights in shocking the younger as much as the younger always has the older. These women, however, can barely contemplate taking liberties that the young may view as theirs by right—but may not countenance in their elders:

Q: Are women you know having affairs?
Connie: *Why ask us? What do we know? None of us has affairs.*
Eleanor: *This is a disgustingly prudish group—nobody has an affair!*
Jean: *Women of all ages are having affairs.*
Sarah: *People are doing that—and living together.*
Bea: *All the young ones are—so why can't the older ones?*
Jean: *How would your grandchildren feel about that?*
Isabel: *They are probably doing it, so why should they mind about us?*
Eleanor: *But they can't see the gran-ma do it.*

—New York, #1

Their reservations about having affairs and living together may come from a supposition that they're not only *at* but also *from* another age:

> **Connie:** *It's a new world today, and it's hard to adjust. You see what the kids are doing, what young couples are doing. My sister lives in Westchester, and she says, "Of course they throw the keys in, everybody exchanges wives, husbands." You know, I am getting hardened to it.*
>
> *—New York, #1*

A certain quaintness colors this picture of alleged suburban mores, for they smack of the 1960s (at least as portrayed in novel and film) more than of the 1980s. Contemporary promiscuity scandalizes Jean too, but she fulminates against some more recent ramifications of it:

> *Today we live in a very immoral world. Take the television commercials about AIDS—I think they're disgraceful. A lady is shown dressed to the hilt going somewhere, and she opens her beautiful evening purse—probably cost $300—and puts a condom in it. "Condom" used to be a forbidden word years ago. The times—it's so blatant! They are advertising everything.*
>
> *—New York, #1*

She sees an irony in how AIDS has led to the rediscovery of celibacy:

> **Jean:** *About AIDS, one thing that bothers me very much is the way the media advises people to abstain. When I grew up everybody abstained. No one was cheap about sex.*
> **Bea:** *You were a bum—*

Jean: Yes, you were a bum if you ever slept with one man before your marriage. You were an immoral woman.

To Jean, young and old live on the opposite slopes of a great emotional divide:

Sex is meaningless to the young. You know, they feel that older people were born in the stone age. Well, we had the feelings that they'll never dream of and we still do! Even today, if we love someone and live together, it's not meaningless like theirs. I know a young girl who has lived together with married men now for at least 15 years. After a while, she throws them off. What is this girl's life?

—*New York, #1*

Decrying the decadence of the times—it's a task the elders of every era have set for themselves, often with ill-concealed enthusiasm. For Dorothy, though, AIDS represents not the wages of modern immorality but a potential menace to her health:

Ida: I don't think it's safe with this AIDS going around now.
Frieda: Types my age wouldn't have AIDS.
Dorothy: Don't be so sure. I heard some stories from a nurse who said she's getting older men—I mean really old—who've been going to prostitutes. So don't be so sure that they don't have AIDS. Give them a blood test first.

—*Miami, #1*

A daughter has demonstrated to Marlene that cohabitation makes sense as a prelude to marriage:

Marlene: I believe in living together because it seems it worked out with my daughter. It's her second marriage, but she lived with him and she waited until she was sure. It took her a while but . . .
Molly: I hear it. I have an ex-in-law who did that.

—*Miami, #1*

Frieda cheers an even younger generation on:

The kids are smart. My grandson is living with a little girl now, and I couldn't be more pleased. She's a doll, they've been together now for almost four years. They're going to be married around the first of

the year. I know that they'll get along because they've been getting along for four years.
Lydia: *Once they get married, they get divorced.*
Frieda: *Maybe, maybe, but they've got a better chance than people that haven't lived together. Because Casey knows all about Dana, Dana knows all about Casey. They know all the bad things about each other; they know all the good things.*

—Miami, #1

And she claims she's poised, if given the chance, to follow their example:

Frieda: *The best thing to do, if you find a man, is to live with him. And then marry him if you want to.*
Lee: *Absolutely.*
Catherine: *I'm just too old for that—I'm 73.*
Frieda: *Oh, hell, I'm older than you are, and I would do it. I'm going to be 80. You think, when we get old, we die? Uh-uh—we come back to haunt the young.*

A more tolerant ghost than the censorious Jean, Frieda embodies the principle that age is at least relatively relative. Once she scorned the attentions of an older man:

Years ago there was a man, much older than me, who wanted to marry me, and I turned him down. When I told my father, he said, "What!" I said, "Look, Pa, if he could play pinochle, at least you could have fun with him. What am I going to do with him?" At that time I was 40; he was 70.

Now, forty years later, when someone is trying to steal her boyfriend, she's as livid as if she's vying with a teenage temptress:

Where I live now, there's a man who is going to be 91. When I moved in, he started making a play for me, and soon we were going all over together. Then in moves a woman, she's there two weeks, you never saw anything like it! She's much younger than I am—I'm going to be 80; she has to be 70, 72. What the hell is she making a play for a man that's past 90? What does she want him for?

She definitely validates Sarah's conjecture:

> **Sarah:** *You see books like "Sex After Forty," "Sex After Fifty," "Sex After Sixty." I think a very fascinating book would be "Sex..."*
> **Bea:** *"After Eighty"?*
> **Sarah:** *"After Eighty."*
>
> —*New York, #1*

There's no reason the goal can't be set—and achieved, regardless of the disapproval of your peers (already observed), of your family (not far ahead), and occasionally even of yourself. When it comes to her looks, a woman is notoriously her own harshest critic, and age isn't reputed to make her less forgiving. But Dorothy is doing her best:

> **Dorothy:** *Why do we downgrade ourselves so much? Some days I feel so nice, and the next time I look in the mirror, I say, "Yuck! Yuck!"*
> **Q:** *Anybody recognize that one? The old "I wish I had a bag for my head" syndrome?*
> **Molly:** *I think you're down on yourself all the time.*
> **Dorothy:** *Not all the time. Sometimes I'm gorgeous. And even when I say, "Yuck," then I tell myself what my psychologist taught me: "Hey, kid, you're not half-bad."*
>
> —*Miami, #1*

Although age in itself may not rule out romance, it definitely steepens the odds of a woman's finding it. Here is Dorothy again, all made up but with no place to go:

> *There isn't anyone around to introduce us to!*

Everyone knows the stark actuarial facts:

> **Lil:** *There are three or four times more women than there are men. Every place I go, they number ten to one.*
> **Judy:** *It's true.*
> **Marilyn:** *It's not easy meeting men. Not at all.*
> **Lil:** *No, because the women outlive the men easy.*
>
> —*Boston, #2*

And Jean's proposal of one way to get acquainted draws some sardonic comments:

> **Jean:** *There are places in the mountains where they have singles groups. Twice a year, 3,000 singles check in at Brown's Hotel in the Catskills.*
> **Connie:** *Yes, 2,999 women!*
> **Jean:** *Of course there are many women, but there are many men too. They advertise it as "Thirty-Five and Up," but you meet people in their 80s.*
> **Sarah:** *"A Hundred and Under" would be more like it.*
> *—New York, #1*

The scarcer a commodity, of course, the more it is prized, and the more fiercely it is sought, as Jean herself acknowledges:

> *The women do run after the men. They just besiege them!*

And the battle can only intensify in the 1990s as the average age of the population increases. Mary grudgingly respects the single-minded-ness of one acquaintance:

> **Mary:** *I have a girlfriend who's always got somebody. She's sweet, she's dear, she never says anything cutting, she'll always agree with you. And yet underneath she's very competitive. There's a certain type of woman that'll never be without a man.*
> **Rose:** *They go for men.*
> **Mary:** *And they find them. That's it, they find them.*
> *—San Francisco*

But Dorothy was much less philosophical after being routed by the predators on the prowl at an affair for singles:

> *Not so long ago I went away on a weekend to the beach, and part of the program was a ballroom called Stardust. Just like you see in the movies, and I went to it. It took me about four weeks to recover [laughter]. I came out of there—no, it wasn't funny—I was so de-pressed, I never should have gone. These women and men come every night, and the women were dressed up. They all looked lovely, and the men were strutting around like peacocks. And there was something*

*called a mixer—you know what that is? The women stand on one line
and the men on another. And as you come up, when it's the man's turn,
he'll take a lady and dance her around for two seconds. And then he's
supposed to go to the end of the line. Well, a man was standing there,
and I thought I was supposed to dance with him. So I walked over to him,
and he said, "It's not your turn!"*

—*Miami, #1*

Enter a peacock. Rude though he may have been, he was just stating
the rules, not enforcing them. That was the job of another species:

Dorothy: *Then I started to walk over to my lady friend who was on the
line. I was going to tell her, "Forget it—I'm going to sit and wait for
you." And two women, young women, said, "Oh, you! Get on the back
of the line!" I said, "I'm not dancing. I just wanted to tell her
something." "Wait your turn!" They were ferocious! They were like—I
don't know what you would say—gorillas! They were fighting for these
men.*
Ida: *It's a jungle, that's the word maybe.*
Dorothy: *Yes, a jungle.*
Laura: *Really hungry for a man.*
Dorothy: *Never again! It practically set me back the ten years that I
had recuperated from my husband's death. I was too vulnerable.*

Any woman ''alone at the dance'' is vulnerability personified,
and other women often seem all too proficient at exploiting it.
Sometimes they are policing the boundaries of the couples' world.
One woman would have denied Betty the favor that Betty had
encouraged her own husband to grant to other women:

*Apropos of sharing, when my husband was alive, we went to a resort.
We both liked to dance, but if there were women sitting around, I'd
say, "Why don't you dance with them?" And he'd get a little angry.
But after he died, I went to a dance and I was sitting at a big table
and one of the men said, "Would you like to dance?" Because I'm
sitting there like a klutz. And his wife whispered to me, "Just once
around!" [laughter]. I think despite her I danced two around [laugh-
ing]. Oh God, if you don't have a sense of humor, you'd just die.*

—*Los Angeles, #2*

At least she made it out onto the dance floor. Frieda never even had a chance at a spin:

> *The first year I lived in Pembrook Pines, they had a New Year's Eve party. Hooray! I went there with a friend of mine, and we sat at a table for eight. There were three couples and Iola and me. And we sit and we sit. This couple gets up to dance and this couple, and Iola and I are sitting there and looking at each other. Finally about an hour later she looked at me, I looked at her, I said, "You ready?" She said, "Yeah." I've never been to a party there since.*
>
> *—Miami, #1*

In the Prologue (page 8) Laura tells Frieda how the same humiliation was rendered all the worse by contrast with what used to be: "remembering how important I was to somebody . . . . and to these people there, I'm dirt!" Is that how she should have felt? Relegated to wallflower in that hothouse atmosphere, you may ask how she could help it. But set Laura's assertion that another dance "would kill me" alongside Betty's: "If you don't have a sense of humor, you'd just die."

Marilyn had to cling even harder to her sense of humor—to keep the men in perspective rather than the women:

> *Marilyn: Men today are a heck of a lot different from the men we used to go out with as kids.*
> *Q: How are they different?*
> *Marilyn: I think they are much more forward. To be very honest, they have one thing in mind. When I went to these dances, boy, that was an experience! There I was, out of circulation for twenty-five years, and suddenly I was listening to lines like you never heard [laughter]! You know, right away, when you first met: "Can you come out to my car?"*
> *Q: Were these stag dances?*
> *Marilyn: Singles dances, for older people like me. In the beginning, I was upset—"My God, I don't believe it. I'm never coming back here again!" Then it got—it was funny. When I could laugh about it, it was okay. I realized that that these people were very lonely too, and it was their way of supposedly making conversation.*
>
> *—Boston, #2*

The undersupply of men does no more to improve their characters than the oversupply of women does theirs. Not that every scene for singles is populated by males so crassly on the make. Jean was comfortably alone at a dance that was a model of decorum (and where age was graciously overlooked):

> *Rae: At our age, to go to a singles weekend up in the mountains—it is really . . . [grimaces].*
>
> *Jean: Rae, this one is put on by the B'nai Zion, it's a charity for homes for the mentally retarded in Israel. You have a marvelous time. They give us wonderful accommodations, we have marvelous food. There are lots of men there. I don't intend to marry them, but it's nice to see them. Some of them are wonderful dancers, some of the best dancers I've danced with. One man—I don't know how old he was—called me "young lady," and I was flattered. "Young lady, would you dance with me?"*
>
> *—New York, #1*

But Marilyn's experience was hardly a fluke:

> *Marlene: Sometimes when I go out and I happen to meet somebody and we go someplace, they say, "Your place or mine?" That's right! I say, "Good night, I'm going home." I mean, when you go out by yourself, they think you're looking to jump into bed with them.*
>
> *—Miami, #1*

Lee is convinced that this sort of swagger is so much bluff:

> *Sometimes, when I hear what some of the men say, I think they're really chicken. They're just as nervous with you as you are with them. But when they meet a woman, they want to make you feel they're macho, you know—hey, they want to take you to bed and all that.*
>
> *—Miami, #1*

Jean, on the other hand, wishes that it were *all* bravado:

> *Jean: If a woman is in her late 60s or early 70s and she meets a man who is in his 80s, she has to think very carefully about aligning herself with him for a love affair. I have a friend who is very direct and sensible and who says she would never marry or even consider having an affair with them. She says, "It would be, every single night, a night of torture [laughter]. It would always be in their minds, and they would persist, and I know I would be tortured night after night." I said,*

"I never thought about it that way" [laughter].
Bea: *Jean, now I know why I never had a love affair.*
Jean: *She has a point, frankly.*

—*New York, #1*

Whatever the truth, we are deep in the domain of sexual stereotypes, and it's only right to let the other side have its say. The men of this retirement community were indeed under siege:

Bud: *Well, I wouldn't join any senior citizens' club. I can tell you honestly, as a single man, you're not lonesome. I never knew so many women could come out of the woodwork [laughter].*
Lillian: *Do you know what they call them in Leisure World, when they know a man is single? "The Casserole Brigade."*
Leonard: *You're talking about casseroles, my wife's been dead for 20 years, and I'm still getting casseroles [laughter].*
Loretta: *He's popular, that's what the matter with him.*
Q: *You didn't remarry?*
Leonard: *No, I didn't remarry.*
Edwin: *He gets all the food he can eat* now.

—*Los Angeles, #1*

Like many war stories, theirs can ooze braggadocio:

Q: *Are you subject to the casserole brigade beating down your door?*
Charlie: *Well, yes, if you break a leg. I went over my bike's handlebars once and broke my kneecap. Then you get a lot of cookies and chicken fricassee. My neighbor said, "I never saw so many women as were coming into your apartment." I said, "That's the biggest little whorehouse in Leisure World."*

Unquestionably a peacock. And Sylvia, in trying to acquit herself of his characterization, convicts all of her neighbors of it:

Sylvia: *Let me tell you, the women in Leisure World have a terrible reputation. Should I tell [our moderator] that little story?*
Irene: *Tell her the story.*
Sylvia: *There was one of our Leisure World ladies who went to the swimming pool. And some man came in that she didn't recognize, so she asked, "Who are you?" He said, "Well, I'm not new here—I've*

just been gone for fifteen years." "Where have you been?" "Well, I've been in the penitentiary." "What did you do?" "I murdered my wife." "Ooohhhh . . . you're single*!" So that's the way they think of us—that we're all out there looking for some man. But it's not true that we're all barracudas.*

Barracudas versus peacocks—not a contest that was ever fought on land or sea, of course. But both images comport closely enough with reality to give them a semblance of life. In another group, Lee confirms how fast the casserole brigade can mobilize:

It's always easier for a man to find someone than a woman, because the women go after him so quickly. If he lives in a complex and his wife dies, almost overnight the other women are inviting him to dinner and giving him this and giving him that.

—Miami, #1

Some of the women in our discussion groups slipped into their roles right on cue:

Lydia: *One man was after me for the longest time. He said, "If you want to go out, we'll go out; if you want to get married, we'll get married." And I said, "I don't date."*
Dorothy: *Where's he live?*
Frieda: *What's his phone number?*

—Miami, #1

These were responding to a proposal that we take their photographs:

Rae: *Are you going to show the pictures to some nice bachelors so that they know what we look like before we meet them?*
Ida: *That's an idea!*
Isabel: *[ironically]* Nobody *wants to meet* anybody! *But then:* "Do you have any nice bachelors?"
Bea: *Where* are *the widowers, for heaven's sake?*

—New York, #1

If the widowers are alone at the dance, they may find it as much of an occasion for ''dying'' as a woman—dying and going to heaven:

Jean: If a man is a good dancer, he will be in great demand. I always tell them to take a course in dancing. It doesn't cost that much to be a really accomplished dancer—you simply go to a studio and learn the latest steps. He will never, never be lonely—ever.

Isabel: How old a man are you talking about?

Jean: Any age if he is in good health, 60s, 70s, 80s.

Isabel: 70s, 80s? They can't even stand on their feet.

Rae: A lot of them can't walk, but they can dance.

Jean: I don't care about their ages, it's wonderful to dance with them. I admire them when they can do that.

—New York, #1

Dance though they may, they're not about to be swept off their feet. Peacocks are as skittish as barracudas are voracious:

Q: Let's get back to the casserole brigade. What about the rest of guys? Ed, how about you?

Edwin: Oh, I got my fill of casseroles. Everybody who invited me for dinner said, "Do you like casseroles?" Well, I've had plenty.

Q: And you haven't remarried, either?

Edwin: No, I don't intend to.

If the women are fed up with men who have "just one thing in mind," so are men with such women—only now that "one thing" is remarriage, or, if not, the kind of economic and social security that go with marriage:

Richard: We're all widowers here. You're telling me you're interviewing widows too?

Q: Oh, sure. Do you think they have the same or different points of view?

Murray: Different.

Richard: I think so too. I think they would prefer to get married again because they need somebody to take care of them.

—New York, #1

Raymond scoffs at Noel's suggestion that women could harbor any other motive:

Noel: I know some women in my neighborhood whom I worked with on Wall Street years ago, and they invite me over for dinner, and I do the same. We're just good friends. And they seem to believe, as I do, that they've got their lives made up. They're comfortable and happy, and they don't need to be married, as every woman years ago thought she had to be.

Raymond: *There's no such thing! You go with a woman, and they all say, "We don't want to get married, we'll just have a relationship." Then, after you've gone with her any length of time, she'll ask you for the ring, and don't let anybody kid you. When you get used to them, and they know you're used to them, you depend on them a little bit, [smiling] then comes the ring part [laughter].*

—New York, #1

But by that time, Edwin warns, you may no longer be able to afford the ring:

I'd say, "Do you want to go to dinner?" And right away, before I finished, they'd picked out the restaurant. I bought some pretty expensive meals in my life as a single man. And when I say "expensive," I'm not talking about $20 meals.

—Los Angeles, #1

Jean maintains that a peacock's chance to unfurl his feathers in front of the ladies is about all that keeps him on his feet:

Don't you notice how women are much brighter, cleaner, nicer than most of the men who are widowers and who fall apart immediately? Even young men. Unless they have a lady that they are courting—then they put their best suits on.

—New York, #1

But Bud saw to it that his finery stayed in the closet on that occasion, for he knew the kind of fish that flashy ornaments can attract:

I was single for five years, and I noticed most of the women wanted the feel of your pocket to see how much you had. In fact, I had plenty of suits because my job required it. But if I met a girl, I always wore the same suit. I didn't want her to know I had more. It was one of my tricks.

—Los Angeles, #1

Female cupidity in a dead heat with male vanity. Had enough of these stereotypes? And of this mishmash of metaphors that they've begotten from battlefield, ballroom, jungle, and reef? So have we, although stereotypes, unfortunately, are the stuff of life, as their power to give birth to metaphor testifies. But a life lived through stereotypes is a life lived secondhand.

Bud found that out when a woman, now his wife, nullified all his preconceptions:

> *But, anyhow, when I met Virginia, money didn't enter into it. She didn't care how much I had, and I didn't care how much she had.*

In any case, even if his fears were merited, they are scarcely the exclusive property of men:

> *Lee: The same for a woman—it works both ways. They're worried the same way as men that they're going to meet someone who is a gold digger and who is going to go after them for whatever they have. That's why there are so many premarital agreements, especially if there are children.*
>
> *—Miami, #1*

> *Edwin: I find most women look for a dollar more than they do happiness.*
> *Sylvia: Well, that's true of both men and women.*
>
> *—Los Angeles, #1*

Nor does every man vaunt himself as a prodigy in the bedroom. This one checked off "widowed" and then added "but keeping steady company":

> *I had some slight problems in beginning dating—but those eased up. (Am still working on some sexual problems.)*
>
> *—Man, 68, 2*

And not every male is swamped by the attentions of females:

> *Dorothy: In a men's group I don't think they would talk as freely as women do.*
> *Marlene: Oh, yes, they would. You'd be surprised how much men talk.*
> *Q: What do you think they would talk about?*
> *Frieda: The same things we do How they're kept busy during the day,*

but at night they go into their apartments, and the four walls . . .
Laura: *I have some friends that are widowers, and they are very lonely, just as we are.*
Lee: *They're lonelier.*

—*Miami, #1*

Because it makes us laugh, men and women can't resist cartooning each other—and themselves. But it tends to set the sexes against each other, and that's pernicious if our subject is how they can best get together again. The scruples and doubts we've come across in this section typically preoccupy survivors who intend to do so only for the short run, or only now and then. And the frivolity of some of their stories mirrors these intentions. We'll close this chapter with the experiences of those who more soberly weighed the prospect of a long-term commitment—and then rejected it or undertook it.

Living Together

We've characterized this section as being about "living together" rather than "remarrying" because quite a few survivors have come to regard the two states as almost interchangeable, especially if they are beyond the child-rearing ages. That seems to be the spirit in which this woman responds to Sarah's suggestion:

Sarah: *Apropos of "why get married?": I went to visit a sick friend in the hospital, and in the bed opposite her was a very lively, happy-go-lucky woman in her mid-80s. And, talking to her, I found she had been married three times.*
Bea: *Imagine how happy she'd be the fourth time!*
Sarah: *Well, I said to her, "I have a feeling you are going to get married again." Because she was so overflowing with life. She looked at me, and she was totally considering my question. Then she said to me in a very serious way, "No. This time, I will just live with him." I was so amused by her answer. A woman of 85 who could still maintain a vital interest, who was still hanging on to being a woman! But she said, "This time I will just live with him."*

—*New York, #1*

Her concession that she will "just" be living with him reveals she's bearing the difference in mind, as was Judy's widowed friend:

She said, although she wouldn't get married again, she would live with someone for companionship. But she didn't want the other stuff that went with it.

—*Boston, #2*

Here we'll concentrate less on the ''other stuff'' than on the fact that living with someone else, under the sanction of matrimony or not, means making room in your life for another like the one you lost.

At the outset of this chapter, we said that desire and fear would be its keynotes. Our first section was given over to those whom desire had left at peace; our second, to those whom fear had all but paralyzed; and our third and fourth, to those who were pressing on despite all the miscellaneous yearnings and apprehensions that can trip up any man or woman trying to do what they were. This section proceeds to some desires and fears unique to survivors—and which this time are held in common by men and women. For both are pondering whether the future can hold some equivalent of what the past did.

Some of that past may be utterly beyond recapture. Lee recalls ''that time'':

When I first got married, I was young, music was playing, everything was beautiful. We all got married during that time. We just went gung ho and married because we loved the girl, we loved her for her beauty and her passion.

—*New York, #2*

Now he's a more timorous man, and not just because he's an older one:

Nowadays most of us over here have paid our dues. So we've got to consider the fear of death, the fear of sex, the fear of insecurity, the fear of loneliness, the fear that they're marrying us just because we have some bread. Sort of five great fears, you know.

But other emotions also bring him up short:

I mean, let's face it, you've got to think of all these things before you get tied up again. And then again, a lot of us are not remarrying because you begin to create your own self—to live by your own self and enjoy your own self.

Your *own* self: as we saw in Chapter 1, it's victory in the struggle of survivors to grow into something larger than "half a couple." Now, ironically, it may be what deters you from reconstituting a couple.

On this round, we'll listen to the men first. Others in Lee's group had once acted as precipitously as he had, and the contrast between then and now bemuses our moderator:

> *Q: Well, is what Lee said true? Is it possible that there is some sort of block to remarrying? I mean, were you guys like this the first time around?*
>
> *Raymond: The first time is altogether different. The first time is a courtship.*
>
> *Q: Noel, were you as hard to catch as you sound like you are now?*
>
> *Noel: No, I was easy. I was a pushover.*
>
> *Al: I met my wife in the country in August, and we got married January 8th that next year.*
>
> *Q: Did you have any of these same feelings—like, "Wait a minute! She said she didn't want marriage, and now she does"?*
>
> *Murray: No.*
>
> *Raymond: When you're young, that's what you go with a woman for, to get married.*
>
> *—New York, #2*

Like Lee's reluctance, theirs intermingles desires and fears. Noel's hemming and hawing overlays one dread in particular:

> *Right now, in my thinking, marriage is not a good thing for me. It's not a normal state. I am too well adjusted now, for me to start with someone and have the same thing happen again, possibly.*

But like Lee, he confides that he enjoys his situation too:

> *I don't want to make that kind of a commitment. I do date somebody, but she doesn't stay over at my house. I'm finally into the pattern of enjoying my life right now, and I don't want to upset the apple cart. I have a lot of faith in feeling satisfied with life, and nothing is going to dissuade me from that. I'm on top of the mountain and I'm going to stay that way.*

Richard has acquired a steady companion and a similar aversion to commitment:

I go with a lady now; it's for companionship. We get along very well, but there's no commitment. I don't say I wouldn't get married, but it's not on my mind at this stage of my life. I don't think I'm too easy to live with anyway. I've got my set way now, you know.

"My set way": John says his is quite literally that, and again not for a lack of choice:

John: *When I got married, I didn't really have any reservations about it at all. It was something I knew I wanted to do.*
Q: *How about now?*
John: *Very different now. I'm up in the air about it. And I don't know if I've really made the attempt to explore as much as I want. Because I'm not into dating a lot, and going to bars, and all that stuff. I've found I've become very sedentary now.*
Noel: *What's wrong with being sedentary?*
Raymond: *Don't you have friends that want to—*
John: *Oh, I have tons of friends. And my family, my mother, my aunts. People become oversolicitous. You get shopping lists, "Call this girl, call that girl," and it's like going to the grocery store.*

With Tom and Lee, just the mention of marriage by a "lady friend" will scuttle that friendship:

Tom: *I'll break the relationship. It sounds kind of crass to say that—it isn't an immediate break, just a clear understanding that nothing was said about marriage. You know, "We've been having a good relationship, and I would like it to continue that way. But I have other lady friends, and I would like to see them, and I don't want to be tied down right now. I'd like to continue to see you, if you can accept those terms." Mostly, nine times out of ten—well, I haven't had that many experiences—they will accept it rather bitterly. And eventually—within not too long a time, call it four weeks—they drop you. They feel rejected, I guess.*
Lee: *That has happened to me, almost the same script. And I did the same thing. I said, "Cool off, cool off." And I find that, since it has cooled off, it is better it happened that way.*
Tom: *And does the lady usually bow out?*
Lee: *Yeah, but very gently, beautifully, you know.*
Tom: *Yeah, no rudeness.*
Lee: *Nice parting, nice parting.*

Those last reflections, we think, betray something deeper than the male jitters about feminine wiles that we witnessed earlier: less a fear of entrapment than of any infringement on one's freedom of action. And many women—in defiance of the men's conventional view—have similar misgivings:

Rose: Just recently, I went with a man a whole year, another man from our chapter whose wife died. But he didn't want to get married, and it was okay with me. A lot of the men don't want to get married. They'll go with you, but they don't want to get married again.

Q: Why is that?

Rose: Well, they just like to fly the coop. And I don't know that I want to get married. Just like Yvette said, you don't mind taking care of your husband's clothes and cooking three meals a day. But if another man came along and you had to start—I'm not part of that anymore. I want just to enjoy myself, really. And if he got sick, you'd have to take care of him. It would have to be someone who would really like your grandchildren, like your children's lifestyle, which might be a little different than ours, you know. There's a lot to think about.

—San Francisco

"A lot" there certainly is, about desires and fears both. We've seen Ann declining to "share my life, my children, my grandchildren, with another man" (page 399). Sharkey and Yvette both shudder at the prospect of seeing a second husband through a terminal illness:

Yvette: If you have lived with someone for a good many years and he gets ill, as many of us have had happen, you're more than happy to do the best that you can for them. But if you marry someone at age 70-something and he gets ill, it's going to be a little bit harder to get as much as you need at that time, when you haven't shared that much.

—San Francisco

Sharkey: If you should meet somebody and he has another illness—to go through that, I just couldn't do it. I would do it for my husband all over again, but I couldn't do it for a . . . you know.

—Boston, #1

"Stranger" may be the word she's searching for, as it was for Irene:

A lot depends on your age. If your husband dies when you are young,

in the 30s, 40s, or early 50s, that's one thing. But if he dies a little older, it makes a difference. If you get married in your 20s, say, you grow up with him, and you grow into all these different things. But to take an older man and a stranger, you know, "Here I am—do these things for me." You just don't want to. You would rather not.
—Boston, #1

Isabel, Jean, and Sarah likewise haven't slipped unthinkingly into becoming set in their ways; they've chosen to, less as a result of their experience of loss than their success at overcoming it:

Isabel: It is nice to be married, but what are the alternatives? Like, what is more important to me? Being with somebody and—gee—taking on new habits and new idiosyncrasies and everything?
Connie: And another family.
Jean: Do you find that, as you grow older, you have less of a desire to marry than when you were younger?
Isabel: Definitely.
Eleanor: You don't even want it, don't even think about it.
Bea: You get set in your own ways.
Jean: Not just so much "set." You begin to count your priorities. And you say, "Well, I am happy the way I am."
Sarah: Especially over the course of the years, after what was very painful for the first year, in learning to adjust, you get an extraordinary building up of confidence. So that after a while you accept the rhythm of being single.
Bea: Your independence.
Sarah: And that becomes very important to you. You find, much to your surprise, that you might discourage marriage even with some-body who could be a fairly desirable human being. You become so attuned to your single life, a second marriage seems almost a threat.
—New York, #1

Hesitations such as these can bode you ill or good: good if they preserve you from making the greatest mistake to which it's legend that survivors are prone; or ill if they prevent you from capitalizing on what may be a survivor's greatest opportunity. Of course, in the absence of hindsight, you may be stumped as to which is which in your case. This woman appears to have come to a conclusion about herself, but adds a rather forlorn exclamation point:

Don't marry just for the sake of being married—frying pan into the fire, you know. I could have married again, but at least I have a good deal of freedom to do and go when and where I please and make personal choices. (Still lonely!)

—*Woman, 77, 15*

This man, however, has all the company he wants:

For some remarriage is the thing to do, even if it is only for companionship. For me, my friends, neighbors, grandchildren, and dog are all I need.

—*Man, 66, 3*

At any rate, we've scattered success stories about living together throughout this chapter so far, and we'll close it with some more. But here we'll make room briefly for the other kind.

Some books on grief are full of tales of the failures, of survivors who seized upon remarriage in foredoomed attempts either to reenact the past or to disown it. We didn't hear too many from our people, and some of those we did were cryptic. Noel discloses his remarriage, and disposes of it, in all of fourteen words:

Q: Did anybody in here remarry?
Noel: I was married before, but only for about two years, to my second wife. But I will never remarry.

—*New York, #2*

But others went into more detail. Frieda lobs a bombshell of a confession into her group—a recital of how a long-time date lured her into an apparently disastrous remarriage:

My husband had a friend, and we two couples used to be together all the time. John's wife died, so the three of us were together, my husband and me and John. When Arthur died, John started taking me out. Well, I wasn't interested in getting married. My father was alive, he wasn't well, and I just wasn't interested. But when my father had died and I was alone, John and I got married. Now, this was after I knew him for ten years. In one week, I knew what I was in for. One week!
Lee: How old were you?
Frieda: By then I was in my forties.

Lee: You could have lived with him and married him.
Frieda: But I didn't. In those years, you didn't do those things. Today people live together, then they didn't. If I had lived with John, I would have known it. Because when he was romancing me, he was dressed to the nines every night, we went to the finest restaurants, he'd open the door for me, bring me candy. After we were married—then you find out whether a man changes his underwear every day [laughter]! You find out if he shaves every day, you find out he's a grouch. I found all those things out in one week, and I put up with it for thirteen years.
Catherine: That's one reason I'd never consider that. I've heard too many stories.

—Miami, #1

Frieda's remarriage is in the classic mold of failed first marriages—old-fashioned illusions colliding with old-fashioned realities, a head-on crash that living together might have averted. But remarriages by survivors can be as easily sabotaged by different hopes—that your partner can accomplish what must be done by someone else. Yourself, for one:

Many widows and especially widowers marry again very quickly. Living in a large retirement community makes this fairly easy, but it often turns out to be a mistake. One needs to be really strong and able to rely on oneself and not expect others to do it.

—Woman, 79, 8

Or by someone else admitted to your life on a different understanding:

For a sudden loss, such as mine, I think I should have sought professional counselling. My remarriage has not fulfilled that function.

—Woman, 58, 3

Even if the remarriages of some survivors work out, they may find other qualms were justified:

I was fortunate to have several men friends available and interested in helping me over the loss of my first husband. I finally married one, and we had some time together before his physical condition became a problem. I paid a price for that long illness. Now I feel alone, but out of that stress.

—Woman, 81, 17

Connie: We were only married about three years when he got sick. He went into the hospital for cancer, and they called me and said, "We didn't touch it. It was in the stomach, and we're going to give him radiation." He had a thirty-day treatment, and then they operated and said, "It went beautifully." But that afternoon he had a heart attack. It was too much for him. All the operations.

—Boston, #1

For some survivors, the absence of another can supersede all other considerations:

Jean: I don't mind being alone, but there are many people who do mind it, very much so.

Isabel: They have to have somebody with them all the time.

Jean: Some of them enter into very unsuccessful marriages because of it. Their cry will be "I cannot live alone!" I would often ask, "Well, how do you feel about this man? Do you like him?" "I don't care, I cannot be by myself!" That's a very poor reason for getting married.

—New York, #1

Edna gloomily bears her out:

Q: You did remarry?

Edna: Yes. A year and a half. That was it!

Q: "That was it"? What was wrong?

Edna: Now I know I'll never marry again. I think I've gotten over it to a certain extent, but not to the point that I'd take another chance, no.

Q: Why would you tell people not to? You're obviously telling us not to, in a way.

Edna: I told a friend not to, a friend of my husband's and mine both. He'd lost his wife. He was talking to me shortly afterwards, and I said, "Don't!"

Q: Because?

Edna: Because I think one reason down deep why I married, I was very lonesome, very lonesome. My husband and I, everywhere we went, we went together. I had nobody to go out with, and so I thought that I could take marriage for the companionship. But you can't.

—San Francisco

That discovery and its aftermath left her seething:

He actually was the one that said, ''Quits!'' He said, ''You may be up-set about it now, but you'll soon find out it's for the best. Because we never should have done it.'' And I'll admit, I was bitter. In fact, I was telling a married friend who wanted to know why I was so bitter, ''I'm not bitter.'' And he said, ''Oh, no, you're not bitter. All we have to do is to bring up that marriage, and you absolutely turn to stone.''

When bitterness descends upon us, however, we have usually laid the blame elsewhere. Now Edna's not so sure:

Rose: Could we find out why it didn't work out? Is that too personal?
Edna: At first, there was no fifty-fifty about it. But now I would say it was fifty-fifty because, as I say, there are times I have a rotten disposition, and that probably interfered. And then, I do think that, in the back of my mind, was my husband.
Rose: Yeah, you were trying to compare, probably.
Edna: I did, and there was no comparison.

Comparisons—they're inevitable, but if they're not drawn intel-ligently, they can torpedo your chances of starting over.

Do not dwell on deceased and past life. (Remember fondly—do not compare). Look to future.
                                                                —Man, 61, 3

Do not compare what you had to a possible present interest in a person. Every relationship in life is quite different. Don't look for a carbon copy of a beloved deceased one.
                                                                —Woman, 73, 9

Perhaps Roger suspects that's what he'd do if he were to look again—which is why he isn't:

Q: Roger, where are you at this point?
Roger: Well, both my wife and I were fairly well along before we got married. She was in her early 30s, I was in my late 30s, so we both had seen enough of the world then. We knew this was what we wanted together, and I don't know if I could find that with anybody else. I'm certainly not looking again.

Q: But you're adamantly opposed?
Roger: *I'm not opposed to it, no. I take it one day at a time.*

—New York, #2

John recognized how self-defeating the impulse was even as he yielded to it:

Once you go out again, I found that you make comparisons. You start stacking this individual with your spouse. You see yourself setting the situation up so it will work against you, rather than just taking it for what it is.
Q: It works against you?
John: *I found it so, yeah: she's not as pretty, she's not as charming, she's not as bright, she's not as this, she's not as that. It's a turnoff.*

—New York, #2

Edith supplies the solution, so obvious as to be embarrassing:

Evelyn: *Well, you compare. I know friends that have met men over the years, and somehow you do compare. And if I ever did meet somebody, he could never take my husband's place, never.*
Edith: *Why do you need somebody to take his place, how about the man taking his own place?*

—Boston, #1

Lee had to remind herself to keep that goal in mind even as a man was achieving it:

When I met my second husband, my mother asked me, "What is he like?" And I said, "He's really very nice." And she said, "But he's not Bernie." I said, "No, Bernie is gone. I had good years with him, but my life with him is over." If you are going to compare someone that you're going out with to your husband, you'll never find anybody. You have to take everyone as they are. We all have faults, we all have shortcomings. And you find someone that likes being with you, that's the most important thing. You can't look for what you had before because no two people that are the same. And unless you decide that's what you're going to do, it's very, very difficult.
Molly: *It's also really unfair to the new man to compare him with your first husband. You can't compare.*

—Miami, #1

As Marilyn discovered, you may not be the only one constrained to compare—and to reject:

> *My daughter is 29, so she should know better. But she did not want anyone in the house because no one is going to take her father's place. I explained to her, "No one is, your father will always be your father, but I am going to go out." And this particular man I met, he has got this patience, it's incredible. Because she was so miserable to him, another man would have turned around and said to me, "Hey, forget it, lady, I really don't need you." But he didn't, and it's getting better, but I don't think she will ever accept another man. And I don't think it's just because of a man taking her father's place. I'm beginning to think that, if she had someone of her own, it might help, but she doesn't.*
> —*Boston, #2*

Perhaps the lack of a man in the daughter's life may indeed be making her so mulish about the one in her mother's. In any case, it lends credence to this warning:

> *Some new opportunities for romantic liaison may surprise and delight you. But be prepared for possible problems of deep-rooted family ties and responsibilities (either or both sides) and try to be understanding and not too demanding.*
> —*Woman, 72, 7*

Marilyn and her friend have been both, so far with no luck:

> *Fran: Maybe she is jealous.*
> *Lil: She's very possessive of you?*
> *Marilyn: Very.*
> *Ellen: Has your friend got a friend for her?*
> *Marilyn: He fixed her up three times. She found something wrong with each one of them, and I don't know if there really was or not. So he tried, and then he said, "You know, she doesn't want anyone."*
> *Virginia: She doesn't want it, she never will.*
> *Marilyn: I think so, and that is a very sad thing.*
> *Ellen: I think "never" is a big word.*
> *Marilyn: Well, I hope, I hope.*

But Judy's son and her new husband thrashed out their differences somehow:

The man that I'm married to now was a friend that my kids knew, but, when he came dressed in a suit to take their mother out, that was different. I know he had a difficult time winning me over, but my oldest son was his biggest foe. Nobody was going to take his father's place, and there was nothing you could say to change his mind. Then one day, after we had been married a couple of years, they went out, and—I don't know what happened. I don't know if they had a knock-down drag-out or what. But then they had a couple of beers and came back and they're the best of buddies. They won't talk about it. They have an understanding, that's all. They call each other up all the time and it's great.

—Boston, #2

On that note, we can let skepticism take a backseat to enthusiasm and move from this,

After seven years of widowhood, I have been happily remarried for three years. I do not believe my case is typical.

—Woman, 73, 12

to this:

Remarry. I was a widow for fourteen years, married at age 74, and have had seven happy years. You are never too old.

—Woman, 82, 22

Find a compatible mate. This worked for me.

—Woman, 71, 7

You've heard of "golf widows"; well, here's a golf wife:

I was introduced to golf, met a wonderful man on the golf course, re-married four years later, and we've been playing golf and enjoying life ever since. (Had a 92 for 18 holes the other day.)

—Woman, 71, 7

If couples like these are deluding themselves, they're content to do so:

My present wife is companionable and sweet, she sometimes makes me believe I'm in charge.

—Man, 76, 5

This group rates at barely zero their chances of having a certain someone happen along:

> *Q: And if somebody came along tomorrow? What would you do?*
> *Yvette: Well . . . it's so out of my thinking that I don't really . . . [laughing] and I like men, too.*
> *Rose: It's out of my thinking too.*
> *Q: Out of your thinking?*
> *Rose: Well, not completely.*
>
> —*San Francisco*

Isabel is also lukewarm, but Jean can get all fired up at the idea of becoming intoxicated once again:

> *Jean: But if you met someone who made you an offer which you couldn't refuse [laughter]? Someone that you really like very much?*
> *Isabel: Well, what's an offer that you can't refuse?*
> *Jean: [with a sweep of the hands] Something marvelous! Things like that happen!*
> *Isabel: Financially, you mean?*
> *Jean: Not financially—*
> *Isabel: Socially?*
> *Jean: A fascinating man! A fascinating companion! Who would really lift your life up to a much happier state. It is not easy to find, but there are people who marry like that.*
>
> —*New York, #1*

If Jean's fantasy is to be realized, the odds are that it will be with another survivor. That prospect holds no enchantment whatever for Noel:

> *I think the worst thing in the world for me was going out with some widows. I met this woman at a party right around the corner. Her husband had been a very famous rabbi, and, God, that's all I heard about—"the Rabbi this and the Rabbi that." And in the process, she claims she lost a $5,000 cocktail ring—it was a disaster! My own thinking is, why should I be going out with someone who has gone through the same thing that I have, and all we do is compare notes about our sorrow and about what we miss in life. There is never going to be a relationship between myself and that type of person.*
>
> —*New York, #2*

Probably best for both, if the hash he made of this occasion is any indication. But this man learned a lot by comparing notes:

> *When a marriage has been good, losing a spouse can be devastating. To eventually adjust, one must be able to talk about it and grieve openly. I was fortunate to meet a good woman who went through the same experience (losing a spouse to cancer). She gave me the chance to vocalize my feelings and understood them from her experience. I needed time, and she understood this better than I did. We are now happily married to each other. Life does not go well without a close companion to share with and love.*
>
> —Man, 63, 6

Lee gambled on a fellow survivor—and hit the jackpot:

> *I'm very, very fortunate because I remarried just about a year ago. Even though friends kept saying, "Lee, we'll introduce you to someone," I said I was married forty-two years and my husband died very suddenly and I just wasn't ready, I didn't want anyone really. But someone introduced us, and the funny thing is, I had met him and his wife before she died. And I'm extremely happy—it's like a new life for me. Really! I met this guy and, I swear, in two months I felt like I was a teenager.*
>
> —Miami, #1

Her bounty includes companionship:

> *We have the same likes, we like to do the same things, and there is always something to talk about. How many times do you get married, and you're married a number of years, and you sit in one chair and he sits in the other, and there's no conversation?*

And she can also flick aside the consensus of the group that sex is "for kids":

> *Well, I guess I'm a kid, because I never enjoyed it as much as I do now.*

In sum:

> **Lee:** *I had a good life before, but this is like utopia.*
> **Dorothy:** *Second time around is better?*
> **Lee:** *Well, when my mother used to see someone holding hands, you*

know what used to say? "Must be a second marriage." It's true—and I'm going to enjoy every single day.

She's settled into the traditional housewifely role:

When I cook a meal for my husband and he says, "Oh, so delicious, you must be so tired," he makes me feel like I'm a queen.

En route to this domestic bliss, they did have their spats:

My husband knew how to do everything except cook, and he used to to tell me how he was going to clean and dust. You know, we laugh at it now, and it's a big joke, but before we got married, you know what we used to have fights about?
Grace: *Recipes?*
Lee: *No. We'd do a wash, and he'd say to me, "I was married for thirty-five years, and all I used was Clorox II." I'd say, "Tough! I was married forty-two years, and all I used was Wisk!" Silly, but you get so set in your ways.*

That unsubmissive streak emerged in other ways too. The woman who counselled us against the folly of trying to make the new spouse match the old (page 441) now confides that she's been able to bring the two into closer alignment:

When I went out with my husband the first time—I mean, my second husband—he came to my door, and I looked at him, and, of course, you say you're not going to think about these things, but you do. And I said to myself, "You know, he's so different-looking from my first husband."
   My first husband was extremely handsome, and he dressed beautifully. My second, he wore clothes that were ten or fifteen years old. Well, we went out the one time, we went out the second time, and if someone likes you and and you offer a suggestion, about clothes or something like that, they change. I think that everyone is open to suggestions. He dresses beautifully now. His wife didn't care what he wore. But I care. I like it when a man is dressed nicely and everything matches.
   And when they look at him now, people who knew him before can't believe it. And he and his first wife never did anything—they never went any place, they always stayed home. I taught him how to play canasta, I have a lot of friends. We're always doing something. So, you know, you can change in certain ways. It was hard to believe he would do it. But you take a chance.

If you do take a chance on acquiring a new spouse and even on changing his or her habits, Judy reminds us that's not all you may acquire:

Q: How old were you when you remarried?

Judy: I was 32, it'll be ten years in September.

Q: Ten years? OK.

Judy: And I had a surprise. I have a 7-year-old daughter! See, you do foolish things when you get older [laughter]! All my other kids are married and have their own. I have six grandchildren—and a daughter that started first grade this week!

Q: That's great, not quite typical.

Judy: No, not your average.

Q: How do you feel about that?

Judy: I think it's great. My grandchildren all call me "Nan." Not "Granny" or "Nana"—just "Nan." They think my name is Nancy, I guess. My daughter likes it, because she is an aunt, she has been one since she was five months old. If she is mad at the kids or something—"I am Auntie Gina to you," she'll say. And they'll have to call her "Auntie Gina." My daughter has three kids, and they are the closest to my little girl's age. And it's really funny being out with them together, the reactions from people. They'll say, "She's their what?" *Because she is only about this high [gesturing].*

Chapter 7

Getting *Through* It: From "Life Goes On" to "Go On With Your Life"

We are all philosophers, if by "philosophy" we mean the possession of an outlook on the world and our place in it. Throughout this book so far—except perhaps in Chapter 1—we've paid more attention to the practical and emotional vicissitudes of being a survivor than to the philosophical ones. Here we'll let the philosophical come to the forefront again.

"Vicissitudes" is the right word for the philosophies propounded by many survivors: those philosophies can change. They can remain constant, of course—most notably, as we'll see, in the realm of religious belief. But the mind can be transformed too, as this woman's was between the days she portrays in her first paragraph and those in her last:

> *At the time of my husband's death, I was devastated. I wept, I wept, from time to time, for a year. I wanted to sell the house and to find another job. In brief, I did not know what I did want. I just kept going "through the motions" of living and working.*
>
> *Now, after nearly twenty-two years of widowhood, I have a busy life, and only within the last two years did I sell the house and make a move. I remember our good days when my husband was living; however, "life hangs by a thread." I am philosophical and more mellow and understanding and extremely grateful for the large share of good things I have had and do have in this world.*
>
> —*Woman, 74, 22*

She seems to have achieved that ambition of so many survivors:

449

I had to resolve to once again become a whole person.
                                                    —*Woman, 70, 3*

But perhaps that achievement must await the day when we see time once again as a whole.

The woman who leads off this chapter seems to have reconciled past and present. Contrast her with the woman who leads off the Epilogue (page 485), for whom what happened then is so hard to reconnect, even eighteen years later, with what transpired "through the years that followed." A death can smash our sense of the wholeness of time into fragments, leaving the past irretrievable, the present intolerable, and the future unimaginable. But survivors again and again recount that, sooner or later, they reassembled those pieces in their minds. Explaining *how*, they very often frame their answers in the intellectual shorthand of the cliché, the platitude, the bromide—like the two that embellish the title of this chapter. Readers expecting more may brush aside these truisms. But remember that a "truism," that contemptuous compound of a word, was born of a truth, and a "cliche" earned its name only because it became the rest home for a widely accepted idea that was once in the prime of life. Just as the self can be reborn after "the seeming death" we watched it suffer in Chapter 1, so truisms and clichés, as wheezing and moribund as they may seem, can be revitalized.

Here (since time is our subject) is an example:

Whether it be a sudden stroke or long and agonizing illness, time will heal us.
                                                    —*Woman, 76, 3*

My old friends were a good source of strength, but time has been the greatest healer.
                                                    —*Woman, 73, 7*

How convenient! If death has robbed time of its value, time itself will make restitution. The patness of the thought make some apologize for it, even as they advance it:

In spite of being a cliché, time does help heal!
                                                    —*Woman, 76, 13*

They admit somewhat lamely that those they most want to solace are those least likely to be convinced:

> *The advice I would offer other widows and widowers is that time is a great healer. I don't know how much this will help them, but it is true.*
> —*Woman, 65, 3*

> *Time is the greatest healer, but new widows find this not very helpful to hear.*
> —*Woman, 72, 11*

Indeed, many don't—and not just new ones:

> *I also get tired of hearing "Time heals all wounds." It doesn't!*
> —*Woman, 68, 2*

> *Some tell you, "Time will heal." But the void and loneliness are still there.*
> —*Woman, 71, 8*

Have we reached a stalemate? It may seem so, until we recall (from Chapter 1) this crucial concession to reality:

> *Nothing will be the same ever, and the pain of loss will always be there, but one copes better as time goes on.*
> —*Woman, NA, NA*

> *We are reduced to the old standbys: time is the great healer; friends and family help. But don't expect things to be the same again.*
> —*Woman, 70, 14*

If "nothing will ever be the same" for those whom time eventually did make whole, then this corollary follows:

> *It's something you never get over—you just have to learn to live with it.*
> —*Woman, 68, 2*

> *The ache is always there. I won't get over it, but hope to live with it.*
> —*Woman, 62, 2*

Getting *over* it would mean leaving the past so decisively behind that it's no longer part of your present. And that would envision some-thing impossible outside science fiction: living in the future.

Such a miracle is beyond the medicinal skills of time. That is why the last two, like so many others, belabor what would seem to be self-evident—that you must live *with* it—and why others insist on a fact so incontestable you might wonder at their bothering to raise it:

> *One does not forget the loss of a loved one; but with time it becomes easier to bear.*
>
> —*Woman, 79, 15*

> *Lil: Eventually, I think, time is a great healer, it really is.*
> *Fran: No, time does not heal.*
> *Lil: You never forget—*
> *Angela: Oh, you never forget, no!*
> *Lil: And there are times, especially around Christmas, the holidays, and birthdays, that you really miss him, but I mean to say, you don't grieve like before. I used to cry my eyes out. You never, ever forget, and the vacancy is always there. Time makes it . . . mellows it, like.*
>
> —*Boston, #2*

By forgetting, of course, you *would* have gotten over it. By never forgetting, however, we must negotiate with one of the least pliable and most unpredictable denizens of the psyche, our memory.

Toward the end of Chapter 1, we glanced at how a survivor's remembrance of a spouse could gradually be transmuted from pain to pleasure, and time's adherents confirm it:

> *Remember that time does heal; the body has a natural urge toward physical and emotional health, if given the opportunity to follow that urge. The loss is never erased, but the sharpness does lessen. Sooner or later, you will begin to remember the good times and be thankful for the days and years that you were blessed.*
>
> —*Woman, 72, 3*

And what seems bad at first may eventually evolve into good. Are these two listening to different messages from the past? If so, that difference probably lies in the mind of the hearer:

Elaine: I have tapes of my husband because he loved to sing. And when you play them or hear a song that he used to sing, that gets to you.
—*Los Angeles, #2*

Enjoy each other as much as possible, live to have as few regrets as possible, and store as many memories as possible. For me, a tape recording (done for another purpose) has been invaluable.
—*Woman, 74, 9*

Recollecting even the good times may seem intolerable if the bad ones are etched in as deeply as they are for this woman:

His long illness deprived him of every factor that contributes to the quality and enjoyment of life—including the deterioration, complete, of a brilliant mind. I don't allow myself to dwell on those terrible years. If I did, I think I'd lose my own sanity.
—*Woman, 73, 4*

This woman can't confront some of the past again either, but she is steeling herself for the day when she may need to:

The grief and pain of his death are just as great as when it happened. There are still some memories too painful to recall and tasks I cannot handle. But when it does become necessary to face them, I will find the strength.
—*Woman, 62, 2*

These survivors are trying to make the good drive out the bad—or at least push the bad into the distance:

After a long illness, the memories foremost in your mind are the recent ones. With effort, reliving happy times brings your loved one into perspective, and the memories become the happy ones.
—*Woman, 80, 3*

Remember the many happy years of marriage, and try to put the hard times and suffering in the background as much as possible.
—*Man, 84, 4*

I have very fond memories of our life together for forty one and a half years. I think of those, and not too often of his long and painful fight with cancer—I was at his side, and I tried to do all I could to help him, and he was trying so hard not to complain about the pain.

—Woman, 76, 8

The concluding words of the last woman betray how swiftly the past can thwart our efforts to be selective. But for some, even the final days have turned to good in retrospect:

My husband kept a writing pad by his bed. And the last words he wrote in this world were written in Latin, meaning: "While we live, let us live." Brave words, written by a person with two failing lungs. I now live by those words.

—Woman, 81, 16

I think what helps me most to continue on is the memory of his strength and courage, and they were never more evident than during his seven months of illness and at his death. If he could make it through those dark months without a single complaint, surely I could face living.

—Woman, 62, 2

Bargaining with memories like these may be easier than with those of bad times of another sort:

I feel that my adjustment to widowhood has been good, because I was fortunate in having a very happy marriage. And so, while lonely, I am not plagued by the guilt and bitterness that I see in friends who were never able to resolve quarrels and bad feelings, and now can never do so.

—Woman, 56, 9

Now and then, of course, we hear a cry to the contrary:

If your marriage was, as mine, as nearly perfect as possible, perhaps survival is more difficult.

—Woman, 74, 9

And though the marriages of these were far from perfect, that seems to have speeded recuperation instead of slowing it:

Barbara: Oh, I felt very bad when he died, yes, but a lot of things had transpired in our lives. We were separated, and I had lost a lot of my feeling. I was glad I was able to help him and forgive him in the final analysis, but it wasn't the same feeling anymore.

—Boston, #1

Q: Do you remember what you needed right away?
Connie: *Well, you have to look at the type of marriage people had. Mine was not good. He was an alcoholic—how can you be happy with somebody like that? So naturally I was able to cope better, because I prepared myself for it and it left me with my own independence—"stand on your own two feet," and stuff like that.*
Sarah: *Well, it is refreshing to hear an honest answer.*

—New York, #1

A great many marriages, perhaps most, have intermingled good and bad all along, and so we are commonly told to hold to the one and cast out the other:

Above all, one must remember the lovely times, things shared. Guilt trips help no one.

—Woman, 76, 3

Try to remember all the happy times you've had and don't fret over what that "might have been."

—Woman, 73, 8

But for some, all the memories may have become benign:

My husband set a good example for living life and meeting life's challenges with dignity and consideration and concern. I was fortunate to have such a husband.

—Woman, 71, 21

My husband taught me how to live and how to die, he changed my life, and I feel rewarded for having lived with him for thirty-eight years.

—Woman, 72, 10

As time goes by, remember the wonderful years, the laughing times, that God allowed you two beautiful people to share together.

—Woman, 82, 3

This woman steeps herself in memorabilia:

> *Soak up and savor all the precious moments and memories. Old love*
> *letters, life story, pictures, tapes, etc., have comforted me.*
> —*Woman, 59, 3*

Another also calls time out from the present to derive strength from
the past:

> *In the field of my husband's endeavors there are so many reminders of*
> *his efforts, his books and his papers and notes, these things give me*
> *great gratification when I take time out to dwell with them. He was a*
> *translator and produced much in the field of literature, especially*
> *poetry—so much richness in life I can still share.*
> —*Woman, 77, 11*

The roads to the lovely or laughing times that you want to
rediscover may lead into the memories of others as well as your own:

> *Continue with your life and see old friends as often as possible, to*
> *remember all the good times you and your husband had. I find if I talk*
> *about him to people who knew him, we always find something happy or*
> *funny to remember.*
> —*Woman, 64, 3*

You may not necessarily be able to respond in the same key:

> *I still get "teary" even after ten years when someone praises my*
> *husband. I can talk about him easily, but go to pieces when others do!*
> —*Woman, 76, 10*

But if you can laugh once again, you may be able to teach others to
do likewise with new memories of their own:

> Don't *hide pictures of those you've lost. And in saying, "That was your*
> *grandpa or dad when he was little," tell something that's funny about*
> *him or her and help them get to know the relative or friend. It helps you,*
> *too. The more you can remember them, the more you still have them.*
> —*Woman, 61, 2*

Others echo that last assertion:

One should talk freely and often about a departed spouse; thus he lives on with us.

—Woman, 86, 8

Bringing the deceased's name into conversation at every opportunity keeps him or her alive in a family. We found this to be true when we lost a 23-year-old son.

—Woman, 79, 4

Reminiscing brought one woman in the Epilogue (page 488) to this revelation: "I did not have to lose him." For some, that confidence issues from their belief in a literal afterlife:

To know that love (even closeness) continues and that there is a hereafter!

—Woman, 73, 3

But for others, the hereafter is now:

I was married for just over twenty-five years to a Scottish physician, teacher, and scholar, and he changed my whole life in those years. In the five years of retirement we shared, he put the house and his estate in the best possible order for me, and his loving influence on my present life does extend beyond the grave.

—Woman, 69, 2

Make a special effort to live the remaining life that is yours—to the best of your ability. Practice living with the best memories of the past, because the past will be yours forever.

—Woman, 74, 3

How do we square this state of mind with the one of the sternest admonitions passed on by one survivor to another?

Do not live in the past! It is entirely up to you whether the years of your widowhood are happy and productive or a time of self-pity and misery both for yourself and those around you.

—Woman, 80, 22

We've been hearing the answer all along—the past must reside in *your* present.

> *Accept what you cannot change. Always remember that nothing can or will be the same, but there is still happiness in life through new and old friends and by doing new things. Always keep a proper perspective. Enjoy the wonderful memories of your life together, but don't live in the past.*
>
> *—Woman, 62, 3*

Only one of those in our survey admitted to ''living in the past,'' and she immediately qualifies that admission:

> *It's a loss I cannot forget, and though I'm ashamed to say it, sometimes I live in the past more than in the present, since my husband and I had a very happy life together. But I feel it is within one's self to adapt to the present and not ask ''why?'' No one can adjust for you.*
>
> *—Woman, 80, 11*

Agreeing with her is the widow of the Scottish doctor who just testified that the grave had not diminished ''his influence on my present life'':

> *One cannot sit back and expect sympathy and comfort from friends and family to do the trick: a new routine is vital and working hard at what is essentially a new life.*
>
> *—Woman, 69, 2*

That new life can depart from the old without deserting it:

> *My memories of my husband are vivid and endearing, but I have made another life for myself that I find rewarding.*
>
> *—Woman, 68, 19*

> *Preserve the memories but do not set up ''shrines.'' One must go forward with a different way of life, hopefully, not without happiness.*
>
> *—Woman, 75, 3*

To this woman, doing that is commemoration at its best:

Grieving for a loved one is an essential part of life. But it must not be extended too long. Making your life meaningful is truly a memorial to the deceased partner.

—Woman, 84, 23

These two have fashioned their days into a tribute ordinarily paid only to the living—a compliment:

Remember they will always be in your heart. So pull up your chin and live a day at a time and keep living as a compliment to the loved one you lost. I was fortunate enough to have a wonderful person and a very gifted artist for a husband. We both were Depression children, and I do not think he would like it if I didn't have guts enough to keep living.

—Woman, 72, 6

We had had nearly forty years of a wonderful *life together. There was so much love and caring. We were each so proud of the other's activities and interests and helped with them. So it was only natural and right to continue our volunteer work, family projects, etc., instead of staying home to mourn. I think it is a compliment to one's mate and shows the strength of the marriage if one continues with what had been shared over the years.*

—Woman, 72, 6

What if you did try to live in the past? You would be chasing after an impossibility as elusive as that of living in the future. And you would be trying to realize a goal that may appear less remote than getting over it but that is equally unattainable—"getting used to it":

There is a chance one can get so used to grief that one finds it easier to live in this state than to change and adjust to a new life.

—Woman, 67, 4

Life will never be the same, and we all know it, a very important part of us is gone. We will never "get used to it," but must learn to adapt to our new situation.

—Woman, 65, 3

If we do succeed in getting used to it, we have failed to adapt or adjust. As we noted in Chapter 1, grief demands a change in us at the same time it makes us face the change in our life. Perhaps that accounts for the beneficial powers ascribed to time—given enough of it, even the most obstinate among us is likely to undergo some alteration. And although change is full of peril, not changing may be more so:

> *Life will never be the same, but you will adjust—the alternative is worse.*
> —*Woman, 74, 3*

Living in the past, could we but achieve it, would exempt us from change. But only the dead enjoy that privilege, and maybe the impulse to dwell in the past finds its most radical expression in the wish that "I were dead too." That's one of the classic utterances of self-pity:

> **Ruth:** *We had always talked about how I would be the one to go. Not him. And how could I be left with all this on my hands? I didn't want it. I'd be very happy if I had died.*
> **Ann:** *[sarcastically] Poor little girl. You're still there, you're still feeling sorry for yourself [nervous laughter].*
> **Ida:** *That's it, tell her!*
> **Ruth:** *I don't feel like that anymore.*
> **Ann:** *Yes, you do—you're still happy on it, you do feel that way.*
> **Ruth:** *I must say, I still sit down, I still cry at times. That's not where it ended. I became self-sufficient, I learned to drive a car, to take care of everything—*
> **Ann:** *You actually grew up a little bit. It makes you grow up.*
> **Ruth:** *But not everybody does. But not everybody does.*
> **Q:** *Well, Ruth, do you feel you have?*
> **Peggy:** *Matured and grown up?*
> **Ruth:** *Yes, I have, to a certain point.*
> —*Miami, #2*

As the swiftness with which Ann pounces on Ruth indicates, self-pity is easy to recognize—in others. But it's hard to define. Like obscenity, it's something we proverbially "know when we see it." And we usually detest it when we do:

> *The worst thing of all is self-pity. Look around you for some one you can help—it won't take long to find him or her!*
> —*Woman, 72, 7*

What makes self-pity so deplorable? Undoubtedly the object upon which that otherwise laudable emotion is lavished. Pitying others may prompt an act of charity, but pitying oneself can lead nowhere except, as this woman suggests, to self-entombment:

> *Look for ways to reach out to people instead of burying yourself in self-pity. There are always people worse off. Don't wait for people always to minister to you.*
>
> *—Woman, 69, NA*

Both our survey and discussion groups yielded many such exhortations against self-pity but amazingly few instances of self-pity in action. In her altercation with Ann, Ruth may have afforded us one such example, but she was caught off her guard and she stands up to her cross-examiner well enough. This woman, unfortunately, lacks a cross-examiner:

> *Die first and avoid the grief*
>   *—OR—*
> *Keep too busy to think and feel.*
>
> *—Woman, 61, 6*

Her second wish prays for death quite as much as her first.

Self-pity is profoundly antisocial, which is why thinking of others is inevitably prescribed as its cure. By doing so, you can make the past serve them as well as you:

> *Allowing oneself to be absorbed in grief and self-pity is selfish and makes things hard for other people. The others are feeling the loss, too, and one needs to be strong to help them. Help them remember the happy times shared and the traits worth remembering.*
>
> *—Woman, 72, 6*

> *I try not to cry when with family and friends. That's for when I'm alone. But I don't allow myself to sit on the "pity pot." I speak of my husband, and I'm always pleased when family and friends do the same. I want him always to be remembered.*
>
> *—Woman, 62, 2*

The image of the "pity pot," with its overtones of the infantile, explains why so many advise us that if we must do the deed, we do it alone:

Just feel sorry for yourself in private.
—Woman, NA, NA

As self-love at its most barren, self-pity subjects us to this merciless catechism:

Marilyn: *I have marvelous friends, and they made sure that I was constantly taken care of. But there came a time when I turned around and said, "Why me?" This selfishness comes over you. I don't know what else to call it. I went through a terrible time of feeling sorry for myself: "How come they have their husbands and I don't?"*
—Boston, #2

As Lee predicates, the question may be inevitable:

You're only thinking of yourself, "Why me?" I think that every widow, everyone who has lost someone dear, says, "Why did this happen to me?" You go out with couples and think, "This one is sick and this one is old. Nothing happened to them. Why did it happen to me?" It's a normal thing. We all say it.
—Miami, #1

But even as we do, we must dismiss the question as unanswerable—at least with respect to the me and, perhaps for the wisest among us, with respect to the why as well:

Acknowledge and accept the death. Don't continually try to figure out "why"—you can't do anything about it.
—Man 61, 3

Whatever answer you do manufacture may turn you against those you need most:

Lil: *A lot of times you go see your friends and then you come home and say, "Why me, why did this happen to me?" I used to have nightmares, wake up at night screaming that.*
—Boston, #2

So you must recognize that you haven't been singled out from the rest of the human race and that you must rejoin it:

Go on living. Don't ask why this happened to me. Remember other people have problems and pains.

—*Man, 81, 12*

Marilyn: *You say, "Why me, why did this have to happen to me, of all the people in the world?"*
Q:. *Marilyn, is there any antidote to that?*
Marilyn: *Is there an antidote? What I said before: you have to force yourself to go out and become part of the world again.*

—*Boston, #2*

A companion that self-love can speedily acquire is a hatred of others, and that may have moved this woman to conclude her essay with this triad:

I love people.
I love life.
I try not to spend time feeling sorry for myself.

—*Woman, 59, 5*

A hatred of others may reach out toward that ultimate Other:

Lee: *"Why would God do something like that to me?" That's what you keep saying, that's what you keep thinking.*

—*New York, #2*

Lee never tells us where the question led him, but it is repudiated by others who proclaim a faith in God:

Be thankful for what you have had—reject any thought of why did this have to happen to me? Be thankful continually! Begin to lean on God for guidance and you will learn to know exactly what to do in making so many decisions you never faced before.

—*Woman, 78, 6*

This book doesn't presume to be a forum for the religious convictions of survivors, a subject on which we made no attempt to sound them out. But they have volunteered those convictions on quite a few occasions, starting with the quote on page 1. The love of God, in one shape or another, lends so much meaning to the lives of some that they can't conceive how others manage without it:

> *The biggest and best help has been living close to the Lord God. With-out spiritual help from God's Word and through prayer, it would be hopeless.*
>
> *—Woman, 63, 2*

> **Mary:** *And what your church can do for you! I know we all have different persuasions, but if it wasn't for my faith, I don't know what I would have done.*
>
> *—San Francisco*

> *No use preaching: ours is a secular society. But I do not know how irreligious people live and survive. I'm not a stoic, nor very brave, but I am a believing Christian and have been supported, deepened, and strengthened in this faith since my husband's death. His life and mine, however imperfect, have been blessed.*
>
> *—Woman, 70, 4*

The days of some can't open or close without a bit of divine intervention:

> *I had and still have a very strong faith in my Lord and Saviour. I could not begin a day without His help.*
>
> *—Woman, 59, 5*

> *Never take your grief or problems to bed with you. Do your best, ask God to take over and do the rest—He will; then relax, go to sleep.*
>
> *—Woman, 77, 3*

As we've already seen, organized religion can open up various byways to a renewed social life:

> *Be active at church—go regularly and gradually become involved in other activities than Sunday morning worship.*
>
> *—Woman, 69, 9*

In fact, half of those we surveyed revealed that they were engaged in some form of "religious activity other than attendance at services." But a primary purpose of faith is to make solitude endurable—and at best enjoyable:

> *Have an inner life (spiritual or religious) so you enjoy solitude as well as social life. I belong to a weekly Meditation Group.*
> —Woman, 82, 4

Being in touch with a Supreme Being bestowed upon the believers among our survivors all the traditional comforts of religion. A relief from loneliness by providing the ultimate Someone to Talk To:

> *Don't forget that God is always available to talk with.*
> —Woman, 68, 4

> *Pray. There's a lot of help "up there" for the asking.*
> —Woman, 78, 21

> Pray—*best and cheapest help there is!*
> —Woman, 73, 15

Guidance in your journey through life:

> *I travel on, in the knowledge I'll never walk alone, as the Psalmist sang, "Though I take the wings of the morning, and dwell in the uttermost parts of the sea, behold, Thou art there. Even there shall thy hand lead me."*
> —Woman, 75, 7

Do not cultivate loneliness: *We do not walk alone. God is always there to help us in our time of need. There are some who would like to have us believe that faith in God and the power of prayer have gone out of style. Don't be deceived:* They never have and they never will.
> —Woman, 77, 3

Courage, and the confidence and serenity that can be born of it:

> *Have faith. There's nothing that's going to happen to you that God and you can't handle.*
> —Woman, 58, 3

*A minister friend gave me these two verses from Scripture, and I keep
a copy of them on my refrigerator:*

> *"Be strong and of good courage,*
> *Be not afraid,*
> *Neither be thou dismayed,*
> *For the Lord thy God is with thee whithersoever thou goest."*
> *Joshua 1:9*

> *"Thou will keep him in perfect peace, whose mind is stayed on
> thee because he trusteth in thee."*
> *Isaiah 26:3*
> *—Woman, 71, 8*

And the knowledge that your life has a point, even though that point
may appear somewhat inscrutable at times:

> *Just remember "God" has a purpose for you. Find that purpose and do
> your best.*
> *—Woman, 56, 2*

> *I'm constantly amazed at the way God prepares us for various phases
> of our lives; and the strength and comfort he provides as we deal with
> trials and tribulations. God does answer prayer—not always to our
> liking or according to our timetable, but according to his plan and in his
> time.*
> *—Woman, 57, 3*

God has somehow reconciled this woman to her manifold losses
(she dictated these words to her son):

> *I am currently recovering from a stroke and am still bedridden. The last
> fifteen years I have been going blind and am now nearly blind. In facing
> the loss of my husband and my illness, I have been greatly aided by a
> deep faith in God. I am a devout, conservative Roman Catholic with a
> solid grasp on life and death.*
> *—Woman, 73, 4*

And God has enhanced the good times of these two as well as
mitigated the bad:

I must begin by saying that I am not a religious fanatic—but I have attended the Episcopal Church all my life, and I am sure that my love of God and a strong faith in his goodness has supported me through all the rough spots and added thankfulness to the joyous ones!

—Woman, 81, 2

Given any situation—be it pleasant or awful—a strong faith in God and human beings (developed before you "need" it) and the desire to keep growing and learning are the most useful tools for a long, healthy, happy active life.

—Woman, 82, 25

The latter woman suggests you should bring that faith (not confined to God, you'll notice) to maturity before the fact. But others discovered it was not too late afterwards:

The most helpful of all was my decision to become a Christian indeed. It has turned my life around.

—Woman, 70, 11

John would probably not style himself a convert, but he comes close:

It was my relationship with God that I found that I needed most, and that's where I got some real answers, if you will. Even though I wasn't ordinarily religious, it has had an effect on me. Some people say it's a crutch, but to me it's a great comfort which I never thought I'd find.

—New York, #2

Some must concede that they are still not all the way there:

The greatest blessing is a strong religious faith, which I am working toward.

—Woman, 72, 5

Such work is demanded of any believer if the death of a spouse has plunged those beliefs into a crisis:

If one's religious faith was a factor and one really believes that there is more to life than one's years on earth, then this is the time to show it.

—Woman, 72, 6

Stay close to your religion; don't be bitter about the loss.
—Woman, 69, 4

We've observed how that bitterness may hurl a "why me?" at God. This woman may be in the throes of that and similar questions:

What made his death bearable was the thought that God had given him to me and had every right to take him away. I keep trying to remind myself that my husband is better off now and I try to be happy for him.
—Woman, 48, NA

Searching for an assurance that God takes away with as much justice as God gives can unsettle even the most devout:

After a while with reflection and faith, I knew that no one could do anything about it. It is the will of God!
—Woman, 82, 4

Very, very difficult indeed to be a survivor. Trust in the providence of God who loves us and guides us and acceptance of his holy will in all our sorrows.
—Woman, 61, 5

This woman views that acceptance not as a matter of moral obligation but as a kind of psychological absolution from that obligation:

Shock, unreality—this can't have happened to me. It bothered me that I couldn't accept "Thy will be done." Suddenly this thought came: "I accept it, not as I ought, but as I am able." It brought peace and release to me. Over the past twenty years, I have said it many times to many people in different situations. I know it has been helpful.
—Woman, 78, 21

"Thy will be done" was the second thought that occurred to Pat when she was told of the death (page 35):

I kept saying, "I don't believe it." And then I got up and said, "I've been preaching for years 'Thy will be done' and it's time I practiced it."
—Los Angeles, #2

She may have found it easier to practice because of this consolation:

> *The thing that helped me was my faith. And the priest said to me, when I told him exactly how it happened, "Just think of your husband having his first feast in Heaven." That was very comforting.*
> *Q: Marvelous, if you can believe in it. Marvelous.*

A surprising number of survivors can. Some, like Pat, anticipate an actual reunion in heaven—and perhaps with a better person, if what Mary's priest assured her group will come to pass:

> *Mary: He said that when we get to Heaven, everything will be absolved and God knows that we have human failings and we do the best we can. And after his lecture, one woman said to him, "Oh, I can't wait to get to heaven and see my husband minus his faults" [laughter].*
> —San Francisco

Others envisage something vaguer but still better in a less definite beyond:

> *I had a strong Christian faith and a belief that we can hope for a better world to come. I feel that it must be very different, but I do hope that my dear husband is joyfully a part of it now.*
> —Woman, 76, 12

> *Noreen: My husband always told me, "Noreen, you'll be fine because you've got your faith." And that's what carries me through. No matter what I do, I always feel like there's something better, a continuation of life or whatever you want to call it, and in the end everything will be all right.*
> —Los Angeles, #2

The miseries of this world can induce the certitude that what comes after must be kinder:

> *When your loved one has an illness that cannot be cured, and you see her in unbearable pain, you have to be convinced that there is life after death and she has gone to a better world.*
> —Man, 68, 3

But for some, it's a prior life that makes the present one more bearable:

> **Roger:** *My wife and I were both into Zen Buddhism, and we both be-lieve in reincarnation, that we've both been here many, many times and that this is just one of them. Although it was a shock when it happened, I still feel that it's just part of the process and that her spirit is with me. So it's not been that terrible an experience for me.*
>
> —*New York, #2*

All beliefs in an afterlife, or a forelife, strive to abolish time as well as death:

> *It is so important not to think of your spouse as being dead. He (or she) is not of the* departed *but he (or she) has* arrived *in Heaven. God is with him (or her) and God is with you, so you are not separated. Recognize that you have a closer link with eternity. This great bond can be a guiding force in your daily life. You do not have a loss—you have a gain and live daily with this goal.*
>
> —*Woman, 78, 6*

But daily life is still what we all must inhabit. Only God, to whom past, present, and future are one, transcends time. Even if you can look forward to sharing the same perspective eventually, you need something more than that expectation to make yourself at home in the land of clocks and calendars:

> **Diane:** *Well, I have a belief that I'll meet my husband in the hereafter and we will be together, and I think that helps an awful lot. I think, well, when I leave this world—*
> **Ann:** *Don't be in a hurry.*
> **Diane:** *I'll see him there.*
> **Clara:** *You're not ready to go yet, are you, Diane?*
>
> —*San Francisco*

On that note, let's go back to the temporal world, the world of death and change. Some survivors say that they have come to accept that world precisely because it does contain death:

Hard though it may be, try to accept death and the loss of a loved one as part of the human condition.

—Woman, 60, 3

Accept as best you can the finality of the separation which is part of the normal life cycle.

—Woman, 80, 9

Others argue that accepting death is no different from accepting any sort of change:

Seek out those experiences which help to reinforce our understanding of life as a constant process of change and renewal: gardening, nature study, travel (to experience ecological diversity), as well as reading about all of the above. For those of us who were privileged to enjoy these experiences with our husbands, the continuation of them can elicit strong, comforting feelings of closeness and connectedness in spirit with him.

—Woman, 61, 2

Noel: *A saying I have used over the years is "There is nothing more constant in life than change," and in that vein the biggest change you can have is the death of anybody, whether it is a spouse or a child. That's a big change to accept, I admit, but I like the concept of accepting things.*

—New York, #2

But speculations like these exude a whiff of abstraction, and we want to focus on some more concrete ideas by means of which survivors—believers and nonbelievers alike—have made peace with the immediate present.

Despite his inclusion of death among life's other changes, Noel rebels at making it a part of his definition of one kind of life:

Death is a finality, it's not part of life, it's a different life maybe, but it's not breathing, it's not eating, it's not dancing, it's not singing. And finding satisfaction out of each day is what life is all about.

—New York, #2

Finding *some* satisfaction in *each* day is how you must get through your grief—your only choice if getting over it or getting used to it are barred to you. And it's a task to which survivors bring outlooks often summed up by the stock phrases opposed in this chapter's title:

> **Irene:** *I was a strong character. I held up during the funeral. I had my family, my three grandchildren came over and they took turns staying with me. And it wasn't long before I really decided that life must go on.*
> **Sylvia:** *Well, I think it takes about two years before you accept the fact.*
> **Irene:** *Yes, it did with me.*
> **Sylvia:** *But when that feeling comes to you, it's like something off of your shoulders. And then you say to yourself, "It was the way it had to be. Now I go on with my life." So that's what I did.*
> —*Los Angeles, #1*

To this woman, the first thought probably brings scant solace:

> *Life goes on. At times I feel like an empty shell.*
> —*Woman, 57, 5*

"Life goes on," however, does pledge an allegiance to life, and that may be why many survivors set such store by it:

> *Life goes on. Do not dwell on the past. Be glad that you can remember the past as a great part of life.*
> —*Woman, 65, 3*

> *Just remember—you are still alive and have a lot to live for and a lot to give. Life* does *go on. Grieve your spouse's death and then get on with the business of living and being productive.*
> —*Woman, 51, 2*

When we liken life to a business, we are thinking of duty rather than pleasure, and being dutiful calls for effort. And a life that goes on may be lived largely at the behest of other people and other things:

> *Remember—life does go on. The bills come, the snow falls, the grass grows, and it all needs our attention.*
> —*Woman, 51, 5*

Concentrating on these demands can be hugely helpful—it's part of keeping busy, after all:

> *Barbara: I had known my husband since I was 15, so I had practically spent my whole life with him, but, you know, life goes on.*
> *Beulah: You don't have a choice.*
> *Barbara: No, there's no choice. I have to get out, I have to go to work. I have to do what I have to do. I think that helps.*
> *Beulah: That helps a little.*
> *Barbara: I think it makes all the difference in the world.*
>
> —Boston, #1

As Beulah and Barbara both note, they're acting under compulsion, with no choice—a precondition or an afterthought with which "life goes on" is repeatedly coupled:

> *Laura: My husband and I always went together on short trips, long trips. I just don't like to go alone.*
> *Frieda: You may not like it, but, honey, there's nothing you can do about it, so you have to do it. Life goes on.*
> *Laura: Yeah, I know.*
> *Frieda: You have to get against that brick wall and knock it down.*
>
> —Miami, #1

With these sentiments, Frieda aligns herself with a great many other fatalists and stoics:

> *Learn to accept what you have no control over.*
>
> —Woman, 78, 8

> *It is not easy, but cope I must, so cope I do.*
>
> —Woman, 77, 2

> *I have no sage advice except get up and get going. There's nothing else to do. Besides, funereal people are a drag.*
>
> —Woman, 59, 12

We're not taking issue with this point of view. If you react to your situation with fatalism and stoicism, that may be your most appropriate possible response, and perhaps your only possible one. But we'd like to close with some who have responded in a somewhat different vein.

A life that goes on may not only be hedged about by constraints and dictated by necessity but may also be consigned to a certain resignation:

> **Rose:** *I just picked up the pieces, and I started doing things, you know, kept busy. There are times you're lonely, you're not always "happy-happy," you know, but you have to make the best of things. Life goes on. That's the way I look at it.*
>
> *—San Francisco*

"Happy-happy" suggests a false buoyancy of spirit, and perhaps that is what Connie is jollying herself into:

> *I enjoy every day. I'm just thankful I'm alive and I can do what I do. I never have a down feeling. If I do, I just keep reminding myself, "Happy! happy! happy!" It's just a silly thing, but it does keep me going.*
>
> *—New York, #1*

Are those like her deluding themselves? Or can some of us *will* ourselves into happiness? This woman would unquestionably have her doubts:

> *My husband was the center pole of my life, and when he died my tent fell down around me. I lost my purpose in living, and happiness and contentment were gone. Happiness I'll never really find again, but I have achieved a livable degree of contentment.*
>
> *—Woman, 80, 5*

Another woman has regained a measure of happiness, but by her own admission not an entirely full one:

> *Losing a beloved spouse after a very happy and long marriage is a painful experience, second to none. Support from loving children and friends, happy memories, and practical common sense make it possible to survive and enjoy a reasonably happy, but very different way of life.*
>
> *—Woman, 76, 6*

Yet others blithely claim they have secured all the happiness they desire through the mere act of choice:

It has been more than two years now, and I now choose to be a happy individual and appreciate what I have—not what I have lost.
—Woman, 74, 3

My husband's death was sudden and unexpected, but from that moment I was grateful for the forty-six years of happiness we had shared. I believe the best way to adjust to the loss of such a loved one is to be happy. I truly believe that even in grief one can be just as happy as he or she WANTS TO BE. Be happy for what you have had. Be happy for all you have now.
—Woman, 72, 5

What divides those who find "happiness" so easily within reach from those who do not? Principally, sheer pleasure in being alive:

Keep busy—feel lucky—you're alive. There is a void in my life, but I am happy. I have always felt if I were unhappy and my husband could know, he would also be unhappy. I feel fortunate to have nice children, grandchildren, and friends, to have fair health, and to be free of money worries.
—Woman, 78, NA

Is she being shallow and self-centered in congratulating herself on her luck? Hardly. This woman clearly isn't when she attributes her felicity to the same good fortune—being the "recipient of life":

In handling sadness we must grapple with a fact of life: we who are left after our loved ones are gone are still the recipient of life and responsible for it. We must do something with it which is worthwhile. It is in completing what God has given us to do that we find real contentment and happiness too.
—Woman, 77, 3

By vowing to go on with our life, we may have arrived at yet another platitude:

Although it may be a cliché, life is for the living.
—Woman, 69, 9

It's a cliché which some survivors instinctively reject:

> **Ida:** *You must remind yourself that you are living, they are gone. We have to think of them with love and kindness, but we are here. I told that to a woman, and she looked very harshly at me: "How could you say that?" This was my neighbor, her husband had passed away six months ago. She's going wacko. She's running around and she's carrying on and she comes in to me and cries and cries. I said, "Look, is banging your head on the wall going to help you? Is that going to bring Bill back? You must face it, it's not easy by any means. It's very difficult. But what are you going to do? We're living and they're gone."*
>
> —Miami, #1

Bowing to that fact need do no disservice to the past, even though you may be committing yourself to the future more decisively than many survivors feel that they can:

> *Find some kind of meaningful activity with which to enrich your life. Although the spouse is dead, the survivor is still alive, and life is to the living. The past is past, and however sweet it was, it is no more. So go forward—life always lies in the future.*
>
> —Man, 75, 5

Welcoming a new life does not constitute an act of treachery:

> *Though it may seem like a betrayal of the love you both felt for one another, you must realize right off that you are embarking on a totally new way of life.*
>
> —Woman, 67, 4

For those heeding that realization, the past rather than the present is the arena where they have no choice:

> **Marilyn:** *It's important for you, for your family, for everybody to realize the dead are dead and there is nothing you can do about it. You must go on with your life, you* don't *forget, you* never *forget, but you must make a new life, you* must.
>
> —Boston, #2

And going on with *your* life puts the burden on one person alone:

You are alive. You are in charge.

—Woman, 84, 5

Only you can make your life meaningful again.

—Woman, 64, 3

One must try very hard to keep faith within one's self. The only person who can help is YOU yourself—it has to come from within.

—Woman, 73, 4

If we believe that, we must take others off the hook:

Do not depend on others to remake your life. Begin right away to make new avenues in your life.

—Woman, 78, 11

Do not depend on family and friends to fill the role of your departed spouses. Assume responsibility for yourself.

—Woman, 80, 12

Such a responsibility can unnerve the boldest of us. Yet these survivors found that their initial fears had evaporated:

The time will come when you realize you are in complete charge of your life—and it will be a pleasant rather than a frightening feeling.

—Woman, 62, 3

Accept that you will make a good many mistakes, but you are in control and must make decisions for yourself. After a long while, you will begin to have a measure of confidence in yourself.

—Woman, 60, 3

With the restoration of self-confidence may come something else—self-discovery:

It was a great *loss for me!!! But I am amazed how I can keep going and am beginning to rebuild my life—as my spouse would want me to. I thought I would not be able to live without him, but I have discovered things about myself I did not know and feel I have learned and am learning to* live *alone triumphantly.*

—Woman, 69, 2

Edith: You've got to start somewhere, and the faster the better. I gave myself a time limit for starting to build my own life. Of course I've gone overboard. I have become narcissistic when I never was. I cut my hair. I had very long hair because that's what he liked. I like short hair—I can be me. I don't owe him anything now except a good memory, which I have. That's all I owe the dead is to remember them. Sounds cruel, but I have to survive. I want more than to survive. I want to live.

—Boston, #1

Edith's statement that "I can be me" doesn't convict her of narcissism in the least. Instead, it prepares her for the kind of self-exploration that this woman is so vigorously engaged in:

Separate from the marriage. Concentrate on yourself. Figure out what you wanted to do but never did, where you wanted to go but did not, and what you never dared dream of doing. Cast aside the idea of compromise, which is essential for a marriage, and instead, focus all your energies and concerns on yourself.

—Woman, 59, 2

Perhaps, to your surprise, you may take a fancy to the self that emerges from such an exercise. In Chapter 1 we reviewed the various injuries that the loss of a spouse inflicts upon a survivor's sense of self, including his or her respect for that self:

The trauma of the grief, loneliness, damage to one's self-esteem, and all the changes facing one cannot be imagined or prepared for. Even accepting the designation "widow" is hard.

—Woman, 75, 3

But widowhood eventually disclosed to Jean that she liked being herself—and that, as a result, not only did others like her, but she could like being by herself as well as with them:

You take good stock of yourself and what your life is going to be like. If you are anywhere an intelligent person, you have to think about those things. One of the most important things you will discover about yourself is something I think all of you ladies probably have: If you like yourself, you are never going to be lonely. But if you despise yourself,

you will be miserable always. You have to think of yourself as a nice person.
Ida: *With a lot to offer.*
Jean: *That's right, and you will find people will be coming to you wherever you go.*
Isabel: *If you are pleasant. If you are not pleasant—*
Eleanor: *Yes, absolutely, if you are a down person—*
Jean: *I have known people in my life who cannot be by themselves at all. They don't like themselves.*
Eleanor: *I like people, but I don't mind being alone.*
Jean: *I like to be alone very much. I love people, but there are times when I love to be by myself.*

—New York, #1

Jean's self-assessment seems to have kept her on the right side of the border between happiness and misery, as this woman's has:

Realize we all have challenges to face—our attitude is what makes the difference. It is easy to get lonely and discouraged and feel sorry for yourself. We all have "down" times, but we must gather ourselves together, make the most of it, and go on. Don't expect others to make you happy. You do your part, and happiness will be contagious.

—Woman, 45, 2

If attitude is everything and if life is the embodiment of change, then this woman's magisterial self-assurance about both should be accessible to us all:

Having my own business, I have always been quite independent, and all my life had to adapt to life and to accept whatever happens. Change is the one thing we know will happen in life. It is, so you accept it. You can always change your attitude about a situation.

—Woman, 73, 13

Alas, many of us can't—at least, not with the apparent ease that she can. As with the woman quoted before her, our ups may seem to war perpetually with our downs. And to survivors whose grief is so new as to leave them wondering whether they will ever know happiness again, this woman may seem guilty of the grossest effrontery:

*As well as a great loss, widowhood can be a great growth experience
and open up all kinds of new learning opportunities.*

—Woman, 49, 3

Optimism at its most asinine? Not for this woman:

*I was a shy, retiring person, content to be in the background and live
vicariously. Now that I am a widow, I have discovered abilities that I
didn't know I had, have become involved in community and volunteer
work and have become someone in my own right. I have made interesting friends outside of my once rather narrow circle, am able to present
a program or contribute to a discussion. I am, in fact, a more self-
reliant, assured, and attractive person. It took determination and effort,
but I have made a satisfying life for myself.*

—Woman, 80, 22

Others, while not reporting such a sweeping self-transfiguration,
stumbled across some agreeable surprises:

*My husband and I had been restoring a twenty-two-room house, built
in 1880. I am continuing the work and this has opened many avenues.
I have learned to make business decisions that I never knew I was
capable of! I am a stronger person because of all my experiences.*

—Woman, 68, 3

***Dorothy:** I say this—and I'm not being funny; I say it with an extreme
sincerity. I'm sorry my husband is gone, I regret it deeply, and I miss
him very much. But I might as well accept the fringe benefits: I can
do what I want to do. Not that he stopped me but—he's not here, so I
might as well take advantage of the fringe benefits. I found out that
I have a lot of talent for things I never knew I had. Now, in this language class, I found out that I'm very good at writing, at writing
spoofs in Yiddish. And, you know, it goes to your head, this applause.
When they wait for you and say, "Did you bring a story, did you bring
a story?" And then they say, "Gee, you're great!" You know, that's
nice. Writing, speaking is my thing, and I didn't know I had it.*

—Miami, #1

"I can do what I want to do"—that latitude amounts to more than
a fringe benefit for some:

For the first time in your life, you are free to do whatever you wish; let it be a heady experience. So try new things—if you fail, you won't disappoint anyone else.

—Woman, 67, 16

That's one of the advantages of being responsible only to yourself. This woman looks upon her life as a reservoir of possibilities—too many of them, in fact:

Actively create a new life for yourself. You can do almost anything you wish (my problem: deciding what to do).

—Woman, 66, 7

Contemplating freedom in the abstract invites grandiose thoughts, and perhaps her indecision springs from overambition. Yvette found her decision easy to make, and modest though her project may appear, it's absorbing her still:

Q: Okay. Yvette, what was the smartest thing you did?
Yvette: One thing was my house. I decided I would make it my house. I mean, it had been our house before, though actually maybe it was his house more—in that I wasn't too fussy and did things the way he wanted to. And I've made it a feminine kind of house because this was a new phase of my life. That's what I've been doing bit by bit, and I'm still working on it six years later. I'm still making it my house—the colors that I want and so forth.

—San Francisco

Look at how this woman has let her own wishes orchestrate her life—not only the little things within it but the big ones as well:

After my husband died suddenly, it was hard to realize at first that doing little things (moving furniture, selecting meals, etc.) could depend entirely on my own wishes. I felt free for the first time in my life, even within the confines of my necessary job and responsibility for my mother and mother-in-law. I decided to continue in the secretarial field where I already had part-time work, and full-time employment was never a problem. My wants have been simple and well within my financial capabilities. The children were educated, I could help—not coddle—them when necessary. They were located at a distance, so there was no

problem with unwanted babysitting. They are independent—and they have never tried to push me into anything I did not want to do.
                                                          —Woman, 77, 20

This woman catalogues the pleasures freedom affords her—again, small items perhaps, but an impressive sum when totaled:

Being older, alone, with infrequent male companionship is often the pits—especially if you look at all the negatives. But there are compensations: I come and go as I please; if I decide to spend an extra day or two on a trip, I only have to let a friend know that I'll be two days late. I can eat cookies in bed, and I don't have to make the bed unless I want to. Since I'm now over 60, I don't have to worry about what the neighbors think. I have a three-bedroom, two-bath home designed for guests, so I've sheltered a number of younger friends for a few weeks or months. It was great to have a young woman of dating age sharing her romantic problems; it was mentally stimulating to have a friend (male) from graduate-school days initiating philosophical arguments. I also cherished the quiet and solitude when they left. I'm completely on my own for the first time in my life, and truly value my freedom.
                                                          —Woman, 62, 12

She can celebrate her freedom because she has refused to let "all the negatives" swallow it up. So must we, if we are to make a haven in the time allotted to us. That time can only be lived day by day—to return to the theme sounded early in Chapter 4. But survivors have two ways of going about it. Believing this:

I don't think anything really helps, except learning day to day to cope with a situation over which you have absolutely no control.
                                                          —Woman, 73, 15

Just take one day at a time and try to keep busy. I don't think you ever get over it, but you can't let it control your life.
                                                          —Woman, 45, 3

Or believing that you are more firmly in control:

I try to take one day at a time and spend it wisely.
                                                          —Woman, 82, 3

Remember, this is not a dress rehearsal. We must continue to live our lives and enjoy every day. And I am nearly 79.

—*Woman, 78, 4*

Most of us are fated to believe both at times: when we can't stride though life, we must trudge. But we also know what separates these two modes of getting through it—the knowledge that, on the one hand, we are merely surviving and, on the other, truly living:

Time is not a great healer and I have no great words of wisdom. Growing older alone is very difficult. I've tried everything widows are supposed to do—even to getting a new puppy, whom I enjoy and love. But the light has gone out, so I run frantically to try all kinds of new ventures and adventures and survive one day at a time.

—*Woman, 73, 3*

I am trying to find out who I am and make my important decisions with self-tolerance. To accept change if it occurs. To take it easy on slips and mistakes. To learn my empty places and their nature and fill them or accept them. To try to cultivate the senses, encourage touch, texture, taste—see the autumn colors, smell the spring flowers. After all, this is what the child does emerging from infancy. The world is ahead. It still is for me at 73. I can only live it one day at a time. So does a 2-year-old.

—*Woman, 73, 9*

The one grows older alone, in a gathering darkness; the other does it in kindred spirit with an infant, in a place where light still dawns. "One day at a time" may define a life that is full or one that is empty. And a full life can be full of contradictions:

Take one day at a time. Think of the good times you have had with one another. Live for the future. Yesterday is gone and tomorrow may never come. I've had a full life and hope for many more years.

—*Woman, 76, 8*

This woman holds forth on the subject with the fervor of an evangelist bearing witness or a politician delivering a stemwinder:

Adjustment is what you yourself make it! You have the choice, either exist in self-pity, or live your life to its fullest. When I became a widow

I saw both types, and I wanted to live my life to its fullest. I wanted people around me, not avoiding me. There are low points in my life, but the high points outnumber them, and I keep reminding myself of my choice. If you look around, you can always see others who are in worse situations than you are. I know now the reality that life can be taken from us in the wink of an eye, and I try to make each day count. And that's what life is all about! So my advice to other widows and widowers is to live life to its fullest. Have your memories, but do not live in them. BE HAPPY AND COUNT EACH MOMENT AS A BLESSING!

—*Woman, 61, 3*

Dorothy is much more terse:

Q: Does this mean anything to anybody: "One day at a time"?
Dorothy: Yes, it means a lot.
Q: What does it mean?
Dorothy: It means I can get through the day. Don't worry about tomorrow. Don't look ahead and don't look back. You're living now, now is the moment, seize it!

—*Miami, #1*

Epilogue

[On the questionnaire, she originally wrote these words.]

I don't know that I can be of much help. We are all so different when concerned with problems. I'm probably more so than many others. I was subject to depressions from age 16. Was able to manage later in life, but most of time could see no reason for great interest in daily life and routine. When I was feeling good, life was good, but such periods were limited.

The head of the psychiatric department suggested after my husband's death that I enter hospital. I was numb after experiences following terrible loss. I had tried mouth-to-mouth resuscitation, called doctor, priest. We both knew he would die, but the reality was more than I could bear. Elder son and younger too were great, handled funeral arrangements—no funeral "receiving line," only funeral. Sister there too, a dear help. The three of us did talk—all feeling the same. This is certainly a dirge! Too much.

[She then pasted over those words a sheet of paper bearing these.]

My sons handled all necessities after my husband's death and rented an apartment for me in the same complex where my married older son lived. Across the hall from me lived a neighbor who has become a dear friend through the years that followed.

We did volunteer work for three years with retarded children. After the three years the institution was converted to housing adults, also retarded. After those three years, we started at Gateway Rehabilitation Center, working with wheelchair adults, young to elderly—

485

ceramics, arts and crafts. All of this volunteer work was as good for Josephine and me as it was for the handicapped.

I made new friends by going to a Bible study group in the apartment complex. Knowing no one there at the time, it was a great help, new friends.

[Finally, she appended this note.]

I found myself writing a long, sad story. Suddenly realized how stupid—you wanted something more like what I have re-done. Sorry.
—Woman, 74, 18

Pat: A year after my husband died, I took a trip by myself. And by the way, tomorrow, October 6th, is the anniversary of the second year of his death. I went with a group, and I went to Death Valley.
Gladys: No pun intended [laughter].
Pat: Because I didn't want to cry at home. I was afraid I would start crying and the phone would ring. My sons can always tell if I've been crying. When I called up the travel agent in Westwood, I explained to her that I was a widow and that it was the anniversary.

I asked what the group was going to do. Did I have to do everything with them? Because I did want to be by myself. I didn't want to ask a close friend along—I wanted to see how I could really cope with it. So I wanted to be sure that I wasn't expected to be with people all the time. I wanted a room by myself. I didn't want a television, a phone, or anything. She said, "This will be perfect—it's very quiet there."

And it worked out. I was so pleased with myself, and my sons were pleased—that I really did it by myself. When I came home I felt good about myself. On our way back, on this trip, I started joining everyone when they had lunch and when they had dinner. And instead of crying in my room, I started going back to my room and laughing!
—Los Angeles, #2

It is my conviction that each individual must, ultimately, formulate solutions to living after the death of a mate. Assistance, advice, sympathy, and compassion are all essential; but the action taken and decisions made are private.

After my husband's death (before retirement), I prepared to accept a minor position with his college, thus continuing alone the kind of life we had shared for over thirty years. Within two months I was totally crippled by spinal arthritis, unable to accept the financial and moral support this position would have provided. Physical therapy eventually restored mobility, but I was and remain unable to perform even simple housekeeping tasks. The usual advice—travel, work, and explore—could not be taken.

Fortunately, I was able to keep our home near the campus; I could continue contacts of long standing within the college. Classes are open to me and I spend time in volunteer work with the Admissions, Alumni, and Development Offices. Under different conditions, a more active life would have been desirable; accepting the alternative, based on foundations already laid, gives me an interesting and rewarding existence.

I am grateful for the opportunity to live among and associate with college students whose friendship I enjoy, to enter again the classroom as a student, and to enjoy making a small contribution to a community of which I have so long been a member. As long as this is possible, I have a sense of security and meaning; beyond this, there is an anxiety about the future, a deep sense of separation, and much physical pain. It seems to me, therefore, that the one who survives must adjust on the bases of time, place, and circumstance—and hope it can be done.

—Woman, 64, 7

My life without my husband is different in many ways. I miss him very much. My new life style, while different, is most interesting and enjoyable in its own right. Many areas I couldn't pursue as fully during my marriage, I have picked up on again. Widowhood doesn't have to mean the end of one's contentment, growth, or friendships.

On days I feel sorry for myself, I remind myself that, even while my husband (who I loved and still love very much) was alive, there were also bad days. I also view things in perspective, being thankful for what I still have and realizing that I could have been asked to give up even more. Look at the poor soul who loses spouse and children or has to endure a major change in life style.

Most important, too, is not relying on others to make things better.

One has to do that oneself. If we expect others to do it, not only do we miss out on much opportunity for growth, self-discovery, and content- ment, but one invariably becomes angry at friends or family, blaming them for one's not feeling better. Friends can pleasantly distract one from one's grief but not resolve it.

Finally, it is important if one enjoyed one's marriage and spouse to reminisce. I have learned, so have our friends, that though my husband cannot still be with us physically, we can still enjoy him and even learn from him as we remember what he might have said or done. Once I realized I did not have to lose him, I was able to resolve my mourning.

—Woman, 49, 5

My husband's sudden and unexpected death was such a devastating experience that for months I just lived from day to day, coping as best I could. Even though it would have been easier to remain home and grieve, I accepted the many invitations and kindnesses our relatives and friends extended. I tried to make myself acceptable company when in their presence. I do not feel as if I have been "dropped" by former friends and couples— although the relationships have changed.

Since my husband's death I have endeavored to conduct myself in a manner that would honor his name. He was a student of the Italian Renaissance (an avocation). He traveled often in Italy and he had taken many slides. Since he was an excellent public speaker, he had planned when he returned to give illustrated lectures on the Renais- sance.

Since my retirement as a mathematics teacher, I have given a series of non-credit courses at the local university on the Renaissance (I am an avid reader and also a student of the Renaissance), using my husband's books, notes, and slides. I do this as a tribute to him—and as a rewarding and worthwhile project for myself. Keep reading. Keep learning. Keep active!

—Woman, 74, 15

I believe that my adjustment was reasonably successful because

1) I moved from a large house to a condo in an adult community (Heritage Village) within three months where I could begin a new life as soon as possible—and where there was a large proportion of widows and single women.

2) I found a full-time job—since I was a professional person with much prior experience, it was not difficult. I worked long hours to keep myself as occupied as possible.

3) I involved myself in community work as a volunteer and I joined appropriate social activities.

4) I traveled by myself in tour groups—sometimes with new friends.

5) After nine years of living alone, I found a compatible woman with whom I share a condo for companionship and expense sharing.

I think it is important for widows to recognize that they must make a new life for themselves and to go about it as soon as possible. Former friends may tire of providing support and being continually reminded of their own mortality. A new life and new people make it possible for you to fit into a social group without the remembrance of memories and depressing associations. It required at least three years before I was able to feel a whole person again.

—Woman, 75, 17

My first bit of advice is to be good to one's spouse throughout the marriage so that one is not haunted by guilt and remorse. The survivor of a good marriage has peace and a special strength to go on alone. My husband was quite a bit older than I. There were things I saved up for when I would be alone, special interests we did not share.

I put myself on a routine, giving myself the first two hours of the day—one hour's walk before breakfast and an hour's reading during breakfast. I had a dog and cannot emphasize enough the importance of a pet. When I couldn't sleep I tried to solve just one thing that was bothering me. I tried to use the time productively and usually fell asleep before the problem was thought through.

I like to cook. I entertained a lot and made special foods for friends who were sick. I did a lot of reaching out to others.

For the first year I held personal mail until the productive part of the day was over, then I read the letters, usually with a drink and a good cry. Grief comes in waves and I could tell when I was "weakening." I would stock up on fruits and juices and hole in until I was ready to meet the world with courage. Most helpful of all were my dog, my family and friends, and a device I found worked for me. First I tried keeping a journal, then I hit upon writing letters to my departed spouse and that worked. *Although I wasn't fooled I was communicating with my beloved.*

After a while the independence of living alone is pretty heady stuff. I began to enjoy it. I missed the quality of mind of my husband but had accepted my loss. Then one evening a stranger—a doctor—came to pick me up to go to a dinner party. We were soon copying our children, living together for six months before marrying. I still grieved at times, but I was happy again. My new husband had been widowed six years. He was very understanding. My last bit of advice is to continue to cherish one's spouse, one's new spouse. These late-in-life marriages can be very good. Our combined incomes allow for more luxuries, and I finally inherited the legacy we had counted on forty years ago when we plotted our future. My elderly parents are tucked underground, and my conscience doesn't bother me.

I guess it all boils down to arranging one's life so that one can live with oneself.

—Woman, 66, 10

I was in the unfortunate (or fortunate?) position of having been divorced and living independently for twelve years prior to my marriage to my late husband. The tremendous feeling of loss of self that I suffered from the divorce set me on the path of investigating ways of dealing with loss and separation. I found that I began to look at myself from a different vantage point. Over the years, with each successive experience of loss or change, my expectations of what my relationship to other people and institutions changed. I became less dependent on them for my well-being.

This slow painful process had led me to a relatively autonomous, comfortable state of being by the time I met my late husband. Our short time together was very intense—wondrous and delightful. He was so much fun to live with! I miss him very much and think often of the enrichment he brought to my life because of the quality of his character and the myriad of experiences, both painful and joyous, we were able to share. Since his death, it has been comparatively easy for me to continue to live a full and satisfying life with less of the trauma I experienced from earlier losses—always grateful for having had even so short an interlude with him.

Suffering loss and change is an inevitable part of living. I have found that doing so—in an age where there is so much information and support to help me grow through the pain to a different level of what it is to be human—has given me much satisfaction.

—*Woman, 63, 2*

Elizabeth: No, I haven't given up! I have used my good silver every day of my life since we were married. I use it today, I've never used anything out of the kitchen to set my table except my silver—knife, fork, spoons, and salad fork. Regardless of the time of day—lunch or dinner—I will not *sit down with anything else. So my friends laugh at me: "What are you doing with your salad fork?" I say, "I like a salad fork and I'm going to use it!"*

And I entertain. I have had the craziest parties sometimes. I bought a piggyback washer-dryer not long ago, and it was supposed to go outside my back door and down the stairs to the utility room. Well, I had part of the floor in the utility room built up for the washer-dryer, so that all I have to do is open the back door and it's right there. I don't go down the steps or anything like that. I had a party for that—an installation party [laughter]!

Ruth: You gave a party for that?

Elizabeth: I gave a party for that. I put a great big red ribbon on the door. So many people bought me—

Ruth: Presents?

Elizabeth: Yes—soap [laughter]. I have enough soap to last a year or more.

Peggy: A party without a reason!

Elizabeth: A party without a reason, that's the idea.

—*Mami, #2*

Many years ago my wife and I learned the importance of doing things together and having fun together. As a result, I have many happy memories.

We planned our retirement well in advance, so we would have lots of varied interests to keep us busy. We bought our old log house on 160 wooded acres, restored the log house, and lived in it during the first two years of retirement while we built a small new house. We lived in the new house for two years before my wife died.

I continue to do all of the things we loved to do together. I have a big garden and can and freeze fruits and vegetables for myself and some for my children. The house is heated with wood, and I cut and split all of it. There is a small greenhouse, and I have flowers, tomatoes, and lettuce all winter. My wife was a home economist and dietician, and I learned something about food and food preparation from helping her in the kitchen. Now I bake all my own bread, do all the cooking, and frequently entertain friends for dinner.

One needs to exercise regularly. I like to hike in the woods, cross-country ski, snowshoe, and ice skate. I walk an average of twenty miles per week in both winter and summer.

A variety of interests keeps one from being bored. In addition to the activities mentioned above, I like to watch wildlife, identify wildflowers, fish, read, and write poetry. I have published a small booklet of poems. I take a lot of pictures and am called on frequently to give slide shows for service organizations and church groups.

Some keys to happiness:

1) Keep busy.
2) Exercise regularly.
3) Eat balanced meals.
4) Take pride in doing your best in whatever you do.
5) Have fun (sometimes it's an attitude or state of mind).
6) Relate to others; help others; sympathize with them in time of sorrow; rejoice with them in times of joy.
7) See and appreciate all of the beauty in our marvelous world.
8) Cherish the past; live in the present; plan for the future.

(If you are ever out this way, stop in for coffee and cookies. Visitors from seven states did just that last summer.)

—Man, 73, 5

Make new friends, as well as keeping the old. Remember the lost person and make him a part, continuing, of your life, thought, and affection. Work as much and as well as strength permits. "We do best homage to our dead when we live our lives most fully, even in the shadow of our loss." I like that quotation, and find it useful even after almost twenty years of widowhood. I will be 88 next summer.

—Woman, 87, 19

Bibliography

GUIDES FOR SURVIVORS

GENERAL

Deits, Bob. *Life After Loss: A Personal Guide Dealing with Death, Divorce, Job Change, and Relocation.* Tucson, Ariz.: Fisher Books, 1988.

Diguilio, Robert. *Beyond Widowhood: From Bereavement to Emergence and Hope.* New York: Macmillan, 1989.

Grollman, Earl A. *Time Remembered: A Journal for Survivors.* Boston: Beacon, 1987.

Stearns, Ann K. *Living Through Personal Crisis.* Chicago: The Thomas More Press, 1984.

Tatlebaum, Judy. *The Courage to Grieve: Creative Living, Recovery, and Growth Through Grief.* New York: Harper & Row, 1980.

Temes, Roberta. *Living with an Empty Chair: A Guide Through Grief.* Amherst, Mass.: Mandala, 1977.

FOR WIDOWS

Antoniak, Helen. *Alone: Emotional, Legal and Financial Help for the Widowed or Divorced Woman.* New York: Simon & Schuster, 1986.

Caine, Lynn. *Being a Widow.* Boston: Morrow, 1988.

Doress, Paula B., and Diana L. Siegel. *Ourselves Growing Older: Women Aging with Knowledge and Power.* New York: Simon & Schuster, 1987.

Fisher, Ida. *The Widow's Guide to Life.* Englewood Cliffs, N.J.: Prentice-Hall, 1981.

Foehner, Charlotte, and Carol Cozart. *The Widow's Handbook.* Golden, Colo.: Fulcrum, 1988.

Gates, Philomene. *Suddenly Alone: A Woman's Guide to Widowhood.* New York: Harper & Row, 1990.

Ginsburg, Genevieve D. *To Live Again: Rebuilding Your Life After You've Become a Widow.* Los Angeles: Tarcher, 1987.

Loewinsohn, Ruth J. *Survival Handbook for Widows (And for Relatives and Friends Who Want to Understand).* Washington, D.C.: American Association of Retired Persons, 1984.

Porcino, Jane. *Growing Older, Getting Better: A Handbook for Women in the Second Half of Life.* Reading, Mass.: Addison-Wesley, 1983.

Seskin, Jane. *Alone—Not Lonely: Independent Living for Women Over Fifty*. Washington, D.C.: American Association of Retired Persons, 1985.

Taves, Isabella. *The Widow's Guide: Practical Advice on How to Deal with Grief, Stress, Health, Children and Family, Money, Work and Finally, Getting Back into the World*. New York: Schocken Books, 1981.

Witkin, Mildred Hope, with Burton Lehrenbaum. *Forty-Five and Single Again*. New York: Dembner Books, 1985.

FOR WIDOWERS

Campbell, Scott, and Phyllis Silverman. *Widower: When Men Are Left Alone*. New York: Prentice-Hall, 1987.

Robertson, John, and Betty Utterback. *Suddenly Single: Learning to Start Over, a Personal Guide through the Experiences of Others*. New York: Simon & Schuster, 1986.

FIRST-HAND ACCOUNTS

FOR WIDOWS

Caine, Lynn. *Widow*. New York: Morrow, 1974; Bantam, 1987.

Graham, Virginia. *Life After Harry: My Adventures in Widowhood*. New York: Simon & Schuster, 1988.

Powell, Mary Clare. *The Widow*. Washington, D.C.: Anaconda Press, 1981.

Robey, Harriet. *There's a Dance in the Old Dame Yet*. Boston: Little, Brown, 1982.

Truman, Jill. *Letter to My Husband: Notes about Mourning and Recovery*. New York: Penguin, 1988.

Weaver, Frances. *The Girls with the Grandmother Faces: Single and Sixty Is Not for Sissies*. Colorado Springs, Colo.: Century One Press, 1987.

FOR WIDOWERS

Lewis, C.S. *A Grief Observed*. New York: Seabury Press, 1961.

Meryman, Richard. *Hope—A Loss Survived*. Boston: Little, Brown, 1984.

Schoen, Elin. *Widower: A Daughter's Compelling Account of How a Man Overcame Grief and Loneliness*. New York: Morrow, 1984.

SPECIAL SUBJECTS

TERMINAL ILLNESS

Ade-Ridder, Linda, and Charles Hennon, eds. *Lifestyles of the Elderly*. New York: Human Sciences Press, 1989.

Moffatt, Betty Clare. *Gifts for the Living: Conversations with Caregivers on Death and Dying*. San Bernardino, Cal.: Borgo Press, 1988.

Saunders, Cicely M., and Mary Baines. *Living with Dying: The Management of Terminal Disease*. New York: Oxford University Press, 1989.

Stafford, Tim. *As Our Years Increase: Loving, Caring, Preparing—A Guide*. Grand Rapids, Mich.: Zondervan Publishing House, 1989.

SUICIDE

Bryant, Betty. *Leaning Into the Wind: The Wilderness of Widowhood.* Philadelphia: Fortress, 1975.

Hewett, John. *After Suicide.* Philadelphia: Westminster Press, 1980.

Ross, Elnora. *After Suicide: A Unique Grief Process.* Springfield, Ill.: Creative Marketing, 1981.

CHILDREN

Brown, Elizabeth B. *Sunrise Tomorrow.* Old Tappan, N.J.: Revell, 1988.

Dodson, Fitzhugh. *How to Single Parent.* New York: Harper & Row, 1987.

Gravelle, Karen, and Charles Haskins. *Teenagers Face to Face with Bereavement.* Englewood Cliffs, N.J.: J. Messner, 1989.

Jewett, Claudia. *Helping Children Cope with Separation and Loss.* Boston: Harvard Common Press, 1982.

Juneau, Barbara Frisbie. *Sad But O.K.: My Daddy Died Today.* Nevada City, Cal.: Blue Dolphin Publisher, 1988.

Krementz, Jill. *How It Feels When a Parent Dies.* New York: Alfred A. Knopf, 1986.

LeShan, Eda. *Learning To Say Goodbye: When a Parent Dies.* New York: Macmillan, 1976.

Osmont, Kelly, and Marilyn McFarlane. *Parting Is Not Goodbye.* Portland, Ore.: Nobility Press, 1987.

Schaefer, Dan, and Christine Lyons. *How Do We Tell the Children? A Parents' Guide to Helping Children Understand and Cope When Someone Dies.* New York: Newmarket Press, 1988.

STORY BOOKS FOR YOUNG CHILDREN

Clifton, Lucille. *Everett Anderson's Goodbye.* New York: Holt, 1983.

DePaola, Tomie. *Nana Upstairs & Nana Downstairs.* New York: Putnam, 1973.

Holden, L. Dwight. *Gran-Gran's Best Trick. A Story for Children Who Have Lost Someone They Love.* New York: Magination Press, 1989.

Miles, Miska. *Annie and the Old One.* Boston: Little, Brown, 1971.

Lee, Jeanne M. *Bá-Nâm.* New York: Holt, 1987.

Viorst, Judith. *The Tenth Good Thing about Barney.* Boston: Atheneum, 1971.

FINANCES AND ESTATE PLANNING

Brown, Judith N., and Christina Baldwin. *A Second Start: A Widow's Guide to Financial Survival at a Time of Emotional Crisis.* New York: Simon & Schuster, 1986.

David, Walter W. *The 50-Plus Guide to Retirement Investing.* New York: Dow-Jones, 1987.

Gatov, Elizabeth S. *Widows in the Dark.* Bolinas, Cal.: Common Knowledge Press, 1985.

Martin, Don and Renee. *Survival Kit for Wives.* New York: Villard Books, 1986.

Starr, Herbert F. *Estate Planning Made Easy*. Blue Ridge Summit, Penn.: Liberty House, 1989.

HOUSING

American Association of Homes for the Aging. *National Continuing Care Directory: Retirement Communities with Nursing Care*. Glenview, Ill.: Scott, Foresman, 1988.

Porcino, Jane. *Living Longer, Living Better: Adventures in Community Housing for Those in the Second Half of Life*. New York: Crossroads/Continuum, 1991.

McCamant, Kathryn, and Charles Durrett. *Cohousing: A Contemporary Approach to Housing Ourselves*. Berkeley: Habitat Press, 1988.

McLaughlin, Corinne, and Gordon Davidson. *Builders of the Dawn: Community Lifestyles in a Changing World*. Shutesbury, Mass.: Sirius Publishing, 1986.

DATING AND REMARRIAGE

Lippi, Otty. *The Second Time Around: An Honest Widow Reveals Her Intimate and Humorous Experiences in the Mating and Dating Game*. New York: Dembner Books, 1981.

PHILOSOPHY

Bouvard, Marguerite, and Evelyn Glada. *The Path Through Grief*. Portland, Ore.: Breitenbush Books, 1988.

Bozarth-Campbell, Alla. *Life Is Goodbye, Life Is Hello: Grieving Well Through All Kinds of Loss*. Minneapolis: Comp-Care Publications, 1982.

Detrich, Richard L., and Nicola J. Steele, *How to Recover from Grief*. Valley Forge, Penn.: Judson Press, 1983.

Kubler-Ross, Elisabeth. *On Death and Dying*. New York: Macmillan, 1969.

Kushner, Harold S. *When Bad Things Happen to Good People*. New York: Avon, 1981.

Kutscher, Austin H., ed. *For the Bereaved: The Road to Recovery*. Philadelphia: Charles Press, 1989.

Moffat, Mary Jane. *In the Midst of Winter: Selections from the Literature of Mourning*. New York: Vintage Books, 1982.

O'Conner, Nancy. *Letting Go with Love: The Grieving Process*. Apache Junction, Ariz.: La Mariposa Press, 1984.

Rando, Therese A. *Grieving: How to Go on Living When Someone You Love Dies*. Lexington, Mass.: Lexington Books, 1988.

Rice, Rebecca. *A Time to Mourn*. New York: New American Library, 1990.

Roth, Deborah, ed. *Stepping Stones to Grief Recovery*. San Bernardino, Cal.: Borgo Press, 1988.

Sanders, Catherine M. *Grief: The Mourning After*. New York: Wiley, 1989.

Shuchter, Stephen R. *Dimensions of Grief: Adjusting to the Death of a Spouse*. San Francisco: Jossey-Bass, 1986.

PSYCHOLOGY AND SOCIOLOGY

Altschul, Sol, ed. *Childhood Bereavement and Its Aftermath*. Madison, Conn.: International Universities Press, 1988.

Bowling, Ann, and Ann Cartwright. *Life After a Death: A Study of the Elderly Widowed.* New York: Tavistock, 1982.

Dietrich, David and Peter Shabad, eds. *The Problem of Loss and Mourning: Psychoanalytic Perspectives.* Madison, Conn.: International Universities Press, 1989.

Lopata, Helena. *Women As Widows: Support Systems.* New York: Elsevier, 1979.

Lund, Dale A., ed. *Older Bereaved Spouses: Research with Practical Applications.* New York: Hemisphere Publishing, 1989.

Kalish, Richard, ed. *Midlife Loss and Coping Strategies.* Newbury Park, Cal.: Sage Publications, 1989.

Parkes, Colin Murray. *Bereavement: Studies of Grief In Adult Life.* Madison, Conn.: International Universities Press, 1987.

Rubenstein, R.L. *Old Men Living Alone.* New York: Columbia University Press, 1986.

Silverman, Phyllis R. *Widow to Widow.* New York: Springer, 1986.

POETRY

Seskin, Jane. *A Time to Love.* Englewood Cliffs, N.J.: Prentice-Hall, 1977.

A PERIODICAL

Bereavement: A Magazine of Hope and Healing. Bereavement Publishing, 350 Gradle Road, Carmel, Indiana 46032.

RESOURCES

The Displaced Homemakers Network
1010 Vermont Avenue, N.W., Suite 817
Washington, D.C. 20005
(202) 628-6767

> A national network that aids widowed and divorced women who have raised families and spent little time in the work force to return to the labor market.

Elderhostel
100 Boylston Street
Boston, Massachusetts 02116
(617) 426-7788

> A program that encourages persons over sixty, single or married, to spend a week on college campus throughout the United States and in several other countries of the world. Participants combine college courses with sightseeing.

International Association for Financial Planning
2 Concourse Parkway, Suite 200
Atlanta, GA 30328
(404) 395-1605

Institute of Certified Financial Planners
Two Denver Highlands
10065 East Harvard Avenue, Suite 320
Denver, CA 80231-5942
1 800 282-7526

> Two sources of information about this field, including the names of professionals in your area.

Institute for Retired Professionals
New School for Social Research
66 West 12th Street
New York, NY 10011
(212) 741-5682

> This educational program is described on page 247.

Institute of Lifetime Learning
1909 K Street, N.W.
Washington, D.C. 20049
(202) 872-4700

> A service of the AARP that promotes opportunities for survivors (and other older people) to pursue educational interests and prepare for new careers.

NAIM, U.S. Catholic Conference
Family Life Division
721 North LaSalle Drive
Chicago, Illinois 60610
(312) 944-1286

An organization for Catholic survivors.

National Hospice Organization
1901 North Moore Street, Suite 901
Arlington, Virginia 22209
(703) 243-5900

A national clearinghouse of information about programs that care for terminally ill people and their families and that offer bereavement counselling.

Parents Without Partners
8807 Colesville Road
Silver Spring, Maryland 20910
1 800 637-7974

An international organization providing social activities and discussion groups for widowed (or divorced) single parents.

Tax Counselling for the Elderly

Free assistance with taxes can be obtained by calling the general IRS number in your state (1 800 424-1040 in most states) and asking about the nearest site at which this program is offered.

THEOS (They Help Each Other Spiritually)
1301 Clark Building
717 Liberty Avenue
Pittsburgh, Pennsylvania 15222
(412) 471-7779

THEOS provides nondenominational spiritual and educational programs for survivors and their families in the United States and Canada. They conduct regional conferences and workshops, publish materials on widowhood, and educate the public on supporting widowed people.

Widowed Persons Service (WPS-TA)
Program Department, American Association of Retired Persons
1909 K Street, N.W.
Washington, D.C. 20049
(202) 728-4370

WPS offers a wide range of services for survivors in the United States: outreach volunteers to visit the newly bereaved, a telephone referral service, group sessions, and assistance and training materials (including the publication *Insights*) for those wanting to form support groups.